The Buildings of DETROIT

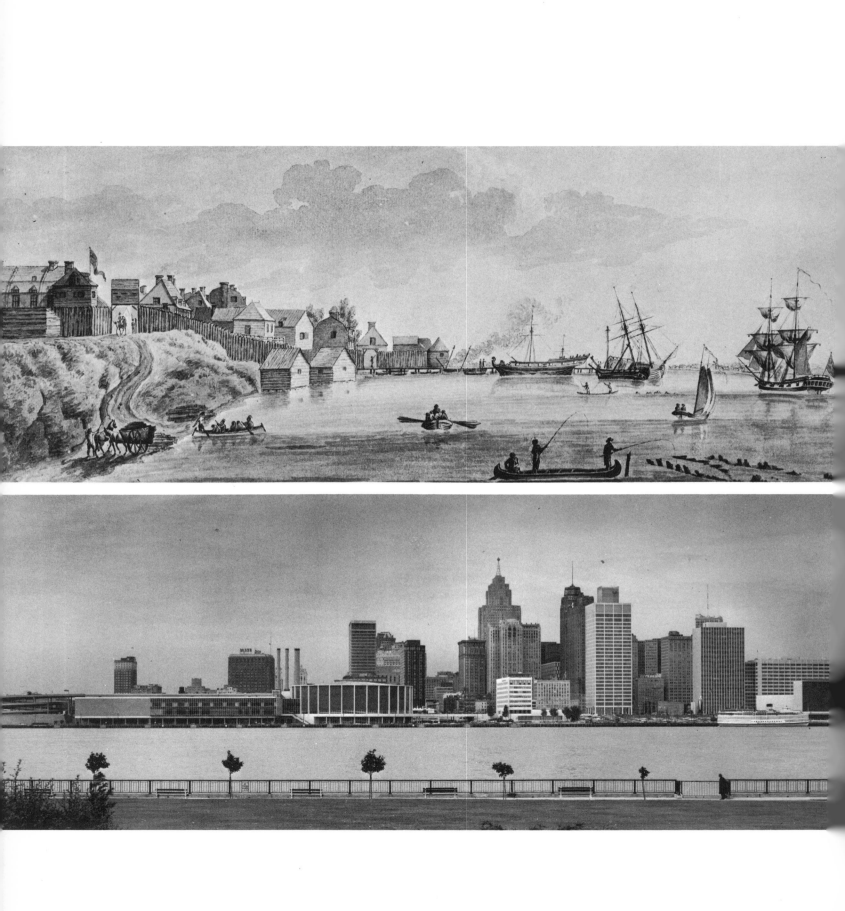

The Buildings of DETROIT

A History   by W. Hawkins Ferry

A Centennial Publication

Wayne State University Press   Detroit 1968

Published simultaneously in Canada by

The Copp Clark Publishing Company

517 Wellington Street, West

Toronto 2B, Canada

Second printing, April 1969

Standard Book Number 8143–1333–7

Library of Congress Catalog Card Number 68–20167

Contents

Illustrations

Illustrations are grouped on pages succeeding the text of each chapter, in which marginal numbers refer to them. In general, date of construction or first completion, not of reproduction, is cited. Condition notes may be but usually are not reflected in the photographs, and may be incomplete: more than one building has been razed or remodeled while this book was in press. Unless otherwise indicated, sites are within the present city limits of Detroit or in Michigan. The picture credit key follows this list.

Frontispiece
View of Detroit, 1794
    Detail of watercolor in the collection of the Burton Historical Collection (see illustration 14).
View of Detroit, 1968

Chapter 1, pp. 19–25
(1) Great Indian Mound
    Destroyed; it was on the north bank of the River Rouge, within half a mile of the Detroit River. Engraving after W. J. Wilson, from Hubbard's *Memorials*.

(2) Fort Pontchartrain du Détroit, 1701
    MS. plan attributed to Cadillac, c. 1702; inscribed 1749, perhaps in reference to de Léry's plan (5) of that year. Locations: (A) church and (B) sacristy; (C) Cadillac's, (D) Tonty's, (E) priest's, and (L-Z) other houses; (F-H) military buildings; (I) main, south or river gate, and (K) small or west gate. In the archives of the Ministry of Colonies, Paris.

(3) Huron Mission House, 1728
    Sandwich, Windsor, Ontario. Destroyed. Engraving in Hubbard's *Memorials*.

(4) Huron Mission Church, c. 1730
    Sandwich, Windsor, Ontario. Destroyed. From "A View of Detroit and the Straits taken from the Huron Church, June 22, 1804," watercolor by Dr. Edward Walsh, in the William L. Clements Library, Ann Arbor (detail).

(5) "Plan du Fort du Détroit" and Map of the Detroit River, 1764
    Engravings after Joseph G. Chaussegros de Léry, 1749 and 1755. The engraver ignored or did not understand the nature of the ribbon farms, for they are clearly indicated as strips, not rectangles, on de Léry's original drawing of 1755 in the archives of the Ministry of Marine, Paris. From Bellin's *Petit Atlas Maritime* (key letters added).

(6) Baudry-Cass House, c. 1745
    Destroyed; reconstruction as of c. 1820. Anonymous drawing, based on an engraving in Farmer's *History*, in the Burton Historical Collection.

(7) Baudry-Cass House, c. 1745
    Destroyed; shown after removal to Larned street. Also known as the St. Martin House.

(8) Jacques Campau House, c. 1757, and Chapel, c. 1778
    Both destroyed. Engraving after Crumb, from Tuttle's *General History of Michigan*.

(9) View of Detroit, 1796
    Copy by C. W. Sumner after a vignette on the "Collot Map" of the Detroit River, in the Ministry of War, Paris; a facsimile copy of the entire map hangs in the Burton Historical Collection. Engraving from Farmer's *History* (detail).

(10) Knaggs Windmill, c. 1815
    Destroyed. "View on Detroit River from Old Knaggs House, Wind-Mill Point, Springwells, 1837." Engraving after W. J. Wilson, from Hubbard's *Memorials*.

(11) Old Moran House, c. 1740 (?)
    Destroyed.

(12) Old Labadie House, c. 1780
    Destroyed.

(404) Norwayne Homes School, *Lyndon & Smith*, 1943
Westland. Lincoln or Jefferson Elementary School, both enlarged.

(405) Lafayette Park Court Houses, *Ludwig Mies van der Rohe*, 1959

(406) Lafayette Park Pavilion Apartments and Town Houses, *Ludwig Mies van der Rohe*, 1959

(407) 1300 Layayette East, *Birkerts & Straub*, 1964

(408) Elmwood Park North, *Eberle M. Smith Assoc.*, 1966

(409) Elmwood Park (project), *Crane & Gorwic*, 1964
Model, looking south from Vernor to Jefferson.

(410) Children's Hospital of Michigan, *Albert Kahn Assoc.*, c. 1970
Architectural rendering by Howard Assoc. Albert Kahn's Brush street addition of 1928 to Harper Hospital is in the background; part of a new parking structure appears to the left (south).

(411) Medical Center (project), *Crane & Gorwic*, 1966
Model, looking north from Mack.

(412) Medical Center (land use plan), *Crane & Gorwic*, 1967
Sites: (A) Maccabees Building (355), (B) Rackham Memorial 1941, (C) St. Paul's Cathedral (316), (D) First Congregational Church (148), (E) Hospital (proposed), (F) Hutzel Hospital 1929, (G) Whitney House (161), (H) Hospital (proposed), (I) W.S.U. Shiffman Medical Library c. 1970, (J) W.S.U. Basic Medical Science Building c. 1970, (K) W.S.U. Medical Research Building (414), (L) Grace Hospital c. 1975, (M) W.S.U. Clinics Building c. 1972, (N) Webber Medical Center c. 1972, (O) Children's Hospital (410), (P) Harper Hospital (115), (Q) Professional Tower (413), (R) Concourse Building (413), (S) Orchestra Hall 1919, (T) Kahn House (295), (U) Brewster-Douglass Homes 1939-55 (base plan courtesy Crane & Gorwic, key letters added).

(413) Medical Center Professional Plaza, *Crane & Gorwic*, 1966
Tower and Concourse.

(414) Medical Center Medical Research Building, *Smith, Hinchman & Grylls*, 1964
Wayne State University.

(415) Cultural Center Park (project), *City Plan Commission*, 1965
Existing buildings, all to the right (west), include: Rackham Memorial, Institute of Arts (with proposed reflecting pool and additions), and Society of Arts and Crafts Art School (lower right).

(416) Detroit Institute of Arts South Wing, *Harley, Ellington, Cowin & Stirton et al.*, 1966

(417) Detroit Institute of Arts Sculpture Court
For main building, see (247).

(418) Wayne University Campus (project), *Pilafian & Montana*, 1948
Old Main, formerly Central High School, is to the south (upper left) at Hancock and Cass; the Insti-

tute of Arts (lower left) and Public Library face one another across Woodward with proposed wings; the Maccabees Building is south and the Historical Museum (not built as shown) north of the library.

(419) Kresge Science Library, *Pilafian & Montana*, 1953
Wayne State University.

(420) College of Education, *Yamasaki, Leinweber & Assoc.*, 1960
Wayne State University.

(421) Meyer and Anna Prentis Building, *M. Yamasaki & Assoc.*, 1964
Wayne State University.

(422) McGregor Memorial Conference Center, *M. Yamasaki & Assoc.*, 1958
Wayne State University.

(423) University Center Building, *Alden B. Dow Assoc.*, 1968
Wayne State University. The university's Chatsworth Apartments, c. 1930, are in the background. Architectural rendering by Rochon.

(424) Shapero Hall of Pharmacy, *Paulsen, Gardner & Assoc.*, 1965
Wayne State University.

(425) Life Sciences Research Center, *Albert Kahn Assoc.*, 1960
Wayne State University.

(426) Ford Life Sciences Building, *Glen Paulsen & Assoc.*, 1967
University of Detroit.

(427) Fisher Administrative Center, *Gunnar Birkerts & Assoc.*, 1966
University of Detroit.

(428) Fleming Elementary School, *Meathe, Kessler & Assoc.*, 1961

(429) Macomb County Community College, *Harley, Ellington, Cowin & Stirton*, 1965
Warren.

(430) Henry Ford Community College, *Eberle M. Smith Assoc.*, 1960
Dearborn.

(431) Glazer Elementary School, *Louis G. Redstone Assoc.*, 1966
Narenda Patel designed the glazed brick mural in the court.

(432) Woodward Elementary School, *Meathe, Kessler & Assoc.*, 1963

(433) Schoolcraft College, *Eberle M. Smith Assoc.*, 1965
Livonia.

(434) Amelia Earhart Junior High School, *Meathe, Kessler & Assoc.*, 1963

(435) Meadowlake Elementary School, *Linn Smith Assoc.*, 1963
Bloomfield Township.

(436) Philip Murray Senior High School, *Eberle M. Smith Assoc.*, 1965

(437) Eastern Senior High School, *Linn Smith Assoc.*, 1966

Picture Credits

Foreword

In the early years of the nineteenth century the stabilization of the frontier permitted the opening up of the interior of the American continent to settlers. The introduction of the railroad and the exploitation of natural resources stimulated economic development. Spawned by the Industrial Revolution, cities sprang up in what had only yesterday been a wilderness.

The late historian Milo M. Quaife pointed out that Detroit is the oldest continuously inhabited community between the Appalachian and the Rocky Mountains. Although founded in 1701, it developed slowly because of primitive conditions and poor transportation. The fire of 1805 left no trace of the early frontier settlement. In contrast, the town grew with unprecedented speed during the nineteenth century. Michigan's vast lumbering and mining operations created a sustained prosperity. Industrialization proceeded apace and was climaxed in the twentieth century by the development of the automobile industry.

Little remains of the architecture of early Detroit. The visitor to the city today is confronted with endless streets lined with garish shops and miles of dreary dwellings. Architectural excellence appears only sporadically. There is something in the raw, unfinished scene that reflects the mobility of the industrial process itself.

Restless change has been a characteristic of the city in the past and has created a sense of impermanence. In the outward thrust of growth, once-fashionable neighborhoods have rapidly deteriorated. Constantly destroying itself, the city has radically changed from generation to generation, and each generation has remolded it to satisfy its own ideals.

After the fire of 1805 a new classical city rose upon the ruins of the pioneer village. The next generation, romanticists at heart, pierced the sky with Gothic spires and sought the seclusion of Gothic and Tuscan villas along the riverbank. More worldly, the late Victorians tried to make their city into another Paris by adorning every building with mansard roofs and filling their houses with French art. Haunted by the memories of the Chicago World's Fair of 1893, the next generation invested their public buildings and their mansions with the restrained elegance of the Renaissance. In the nineteen-twenties the pendulum swung again, and the Gothic returned in a blaze of glory. Thus Detroit was a mirror that reflected the changing panorama of American architecture.

It was not until the local architects were able to resist the temptation of imitating historical styles and began working in the contemporary idiom that they began to play a significant role nationally. The inventiveness that had nurtured the automobile soon spread into the field of architecture, and Detroit became a laboratory not only for new automobiles, but for new architecture. Albert Kahn, Eero Saarinen, and Minoru Yamasaki set a new pace in adapting form to function and became eminent leaders in the development of American architecture.

Coming to terms with the twentieth century, the present generation of Detroiters is attempting to build a modern city that will satisfy the demands of modern living. It is the task of this book to resurrect the vanished worlds of Detroit's past and to find in the continuity of the evolutionary process the promise of a brilliant future.

W. H. F.

Acknowledgments

My interest in local architecture began in 1939 when I returned to Detroit from Harvard University where I had majored in the history of art and architecture as an undergraduate. I was attracted by the old buildings of architectural interest that were rapidly disappearing from the local scene and arranged to have professional photographers make a permanent record of them. This was the basis of an architectural exhibition which I organized at the Detroit Institute of Arts in March 1943. In connection with the exhibition I wrote an article in the current issue of the *Bulletin of the Detroit Institute of Arts* entitled "Representative Detroit Buildings, a Cross Section of Architecture, 1823–1943."

In this project I was guided and encouraged by Professor Emil Lorch of the University of Michigan. Also helpful was Professor Buford L. Pickens, then at Wayne State University, who wrote articles about Detroit architecture in *The Art Quarterly* and *The Architectural Review*. Valuable information was obtained by interviewing George D. Mason, Louis Kamper, and Albert Kahn, architects of the older generation. Professor Lorch introduced me to Ernest F. Lloyd in Ann Arbor, and I am indebted to the latter for supplying much valuable information about the work of his father, architect Gordon W. Lloyd, who designed several of Detroit's Gothic Revival churches. At about this time Wayne Andrews drew my attention to references to Italian villas built in Detroit by architect A. J. Davis in the Davis papers at the Metropolitan Museum of Art in New York. These two sources of information provided the basis for an article, "The Gothic and Tuscan Revivals in Detroit, 1828–1875," which appeared in *The Art Quarterly* in the summer of 1946. In preparation for this article interviews were held with Mrs. Alanson Brooks of Detroit and Mrs. Louis Hall of Ann Arbor, whose fathers Bela Hubbard and Judge Samuel Douglass, respectively, owned two of the houses described.

In 1955 I gave a lecture at the Grosse Pointe War Memorial for the Grosse Pointe Historical Society on "The Mansions of Grosse Pointe." This was published in the March 1956 issue of the *Monthly Bulletin of the Michigan Society of Architects*.

Also in 1955 the Wayne State University Press asked me if I would write a history of Detroit architecture to be published by the Press and I agreed, little realizing how much time it would consume. The research on the subject which I had already done provided the groundwork for the project, and I proceeded to fill in the gaps. Interviews were arranged with Clarence Smith, the son of a leading local nineteenth century architect, Mortimer L. Smith; Ernest Wilby, who had worked in Albert Kahn's office; and William E. Kapp, who had been the head of the architectural department of Smith, Hinchman and Grylls, one of Detroit's most prominent architectural firms. Miss Florence Davies, former art critic of the *Detroit News*, was kind enough to lend me a manuscript, "A Letter on Gothic Architecture," by Wirt Rowland, one of the principal architectural designers for Smith, Hinchman and Grylls during the twenties.

Most of the information about early Detroit buildings was obtained from old newspapers and periodicals, and for this I relied heavily upon the Burton Historical Collection of the Detroit Public Library. This was also the source of most of the photographs of early buildings, many of which are no longer standing. My thanks are due to the staff of the Burton Collection for their helpful assistance. I am also indebted to the library of the Henry Ford Museum in Dearborn and to the Chrysler Corporation for providing information and photographs. I am obliged to Wayne Andrews and Henry Hope Reed for allowing me to use their photographs and to Robert Kozlow for assembling photographs.

In writing the contemporary section of the book, I received the cooperation and assistance of many local architects; and I wish to express my appreciation to them for supplying information and photographs. I am also grateful for information from the Detroit City Plan Commission, Housing Commission, Public Schools, Department of Reports and Information, and also from the Office of Capital Programs of Wayne State University. Thanks go to James Dunn for collecting biographical material and to photographer Joseph P. Messana for pointing out local examples of modern religious architecture. Finally, I am particularly grateful to Robert P. Metzger for doing research and assembling literature and photographs.

W. H. F.

The Buildings of DETROIT

1. The Frontier Community

The Frontier Era

The location of a great city on the Detroit River seems to have been predestined. The site commands one of the most heavily traveled waterways in the Great Lakes area and one of the few river crossings between the lakes. It was precisely these advantages that led Antoine de la Mothe Cadillac to establish *Fort Pontchartrain du Détroit* in 1701 on the broad strait that connects Lake St. Clair and Lake Erie.

The frontier era of Detroit lasted roughly from its founding by Cadillac in 1701 to the removal of the stockade around the town in 1827. Besides being the center of the fur trade with the Indians, it was also the key military post of the Great Lakes area. Figuring prominently in the international struggle for the continent, it was successively occupied by the French, British, and Americans. It was also a target for repeated Indian attacks. Until these hostilities had subsided and Michigan had become an integrated part of the American republic, it was not a desirable place for permanent settlement. The uncertain profit of the fur trade was a meager reward for the isolation, the hardship, and the danger of the frontier.

For over a century the town was but a cluster of log buildings lost in the immensity of the wilderness. Each primitive structure bore the unmistakable imprint of the French, English, or Yankee mentality. The community as a whole was the product of unique environmental and historical circumstances.[1]

Before the White Man

Before the coming of the white man, Michigan was a vast area of virgin forest. An aboriginal population of about fifteen thousand souls was thinly scattered over the gently rolling terrain. The majority of settlements were along the Saginaw and St. Joseph River valleys where transportation by canoe was possible and the fish supply was abundant. This dietary item was supplemented by game from the forests and corn and other vegetables cultivated in small clearings. The Indians had learned the advantages of living together in small communities, but the crude weapons and implements at their disposal necessarily limited the number of persons a given area could support. So the villages were relatively impermanent and except two or three very populous areas widely separated. In addition to the waterways, trails located with great sagacity formed a secondary network of communication throughout the area. The principal tribes living in the Michigan area were the Chippewas or Ojibways, the Ottawas, the Potawatomies, and later the Hurons.[2]

According to Judge Charles I. Walker, "The region around Detroit was not favorable residence ground for the tribes because it was on the warpath of the Iroquois who carried their terrors as far west as the Illinois country."[3] This, however, did not prevent the Indians from choosing the future site of Detroit for burial purposes. Their burial mounds were the first human monuments along the Detroit River, lasting well into the nineteenth century. The most imposing *(1)* of these, the Great Mound of the River Rouge at Delray was, according to Bela Hubbard, "700 or 800 feet long, 400 feet wide, and not less than forty feet high."[4]

Enter the French

The Great Lakes area with its inhospitable forests and extremes of climate was long ignored by European explorers and might have remained indefinitely in its primordial condition if a series of unusual circumstances had not prompted the French to penetrate it in the early seventeenth century. Jacques Cartier had discovered and explored the St. Lawrence River in the years 1534–42, and so France quite justifiably laid claim to the lands adjoining the river. One of the principal motivations of the early explorers, beginning with Cartier, was the desire to discover the legendary passage to the Western Sea and the Indies. It was this vision that lured them up the St. Lawrence to the Great Lakes and the Northwest.

Quebec, the first permanent French settlement, was founded by Samuel de Champlain in 1608. From the beginning the French were friendly with the Huron Indians, whom they encountered near Quebec. Before the founding of Quebec there had been a feud between the Hurons and the Five Nations of the Iroquois who lived south of the St. Lawrence and Lake Ontario. Therefore the Iroquois were hostile to the French. It was the menace of the warlike Iroquois to the south that prevented French expansion in that direction and forced French explorers to head toward the northwest. To reach the Great Lakes it was necessary for them to follow the Ottawa and French Rivers to Georgian Bay, instead of taking the more direct route by way of Lakes Ontario and Erie.

Étienne Brulé and his companion Grenoble were the first Europeans to visit Michigan. Searching for a water route to the Pacific, they reached the Upper Peninsula by canoe in 1622. With the same objective, Jean Nicolet pushed farther on to Green Bay in Lake Michigan in 1634. Hard upon the heels of the explorers came the *coureurs de bois*. They hunted, trapped, and bargained with the Indians for furs in the remote recesses of the forest. In the spring they would return to Montreal, their canoes laden with furs which they would sell at a handsome profit.

Among all the Frenchmen to invade the forest, the intrepid missionaries were perhaps the most effective in establishing the foothold of France in the wilderness. Fired with a zeal to convert the natives and teach them the ways of civilization, they were responsible for establishing and maintaining many of the earliest communities in the Great Lakes area.

In 1615 a Huron mission was established at the head of Georgian Bay in the midst of the fortified villages of the Huron Indians. However, in 1649 this stronghold of the Hurons was attacked by the Iroquois. The Hurons fled to various points in the north and the post was abandoned. In 1665 Father René Ménard founded the Mission of La Pointe du Saint Esprit on Lake Superior in what is now northern Wisconsin. In 1668 Father Jacques Marquette founded Sault Ste. Marie, the first permanent settlement in Michigan. Three years later he founded the Mission of St. Ignace among the Hurons on the northern shore of the Straits of Mackinac. The same year a military post was located there, and the community which grew up around these establishments became known as Michilimackinac (now St. Ignace).

There are no reports of any Frenchmen visiting the Lower Peninsula of Michigan before 1669. The danger of the Iroquois war parties ranging along the lower lakes was too great. However, in that year a French regiment decisively defeated the Iroquois who then agreed to a treaty of peace allowing the French to travel on the lower lakes. In the same year Adrien Joliet discovered for the first time the route through Lakes St. Clair, Erie and Ontario to the St. Lawrence. Fathers Dollier and Gallinée took the same route in the opposite direction in 1670. By 1671 the French were in a position to take formal possession of the Great West. Simon Daumont, Sieur de St. Lusson, representing the French king, officiated at an elaborate ceremony at Sault Ste. Marie calculated to impress an assembled throng of two thousand savages.

Still, however, the legendary passage to the Western Sea had not been discovered. In 1673 Louis Joliet, the brother of Adrien, was sent by the French government to explore the Mississippi River. Father Marquette accompanied him as a missionary to the Indians. Paddling downstream as far as the mouth of the Arkansas River, they came to the conclusion that the Mississippi emptied into the Gulf of Mexico.

More ambitious in his plans, Robert Cavelier, Sieur de La Salle, conceived the idea of exploring the Mississippi to its mouth and erecting a chain of forts which would prevent the English from settling in the middle of the continent. For travel on the Great Lakes, La Salle's men built the sailing vessel the *Griffon* at the mouth of the Niagara River. Father Louis Hennepin, who accompanied him, has left us a delightful account of the scenery and the native Indians.

No inhabitants were encountered along the banks of the Detroit River. This area was glowingly described as an earthly paradise abounding in game and hardwood trees. "One would think," said Father Hennepin, "Nature alone could not have made, without the help of Art, so charming a prospect."[5] He tried to persuade La Salle to found a settlement there, but the latter was too intent upon the objectives that lay ahead to pause for such an undertaking at so early a stage in the expedition.

After the sinking of his *Griffon*, in 1679 La Salle erected Fort Miami at the mouth of the St. Joseph River. In 1682 he erected Fort St. Louis at Starved Rock in the Illinois country and gathered about him three thousand friendly Indians as a protection against the Iroquois. He reached the mouth of the Mississippi in 1682 and would have carried his plans further if he had not been killed by disaffected followers in 1687.

In the meantime the English traders were becoming serious competitors in the fur trade. They found the Indians eager to exchange furs for English goods, which were cheaper than the French. Before long they had passed up Lake Huron and were trading with the Indians at Michilimackinac (St. Ignace). To prevent the English from reaching the upper lakes, Daniel Greysolon, Sieur Duluth, built Fort St. Joseph at the head of the St. Clair River in 1686. However, this was abandoned two years later. In 1690 Fort de Buade was erected at

Michilimackinac and in 1691 another Fort St. Joseph was built twenty-five miles up the St. Joseph River from where La Salle had established Fort Miami in 1679.

Michilimackinac was the most important place in the West. The commandant of Fort de Buade had supervision of all the other forts, and the superior of all the western missions had his headquarters at the Mission of St. Ignace. Near the fort was a French village of sixty houses, and the Hurons and Ottawas each had a large town close to the mission. The Indian communities contained seven thousand inhabitants. During the summer more than five thousand additional Indians camped in the neighborhood and the settlement was crowded with several hundred *coureurs de bois*.

From 1694 to 1698 Antoine de la Mothe Cadillac was commandant of Michilimackinac. When not preoccupied with military duties, he had time to write a memoir in which he made a detailed study of the geography and the Indian life in the area. He described the Huron and Ottawa towns as being surrounded by triple stockades. The streets were regular, like those in French villages. The cabins were one hundred or more feet long by twenty-four feet wide with a door at each end. They were rounded like arbors and each consisted of a framework of poles to which was attached a covering of bark. Each family had its own apartment. The French houses were built of wood, "one log upon another," but the roofs were made of bark. Only the houses of the Jesuits were roofed with planks. Surrounding the settlement as a whole were the cultivated fields of the Indians.[6]

Michilimackinac had grown from a small missionary outpost to a busy trading center. All of New France was thriving under the able guidance at Quebec of Governor Louis de Buade, Comte de Frontenac. However, many in the colony were not in accord with his imperialist policy. The most powerful element to oppose him was the Jesuit order. Intent upon saving the souls of the Indians, the missionaries were distressed at the way their charges were being demoralized by the ample supply of brandy provided by the white traders. As a result, in 1696 Louis XIV issued a royal decree commanding all Frenchmen except the missionaries to leave the upper country. Thus in 1698 Fort de Buade and Fort St. Joseph were abandoned.

Antoine de la Mothe Cadillac was not one to stand idly by and watch New France crumble. It was hardly a pleasing prospect to him to lose the command of an important military post and, along with it, an enviable opportunity to make a fortune in the fur trade. It was fortunate for New France that Cadillac was as imaginative as he was enterprising and that his intimate knowledge of local conditions was coupled with a high degree of statesmanship. In Paris he persuaded the king to allow him to establish a new post on the strait between Lake St. Clair and Lake Erie. This, he argued, was necessary to hold in check the English and subdue the Iroquois. Furthermore, the new location would be far more strategic than that of Michilimackinac.

Early in June 1701 Cadillac set out from Montreal in twenty-five canoes with two priests, fifty soldiers, fifty *coureurs de bois*, and one hundred Indians. Alphonse de Tonty was second in command. Since the treaty of peace with the Iroquois had not yet been signed, Cadillac followed the old route by way of the Ottawa River, Georgian Bay, and Lake Huron, reaching the Detroit River on July 23.

After spending the night on Grosse Ile, Cadillac located an ideal site for the fort some distance above the island at the narrowest stretch of the river. Here there was a level expanse of ground at the tip of a forty-foot clay bank, and a small creek ran parallel to the river, then turned and joined it. On this peninsula of high ground Cadillac built *Fort Pontchartrain du Détroit* or Fort Pontchartrain of the Strait. It was named in honor of Jérôme Phélypeaux, Comte de Pontchartrain, Louis XIV's minister of marine.

Cadillac's men quickly set to work felling trees in the virgin forest and shaping them into logs. The large logs were used for the church and the small ones, cut into twenty-foot lengths and sharpened at the ends, were used for the palisade. The walls of all the buildings were formed of logs placed side by side vertically, the roofs being covered with grass.[7]

Cadillac's map of 1702 shows a fort about two hundred feet square with *(2)* bastions at each corner.[8] There was a large gate toward the river and a small one to the west. The most prominent buildings were the church, the priest's house, Cadillac's and Tonty's houses, a warehouse, and two guard houses. There were also thirteen smaller houses. The fort was located in an area bounded today by the southern side of Jefferson avenue, and Griswold, Larned, and Shelby streets in modern Detroit. The palisades were later extended to the west to what is now Washington boulevard.

In addition to being commandant of the fort, Cadillac played the role of a feudal lord. He distributed lots within the stockade and farms along the river above the fort on the basis of feudal tenure. So long and narrow that they are often called ribbon farms, they varied from four to six hundred feet in width and from one and a half to three miles in depth. He also built a windmill on the river bank and charged one-fourteenth for grinding.

Partly to facilitate fur trading and partly as a protection against hostile Indians, Cadillac invited friendly Indian tribes to build their villages near the fort. The Ottawas and Hurons from Michilimackinac and the Potawatomies from the St. Joseph River valley settled close to the fort. The Chippewas came from various points to Harsen's Island at the mouth of the St. Clair River, and the Miamis from the St. Joseph River valley settled at the mouth of the Maumee River. During the winter of 1701–02 there were six thousand Indians living in the Detroit area. Trouble with the Ottawas forced the Miamis to move away in 1712.[8]

The Potawatomi village was located on the river a short distance below the fort. Made of mats of woven reeds, their huts were conical with rounded tops. The Huron village was nearer the fort at the mouth of the Savoyard River. It was enclosed with a double row of palisades with bastions and gates. The houses were forty to sixty feet long and about twenty feet wide. They were built with a pole framework covered with elm bark, the tops being rounded like arbors. In each house there were compartments for four or five families. The Ottawa huts were similar. They had built a palisaded fort across the river on the present site of Walkerville, Windsor, Ontario.[9] During the summer months the Indians remained in their villages, but throughout the winter the male population invaded the forests in search of wild animals for meat and furs. In the spring they would return with pelts to trade with the white man for guns, ammunition, blankets, kettles, trinkets, and many other items.[8]

So many Indians had left Michilimackinac to settle around Detroit that the Jesuit priest there burned the mission at Saint Ignace and withdrew to Quebec in 1705. The Jesuits were not pleased at the prospect of a new settlement being established where the Indians would be debauched by the *coureurs de bois*, and the merchants of Montreal and Quebec feared that the new post would injure their trade. Finally pressure was brought to bear on the government, and Cadillac was removed from his post and made governor of Louisiana in 1710. It was a major disaster for Cadillac and for the community which he had founded with such high hopes.

Upon the recommendation of Pierre François de Charlevoix, who had visited Detroit in 1721, the Jesuits of Quebec established a Huron mission near Detroit in 1728. It was located on the opposite shore from the fort where Sandwich, Windsor, Ontario, now stands. That side of the strait was chosen to avoid the conflict of ecclesiastical jurisdiction with the Recollets who were in charge at Detroit. In 1747 the Hurons located their village in the immediate vicinity of the mission. There they learned from the Jesuits how to make their houses out of squared logs.

(3) The mission house was a long narrow building ninety by thirty feet facing the river. It was one and a half stories high with a steeply pitched roof and dormer windows. Hewed pine and sawed lumber were used throughout the structure, although the cellar and two chimneys were of stone. The oldest part of the house was built in 1728, but this was extended fifty feet to the west in 1743. It remained standing until about the beginning of the twentieth century.[10]

(4) The Huron church, built shortly after the founding of the mission, stood to the west of the mission house until the middle of the nineteenth century. A charming watercolor drawing, painted by Dr. Edward Walsh in 1804, shows it to have been a simple wooden structure with a steep roof surmounted by a belfry, above which was a weathervane in the shape of a cock.[11] A series of slanting poles propped up the aging walls.

In 1736 a store and warehouse were established at the mission. There the Hurons could store their foods and furs and deal with the traders under the watchful eyes of the Jesuits who prevented them from being swindled or debauched by liquor.

The Recollet church at Detroit was known as Ste. Anne's. First built by Cadillac in 1701, it was rebuilt four times before the entire town was burned in 1805. In 1711 the church was described as being thirty-five by twenty-four and a half feet wide, and ten high, "boarded entirely above, with oak joists in a good ridge, and below of beams with square joists; with its doors window [sic] and shutters, and sash-frames between of twenty squares each."[12] This was evidently the church built in 1709. A view of Detroit in 1796 shows the small stockaded *(9)* town; Ste. Anne's of 1755 with its belfry stands out prominently like a church in a medieval walled town.[13]

During the eighteenth century the little town of Detroit grew very slowly. It remained a small outpost in the wilderness. Too few Frenchmen found the West attractive enough to go there and settle, and so the West was largely the domain of the shiftless *coureurs de bois.*

The conclusion of peace with the Iroquois shortly after the arrival of Cadillac brought the first trickle of settlers to Detroit, since travel by way of the lower lakes was finally permitted. When Mmes. Cadillac and Tonty landed in Detroit in the fall of 1701, an example was set for some of the colonists to bring their families to the new community. However, when Cadillac was removed in 1710, many of his followers deserted the town and there was a notable decline in population. In 1749 the governor of New France attempted to stimulate colonization in Detroit by offering farm animals and equipment to any family who would occupy a farm there, but this plan was not a success. The total population of the fort and the neighboring farms was then only about nine hundred.

The De Léry map of 1749 shows that the picket lines had been pushed somewhat further north and south from where they had been toward the end of

Cadillac's regime.[14] Houses were crowded together on narrow unpaved streets. *(5)*
The four principal streets, which ran east and west, were named *Rue St. Joseph,*
Rue St. Jacques, Rue Ste. Anne, and *Rue St. Louis.* Just below the top of the
pickets was a runway for soldiers and below that on the ground was a foot path
called the *chemin de ronde* or road around the village.[15]

As mentioned before, the earliest houses were one and a half stories built of
logs driven vertically into the ground. Steeply pitched roofs with low eaves were
covered with shingles of white cedar and penetrated by dormer windows. At
first chimneys were made of sticks and clay, but later stone from nearby quarries
was relied upon. The earliest windows were merely open holes closed by solid
wood shutters, but eventually they were covered with thin buckskin or panes of
glass. The doors were often divided like Dutch doors, the upper half being left
open in pleasant weather. Floors were of beaten clay or logs flattened on one
side.[16] With increasing prosperity the houses and palings were whitewashed and
the doors painted bright green. The inside furnishing was simple in the extreme.
Indian mats were used as rugs. There were wood or rush chairs and wooden beds,
tables, dressers, and chests. Invariably a crucifix hung on the wall.[17]

The French had no tradition of building log cabins, but the habitants of
Detroit soon learned by experience the imprudence of building the walls of their
houses by driving logs into the ground. In addition to being laborious, this
method was also impractical, since the absorption of moisture from the ground
caused the logs to decay. Placing the logs horizontally on top of one another and
mortising them at the corners soon became the accepted mode of construction.[18]
By the middle of the eighteenth century it became common practice to cover
the logs with clapboards cut at a sawmill.[19] Since all the houses inside the palisade
were destroyed in the conflagration of 1805, our knowledge of the French colonial character of their architecture derives mainly from descriptions and illustrations of outlying farmhouses that survived well into the nineteenth century.

A simple gabled structure built of vertical logs, the Jacques Campau house, *(8)*
dating from about 1757, was an example of the earlier type of construction. It
stood on the river bank opposite Belle Isle. About 1778 Campau built a little
chapel near his house.[20]

The first farmhouse west of the fort was built by Jean Baptiste Baudry *(7)*
between 1740 and 1750. Later occupied by General Lewis Cass, it became known
as the Cass house. It was a one-and-a-half story building of cedar logs covered
with clapboards; out of a high sharp roof with dormers emerged a short massive
stone chimney.[18] For many years it exhibited the tomahawk and bullet marks
received during the Indian wars.[21] Other well-known owners were William
Macomb and Oliver Newberry. In 1836 it was moved north to Larned street,
where it remained until it was demolished in 1882.[22]

The Moran house on Woodbridge street between St. Antoine and Hastings *(11)*
was reputedly built in 1734 but probably was of later date.[23] Somewhat similar to
the Cass house, it was made of logs covered with clapboards. All nails used in the
house were of wrought-iron, as were also the locks on the doors and their keys.
It was demolished in 1886.[24] The Lafferty house was built in 1747. Located on
the river between what is now Twelfth and Thirteenth streets, it was demolished in 1861.[25] Built about 1780, the Labadie house on River street at *(12)*
Twenty-fourth was razed in 1910.[23] The old central part was made of logs
covered with clapboards; two circular wings were added in 1830.[26]

A type of structure rarely found in eighteenth century America but very *(10)*
common in early Detroit was the windmill. The shore line of the Detroit River
was not as straight as it is today and there were innumerable shallow bays and

9

points. On every prominent point was a windmill, the base of stone and the upper part of wood surmounted by a conical shingled roof.[27] Many of these were in operation well into the nineteenth century. Recalling his first impression of them upon reaching Detroit by boat in 1827, Friend Palmer declared that they "presented to us a wonderful sight on that bright May morning. They were in full operation; their four immense arms, covered with white sail-cloth, were whirled through the air by the force of the wind, and . . . filled us with delightful amazement as all New York state could not produce a scene to match it."[28] In his enthusiasm over the picturesque aspects of the windmill, Palmer omitted mention of an equally important if less conspicuous type of mill characteristic of early Detroit—the watermill. There were several of these located on the small creeks which once drained into the Detroit River but have since disappeared. Some of these watermills were gristmills and some sawmills.[29]

After the dismissal of Cadillac the land titles which he had granted were nullified. This gave scant encouragement to prospective settlers. After a period of negligence the Quebec government changed its attitude and took measures to encourage and strengthen the small outpost. Good land titles were again obtainable. As the population increased, more farms were established for some distance on both banks of the river. Each farm had a narrow frontage on the river to provide access by canoe and a convenient water supply. Near each log cabin was a small cultivated area with an orchard. Farmers owned cattle, sheep, and small shaggy ponies. In dry weather the farmer could drive his little springless two-wheeled cart into town along the dirt road that skirted the river.

One might imagine life to have been rather dreary in the infant community cut off from the outside world by a vast wilderness, but the French *joie de vivre* gave the place a very lively atmosphere. There was horse-racing, dancing, or gambling, and frequently the strains of a violin floated in the air. In the winter there were trotting races on the river ice, the ponies pulling little sleighs or carryalls behind them.

But the carefree existence of the frontier outpost could not last forever. The foresight of Cadillac in establishing Detroit had kept the French in control of the Great Lakes, but French dreams of empire were foundering in the mire of complacency and political corruption. Again the more enterprising British were becoming disturbingly competitive. British traders were pushing westward along the Ohio valley. Here they came into conflict with the French who realized that this area was the weakest and most defenseless link in the vast French empire which extended from the mouth of the St. Lawrence to the mouth of the Mississippi. At first the French were successful in establishing forts at strategic locations in the Ohio valley. The conflict that developed was the American counterpart of the Seven Years' War in Europe. It was the crucial moment to decide who would control the American continent. In America the English had the advantage of a much greater population.

In 1758 the English captured Fort Duquesne and in 1759 they took the forts at Ticonderoga, Crown Point, and Niagara. After the fall of Quebec and Montreal, all of Canada was surrendered to the British in 1760. Shortly thereafter the British occupied all the French posts in the Northwest, including Detroit.

British Ascendency

In Detroit the transfer from French to British sovereignty was made with no apparent difficulty. The British soldiers behaved well and the habitants were friendly. The French merchants invited the new commandant and his officers to their dances, and he in turn entertained them and their wives and daughters at parties and balls. At these functions the style of clothing approximated what might have been seen in London or Paris.

The French had always considered the Indians as friends, but the unscrupulous British traders swarmed over the country cheating the Indians and robbing them of their furs. The promises of friendship and gifts proffered by British officialdom did nothing to assuage the growing resentment of the Indians. The Ottawa Chief Pontiac conceived a plan for obliterating Detroit. In 1763 he held the little stockaded town in a state of siege for five months. It was only due to the pertinacity and good judgment of Commandant Major Henry Gladwin and the assistance of the loyal French that Detroit survived, and Pontiac finally offered to make peace. Aroused against the British, the Indians attacked all the forts west of the Alleghenies. Detroit, Niagara, and Pitt were the only forts that were able to hold out against their depredations.

Because of their congeniality with the Indians, the French had never found it necessary to keep a large garrison at Detroit. On the other hand, after the tribulations of the Pontiac War, the English deemed it necessary to maintain a large garrison permanently. Consequently in 1764 a large parade ground and barracks were added to the west of the town. All the buildings were constructed of timber except the powder magazine, which was of stone. The old picket line was extended to enclose this area, known as the Citadel. At the beginning of the Revolutionary War, between two and three hundred soldiers occupied this enclosure, and during the war it was used partly to hold prisoners of war. Detroit became the base of operations for murderous raids into the western country by both whites and Indians. American settlers were murdered and scalped and some were brought as prisoners to Detroit.[30]

To prevent further raids, Colonel George Rogers Clark, commandant in Kentucky, captured several Illinois towns and was planning to attack Detroit. This alarmed the authorities at Detroit who realized that their stockaded town would be defenseless under an artillery barrage. Consequently, in 1779 Captain Richard B. Lernoult built a fort back of the town about where the Federal Building now *(13)* stands.[31] Inside there were officers' quarters, barracks, and other buildings. According to F. Clever Bald:

It had a high earthen rampart with half-bastions so that fire could be directed against enemy soldiers who might penetrate the outer defenses. In front of the rampart was a ditch with a palisade in the middle, then the glacis, a low rampart of earth. Outside the glacis an abatis of felled trees, with the branches cut short and sharpened, served the purpose of a present day barbed-wire entanglement. The stockade of the town was extended back to the forward extremities of Fort Lernoult.[32]

An accurate impression of Detroit in 1794 may be obtained from a watercolor by an unknown contemporary artist.[33] In the foreground may be seen the government wharf and the royal naval vessels, while in the background are shown the west gate and bastion, and the Citadel within the fort. The houses *(14)* crowded behind the stockade are all characteristically *Québec* types with steeply pitched roofs. There are gabled, hipped, and gambrel roofs, all of which have small dormer windows placed low above the eaves.[34]

Thus it may be seen that, except for the modernization of the military installations, the British did not materially change the aspect of the town. It was still merely an outpost in the wilderness, and the uncertainty of the future did little to promote a more permanent and monumental architecture. Notwithstanding its importance officially and commercially, the Anglo-Saxon element of the population remained relatively small. For the time being the crude frontier buildings inherited from the French regime were adequate.

In spite of the rusticity of the surroundings and the provincialism of the majority of the habitants, the importance of the town as the administrative and commercial center of a vast area brought it in touch with the great outside world. Among the military officers and the wealthier merchant families there always could be found people of varied backgrounds and cultivated tastes. William Macomb might be cited as an example of a prosperous British merchant of the day. Furnishing the British army with supplies enabled him to aspire to a scale of living that was uncommon in the West. He owned the old Baudry house (7) which later became known as the Cass house. It was on the first farm below the fort. In addition to the house, the farm had a barn, a sheep house, a cider press, a root cellar, and a bakehouse. The land was utilized for an orchard, a garden, and a 'deer park' with a 'look-out house.' At Macomb's disposal were twenty-six slaves, mostly Negro. For his intellectual needs he had acquired a two-hundred volume library of English classics.[35]

Perhaps one of the most enterprising merchants of the period in the fur trade was John Askin. Having begun his career at Mackinac, he moved to Detroit in 1780. He married Marie Archange Barthe and became the owner of her ancestral home, the first farm above the fort. Disconsolate over the victory of the Americans, he moved to the Canadian side of the river in 1802.[36] Mrs. Askin's sister Therese Barthe married Commodore Alexander Grant, commander of the Royal Navy fleet of the upper lakes. For his wife, ten daughters and two sons he conceived a truly fabulous domicile on the shores of Lake St. Clair in Grosse Pointe. Aspiring to found a seigneury similar to the old French claims on the St. Lawrence, he acquired a tract of about four hundred **acres, and** during the winter when the lakes were frozen employed his sailors and soldiers in clearing off the forest trees. On this tract, according to Theodore P. Hall:

He erected a large manor-house known in its day as "Grant's Castle." It was built of hewn oaken timbers taken from the surrounding forest. These were neatly dovetailed at the corners, and the interstices between the logs carefully filled with plaster. It was about 160 feet long, two stories in height, and surrounded on all sides by huge two-story verandas or "galleries," as the French termed them, and in shape resembled a great barrack.[37]

From his castle Grant distributed bounties and pensions to the Indians. The great Chief Tecumseh was a frequent visitor. Even after the American occupation Grant continued living in his unique establishment until his death in 1813.

When the Revolution terminated in 1783 the Americans were pledged by treaty to compensate for property taken from exiled Tories. Since the war-weary American people failed to carry out their part of the bargain, the British government retaliated by withholding the surrender of Detroit and several other frontier forts. Thus Detroit remained under Canadian rule until 1796.

In the meantime it became the center for the distribution of goods to the Indians and the point of departure for continuing Indian raids on the American settlers in the Ohio valley. The defeat of the Indians in 1794 by General Anthony Wayne at the Battle of Fallen Timbers, several miles south of present-day Toledo, paved the way for the Jay Treaty with Great Britain in 1796, by which

Detroit and other forts were formally surrendered to the Americans. On July 11 the British hauled down the Union Jack and embarked for Lower Canada, and the American flag was raised above Fort Lernoult. Two days later Colonel John Francis Hamtramck arrived at Detroit and took command with a garrison of four hundred men. At last, thirteen years after the ratification of the Treaty of Paris, Michigan became a part of the United States.

American Beginnings

At the time of the American occupation Detroit was the largest town in the West. There were about five hundred persons living in the stockaded town and about twenty-one hundred living on the farms. By this time the ribbon farms had reached up to the St. Clair River and down to the River Rouge. About two-thirds of the population was of French extraction. Three months after the British evacuation Isaac Weld described the appearance of the town. He noted that the narrow streets were still unpaved and were very muddy after a rain. However, on most of the streets there were sidewalks made of squared logs placed close together transversely. He found that the shops were well stocked with commodities. At the foot of the river bank were wooden wharfs to accommodate twelve sailing vessels belonging to the traders.[38]

Colonel John F. Hamtramck was made commandant at Detroit in 1796. In *(8)* 1802 he purchased the Jacques Campau farm and erected a house on the river bank. It was built of logs and covered with weatherboard. At each end were *(18)* stone chimneys. Hamtramck did not have very long to enjoy his new home, as he died in 1803. The house was demolished in 1898.[39]

There were still many Indians living more or less permanently in the vicinity. Others came to trade or receive presents from the commandant. "In the early summer, when they came from the woods with their winter's catch of furs," wrote F. Clever Bald, "the red men outnumbered the whites. Camping along the river bank, they slept under their overturned canoes, or in dome-shaped wigwams made of saplings covered with bark or with mats woven from reeds."[40] During the day the streets of the village teemed with Indians who had come to trade with the merchants. Not to be trusted because of their partiality to the British, the Indians were required to leave town at nightfall and the gates of the stockade were closed behind them.

Under the American flag Detroit was located in an area designated by the Ordinance of 1787 as the Northwest Territory. Out of this area were eventually to be carved the states of Ohio, Indiana, Illinois, Michigan, Wisconsin, and part of Minnesota. By 1798 the population of the Northwest Territory was sufficiently large for the establishment of a territorial legislature which met first at Cincinnati and later at Chillicothe. Wayne County was entitled to three elected members of the new assembly. In 1802 one of these members, a young lawyer named Solomon Sibley, procured the passage of an act at Chillicothe incorporating the "Town of Detroit," the county seat.

In 1805 a bill was enacted in Washington creating Michigan Territory, which included approximately the present area of the Lower Peninsula and a small portion of the Upper Peninsula. The territory was to be administered by a governor and three judges. President Jefferson appointed William Hull of Massachusetts as governor and Augustus B. Woodward of Washington as chief justice. In 1818 Michigan Territory was extended to include what is now Wisconsin and part of Minnesota.

Detroit was completely destroyed by fire on June 11, 1805, and the new territorial rulers arrived to find nothing left of their capital but charred debris and a few tottering stone chimneys. The inhabitants had sought refuge in nearby farmhouses or were living in tents or improvised shelters on the Commons. It was fortunate that fate brought Augustus B. Woodward to Detroit at this grave moment in its history. A man of extraordinary intellectual curiosity, he was aware of the latest developments in city planning and had the imagination to visualize a model metropolis of the future on the site of the ruined frontier post. A native of New York, he had graduated from Columbia College, studied law in Virginia, and was practicing law in Washington when he was called to his new post in Detroit. He was a friend of Thomas Jefferson and knew Major L'Enfant, who was responsible for the plan of Washington. In Detroit he was able to persuade the governor and the citizens to postpone building operations until authority could be gained from Congress to follow a suitable plan.

(16) Woodward's plan for Detroit was not, as Buford Pickens points out, merely a copy of the Washington plan.[41] L'Enfant's plan was a gridiron system of streets overlaid by diagonals, whereas Woodward's was based on a hexagon, divided into twelve sections, which could be repeated ad infinitum. It was a better integrated plan than L'Enfant's. There were principal parkways two hundred feet wide and secondary diagonals one hundred and twenty feet wide with circles or circuses and other open spaces.[42] In 1805-06 Congress passed laws authorizing the platting of the new plan. The work of surveying and laying out the streets proceeded slowly. Unfortunately, uncooperative land owners prevented all but a fragment of the original plan from being carried out. However, *(17)* we are indebted to Woodward for the broad avenues and open spaces which today give the downtown area of Detroit a distinctive quality.

After the fire of 1805 the elegant metropolis of Woodward's imagination was far from realization. Slowly buildings arose on the newly platted lots. The Coun- *(19)* cil House is known to have existed as early as 1807 on the southwest corner of Jefferson avenue and Randolph. A rugged unadorned stone building with a mansard roof, it connoted the immediacy of life in Detroit in those unsettled times. It was used for courts, fairs, elections, and meetings of religious and political societies. The Indian Department occupied a portion of it as late as 1831. In 1848 the building was burned.[43]

Among the prominent citizens of the day was James May, a British merchant and lawyer who had become an American citizen. After the fire of 1805 he gathered up stones previously used for chimneys and built a stone house on the north side of Jefferson avenue west of Cass. A description of the house by William Woodbridge gives the impression that it was similar to the traditional French dwelling. "It is a one-story gable-roof house," observed Woodbridge, "having four rooms on the first floor, beside a hall or front entry running through the house opening on a piazza." From the latter could be viewed a magnificent panorama of the river.[44]

When John Askin moved from Detroit to the Canadian side of the river his farm was occupied by his daughter Adelaide and her husband Elijah Brush, a lawyer who came to Detroit from Vermont in 1789. In 1806 Brush bought the property. The first farm above town, it became known as the Brush farm, the location of which is now permanently identified by Brush street.[45]

Before the house was torn down in 1876 the *Free Press* noted that it was "constructed of hewn logs a foot broad and five or six inches thick, tenoned at the side and dropped into grooved corner posts at the doors and windows. These logs were imbedded in mortar. The house was a story and a half high. The interior was neatly plastered, the lath having been split by hand from white cedar wood, and all the nails used were wrought by hand." Elijah Brush became prominent in the legal, political, and military life of the city. All the distinguished visitors to the Northwest Territory were wined and dined at his house. At one time he was the possessor of twenty slaves who ministered to the comfort of the guests, among whom were Governor Hull, Governor Cass, and Commodore Perry.[46]

In 1807 Governor William Hull built for himself what was then considered a *(20)* "grand mansion" on the southeast corner of Jefferson avenue and Randolph.[47] No longer standing, it was the first brick house in Detroit and the only one until 1820. It was fifty feet square, two stories in height on a stone basement, crowned by a truncated hip roof. There were balustrades on the roof deck and the entrance portico.[48] Clearly the derivation was from New England Georgian prototypes, although the proportions and details revealed an inexperienced hand.

The same year Hull built his mansion he also completed a new log stockade around the town and the fort (1807).[49] Repeated visits of large bands of Indians to Fort Malden at present-day Amherstburg, across the Detroit River at its mouth, caused alarm in Detroit. There the British authorities gave the Indians presents far in excess of those they received from the Americans. The growing tension with the Indians throughout the Northwest Territory was marked by more and more frequent acts of violence. In November 1811 General William Henry Harrison defeated the Indians at the Battle of Tippecanoe near the present-day city of Terre Haute, Indiana. At this time England was at war with France. In addition to nourishing the hostile feelings of the Indians toward the Americans, England was also interfering with American commerce at sea. The United States finally declared war against Britain in June 1812.

Governor Hull was placed in command on the Detroit front. Although he had made an excellent record in the Revolutionary War, he had since aged and lacked the aggressiveness for the task at hand. In August 1812 he meekly surrendered Detroit to the attacking forces of General Isaac Brock. Detroit then remained in British hands for over a year. Finally in September 1813 Commodore Oliver H. Perry defeated the British fleet in the Battle of Lake Erie, and in October General Harrison overwhelmed General Proctor's army and Tecumseh's Indians at the Battle of the Thames near the present-day town of Thamesville, Ontario. The victory of the Americans over the British at the Battle of Plattsburg brought the War of 1812 to a close, and peace was concluded by the Treaty of Ghent in December 1814. Feeling themselves betrayed by the British, the Indians of the Northwest Territory meekly submitted to peace treaties with the Americans.

Charting a New Empire

The dawn of 1815 found Detroit prostrate from the ravages of war, but the coming of peace brought new hope. President Madison appointed Lewis Cass governor of Michigan Territory. During the fifteen years of his administration he was to convert a wilderness outpost into the capital of an empire. He opened up Michigan to settlers by buying up land for the government from the Indians and building roads.

Born in New Hampshire, Cass had been a United States marshal in Ohio and a colonel under Governor Hull in the War of 1812. In 1815 he brought his family from Ohio to Detroit in an elegant carriage, completely overawing the rustics of the town by such a display. The vehicle was the first of its kind in Detroit and Cass, feeling that it was in bad taste to flaunt it before the impoverished inhabitants, sold it to a liveryman.[50] As a home for his family Cass bought *(7)* the first farm below the town, thereafter known as the Cass farm, from William Macomb. Thomas L. McKenney wrote about it in 1826:

You enter first into a room or saloon, in which the governor receives his business visitors and where lie scattered about, in some tolerable confusion, newspapers and the remains of pamphlets of all sorts, whilst its sides are ornamented with Indian likenesses, pipes, snowshoes, medals, bows, arrows, etc. On your left is a door which leads into the dining apartment, back of which is another room of about the same size, divided from it by folding doors. . . .

From the right of the audience room you enter the drawing room; and in place of the back room in the left division, two rooms are arranged, one of which serves for the library and the other for a lodging room. These rooms being well carpeted and curtained and furnished in excellent but plain style . . .

"It had," thought McKenney, "much of the simplicity of republicanism."[51] *(6)* On the front of the house overlooking the river was an incongruous pagoda-like porch which had at one time been a garden pavilion—possibly William Macomb's 'look-out house'—and was later attached to the house.

At Springwells, two miles down the river from the Cass farm, was the *(15)* Knaggs farm. Its owner Whitmore Knaggs spoke six Indian dialects, as well as English and French. He was Indian agent under Cass and was invaluable in treating with the Indian tribes.[52] Several times Tecumseh and his brother 'the Prophet' made friendly visits to the house. It had been built in 1790 and Knaggs bought it some time after the American occupation from a Frenchman named Gobelle.[53] Long since vanished, it was made of clapboarded squared pine timbers. The main portion was a story and a half with dormer windows. It contained three large rooms separated by a central hall. A low one-story wing contained two rooms and a kitchen. A square portico commanded a fine view of the *(10)* river.[54] About 1815 a windmill was built in front of the house on the river bank. This was taken down in 1854.

The final and most fully developed phase of the French architectural tradi- *(21)* tion in Detroit was represented by the Joseph Campau house (1813) located on the south side of Jefferson avenue between Griswold and Shelby streets.[55] It was a story and a half with a gambrel roof, small dormer windows, and two brick chimneys. There were heavy oak posts at each corner and the walls were composed of oak planks, hickory pegs being used throughout.[56] The exterior clapboards were painted yellow, the paneled shutters white.

For many years Joseph Campau carried on a thriving fur trade with the Indians and maintained several posts throughout Michigan. Always on friendly terms with them, he learned many of their dialects.[57] Frequently a score of dusky braves with their squaws and papooses could be seen lounging about in front of his house, since a front room was used as a store with an office at the rear. Behind the house were a storehouse and a dock on the river to accommodate the batteaux, of which Campau had several in the Montreal trade.[58] By 1840, when most of the Indians had been moved west of the Mississippi by the government, Joseph Campau had retired from active business and devoted the remainder of his long life to looking after his numerous real estate holdings and investments. His account books were meticulously kept in French, as he was never completely at home with the English language. Toward the end of his life he became the wealthiest man in Michigan.[59]

Joseph Campau's fur trading business represented the traditional interdependence of the white man and the Indian. But now that Michigan Territory was to be opened to American settlers, the Indian no longer fitted into the economic scheme of things and was regarded as a menace that must be eradicated. The government in Washington counted upon Governor Cass to keep the Indians off the warpath and to obtain land cessions from them by treaty. He was ex-officio superintendent of Indian affairs for the original area of the Northwest Territory. Not only did he obtain most of Michigan, Wisconsin, and northern Minnesota without resorting to war, but he also won the respect of the Indians for his fairness and kindness.

Educated explorers and travelers had from time to time recorded their impressions of the physical aspects of the Great Lakes area, but now that a new empire was opening up for permanent habitation, the government and citizens alike were eager to know more about their new domain. Enterprising young men eagerly turned to a study of the geography, geology, botany, and ethnology of the region. In 1820 Governor Cass obtained the consent of the government to organize an expedition to explore the territory that had recently been committed to his care. He wanted to learn more about the geography and mineralogy of the area, and about the condition of the more remote Indian tribes. Starting out from Detroit in May in three large canoes, the members of the expedition explored the shores of Lakes Huron, Superior and Michigan, and the upper reaches of the Mississippi River.[60]

Instead of completing the trip by canoe with the rest of the party, Cass returned to Detroit from Chicago on horseback by Indian trail. Chicago at the time consisted of a stockade occupied by one hundred and sixty men, and a cluster of ten or twelve dwellings which housed about sixty people. The community, originally called Fort Dearborn, had been founded as recently as 1803.[61]

The men on the expedition were well qualified to fulfill their objectives. Henry Rowe Schoolcraft, an Albany glass blower turned geologist, had been selected by the War Department to go along as the government's natural historian; Captain David B. Douglass, a professor of engineering at West Point, was chief topographer; and Charles C. Trowbridge, who had come to Detroit the previous year from New York State, was assistant topographer. Cass left for himself the task of observing the Indians.[62]

When the expedition stopped at Sault Ste. Marie, Cass obtained a site for a military post from the Indians, and two years later Fort Brady was built there. Schoolcraft became interested in Indians in 1820, and was Indian agent at the Sault in 1822–33 and at Mackinac Island in 1833–41. During this period he made an intensive study of Indian life and wrote many books on the subject, learning at the same time the Chippewa language. Next to Schoolcraft, Cass himself was the greatest authority in the United States on the customs and languages of the northern tribes. In Detroit and on his travels in the wilderness he was constantly gathering first-hand information and making notes, and he encouraged Charles C. Trowbridge, who became his secretary, to do likewise.[63]

In 1826 Thomas L. McKenney of the Indian Department journeyed to Lake Superior to negotiate jointly with Lewis Cass the Treaty of Fond du Lac with the Chippewa Indians. In 1827 he published his *Sketches of a Tour to the Lakes* and in 1844, with James Hall, *The Indian Tribes of North America*, a collection of biographies and portraits of distinguished Indians. James Otto Lewis accompanied Cass and McKenney on several of their treaty-making expeditions and did many of the illustrations for McKenney's works, as well as for his own *Aboriginal Port-Folio* of 1835. He painted many portraits of Indians in Detroit, including one of the Prophet the brother of Tecumseh.[64]

In 1830 a group of leading citizens invited a young scientist named Douglass Houghton to come to Detroit to lecture on geology, botany, chemistry, electricity, and magnetism. Houghton had been a professor at the Rensselaer Polytechnic Institute of Troy, New York. The lectures he gave in the old Council House on Jefferson avenue were a great success. In 1831–32 Houghton was appointed surgeon and botanist on an expedition organized by Schoolcraft to attempt to locate the source of the Mississippi. This was found to be a small lake which Schoolcraft named Lake Itasca. While classifying the flora of the area traversed by the expedition, Houghton became convinced that the region was rich in mineral resources. When Michigan became a state in 1837 and acquired the Upper Peninsula, Houghton secured the authorization of the state to make a geological survey. Unfortunately it was never completed because of his untimely death by drowning in Lake Superior in 1845. However, the report which he made following an expedition to Lake Superior in 1840 is important because it acquainted the people of Michigan with the extent and location of the state's rich copper deposits.[65]

(19)

Bela Hubbard was assistant geologist with Houghton on the expedition of 1840 and also on an earlier expedition in 1837 to examine the salt springs of the Saginaw valley.[66] A native of New York State, he had come to Detroit in 1835, a year after graduating from Hamilton College. For several years after his arrival he lived in the old Knaggs house at Springwells.[67] In his memoirs he recalls seeing the Detroit River alive with the canoes of Indians on their way to receive annuities from the British government at Amherstburg. This practice was continued by the British until 1836.[68]

(15)

By the twenties the English and the Indians were no longer considered a serious threat. Fort Lernoult, renamed Fort Shelby after the War of 1812, was allowed to fall into disrepair and in 1826 it was demolished; Fort, Shelby, Wayne and Cass streets were laid out on its site.[69] In 1830 the United States government accommodated settlers in the western wilderness by passing the brutal Removal Act. This act provided for the exchange of the Indians' eastern holdings for lands beyond the Mississippi River. By 1840 most of the Indians in Michigan had moved west or else sought refuge in Canada.[70]

In 1827 the stockade around Detroit was removed.[71] At last the town was breaking out of its chrysalis, where it had been slumbering for so long. The frontier era was drawing to a close. Behind were years of isolation and sanguinary conflict, while ahead lay a new era of peaceful growth and prosperity.

(1) River Rouge Indian Mound (BHC/JKJ)

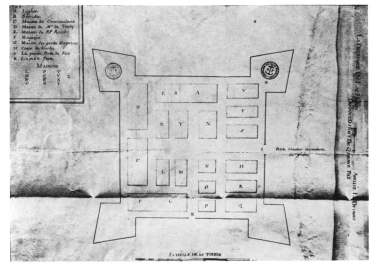

(2) Fort Pontchartrain (Cadillac's plan), 1701 (BHC)

(3) Huron Mission House, 1728 (BHC)

(4) Huron Mission Church (by Walsh, 1804), c. 1730 (BHC)

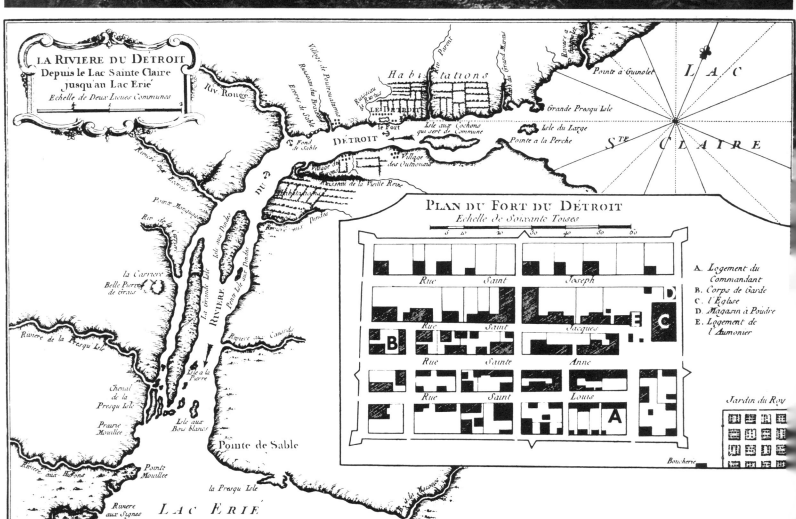

(5) Detroit River and Fort (de Léry maps), 1764 (BHC)

(6-7) Baudry-Cass House, c. 1745 (BHC/JKJ)

(8) Old Campau House, c. 1757, and Chapel, c. 1778 (BHC)

(9) View of Detroit, 1796 (BHC/JKJ)

(10) Knaggs Windmill, c. 1815 (BHC)

(11) Old Moran House, c. 1740 (BHC)

(12) Old Labadie House, c. 1780 (BHC)

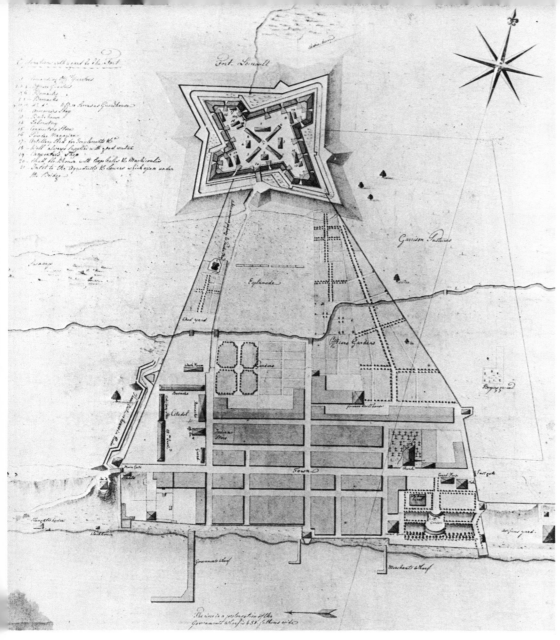

(13) Detroit and Fort Lernoult
(Rivardi map), 1799 (BHC)

(14) Citadel, 1764 (BHC)

(15) Knaggs-Hubbard House,
c. 1790 (BHC)

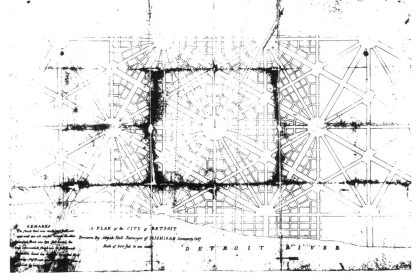

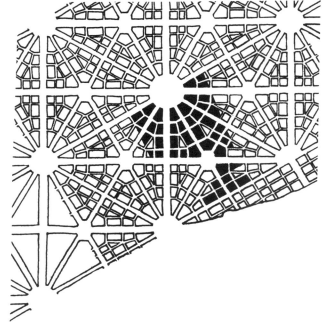

(16-17) Woodward Plan (Hull map), 1807 (BHC/JKJ) (BLP)

(18) John F. Hamtramck House, 1802 (BHC)

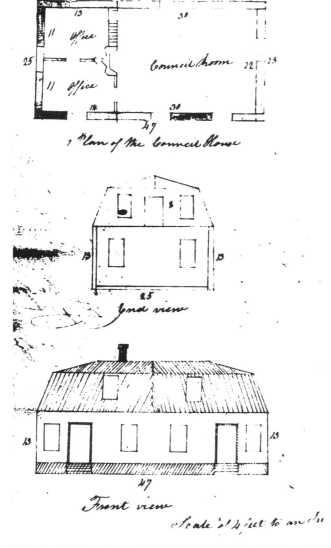

(19) Council House, c. 1807 (BHC)

(20) William Hull House, 1807 (BHC)

(21) Joseph Campau House (by Cohen, 1853), 1813 (BHC)

2. The Classic Ideal

The Vanishing Frontier

The Ohio River was a natural thoroughfare for the settlers who began moving west at the beginning of the nineteenth century. Consequently the river cities grew faster than the cities of the Great Lakes area. Cincinnati and St. Louis became the largest and most important centers of the West and maintained this hegemony as long as the rivers remained the major arteries of transportation. The early nineteenth century character of many sections of Cincinnati and St. Louis attest to their growth during this period.

Thus the main stream of westward immigration flowed past Michigan into the new states of Ohio, Indiana, Illinois, and Missouri. In 1815 Edward Tiffin, the surveyor-general of the United States land office, issued a report based on misinformation that Michigan consisted of nothing but lakes, swamps, and poor sandy land. This further retarded the development of the state.[1] To reach Michigan settlers from the East came along the Mohawk Trail to Buffalo where they embarked on sailing vessels for Detroit. The first steamship on the Great Lakes was the *Walk-in-the-Water*, named after a Wyandotte chief. Its initial trip from Buffalo to Detroit was made in 1818, thus opening a new era of steam navigation.[2] The Industrial Revolution had produced a germinating agent that would accelerate the growth and development of the Great Lakes area.

Also in 1818 a government land office was opened in Detroit and recently surveyed land was offered for sale to the public. At this time there were no settlements back from the river, and directly behind the town stretched the endless primitive forest.[3] Indian trails were not suitable for wagons, so horses fitted with pack saddles were still the only means of transportation.[4] Settlers with wagons filled with farm implements and household goods needed roads to reach the interior of Michigan. Governor Cass appealed to the government for financial aid, and by the twenties roads began fanning out in all directions from Detroit. New towns sprang up along these routes. By 1835 two stagecoaches a week made the round trip from Detroit to Chicago. Since these mud roads were frequently impassable, plank roads were provided after the Michigan Plank Road Act of 1848. Although the planks were an improvement, they also proved unsatisfactory, so later gravel surfacing was substituted.

It was not until after the completion of the Erie Canal in 1825 that the full tide of immigrants reached Michigan. During 1836 as many as two thousand arrived at Detroit in a single day on steamships and sailing vessels. The hotels were crowded, and the streets were jammed with wagons drawn by horses or oxen. Most of the settlers did not linger long in town, as they were bound for the interior.[5] Nevertheless, there was a steady increase of population in Detroit; it was 1,650 in 1820, 6,927 in 1836, 21,019 in 1850, and 45,619 in 1860.[6]

Although some of the newcomers were German or Irish, most were from New England and New York State. They brought their own predilections for religion, education, and cultural pursuits with them. Churches were built and schools established, although free public schools under a board of education were not provided until 1842. In 1817 the Detroit City Library was incorporated, and the first successful newspaper, the *Detroit Gazette,* was founded.[7]

Also in 1817 Judge Augustus B. Woodward drew up an educational plan which was adopted as law by the governor and judges. The organization provided for was named by Woodward the Catholepistemiad or University of Michigania. The Reverend John Monteith, a Presbyterian minister, was appointed president, and the Reverend Gabriel Richard, a Roman Catholic priest, vice president. Woodward's scheme was too elaborate and advanced for its day, so the legislative council abolished the Catholepistemiad and established the University of Michigan in 1821, but there was no real university until after Michigan became a state in 1837.[7] At that time the question of where to locate the university was solved when the growing community of Ann Arbor offered a forty-acre tract for the future campus.[8]

(25) In 1817–18 a building for the Catholepistemiad was erected in Detroit on the west side of Bates near Congress street. For several years it was occupied by a primary school and a classical academy operated under the supervision of the university trustees. It was an unpretentious gabled two-story brick building unmistakably showing New England Georgian lineage. Later used as a branch of the University of Michigan and a school by the Detroit Board of Education, it was torn down in 1858.[9]

The Federal Style

(23) The delightful painting, A View of Detroit in 1836, by William James Bennett shows the Detroit River alive with churning side-wheeler steamboats.[10] In the background is the new town that had sprung from the ashes of its predecessor.[11] The busy water front, the neat white buildings, and the skyline, punctuated by church steeples, give the unmistakable impression of a prosperous contemporary New England seaport.[12] More than at any other time in its history, the architectural aggregate of the city was homogeneous and of uniformly good design.

As the frontier receded, the increasing tempo of business enterprise in Detroit permitted architecture to consist of more than just the barest essentials. Form, proportion, and detail became important considerations after over a century of primitive makeshift structures. The immigrants from New England brought with them the architectural concepts then popular in the East. It was the beginning of a process of nationalization of architecture, always, of course, involving a certain time lag for the dissemination of ideas from their point of origin.

After the American Revolution there was a reaction in the United States against the Colonial Georgian architecture. To be sure, the Georgian tradition lingered on, especially in the more conservative areas like New England, but this tradition was modified by the influence of the Adam brothers in England. The delicate curvilinear Adam detail had been largely relegated to interiors in England, but in America such men as Samuel McIntire and Charles Bulfinch in Massachusetts applied the same principles of design to the exteriors of their buildings. The style thus evolved came to be known as the Federal style.[13]

By the thirties a building boom began in Detroit that has never since abated. The first *City Directory* (1837) listed a considerable number of builders and others who called themselves architects. Among them was Francis Letourno, a native of Mt. Clemens. Enterprising and versatile, he built the Michigan Exchange Hotel (1835), SS. Peter and Paul's Church (1848), and several houses, as well as a number of lighthouses on the lakes, and even steamboats.[14] According to Friend Palmer, Letourno (F. M. Latourneau) also built "the wooden dwelling of Thomas Palmer, corner of Fort and Shelby Streets, conceded to be at that time the finest and best constructed wooden residence in the city. The carved mantels, the carved fanlight over the front entrance on Fort Street, as well as the covering for the attic window in the gable on the same street, were wonders in their way."[15]

A successful merchant, Thomas Palmer had built the first brick store in Detroit in 1820 on Jefferson avenue. Associated with him in business was his brother John Palmer, whose house was located on the southwest corner of Griswold and Fort streets. It is likely that Letourno also built this house, which *(26)* was erected in 1829. With a finely detailed cornice and a semi-circular window in the tympanum, it consisted of a pedimented main mass and a low side wing. The house was razed in 1869.[16] The Penobscot Building now stands on the site. *(354)*

Letourno also built the Indian Agency house at Sault Ste. Marie for Henry Rowe Schoolcraft in 1827.[14] Before it was disfigured by later alterations it was a charming example of Federal architecture.[17] Originally it consisted of a two-story main block with two symmetrical dependencies. The door was framed with an elliptical fanlight and sidelights. On the interior, mantels with delicate elliptical sunbursts and moldings have remained intact to the present day. A recently discovered letter from Obed Wait to Schoolcraft indicates that the former built the agency house.[18] Perhaps Letourno worked with him.

Now that steam navigation had made the Great Lakes area accessible to the more populous regions of the East and to Europe, there was a considerable curiosity among the intelligentsia as well as among travel-minded citizens to see for themselves the wonders of the new inland empire that held so much promise for the future. Detroit was then the gateway to the Northwest, and many large hotels sprang up to accommodate the stream of immigrants and curious visitors that funneled through the town. In the days before the Civil War it was unthinkable for the traveler not to record his impressions. Michigan was probably visited by more literate travelers than any other area in the United States, and the still largely unexplored fund of books and documents they produced provides an invaluable source of information for the student of early times in the state.[19]

Alexis de Tocqueville passed through Detroit in 1831, burning to reach "the last limits of civilization" and "to find there Indian tribes entirely barbaric."[20] Harriet Martineau, the English authoress, not such an avid student of aboriginal mores, paused long enough at Detroit in 1836 to observe that "the streets of the town are wide and airy but the houses, churches, and stores are poor for the capital city of a territory or state. Wooden planks, laid on grass, form the pavement in all the outskirts of the place. The deficiency is of stone, not of labor." Miss Martineau failed to mention that nonetheless some of the downtown streets were paved with cobblestones. However, she sounded a more hopeful note by saying, "The society of Detroit is very choice. It has continued so since the old colonial days and there is every reason to think that it will become, under its new dignities of statehood, a more desirable place of residence."[21]

(22)
(20)
While in Detroit, Miss Martineau stayed at the American before setting out on her arduous journey by stagecoach to Chicago. The hotel was built in 1835 on the south side of Jefferson avenue east of Randolph. It incorporated as a nucleus Governor Hull's old residence. An early engraving in Farmer's *History*, made after the name had been changed to Wales' Hotel, shows a stagecoach filled with passengers at the entrance. The Jefferson avenue façade, charmingly domestic in scale, displayed typically Federal characteristics: the low roof lines concealed behind balustrades, the entrance framed with an elliptical fanlight and sidelights, the front porch with its slender columns, and the pilasters that graced the eastern extension.[22] In the fire of 1848 Detroit lost one of its finer hostelries.

(28)
Another visitor at the American in 1836 was Anna Jameson, the English authoress and art critic. She attended services at the First Brick Baptist Church which had been completed the year before on the northwest corner of Fort and Griswold streets.[23] "The church is one of the largest in town," she wrote, "plain in appearance, but the interior handsome, and in good taste."[24] Mrs. Jameson failed to notice a particularly graceful terraced clock tower above the pediment. The Federal subtlety of its design made a pleasing contrast with the plainness of the main mass of the church. In 1859 the old church was torn down to make way for a new church on the same site.

(24)
When Detroit was burned in 1805 old Ste. Anne's Church was swept away. After many vicissitudes the parish, led by the beloved priest Father Gabriel Richard, collected its forces to erect a new Ste. Anne's on the north side of Larned street between Randolph and Bates.[25] The cornerstone was laid in 1818 and the first services were held in 1828.[26]

An engraving in the first *Detroit City Directory* (1837) shows a plain cobblestone building with round-arched windows on the sides and back.[27] It had a small central octagonal dome and two small cupolas in the rear. In front rose two graceful Federal spires with open belfries. Rexford Newcomb has pointed out the similarity between these towers and the towers on St. Joseph's in Bardstown, Kentucky.[28] Detroit was then included in the diocese of Bardstown, and Bishop Flaget of Bardstown, who witnessed the cornerstone laying of Ste. Anne's, may have had something to say about the design of the Detroit church. In 1842 the center dome and the cupolas were removed. The next year a handsome Greek Revival porch, consisting of paired Doric columns supporting an entablature and pediment, was added onto the front of the church. At that time also the belfries were enclosed.[26]

In 1832 a cholera plague broke out in Detroit. After administering aid to many sufferers Father Richard died, a victim of the plague, and was buried in the crypt of Ste. Anne's. In 1886 Ste. Anne's was torn down and the land sold for commercial purposes. In the following year services were held in the new *(122)* Ste. Anne's erected at Nineteenth and Howard streets. The remains of Father Richard were transferred there.

(31)
The oldest existing church building in Detroit is the Church of SS. Peter and Paul (1844-48) on the northeast corner of Jefferson avenue and St. Antoine street.[29] Designed by Francis Letourno, it is a restrained but monumental brick building, lacking in any of the bold classical features that were becoming increasingly popular.[30] After all, the New England meetinghouse was a distinctly Protestant development, so it is not surprising to find Letourno turning to Italian Renaissance forms for a Roman Catholic church.[31] Forty years earlier Charles

Bulfinch had done likewise for both St. Stephen's Church and Holy Cross Church in Boston.[32]

The walls of SS. Peter and Paul's are broken into bays by Ionic pilasters supporting an entablature. Between the pilasters are round-arched windows set in blind arches. On the front of the church is a projecting bay, in the center of which is an entrance framed by a pediment supported by Ionic pilasters. The architect's original perspective drawing included a Wren-like tower, but this was never constructed.[33] On the interior the three-aisled basilica has barrel vaults in plaster.

One of the most monumental buildings of the Federal period is the old *(29)* barracks (1848) still standing within the ramparts of Fort Wayne. Lieutenant Montgomery C. Meigs, who supervised the construction of the fort, is credited with designing the barracks.[34] It is a three-and-a-half story stone structure divided into five bays or sections separated by two-foot fire-walls. There are quoins at the corners of the building and on each side of the central bay. In general outline the building harks back to the stern New England institutional tradition of the previous century, and the only token of Federal elegance is the elliptical window in the central pediment.

The fort as a whole represents the last phase of military architecture in *(30)* Detroit. Fort Shelby had been demolished in 1826. However, tensions developed between the United States and Canada with the outbreak of the Patriot War or rebellion in Canada in 1837. Since the vulnerability of Detroit was apparent, Congress allocated funds for the construction of Fort Wayne. Although the fort has never been attacked, it served as a training center during the Civil War and was heavily garrisoned during World War I. With the advent of World War II it became an ordnance depot.

Built at the bend of the Detroit River three and a half miles below the City Hall, Fort Wayne owed much to the principles of fortification laid down by Sébastien Vauban, the great French military engineer. When first erected (c. 1845–50), it was a square bastioned fort with sand embankments and a red cedar scarp with embrasures of oak. In 1864 the cedar scarp was replaced by a brick and concrete scarp wall twenty-two feet high and seven and a half feet thick, the oak embrasures having been replaced with masonry. The redan designed by Meigs was completed and the casemates were altered. After a century of service the fort was transferred to the city of Detroit in 1949 and is now a military museum.[35]

The Greek Revival

The fragile Federal style was but the first timid gesture of a young nation. As the country gained in strength and self-assurance, Washington and Jefferson became convinced that the architecture of Greece and Rome best expressed the ideals of the young republic. The ancient world had been an inspiration to the architects of the Renaissance and the stimulus was renewed in the eighteenth century by the beginnings of scientific archeological research. Jefferson, however, received the direct impact of antiquity when he viewed the best-preserved Roman temple, the Maison Carée at Nìmes in France. The buildings which he later designed revealed how deeply he was imbued with the Roman spirit.

Since the full degree of Roman sumptuousness could never be attained by the architects of so young a republic, they turned increasingly to the serene dignity of the Greek ideal. Latrobe, Mills, Strickland, and Davis, and Bulfinch in his later years, led the way in the large cities of the eastern seaboard. Never mere plagiarists, their use of classical proportions and details never blinded them to the utilitarian requirements of their buildings. With skill and taste they went about creating a new American architecture. Measured drawings in the handbooks of Asher Benjamin and Minard Lafever were useful in spreading the new style to the remotest corners of the nation and eventually across the continent. The classical fervor continued until it was mitigated by increasing romanticism and materialism, and finally extinguished by the turmoil of the Civil War.[36]

Judge Woodward had done more than anyone else to provide an appropriate atmosphere for classical architecture in Detroit. His enthusiasm for the classic world had prompted him early in his career to change his own name from Elias to the Roman Augustus and later to name the town of Ypsilanti after a hero of the Greek war for independence. His scheme for the Catholopistemiad was a masterpiece of Greek scholarship; even if it never materialized, it is noteworthy that Greek and Latin actually were taught in the building intended for his university.[37] In his plan for Detroit the Campus Martius and Grand Circus were Roman in concept. The open spaces and the broad avenues of the city only needed imposing classical façades to create the desired effect.

(25)

(17)

One of the first buildings to fulfill this need was the Court House or Capitol built in 1823–28 at the head of Griswold street in what is now Capitol Park.[38] Designed by Obed Wait, this handsome brick structure with an Ionic hexastyle portico heralded a new era of Greek Revival architecture. However, the domestic quality of the typically Federal entrance with its fanlight and sidelights and of the small shuttered windows gave evidence of its early date.[39] A tall three-staged steeple carried on the New England tradition.

(35)

Originally intended to serve only as a courthouse, the building housed the Legislative Council of Michigan from 1828 to 1847. By 1823 Michigan Territory had become sufficiently populous to entitle it to a legislative council and the rule of the governor and judges came to an end. Lewis Cass, however, remained in office as governor until 1831 when he resigned to become secretary of war in Jackson's cabinet. During the governorship of Stevens T. Mason, Michigan became a state in 1837 with a new state constitution. In 1847 Lansing became the state capital, as the legislature had decided that a location in the center of the state was more desirable.[40] The old capitol building in Detroit was later used as a high school and in 1893 it burned.[41]

When Frederick Rese came to Detroit in 1834 as the first bishop of the new diocese of Michigan, he brought with him from Cincinnati Captain Alpheus White in the capacity of architect. Previously White had received architectural training in New Orleans following his military exploits in the War of 1812. One of his first jobs in Detroit was some remodeling at Ste. Anne's. In 1840 Bishop Rese was summoned to Rome, never to return, and shortly thereafter White went back to Cincinnati.[42] While in Detroit, White also designed the City Hall which was built in 1835 just east of Woodward avenue in the middle of what is now Cadillac Square.[38] It was a two-story Greek Revival structure of brick with pilasters supporting the entablature. Above the pediment was an octagonal belfry on a square base. The building was torn down after a new City Hall was built.

(33)

(85)

According to the *Detroit Directory* of 1850, the First Presbyterian Church (1834–35) was "deemed one of the best churches in the western states."[43] Located on the northeast corner of Woodward avenue and Larned, it was a Greek Revival two-story brick structure designed by Alonzo Merrill.[44] On the front was a Corinthian hexastyle portico, and above the pediment rose a staged steeple

(32)

with a spire. On the interior there were galleries on three sides. In 1854 this beautiful building was completely destroyed by fire.

Alonzo Merrill also designed the First Methodist Episcopal Church erected *(36)* on the southwest corner of Woodward avenue and State street in 1849–50.[45] It was a rather free interpretation of the distyle-in-antis temple with massive Ionic columns. Stuccoed and colored to resemble granite, the exterior walls were divided into bays by pilasters supporting an entablature. A steeple, part of the original design, was never constructed.[46] On the interior there were galleries on three sides. When it was decided in 1864 to build the Central Methodist Church *(61)* uptown, the old church was sold and later replaced by a business building.[47]

The Congregational Unitarian Church, erected in 1853 on the northwest *(45)* corner of Lafayette and Shelby streets, represented the culmination of Greek Revival church architecture in Detroit.[48] The Greek temple was more closely approximated than heretofore with a handsome Ionic hexastyle portico behind which was a bare wall penetrated by a single large entrance.[49] Even the steeple, so much a part of the Christian tradition, was omitted. Archeological verisimilitude was not carried to extremes, however, and tall windows on the sides of the building assured a cheerful interior. The church was abandoned by its congregation in 1890 and thereafter served as a music hall and later a theater. Eventually it was razed and replaced by a commercial building.[50]

The rising tides of commerce prompted the organization of the Bank of Michigan in 1818. Reputed to be the first structure of dressed stone in Detroit, the second building of the Bank of Michigan was erected on the southwest *(34)* corner of Jefferson avenue and Griswold in 1836.[51] Built of shell limestone, it was a simple two-story flat-roofed building with corner pilasters supporting an entablature. A recessed entrance was framed by two Doric columns set in antis. The architect for the Bank of Michigan was Charles Lum according to the *Detroit Directory* of 1850. After the bank failed in 1842 the building was used as a federal courthouse and post office. Later it was occupied by the First National Bank and finally by the Michigan Mutual Life Insurance Company. When the building was torn down in the early twentieth century the handsome entrance way was moved to the garden of the Architectural College in Ann Arbor.

Charles C. Trowbridge became a cashier at the Bank of Michigan in 1825 and president in 1839.[52] He also became actively interested in railroads and real estate. The shift during one man's life from ethnological to business interests was indicative of the rapid transformation of Detroit from a frontier community to the heart of a thriving empire. The period of exploration and scientific investigation had paved the way for the exploitation of natural resources. In 1826 Trowbridge built for himself what was considered the finest frame house in the *(37)* territory. Considerably altered and reduced in size, it stands today on the south side of Jefferson avenue between Rivard and Riopelle. When it was built Jefferson avenue as we know it today existed only on paper and to reach the house it was necessary to use the River road.[53]

In 1835 Griswold street was opened north to State street. In the same year James Abbott II built a house on the southeast corner of Griswold and Fort *(44)* streets.[54] It was described as "one of the most substantial, costly, and elegant buildings in Detroit."[55] Increasing commercialism had driven Abbott from his former house on lower Woodward avenue to seek peace and quiet in what was then a country atmosphere. His position as postmaster of Detroit and agent of the American Fur Company enabled him to make his home a social center of the day. The house was a simple gabled brick mass devoid of any ornamental detail.

(176) It had a Greek Revival doorway with a rectangular transom and sidelights, and shuttered windows with stone caps and sills. The Hammond Building was later built on the same site which is today in the heart of Detroit's financial district.

(43) Although restrained and conservative, the Francis Palms house (1848) was more sophisticated than the earlier Abbott house. The architect, Henry Leroy, came from western New York.[56] Talbot Hamlin has pointed out the similarity between the Palms house and the Starbuck houses built in Nantucket ten years earlier or some of the Salem houses of thirty years before.[57] Located on the north side of Jefferson avenue between St. Antoine and Hastings, it was a monumental brick structure with end chimneys and a balustrade above the cornice. There was a central Ionic porch in front of the doorway with leaded transom and sidelights. Francis Palms was born in Antwerp, Belgium, and came to Detroit in 1832. A quiet and unassuming man, he amassed a large fortune in banking, real estate, and other business interests.[58] When he died in 1886 his house was pur-
(168) chased by the Detroit College and torn down to make way for a new college building.

(39) Further out Jefferson avenue than the Palms house, the somewhat similar Alexander Chene house must have been built about the same time. From 1901 to 1914 the house was owned by Charles B. Warren who made an addition to the rear. Still standing today, the house is now Little Harry's Restaurant.

The Oliver Newberry house on the northeast corner of Fort and Shelby streets carried the tradition of the Palms and Chene houses into the early fifties.[59]
(48) A hipped instead of a gabled roof permitted a continuous cornice, and the parapet was broken by dormer windows. Newberry's success in shipping and shipbuilding won him the sobriquet, Admiral of the Great Lakes. A bachelor, he lived with his brother Henry and his nephew Henry L.[60] After his death in 1860, the house was sold to Hiram Walker, and from 1909 to 1913 it was occupied by the University Club. Finally in 1914 it was torn down and replaced by a commercial structure.

(41) Recently the old Newberry warehouse at the foot of Wayne street was demolished to make way for the Civic Center. When erected in 1854 it was the tallest and largest building west of Buffalo.[61] For many years it housed the offices of the Detroit and Cleveland Steam Navigation Company. On the end walls of the fourth and fifth floors were doors to which supplies were hoisted. While the fortress-like exterior walls were of solid brick, the interior framework was made up of massive pine timbers put together with remarkable craftsmanship.[62]

(38) In 1848 the widow of Judge Solomon Sibley built a house for herself and her two daughters on the south side of Jefferson avenue next door to Christ Church.[63] It is a frame version of the Palms and Chene houses. Along with the Chene and Trowbridge houses, it is one of the few surviving early nineteenth century houses in Detroit.[64] It is now owned by Christ Church.

As Greek Revival architecture evolved from its simple beginnings, we have seen that churches and public buildings tended to approximate more closely the historic Greek temple. An example of this trend in domestic architecture was the
(40) David Preston house (1860) which once stood on Bagg street. It was a two-story temple-type house with a tetrastyle Ionic portico and side wings. Similar to many houses to be found in western New York and Ohio, the Preston house was probably based on designs in some architectural handbook.[65]

(42) Dr. George B. Russel's house on East Jefferson avenue at Beaufait brought the Greek Revival tradition in domestic architecture to a grand finale in the sixties. Reminiscent of the grandeur of the Old South, the two-story Corinthian

portico was unique in Detroit, as was the continuous balustrade above the cornice.

In the sixties the classical style was gradually being supplanted by more romantic forms. The James F. Joy house still retained the classical porch, but the *(46)* bracketed cornice and cupola were already showing the new Italian influence. Built in 1862, the Joy house was located on the northeast corner of Fort and First streets. Joy later became president of the Michigan Central Railroad. After his death in 1896 the house was demolished.[66]

One of Detroit's leading hostelries of the fifties and sixties was the Biddle *(47)* House which stood on the southeast corner of Jefferson avenue and Randolph. Built in 1849, it resembled the Tremont House in Boston by Isaiah Rogers (1829). At the western end of the Jefferson avenue façade was a two-story recessed portico with a balcony. The massive Doric columns on the front of the portico were a token of the widespread popularity of Greek forms during this period. In its heyday the Biddle House entertained many distinguished guests, including President Andrew Johnson, General U. S. Grant, and Admiral Farragut. Frequently the balcony was used by visiting celebrities when they addressed crowds gathered in the street to greet them. The shift of business interests from Jefferson to Woodward avenue caused the gradual decline of the hotel. After many vicissitudes it was finally demolished in 1917.[67]

Even the Michigan Central Depot of 1848 assumed a classical garb. The front *(49)* of the large gabled structure at the foot of Third street was faced with pilasters and a pediment vaguely suggesting the Greek temple. To the rear of the station was the massive brick dome of the engine house, a striking landmark from the *(50)* river. Originally the Michigan Central Railroad came in on Michigan avenue to a station just beyond Griswold street on the site of the future City Hall, but in 1848 the tracks were diverted along the bed of May's Creek to the new depot on Third street.[68] Subsequently considerable river frontage was acquired for sidings. In their early years the railroad interests encountered much opposition, culminating between 1854 and 1865 in the destruction of the depot, roundhouse, and freight house by arsonists.[69] It was not until 1882–83 that a new depot was built. *(123)*

Possibly the greatest stimulus to the growth and development of Michigan during the nineteenth century was the railroad. Settlers were distributed throughout the interior, towns were developed, and an outlet was provided to the markets of the world. The railroad system of Michigan became a part of a vast network that laced the continent and became the mainspring of the American economy. Even before the Civil War, Detroit was well on its way to becoming an important railroad center. When Michigan was admitted to the Union in 1837 a plan was proposed to extend three parallel east-and-west rail routes across the state. The Michigan Southern and the Michigan Central both reached Chicago in 1852, and the Detroit and Milwaukee Railroad reached Grand Haven on Lake Michigan in 1858. Detroit was linked to the East by the completion of lines from Buffalo to Windsor in 1854 and from Buffalo to Toledo in 1855.[70]

The prosperity of Michigan and of the nation as a whole was reflected in Detroit. Old buildings were outgrown and replaced, and commercial and industrial areas spread into what had previously been residential areas. Today almost nothing remains of the 'Classic City' that rose so proudly from the ashes of the fire of 1805. One by one its buildings have fallen prey to the demands of an expanding commerce. "Up to the time of the Civil War," wrote Talbot Hamlin, "Detroit was a town as distinguished in its buildings as in its original layout."[71]

(22) American (Wales') Hotel, 1835 (BHC/JKJ)
(23) View of Detroit (by Bennett), 1836 (DIA/JKJ)
(24) View of Detroit (by Macomb), 1821 (DIA/JKJ)

(25) Catholepistemiad, 1818 (BHC/JKJ)

(26) John Palmer House, *F. Letourno(?)*
1829 (BHC/JKJ)

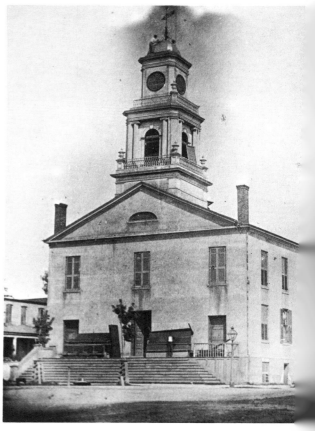

(28) First Brick Baptist Church, 1835 (BHC/JKJ)

(27) Ste. Anne's R.C. Church, 1828 (BHC/JKJ)

(29-30) Fort Wayne, *M.C. Meigs*, c. 1850
(BHC/JKJ) (DHM)

31) Saints Peter and Paul's R.C. Church, *F. Letourno*, 1848 (BHC/JKJ)

(32) First Presbyterian Church, *A. Merrill*, 1835
(BHC/JKJ)

33) City Hall, *A. White*, 1835; Russell
House, *Jordan & Anderson*, 1857
(BHC/JKJ)

(34) Bank of Michigan, *C. Lum*, 1836 (BHC/JKJ)

(35) Court House and Capitol, *O. Wait*, 1828 (BHC/JKJ)

(36) First Methodist Church, *A. Merrill*, 1850 (BHC/JKJ)

(37) Charles C. Trowbridge House, 1826 (JPM)

(38) Mrs. Solomon Sibley House, 1848 (HAL)

(39) Alexander Chene House, c. 1850 (JPM)

(40) David Preston House, 1860 (BHC/JKJ)

(41) Newberry Warehouse, 1854 (BHC)

(42) George B. Russel House, c. 1860 (BHC/JKJ) (43) Francis Palms House, *H. Leroy*, 1848 (BHC/JKJ)

(44) James Abbott House, 1835 (BHC/JKJ) (45) Congregational Unitarian Church, 1853 (BHC/JKJ)

(46) James F. Joy House, 1862 (BHC/JKJ)

(47) Biddle House, 1849 (BHC/JKJ)

(48) Newberry-Walker House, c. 1850 (BHC/JKJ)

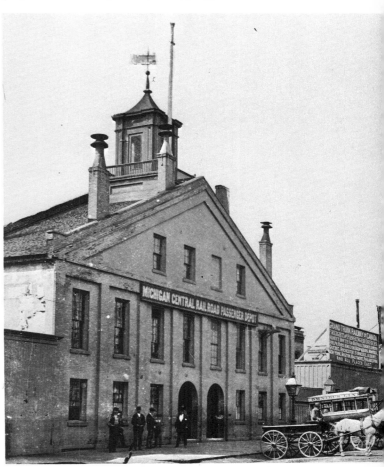

(49) Michigan Central R.R. Depot, 1848 (BHC/JKJ)

(50) View of Detroit (by Lange), c. 1860 (BHC/JKJ)

3. The Romantic Idyll

The Romantic Background

Romanticism prevailed in Europe during the first half of the nineteenth century. It represented a reaction of the introspective Northern spirit against the classicism and rationalism of the Mediterranean spirit.[1] The French Revolution had sounded the death knell of the old regime and a new era of political liberty had dawned. The individual was free to express himself unfettered by the artistic dogmas of an aristocratic minority.

Although the Classical Revival may be considered a continuation of the rationalist tradition in the arts, nevertheless romantic overtones were manifested in a heightened nostalgia for the past. Antiquarianism began with the excavations at Pompeii and Herculaneum. Never before had modern man been treated to such an intimate glimpse of the daily living habits of the ancient world. From then on historical resuscitation was to color the arts for many years. When the vogue for classicism had run its course it was inevitable that stylistic innovators should search for other remote civilizations for their inspiration. The wave of nationalism that followed the Napoleonic Wars prompted each country to reexamine its own cultural heritage, and the accomplishments of the Middle Ages, which had been so ignored in the Age of Reason, were admired with a chauvinistic fervor.

Literature was the parent art of the Romantic period. In an age of emotional expression specific images were needed to arouse these emotions. Brought to life by prose, poetry, and drama, the colorful heroes and heroines of the legendary past occupied the center of the public's imagination. Music, painting, and architecture were readily attuned to the imagery of literature, and all the arts were drawn into the magic circle of romance. In England, where the classical spirit had never been very strong, the impact of romanticism was overwhelming. Scott, Byron, and Tennyson were enchanting the public with rhapsodies over the glories of the past, and Shakespeare rose from the grave to captivate his audiences again. English Gothic architecture, which had merely amused a few dilettantes in the previous century, was recognized as a great national expression.

Appointing himself as the apostle of the Gothic Revival, Augustus W. Pugin turned out a series of eulogistic treatises on the subject which were illustrated with detailed drawings. Handbooks such as these became the bibles of the oncoming generation of architects. Also furthering the Gothic cause were the religious zealots of the day. Adherents of the Oxford movement and members of the Ecclesiological Society demanded a return to medieval ritual and insisted upon medieval church design as a necessary concomitant.[2]

In the meantime, romanticism was gaining ground in America. Authors like Hawthorne, Irving and Poe, and artists like Washington Allston and Thomas Cole were conjuring up strange and colorful visions from the past. Crenelated towers were rising along the banks of the Hudson River and converting it into an American Rhine. Spires, crockets, and finials were sprouting in towns and villages where only recently the supremacy of columned temples was unchallenged. In 1846 two masterpieces of Gothic architecture were completed in New York: James Renwick's Grace Church and Richard Upjohn's Trinity Church.

The Gothic Revival: Churches

Even Detroit, so recently drawn into the mainstream of circulation by the miracle of modern transportation, was affected by the prevailing romantic mood. Book shelves of the well-to-do were lined with choice romantic readings, and an emergent theater brought life to the heroes of fiction. Edwin and Wilkes Booth and Charlotte Cushman appeared in many Shakespearean roles. Devotees of Scott were treated to a dramatization of *Rob Roy*, and Byron enthusiasts were thrilled when Adah Isaacs Menken, lashed to the back of a racing steed, was borne across artificial stage hills in the role of Mazeppa.[3]

Small wonder that a citizenry so dazzled by the world of romantic literature should become impatient with the Olympian serenity of Greek Revival architecture. It seemed as if the Gothic style had been expressly invented to satisfy their newly-acquired taste for the picturesque and extravagant. Little did it matter if the principal building materials in Detroit had hitherto been brick and timber and if the meager supply of stone in the nearby quarries was not suited for traditional stonework.

In any event the Protestant Episcopalians could hardly be satisfied for long with St. Paul's Church,[4] a plain brick structure Alonzo Merrill had built for them in 1828 on Woodward avenue between Larned and Congress streets.[5] Detroit's most Anglican congregation was growing in size and prestige, so in 1836 *(53)* Captain Robert T. Elliott enlarged and Gothicized their church, adding a two-stage tower. Pinnacles, crockets, moldings, and battlements were applied to the structure like so much frosting on a wedding cake. If these details were superficial, they at least displayed a certain skill in execution. It was unfortunate that Captain Elliott's talents could not have been directed to some more ambitious project than the mere task of remodeling, for he appears to have been an architect of more than usual ability for the time and place.

Elliott was born in Ireland and educated there as an architect and civil engineer. In 1819 he sailed for Canada and began his career doing reconstruction work on the Citadel of Quebec. In 1827 he moved to Rochester, New York, where he was the architect for St. Patrick's Church, a Gothic structure in native bluestone. Leaving Rochester in 1834, he resided in Detroit until his death in 1841. During the winter evenings of 1836 he gave lessons in architecture, drawing, and building to a class of adult pupils which included Henry Leroy. One of his most important commissions in Detroit was a mansion for John A. Welles, no trace of which remains today. Among his other talents was the ability to converse freely in French or Gaelic with his wife, who was also from Ireland.[6]

The remodeled architecture of St. Paul's Church won such acclaim that overnight the Gothic became the favored style for churches in Detroit. Unfortunately, Captain Elliott did not live to further realize his gifts; so Calvin N. Otis of Buffalo was called upon by the Episcopalians to be the architect of the *(54)* Mariners' Church, which was completed in 1849 on the northwest corner of

Woodward avenue and Woodbridge.[7] Otis had first learned the trade of carpenter and joiner which prepared him for the profession of architecture.[8] In 1847 he built Grace Episcopal Church in Galena, Illinois, then the metropolis of that region.[9]

The idea of establishing a sailors' mission germinated in the minds of Miss Charlotte Ann Taylor and her sister Mrs. Julia Ann Anderson who bequeathed their entire property to establish the Mariners' Church. The will directed that it be built of stone.[10] This was the first of a series of gray limestone churches that were to form the main body of Gothic Revival work done in Detroit during the next twenty-five years. The stone was obtained from quarries down the Detroit River at Malden and Trenton and sent upstream by barge. Since this stone was unsuitable for anything but rubble walls, sandstone good enough for trim and carved ornament was later obtained from quarries on Lake Erie in Ohio.

On the Mariners' Church, however, wooden pinnacles, battlements, and belfry were added to the buttressed limestone walls. In the course of time these wooden elements have disappeared. The building is a box-like structure with a sloping roof supported on Howe trusses. The Tudor-arched windows give it its claim to being called Perpendicular Gothic. To aid in maintaining the building the lower story was first used as a post office and was later rented to various business firms. Adding to Detroit's lengthy list of fugitive churches, old Mariners' was moved in its entirety to the southwest corner of Randolph and Jefferson in 1955 to make way for the Civic Center. Remodeling of the church to suit *(380)* its new location gave it a new dignity, but deprived it of some of its quaint early nineteenth century character.

Calvin N. Otis was also the architect of the second St. Paul's Episcopal *(51)* Church.[11] The congregation had grown too large for the old St. Paul's Church on Woodward avenue, so a new church was built in 1852 on the northeast corner of Congress and Shelby streets. It was a much more ambitious project than Mariners' Church. Early English Gothic with lancet windows was chosen in preference to Mariners' Perpendicular Gothic. Undoubtedly Otis was strongly influenced by Richard Upjohn's St. Paul's Church (1850-51) in Buffalo,[12] to which the Detroit church bore a striking resemblance. A handsome steeple with a spire was placed at the corner of the building where it could be seen to advantage from both converging streets. On the opposite side of the asymmetrical façade was a small turret terminating in a pinnacle. The proportions of the church were good, even if the details were simple in the extreme. The audience chamber of the building was unobstructed by columns or galleries and was spanned by large hammerbeam trusses. A small chancel provided a setting for the altar.[13] Basically the church was still the New England meetinghouse, the only change being the substitution of Gothic for Georgian motifs. Eventually outgrown, the church was moved stone by stone in 1901 to the corner of Lafayette and East Grand boulevard where it became the Church of the Messiah.[14] The new St. Paul's Cathedral was finally built on Woodward avenue in 1908–19. *(316)*

Two other architects who were responsible for some of Detroit's churches of the early fifties were Octavius and Albert H. Jordan from Hartford, Connecticut. Albert Jordan is first mentioned as a resident of Detroit in the *City Directory* of 1852–53. After a short stay in 1853, Octavius Jordan returned to his practice in Hartford, but Albert Jordan remained in Detroit until 1861, doing most of the work on the Detroit churches and eventually becoming independent of the Hartford firm.[15] The Jordans do not appear to have specialized in church building in Hartford, where churches were already plentiful. Fast-growing Detroit offered much greater opportunities for ambitious young architects.

(52)   The Fort Street Presbyterian Church, still standing on the southeast corner at Third, was completed by the firm of O. and A. Jordan in 1855 under the supervision of Albert H. Jordan.[16] The main body of the church resembles the second St. Paul's with its vast hammerbeam trusses, yet the façade struck a new note by being ornamented with a plethora of archeologically correct stone details rather incongruously juxtaposed. Probably the architects culled these motifs from the pages of Pugin or Britton and applied them superficially with little understanding of true Gothic form or structure. Out of this welter of ornament it is possible to recognize a facsimile of a corner turret of King's College Chapel, Cambridge, and also of the extraordinarily slender spire of St. James at Louth, Lincolnshire, both in England.[17] Certainly the little pepper-box belfry placed awkwardly at the top of the front gable does nothing to improve the overall effect of the main façade. Yet, in spite of these discrepancies, the church has been much admired for its lacy stonework and graceful silhouette.[18] To be sure, there were the first stirrings here of that desire for novelty and ostentation which characterized the later Victorian Gothic work, yet the papery quality of the detail and the simplicity of plan ally the church more closely to the early Gothic Revival.

(60)   In contrast to the Fort Street Presbyterian Church, Albert Jordan chose a symmetrical rather than an asymmetrical scheme for his Jefferson Avenue Presbyterian Church of 1855, now no longer standing.[19] There was a salient axial tower in front of the gable end of the building. The coffers of this congregation were not overflowing, so there could be no flights of fancy in stone. The exterior walls were of brick covered with stucco. On the interior wood and plaster

(59) were employed to simulate a fully articulated medieval structure. There were clustered piers and ribbed vaults, and above the nave arcade were triple windows lighted from skylights in the sloping roof.

    By 1855 Albert Jordan had become independent of the Hartford firm. A young Scots draftsman named James Anderson, who had learned architecture in the Jordan office, is known to have done a large portion of the work on the Fort Street Presbyterian Church. Still in his twenties, Anderson became a partner of

(56) Jordan in 1857.[20] In 1861 they built St. John's Episcopal Church on the southeast corner of Woodward avenue and High street, now Vernor highway or Fisher freeway.[21] There was no need for economizing as Henry P. Baldwin, a shoe

(97) manufacturer, unstintingly provided the funds for the construction of the church.[22] There is an unmistakable family resemblance to the Fort Street Presbyterian Church, but the frenzied copyism of the earlier church has been watered down and tempered by a better sense of design. In short, here we recognize all the earmarks of Victorian Gothic at its best.

    The sandstone trim of St. John's contrasts agreeably with the rich texture of the limestone rubble walls, and an unusual variety of Flamboyant stone tracery adds a touch of Victorian novelty to the well-composed façade. The main mass of the church is broken by wings that appear to be transepts but are actually occupied by vestry rooms, a library, and a minister's study. At the rear of the

(55) church is a picturesque chapel that recalls one Jordan built in Elmwood Cemetery in 1856. On the interior of the church there were galleries on three sides of the audience chamber, their only support being brackets extended from the walls. Large hammerbeam trusses above originally extended from wall to wall. However, in 1935 the entire church had to be moved back sixty feet because of the widening of Woodward and it was necessary to build steel and plaster piers on either side of the nave for additional roof support. The tower was pulled down and rebuilt stone by stone in the new location.[23]

In 1858 the position of Jordan and Anderson as Detroit's ranking church architects was challenged by the arrival in the city of a young English architect, Gordon W. Lloyd, who was not, however, a stranger to the New World. Although born in Cambridge, England, Lloyd had come to Canada when six years of age with his parents who settled in Sherbrooke, Quebec, in 1838. He returned to England in 1847 upon the death of his father Lieutenant William Lloyd, R.N. After completing his education he entered the architectural office of his uncle Ewan Christian, a well-known church builder and restorer who was later president of the Royal Institute of British Architects.[24] Although Christian's work had no particular claim to distinction, "his hatred of shams was proverbial."[25] While working in his uncle's office Lloyd attended night classes at the Royal Academy.[26] During this period he did some Puginesque drawings of Gothic detail.[27] However, the supremacy of Pugin was waning and a new generation of architects, rebelling against the insularity of English Gothic, were not averse to foreign influence. One of these rebels was Sir George Gilbert Scott, who probably influenced Lloyd, as he began giving lectures at the Royal Academy in 1855.[28]

It was a period when the young English architect felt obliged to finish off his professional training with a sketching tour of the Continent. Lloyd was no exception. He toured Brittany, Normandy, and Touraine in the fall of 1856. The following fall he went from town to town by steamboat along the Moselle and the upper Rhine. Like Scott, Lloyd was attracted mostly by the northern Gothic. The sketches which he brought back revealed a romantic interest in medieval churches, houses, and castles with their crisp Gothic detail, steep roofs, and picturesque aspects.[27] Well prepared for his future career, Lloyd sailed for America in 1858. It is interesting to speculate as to why he chose Detroit as the scene of his endeavors. While living in Canada he had probably heard of this youthful fast-growing city that held such promise for the future. Certainly there would be less professional competition than in the older centers of England and America. Then, too, since Detroit is a border city, he could still be near Canada, which had been his boyhood home and to which he felt a strong allegiance.

Lloyd's choice of Detroit was justified, as he soon received several important commissions. He began Christ Episcopal Church on East Jefferson avenue between Hastings and Rivard in 1861.[29] Upon its dedication in 1863 the *Detroit Free Press* noted, "The style of architecture is Gothic, of the early part of the fourteenth century, adapted and kept subordinate in all respects to modern requirements."[30] Yet in view of Lloyd's orthodox background and his familiarity with authentic Gothic monuments, it is not surprising that Christ Church is more medieval in character than the Jordan churches. There are transepts with galleries, and a lofty nave arcade supporting graceful hammerbeam trusses. It was a disappointment to Lloyd that for economic reasons it was necessary to construct the round arcade piers of plaster furred from a chamfered pine core. With such a light timber construction, Lloyd must have felt that, although a nave arcade was required to create the proper Episcopalian atmosphere, a clerestory was not appropriate. He therefore resorted to an unusual lighting expedient: spherical-triangular windows jutting into the roof as dormers were placed high in each bay of the lateral nave walls. If the chancel was originally no deeper than its predecessor at St. John's, it was only because at that time it was customary for the choir to occupy the side or rear galleries. The practice of placing a vested choir in the chancel was not introduced into the American Episcopalian service until comparatively recently, necessitating a lengthening of the chancel of Christ Church in 1903.

(57)

On the front of the church, providing most of the illumination, is a large single window with elaborate Decorated tracery. To the right is a handsome tower with an arcaded belfry and a Germanic wedge-shaped roof, while on the left subordinate interest is provided by two prominent crocketed pinnacles crowning the buttresses. The rock-faced limestone walls, contrasting with the dressed sandstone trim, add richness of texture to this charmingly original yet discreet example of Victorian Gothic.

(61)   Lloyd was allowed an even greater opportunity for originality in the construction of the Central Methodist Episcopal Church in 1866–67 on the northeast corner of Woodward and Adams avenues.[31] Unlike the Episcopalians, the Methodists were not bound to a traditional architectural concept. Advantageous for both seating and lighting are the broad semi-octagonal transepts. Large gables on the faces of the transepts serve to break up the external mass of the building. This increasing tendency toward multiplicity of forms is also evident in the diversity of window openings. Nevertheless, an interesting three-dimensional quality was achieved and triviality avoided by the restrained ornament and rugged masonry. A strong vertical accent was provided by a corner tower with a broach spire. During the widening of Woodward avenue in 1935–36 this steeple was rolled eastward twenty-six feet and the front wall was moved back, the nave being thus shortened by twenty-eight feet.[32] Although this disfigured the church considerably, its character was not essentially altered.

The Central Methodist Church brings to mind Richard Upjohn's St. Thomas's Church which rose in 1868–70 on Fifth avenue in New York on the site of the present edifice of the same name by Goodhue. Here could be found the anomalous semi-octagonal transepts that appeared earlier in Lloyd's work. St. Thomas's was a commendable example of the Victorian phase of Upjohn's Gothic, even if it lacked the stylistic purity of his earlier masterpiece, Trinity.[33]

Although Lloyd was thirty years younger than Upjohn, a similarity of approach is especially noticeable in their smaller churches, which are characterized by a simplicity of primary masses, a sensitivity to proportion, and a restraint of detail. Lloyd's early success in Detroit brought him many commissions throughout Michigan and Ohio.[34] Trinity Episcopal Church (1861) in Marshall, Michigan, has the charm of a small English parish church. Built of yellowish local limestone, the simple mass of the church was relieved by a chancel and a steeple. The façade was ornamented by a central window containing plate tracery.

On a larger scale are Lloyd's St. Andrew's Church (1867) and Congregational Church (1872), both in Ann Arbor, Michigan. Originally these buildings were without towers, but in 1901–03 he added a fine battlemented tower to St. Andrew's.[35] There being no quarry near Ann Arbor, these churches were built of granitic fieldstone, roughly squared to form charmingly variegated wall surfaces that blend agreeably with their polychromatic slate roofs. Narrow lancet windows penetrate the fieldstone directly, requiring no trim or tracery. An instance of the experimental turn of Lloyd's mind is seen in his use of cast stone for the water table of St. Andrew's. Obsessed with the problem of eliminating the excessive cost of dressed stone, Lloyd considered at one time going into the business of making cast stone.[26] The necessity of economizing also led him unwillingly to utilize cast-iron Gothic columns to support galleries, as in the Ann Arbor Congregational Church. In St. Andrew's membered wooden piers support a small clerestory resembling a continuous dormer, penetrated by a series of quatrefoil openings.

Lloyd's St. Paul's Episcopal Church (1873) in Flint, Michigan, is a more elaborate version of St. Andrew's.[36] There is the same type of clerestory, but in addition there are full transepts and a broach spire. Fine plate tracery of dressed stone contrasts with the rusticated limestone walls. In 1873 Lloyd also built St. Paul's Episcopal Church in Marquette, Michigan. Unusual features were the use of local brownstone and a tower placed diagonally at the corner of the building. Among Lloyd's Ohio churches, Trinity (1866–69) in Columbus is an almost exact duplicate of Christ Church in Detroit, and Christ Episcopal Church (1872) in Springfield chiefly differs from the Ann Arbor Congregational Church of the same year in the addition of a steeple.

In 1870–71 Lloyd erected the Trinity Episcopal Church in Pittsburgh.[37] The Pennsylvania city, at this time looming larger in the industrial world than Detroit, was in a better position to loosen its purse strings for a really large undertaking. Not limited in his use of cut stone, Lloyd could at last realize his ideal of a fully articulated academic Gothic church in his favorite Decorated style. There is a magnificent tower in four stages with a crocketed stone spire. Fine Geometric tracery adorns the large window on the façade, while on each transept appear ornate rose windows. A chancel forty feet in length terminates in a French polygonal apse, while clustered stone piers support a full clerestory beneath a timber barrel roof. In spite of this, the interior of the church is disappointingly lacking in medieval feeling since the nave is too wide for its height. Barring this discrepancy, the church compares favorably with the best work of Renwick and Upjohn.

The original chapel of Trinity Church with its bell cote flanked by two gables recalls the original chapel of the Central Methodist Church in Detroit. Both these chapels were later replaced by church houses. Only the charming cruciform chapel of Christ Church in Detroit remains with its picturesque arrangement of lancet windows and bell cote. This chapel was disfigured, however, by the extension of the chancel of the church proper in 1901–03. The motif of the bell cote above the façade was engagingly translated into wood in Lloyd's St. James Episcopal Church (1867) on Grosse Ile near Detroit.[38] The side walls are of battened boards broken by wood buttresses corresponding to the roof trusses. Less distinguished versions of wooden churches with vertical siding were common in Detroit at the time.

(58)

The panic of 1873 seriously curtailed Lloyd's church building activities. With the exception of St. Paul's Episcopal Church of 1875 in Cleveland (now St. Paul's Shrine of the Blessed Sacrament), he did not build any more important Gothic churches. The popularity of the Gothic was waning and the relative purity of the earlier revival styles was being submerged in the stylistic melee of the seventies. The Cleveland church falls far below the mark of Lloyd's previous churches. Novelty for the sake of novelty was introduced in a half-hearted manner. The tower was crowned with an octagonal belfry joined by flying buttresses to corner pinnacles. Rising too high above the belfry parapet, the pinnacles failed to provide a satisfactory tapering effect. Elsewhere on the church flaring eaves and Swiss gables added to the confusion.

Lloyd was so unmistakably Anglican in his tastes that it is not surprising that one of Detroit's leading German Roman Catholic congregations looked elsewhere for an architect to satisfy its religious needs. Francis G. Himpler of New York was chosen to build St. Joseph's Church (1870–73) on Orleans street south of Gratiot at the southeast corner of Jay.[39] Its tall windows, steep roof, and soaring frontal tower bring to mind the *Hallenkirchen* of southern Germany. It was the last in the cycle of Detroit's native limestone churches.

(62)

The Gothic Revival: Villas

It was inevitable that Americans would soon tire of the cool formality of their Grecian villas and pine for more romantic dwellings. England, that great nineteenth century incubator of styles, had developed a wide variety of formulas for domestic architecture calculated to satisfy the most demanding romantic tastes. On this side of the Atlantic, Alexander Jackson Davis of New York took up the torch and began providing wealthy merchants with fastidious villas in the Gothic or Tuscan modes. Steeped in the lore of romantic literature, he relied upon a fertile imagination and an unerring artistic sense to produce some of the most charming architectural creations of the period.

Davis's architecture implied a new philosophy of the domestic. This was precisely what hundreds of home-builders from Maine to Missouri needed. Andrew Jackson Downing, a friend of Davis, understood this need and took it upon himself to explain the new philosophy in a series of volumes amply illustrated with examples of Davis's work. A native of Newburgh-on-the-Hudson, Downing was primarily a landscape architect. To his readers he presented a glowing vision of picturesque villas nestled in a landscape that was a "refined imitation" of nature in such books as *A Treatise on the Theory and Practice of Landscape Gardening* (1841), *Cottage Residences* (1842), and *The Architecture of Country Houses* (1850).[40] To those contemplating the erection of a new home Downing offered a choice of styles: Roman, Italian, Swiss, Venetian, Rural Gothic, or Bracketed. The Greek style was too formal for anything but a public building. "Domestic architecture," he declared, "should be less severe, less rigidly scientific, and it should exhibit more of the freedom and play of feeling of every-day life." Style should come from the creative adaptation of past forms. "So far as an admiration of foreign style in architecture arises from the mere love of novelty, it is poor and contemptible," he warned.[41]

Downing left no doubt as to his personal preference. His own home at Newburgh, which he called Highland Gardens, was a Tudor Gothic villa. Dark furniture and woodwork did little to brighten the somber interiors. In the library busts of worthies hovered above the Gothic bookcases in ghostly silence.[42] To Downing, at least, the Rural Gothic style expressed "as large a union of domestic feeling and artistic knowledge as any other known."[43] The teachings of Downing were so irresistible that Gothic villas and cottages began to dot the American landscape. When architects were not available, carpenters could consult his and other similar books directly. As the domestic counterpart of the Gothic church, the Gothic house was the first to become widely popular. Other styles followed suit. It was the beginning of a long and complex period of eclectic architecture. Pandora's box had been opened, and Americans would be bedeviled for many a generation with a mounting desire for the picturesque.

(64) One of the first Gothic houses in Detroit was built in 1845 by Charles Stewart, an Irish lawyer closely associated with Governor Mason. Located on the southwest corner of Fort street and Second, when new it was considered the finest wooden house in the city. Stewart, who was what today might be called a promoter, designed this house for his family; but he only lived there for a few years, business calling him to the East. It was later occupied by Henry A. Newland who had made a fortune in the fur business.[44] Architecturally speaking, the house was merely the box-like dwelling of New England tradition dressed up in Gothic instead of Greek trimmings. The roof line was broken by gables trimmed with scalloped vergeboards. There were drip moldings and a hint of

tracery in the central window. On the inside there was a steep narrow flight of steps in the central hallway. The Theodore H. Hinchman house (1848), also on Fort street, was very similar.[45] It was removed in 1868, and the Stewart or Newland house was torn down in 1905.

In 1848 the new Michigan Central Depot was completed west of Third *(49)* street and then some of the most desirable residential frontage in the city was by degrees choked off by railroad sidings along the river. This and the increasing commercial expansion forced prosperous merchants to seek sites for new houses further and further out Fort street and Jefferson avenue. Town houses became less popular as more and more followers of Downing sought countrified surroundings.

During the period between his arrival in Detroit in 1858 and the panic of 1873, Gordon W. Lloyd produced a series of residences. His early indoctrination in England had dedicated him to the Gothic and his uncompromising standard of monumentality applied as much to his domestic work as it did to his churches. The use of native limestone lent a note of sober dignity to his houses which were, nevertheless, varied by occasional light-hearted moods. Although he was never a mere copyist, yet it is not difficult to detect Downing's influence.

Lloyd's Alexander H. Dey house of 1862 and his Thomas A. Parker house of 1868, next-door neighbors on East Jefferson avenue, were still rather formal town houses. The Elizabethan details of the Dey house, although interesting in *(68)* themselves, failed to compensate for the cramped and incongruous windows in the street front.[46] The proportions of the Parker house were more satisfactory, *(70)* but even here the architect was handicapped in attempting to recall the glories of Sir Walter Scott's abode at Abbotsford on a restricted site. The Dey house was recently torn down, but the Parker house still survives as a part of the Lakeside General Hospital.

On the other hand, the Sidney D. Miller house of 1864 marked a new depar- *(63)* ture in Lloyd's work toward a more rural type of dwelling. Downing's ideal had unmistakably come to life on East Jefferson avenue. The house was built back from the street in a landscaped setting, and a curved walk swept between stone Gothic gateposts toward the entrance. Although still symmetrical, the main rectangular mass of the house was broken up by bay windows, pavilions, and dormers. To complete the Gothic ensemble there were trefoil motifs in the vergeboards and tracery, ornamental brick chimneys, and a pointed-arch entrance. Sidney D. Miller, a railroad attorney, married the daughter of Charles C. Trowbridge. Jefferson avenue had seen better days as a residential area when their son Sidney T. Miller, also a lawyer, built a house on Beverly road in Grosse Pointe at the beginning of the twentieth century. The paneling from the library of the old Jefferson avenue house was installed in the Grosse Pointe house, now owned by Edward B. Caulkins Jr. Made of butternut, it was originally stained dark brown. Above the bookcases is a band of quatrefoils, and handles project from quatrefoils on the drawers beneath the shelves. Elsewhere there are finely carved details. This room is the only vestige left from the old house on East Jefferson which was torn down in 1955. Built of limestone left over from the construction of nearby Christ Church, the building was one of Detroit's architectural landmarks.

In 1863 Lloyd built a little cruciform stone cottage for Judge Samuel T. *(69)* Douglass on Grosse Ile overlooking the lower reaches of the Detroit River.[47] Far from the bustle of the city, it epitomized the new vogue for country living. Scalloped vergeboards, ornamental brick chimneys, and an assortment of porches added interest to this charmingly rustic dwelling. Inside, Gothic touches included pointed-arch bookcases recessed in the walls and white pine mantelpieces carved with Gothic detail. Later Judge Douglass added a wing for his library.

Although a lawyer by profession, Judge Douglass was much interested in science, having been on expeditions with his friend and cousin Douglass Houghton. For mental relaxation he read liberally in the field of science. The theories of Darwin won his approbation at a time when they were considered heretical. He also had time to indulge in practical farming, finding counsel in the pages of *The Country Gentleman.* In those days Grosse Ile was so remote from Detroit that Douglass used to remain in town all week, returning weekends in the steamer *Dove* during the warm months. In winter he would drive a cutter across the ice-covered river to Trenton where he would catch the train to Detroit. Later, when Grosse Ile was linked to the mainland by rail, he could commute daily to the city.[48]

(67)
(88)
Downing would have been delighted with the Rural Gothic villa of S. Dow Elwood, a book dealer who turned to banking later in life. It was built in 1870 on a large semi-wooded tract of land that sloped down from East Jefferson avenue toward the river opposite Belle Isle. A curved carriage drive looped around in front of the house, the exterior walls of which were composed of flush wooden siding. The architect displayed skill in the handling of proportions and details. Lacy vergeboards and long drooping pendants on the gables created a melancholy effect. The first-floor windows were shaded by the porch roof or by hoods above projecting balconies.

"As regularity and proportion are fundamental ideas of absolute beauty," wrote Downing, "the Picturesque will be found to depend on the opposite conditions of matter—irregularity, and a partial want of proportion and symmetry."[49] The Elwood house certainly fulfilled these qualifications for the picturesque. In departing from the rigid symmetry of the traditional dwelling, it represented a new flexibility of plan and mass that were to provide the basis for modern domestic architecture. Today the Alden Park Manor stands on the site of this outstanding example of the Gothic villa. Judging from the similarity of
(65)
details, the Franklin Moore house must have been designed by the same architect who did the Elwood house at about the same time. Located far out Fort street, it also looked like something out of the pages of Downing, albeit the view from the octagonal tower was of the Detroit River instead of the Hudson.

Even Downing had admitted that the Gothic style was best suited to churches and villas. In view of the popularity of the Gothic in Detroit, however,
(83)
it is not surprising that at least one public building succumbed to its pervasive influence. Erected in 1850–51 on the southwest corner of Jefferson avenue and
(19)
Randolph, the site of the old Council House, the Firemen's Hall was notable for its restraint of detail. It was a simple three-story brick structure with shops on the first floor, offices and a concert hall on the second, and a magnificent hall on the third.[50] Above the tall windows on each floor there were pointed ogival arches. Window caps and sills were of iron. On the front of the building were cast-iron clustered Gothic columns supporting a heavy iron cap and molding. Beneath the third floor windows was an iron balcony extending across the entire front.[51] Since it was flat-roofed, the architect seems to have felt the necessity of finishing off the top of the building with a bracketed Italianate cornice. It was perhaps this rather anachronistic feature that prompted the *Detroit Directory* (1850) to refer to the building as Anglo-Tuscan.

Firemen's Hall was erected by the Fire Department Society. The objectives of this organization were to "harmonize the interests of the firemen, and to provide for the relief of disabled and indigent firemen and their families." Funds were raised from membership fees and entertainments of various kinds. On many a gas-lit evening there were gala balls and concerts.[52] Lola Montez, the favorite of Ludwig II of Bavaria, gave a lecture there.[53] In 1852 and 1853 art exhibitions were held which included works by artists still revered locally, such as Frederick E. Cohen, Robert Hopkin, Lewis T. Ives, and Robert S. Duncanson.[54] After many years of service there was no longer any need for the society, so in 1886 the building was sold to the Water Board. In 1955 the structure was torn down to make way for the new Civic Center. *(54)*

The Tuscan Revival

In the early nineteenth century not all the moneyed bourgeoisie in England who longed to live in the country were inclined to indulge in the Gothic. Searching for other formulas for the picturesque dwelling, architects discovered the rural Italian villa—a type which had been overlooked during the previous century in the enthusiasm over the classical temple.[55] It would be futile to search the Italian countryside for prototypes of the romantic version of the Italian villa, since the inspiration came largely from the architectural fabrications to be found in the landscape paintings of Claude Lorrain and Nicolas Poussin. From these nebulous sources designers developed asymmetrical houses composed around central towers.[56] Roofs of low pitch projected out on brackets. Other vaguely Italian details were massive window dressings, round arches, and verandas with arcades or simple columns.

Andrew Jackson Downing wrote that in America "there is a strong and growing partiality among us for the Italian style." It was expressive, he explained, "of the elegant culture and variety of accomplishments of the retired citizen or man of the world," and connoted, "not wholly the spirit of country life nor of town life, but something between both."[57] Alexander Jackson Davis was soon designing some of his finest residences in the new mode. In 1851 he built an Italian villa for Llewellyn P. Haskell, a wealthy chemist, at Orange, New Jersey. It was part of a residential development called Llewellyn Park, which Haskell had appointed Davis to lay out according to the precepts of Downing. Half-hidden in the sylvan solitudes were all manner of rustic and picturesque villas. In this grandiose real-estate scheme lay the germ of the modern garden city.[58]

In Detroit the works of Downing were eagerly consumed by Bela Hubbard.[59] The adventurous days of his scientific explorations were over and his alert mind now turned to less rigorous pursuits. As if making a fortune in real estate were not enough, he also took a turn at the lumber business. Shortly after he arrived in Detroit in 1835 Hubbard had bought the two-hundred-and-fifty acre Knaggs *(15)* farm at Springwells on the river below Detroit and for several years lived in the old Knaggs log cabin.[60] As the owner of such a large farm, horticultural matters were of considerable interest to him. He consulted Downing's works on the subject and became imbued with the author's philosophy of country living. Soon he imagined himself living in a romantic villa surrounded by semi-natural parks and gardens. It is not surprising, then, that by 1853 he had asked Davis in New York to be the architect for his future home. Davis advised him to visit Llewellyn Park in New Jersey and to inspect Haskell's Italian villa.

Hubbard's enthusiasm was contagious. He persuaded both his brother-in-law John C. Baughman and a friend Christopher Reeve also to commission Davis to build Italian villas for themselves near his. It would be a little colony like Llewellyn Park. He would need only eighteen acres for himself between Fort street and the river. This included a small pond. A diagram of his estate which he sent to Davis resembled a plan from the pages of Downing's *Landscape Gardening.* The location of the house was indicated, as were areas devoted to gardens, orchards, and lawns, all connected by curving driveways and walks.[61]

(73) From then on Hubbard took over the supervision of the construction. Letters concerning many practical and aesthetic problems were exchanged between the owner and the architect in New York. It is evident from this correspondence that Hubbard had a great deal to do with the plan and details of the house, giving it a distinctive personal quality. Vinewood, as it was called, was completed in 1856. The main mass of the house, the tower, and the veranda were well related in a simple yet monumental composition.[62] Italian influence was evident in the round-arched windows, the Tuscan columns, the balustrades, and the bracketed cornices. A wide diversity of window openings added to the theatrical effect, even if it detracted from the purity of the design. In the center of the house was an octagonal hallway. At the head of the stairs the Hubbard crest glowed luminously in stained glass. At the base of the tower was the library modeled after Sir Walter Scott's library at Abbotsford, and busts of worthies were inserted in niches above the bookcases. In addition to scientific books the library contained classics of American, English, French, and Italian literature.[59] At the opposite end of the house were the parlor and the dining room, both opening on the conservatory. Hubbard was an inveterate traveler, having first crossed the Atlantic on a side-wheeler. From Italy he brought back marble sculptures and oil copies of Renaissance paintings to adorn the rooms of his new home.[63]

Toward the end of his long and eventful life the squire of Vinewood lived in semi-retirement. The city which he had known as a small stockaded town had reached out to encompass the property he had owned for so many years. His mind was a repository of scientific, historical, literary, and artistic information, but closest to his heart was a thorough knowledge of every aspect of the state which he had watched grow from primitive beginnings to a vast commonwealth. This rich store of memories he preserved for posterity in the pages of *Memorials of a Half-Century* which was published in 1888. Toward the close of the century Hubbard died; Vinewood was torn down in 1933. Today nothing remains of the semi-wild acres that Hubbard loved so much, for they are lost in the miles of dreary closely-built residential areas on the West Side.

(66) In 1856 Davis completed his Italian villa for John C. Baughman on a tract on Fort street next door to Bela Hubbard.[64] As he had been given a much freer rein than with Hubbard, the house was more typically Davisian, resembling in many ways the Haskell villa in Llewellyn Park.[65] It was a skillful exercise in three-dimensional design in the grand picturesque manner. Varying roof levels built up to two central towers—a massive one above the entrance hall and a slender contiguous one containing a spiral staircase. In contrast to this vertical element was the horizontal sweep of verandas casting deep shadows. This house was generally associated with its second owner Daniel Scotten, a tobacco magnate who moved into it in 1864. Surrounded by densely wooded areas interspersed with broad lawns, it was the ideal retreat for hard-working Scotten. Somewhat of a hermit in his private life, he tried to make up for a scanty education by becoming an omniverous reader. For years he bought books by the thousands covering every subject. He considered Shakespeare the world's greatest man and chose as his favorite poem Gray's *Elegy Written in a Country Churchyard.* Like

Hubbard a horticulturist, he could even give the Latin names of the weeds in his garden. Although indifferent to social life, he showed his concern for his fellow men by providing indigent neighbors with free turkeys and firewood.[66]

The Christopher Reeve house rounded out Davis's triad of Italian villas in Detroit, all of which have since been demolished.[67] The modest scale of the Reeve residence seems to have dampened his enthusiasm and resulted in a rather perfunctory reliance upon the usual clichés. Although the performance was clearly not up to the level of his other two endeavors, yet it displayed a standard of architectural discipline that put it in a class apart from other specimens of domestic architecture in Detroit.

Perhaps the best example of an Italian villa by a local architect belonged to John J. Bagley who had been very successful in the tobacco business and was later elected governor of the state. It was built in 1869 on the corner of Washington boulevard and Park avenue, now the site of the Statler Hotel. The *Free Press* of the day called it a "monument of elegance and cultivated taste."[68] For the first time in Michigan plate glass was used in the windows of a residence. Aside from this innovation the design of the house followed the generally accepted pattern for the Italian villa. It was an L-shaped structure wrapped around a lofty tower and a veranda. There were bracketed cornices, balustrades, and round-arched windows. If it lacked the subtlety of a Davis masterpiece, nevertheless the design was consistent and harmonious. *(71)* *(231)*

The principal room in the house was a vast high-ceilinged parlor. A chandelier of frosted glass globes with crystal pendants hung from an ornate plaster medallion in the center of the room. Gilt-framed paintings on the walls gave evidence of the Bagleys' artistic leanings, while overstuffed tasseled divans accommodated their guests. It was an ideal setting for the receptions they gave for the distinguished visitors who came to Detroit to lecture. Ralph Waldo Emerson, Bronson Alcott, Matthew Arnold, and the East Indian Swami Vive Kananda were among those who enjoyed the Bagleys' hospitality.[69] *(74)*

One of the most colorful figures of the period was Senator Thomas W. Palmer, son of Thomas Palmer. He was in the lumber and real estate business in partnership with his father-in-law Charles Merrill. Later in life he became a United States senator and then ambassador to Spain.[70] The Palmer house was built in 1864–74 on Woodward avenue on the site of the Detroit Institute of Arts. The formula of the Italian villa was still apparent, but it had been freely translated into a wooden vernacular. This rambling country dwelling contained the senator's art collection, including oil copies after Murillo, and Randolph Rogers' marble Nydia the Blind Girl of Pompeii.[63] *(72)* *(82)* *(247)*

In general the Italian villa type, even more than the Gothic villa, caused the breakdown of the tradition of symmetry in American house design and provided an unprecedented opportunity for flexibility of plan.[71] If, however, rustic irregularity did not suit the taste of all, there was also an opportunity for formal symmetry within the broad framework of the Tuscan idiom. In the thirties and forties Sir Charles Barry built a series of clubs and mansions in London, modeled after sixteenth century Florentine *palazzi*. It was evident that this was the direction indicated for Americans with formal inclinations.[72]

Perhaps the most academic of Detroit's Barryesque mansions was the one built in 1864 for the fur and hat merchant Frederick Buhl.[73] Located at the intersection of Fort street and West Grand boulevard, it was surrounded by beautifully landscaped grounds and was approached by a carriage driveway that circled around an iron fountain of Neptune. Built of brick painted gray, this handsome symmetrical house was embellished with bracketed cornices, heavy *(75)* architraves, and balustrades. A Palladian window graced the façade above a classical entrance portico.

(76)
(358) Somewhat similar in style was Senator Zachariah Chandler's house built in 1858 at the northwest corner of Fort street and Second on the present site of the Detroit News Building. It was a square three-story block made of brick covered with stucco. Although it resembled in plan the traditional New England house, a denticulated cornice, a round-arched porte-cochere, and an extensive use of balustrades brought it in line with the current vogue. Jordan and Anderson, the architects, seem to have had a rather vague notion of academic detail, for only the traceried windows of the sun porch gave any suggestion of early Italian Renaissance precedent.[74]

(77) The Eber Brock Ward house of about 1860 on West Fort and Nineteenth streets announced to the world the economic success of its owner. Here ornamental details added to the impression of grandeur. Ship owner and steel magnate, Captain Ward was the most enterprising and the wealthiest man in Michigan upon his death in 1875.[75] Considerably altered and enlarged, his former residence became the House of the Good Shepherd.

(79)
(78) In 1860 Jordan and Anderson supervised the construction of the former Custom House and Post Office which stood until recently on the northwest corner of Griswold and Larned streets.[76] The plans were drawn by Ammi B. Young, supervising architect of the Treasury Department, who designed many courthouses and post offices throughout the United States.[77] The building was faced with monumental sandstone ashlar. The basement rustication, the string courses at each floor level, and the dressings of the round-arched windows were executed with fine traditional craftsmanship. Unlike Barry, the architect did not attempt a literal resuscitation of the Florentine *palazzi* and the building lacked the subtlety of detail and proportion of this prototype. Its most remarkable feature was the internal structural system which was extremely advanced for its day. The floors were composed of rolled-iron beams supporting brick arches covered with concrete. Iron columns provided interior support.

The same construction was used for the former Marine Hospital on the southwest corner of Jefferson and Mt. Elliott avenues.[78] This might indicate that Young also provided the plans. In any case, Jordan and Anderson were the supervising architects. Upon the completion of the building in 1857 the *Detroit Free Press* asserted: "The character of the work is in advance of anything heretofore built in the city."[79] It was a rectangular brick edifice with a string course above the ground story, a cornice, and quoins at the wall corners. The front and rear of the building were faced with iron balconies originally covered with iron scrollwork.

(82) Italian Renaissance details appeared on the Merrill Block built in 1854–59 by Charles Merrill on the northeast corner of Woodward and Jefferson avenues. A monumental effect was achieved by the simplification and adaptation of Italian forms to a commercial structure. The bold architraves of the series of triple windows stood out against the plain brick walls and a heavy cornice provided a unifying element. This block was torn down to make way for the City-County (382) Building. Later commercial buildings displayed an increasing fussiness of detail.

The taste for Italian Renaissance forms was soon to invade the field of church architecture as a challenge to the Gothic monopoly. With his usual self-assurance Albert Jordan stood ready to accommodate the public. Perhaps it is fortunate that he allotted no time to the study of the smaller Italian Renaissance churches but preferred to tread on ground with which he was more or less familiar. Carefully avoiding any Greek Revival details, he relied upon the New

England church tradition. A return to the use of the round arch was enough to convince the public that they were indulging in Roman architecture.

In 1854 Jordan completed a new First Congregational Church on the south- *(80)* west corner of Fort and Wayne streets.[80] It is not difficult to trace the lineage of this church back to Minard Lafever's Pearl Street Congregational Church (1851–52) in Hartford,[81] or even further back to Ithiel Town's First Congregational Church (1812–18) in New Haven.[82] On the front of the Detroit church was a Wren-like steeple. There were round-arched doors and windows, Tuscan pilasters, and thin blind arches. The walls were of brick covered with stucco and painted a somber brown. On the interior there were no galleries except one for the choir.[83] After many years of misuse the remains of the church were recently demolished and replaced by a parking garage. It is interesting to notice that *(60)* Jordan's Jefferson Avenue Presbyterian Church, completed a year after the First Congregational Church, was similar in general configuration. He must have been in a hurry to complete the drawings, for he merely converted the Roman details of the earlier church into Gothic details.

After the destruction by fire of the old First Presbyterian Church on Wood- *(32)* ward avenue in 1854, it was decided to build a new church further uptown on *(81)* the northwest corner of Farmer and State streets, the present site of the J. L. *(175)* Hudson Company store. Albert Jordan having been chosen as architect, the new First Presbyterian Church was completed in 1855.[84] Using the same technique just mentioned above, he merely translated the Gothic vocabulary of the Fort *(52)* Street Presbyterian Church, which was also completed in 1855, into the Roman idiom. Straying too far from historical precedent, Jordan seems to have become confused, especially in his treatment of the façade. The exterior walls were brick covered with stucco.[85] The interior had galleries on three sides. The saving grace of the church was the handsome Wren-like steeple with its slender spire.

Before the days of multi-storied buildings the skyline of Detroit was domi- *(84)* nated by soaring church spires. As a whole the city must have been a pleasing sight. Here and there the romantic architectural repertories added variety to the earlier classical matrix. The city's architecture was inherently symbolic, reflecting the political, religious, and literary ideologies of the day. To further complicate matters, Downing had invented a new architectural vocabulary symbolic of domestic virtues. Nevertheless, a certain homogeneity still prevailed; for, although buildings were varied in style, they were individually consistent and collectively uniform in scale. The scars of industrialism were still relatively unobtrusive, and life assumed an easy balance between the stimulus of the city and the rustic joys of the nearby countryside. In the daily round of activities there was time for study and meditation and individualism was given a free rein. Even after the Civil War the romantic spirit lingered on, until it was finally engulfed by the materialism of the seventies and eighties.

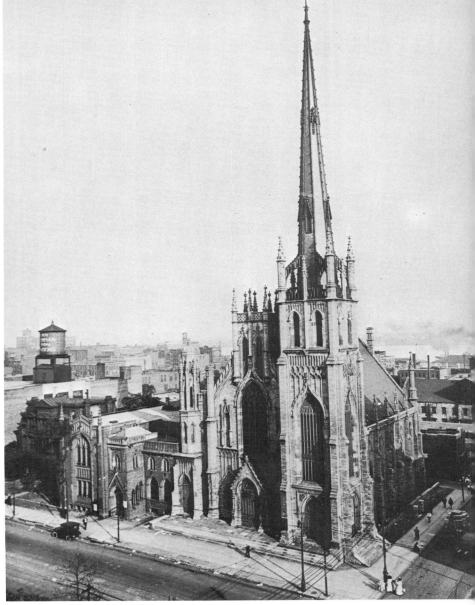

(52) Fort Street Presbyterian Church, *O. & A. Jordan,* 1855 (DIA)

1) St. Paul's P.E. Church, *C. N. Otis,* 1852 (BHC)

(54) Mariners' P.E. Church, *C. N. Otis*, 1849 (BHC/JKJ)

(53) St. Paul's P.E. Church, *R. T. Elliott*, 1836 (BHC/JKJ)

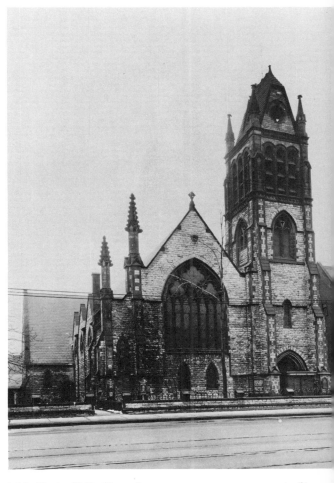

(57) Christ P.E. Church

(55-56) St. John's P.E. Church, *Jordan & Anderson*, 1861
(JSC)(DIA/JKJ)

(57-58) Christ P.E. Church, *G. W. Lloyd*, 1863
(MB)(JSC)

(59-60) Jefferson Avenue Presbyterian Church, *A. H. Jordan*, 1855 (BHC/JKJ)

(61) Central Methodist Church, *G. W. Lloyd*, 1867 (DIA/J

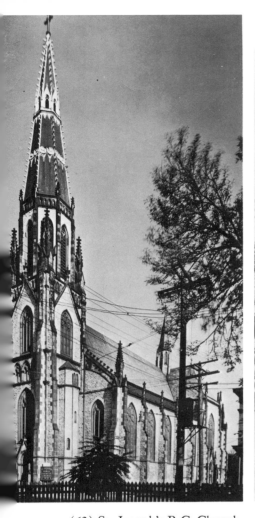

(62) St. Joseph's R.C. Church,
F. G. Himpler, 1873 (JSC)

(63) Sidney D. Miller House, *G. W. Lloyd,* 1864 (ELA)

(64) Stewart-Newland House, *C. Stewart,* 1845 (BHC/JKJ)

(65) Franklin Moore House, c. 1870 (BHC/JKJ)

(66) Baughman-Scotten House, *A. J. Davis*, 1856 (BHC/JKJ)

(67) S. Dow Elwood House, 1870 (BHC/JKJ)

(68) Alexander H. Dey House, *G. W. Lloyd*, 1862 (HAL)　(69) Samuel T. Douglass House, *G. W. Lloyd*, 1863 (MLH/JKJ)

(70) Thomas A. Parker House, *G. W. Lloyd*, 1868 (HAL)

(71) John J. Bagley House, 1869 (BHC/JKJ)

(72) Thomas W. Palmer House, 1874 (BHC/JKJ)

(73) Vinewood, *A. J. Davis*, 1856 (BHC/JKJ)

(74) John J. Bagley House (DIA)

(75) Frederick Buhl House, 1864 (BHC)

(76) Zachariah Chandler House, *Jordan & Anderson*, 1858 (BHC/JKJ)

(77) Eber B. Ward House, c. 1860 (DN)

(78-79) Custom House, *Young, Jordan & Anderson*, 1860 (BHC/JKJ)

(81) First Presbyterian Church, *A. H. Jordan*, 1855 (BHC)

(80) First Congregational Church, *A. H. Jordan*, 1854 (BHC/JKJ)

(82) Merrill Block, 1859 (ELA)

(83) Firemen's Hall, 1851 (BHC/JKJ)

(84) View of Detroit (by Robertson), c. 1855 (BHC)

4. Victorian Potpourri

Industrial and Commercial Growth

During the second half of the nineteenth century the exploitation of the natural resources of Michigan reached a peak. In the early years of the century the fur trade began to decline owing to the depletion of fur-bearing animals. The men who had been active in this field shifted into the new industry of lumbering. Sawmills had always supplied the local needs of Michigan towns, but it was not until the forties and fifties that commercial lumbering began.[1] By 1873 it had become the second largest industry in the state following agriculture. In 1890 Michigan led all the states in the union in the production of lumber.[2]

In his geological reports Douglass Houghton had drawn attention to the extensive copper deposits in the Upper Peninsula; even before his death in 1845, prospectors began pouring into the area. Mining operations were begun on the Keweenaw Peninsula in 1842, and by 1889 Michigan had become the greatest copper-producing state in the nation. The presence of vast iron deposits in the Upper Peninsula was not known until 1844. On a surveying expedition in that year William A. Burt noted the erratic movements of the needle of his magnetic compass. The site was south of Teal Lake where Negaunee now stands, and it was there that the first iron mining operations began in 1847. High transportation costs made mining unprofitable at first, but the completion of the Sault Canal in 1855 facilitated the shipment of ore to such an extent that mine production steadily increased.[3] By 1889 Michigan mined more iron ore than any other state.[4]

The development of extractive industries in Michigan was a stimulus to the industrial growth of Detroit, especially in the manufacture of products that involved the use of wood and iron. While the forests lasted to supply charcoal, iron furnaces produced charcoal pig iron and wrought iron. Later, when coke iron superseded charcoal iron, the iron industry shifted to centers nearer the coal beds.[5] In the meantime large-scaled manufacturing proceeded apace in Detroit. Large industrial complexes with towering smokestacks were erected wherever rail or water transportation was accessible. Thus began the scattered industrial development that has been characteristic of the city ever since.

During the period of railroad expansion the manufacture of railroad cars became a leading industry in Detroit. In 1853 Dr. George B. Russel organized the Detroit Car and Manufacturing Company which was later bought by George M. Pullman of Chicago. In 1864 James McMillan and John S. Newberry organized the Michigan Car Company to manufacture freight cars. This was later merged with the Peninsular Car Company which had been founded by Colonel Frank J. Hecker and Charles L. Freer in 1885.[6] For many years Detroit ranked as the leading stove-producing city in the world. Jeremiah Dwyer organized the Detroit Stove Works in 1864 and the Michigan Stove Company in 1871. The Peninsular Stove Company was founded in 1881.[7] Other large industries that became prominent in the early industrial scene in the city were D. M. Ferry and Company, the seed firm founded in 1856, and Parke, Davis and Company, the pharmaceutical laboratory founded in 1867.

These and many other new industries attracted immigrants to Detroit from New England, New York State, and Europe. The population rose from 45,619 in 1860 to 205,876 in 1890.[8] An increased population meant greater purchasing power. Wholesale and retail houses increased in size and number, utilizing such modern phenomena as traveling salesmen, delivery wagons, and newspaper advertising. The introduction of plate glass about 1860 encouraged attractive window displays. It was in this period that the large department stores were founded: Newcomb, Endicott and Company in 1868, Mabley and Company in 1870, and the J. L. Hudson Company, the sole survivor today, in 1881. From 1830 to 1850 Jefferson avenue had been the principal retail district, but after 1860 business began to travel up Woodward avenue. By 1870 it had swept by the Campus Martius and was well on its way to Grand Circus Park.[9]

The Rewards of Ambition

After the Civil War the horse-drawn streetcar system was extended to every part of the city. A jingling bell on the collar of each horse warned pedestrians and other vehicles off the tracks.[10] Spans of horses drew shiny broughams or victorias over the cedar-block pavements to the large mansions that kept pushing farther and farther out East Jefferson avenue and West Fort street. Lafayette street and Woodward avenue above Grand Circus Park also became fashionable addresses.[11] The *Michigan State Gazeteer and Business Directory* of 1875 was thoroughly complacent about the Michigan metropolis:

Detroit is without doubt the best drained, the best paved, the best shaded, the cleanest, and in general the healthiest city in the West. It covers an area some six miles in length up and down the river, by a depth of about two and a half miles. Having so much ground, the dwellings are not crowded together in solid blocks but are mostly detached with intervening space. This, with the wideness of the streets and the prevalence of shade trees, gives the place more of a village than a city air and contributes much to its pleasantness as a place of residence.

Society, too, from the less frequent changes that obtain here over other western cities, is more settled, refined, and truly genteel. Thus as a place of residence it is unsurpassed by any place west of Boston. Indeed, while the business activity and stir of Chicago is lacking, Detroit resembles Boston not a little in its social and literary atmosphere.

It is doubtful if Bostonians would have shared this opinion, least of all President Charles W. Eliot of Harvard University. Visiting Detroit in 1883, he jotted in his journal:

The city and people very interesting to me. Rectangular and radial system of streets and all avenues planted with trees—mostly maples. Considerable variety in plan of planting. Very few dwellings built in blocks. Miles upon miles of cheap but decent houses, each with its little plot of land. A few streets of more pretentious houses—but these are also of an appalling architectural sameness. French-roofed, square, brick, stone-trimmed buildings. Unhomelike and "stuck-up" dwellings. No Greek-portico houses, and as yet no "Queen Anne." A commonplace and very communistic-looking city—but, I suppose, a fair type of many a city in the West. The dull flatness of the country in which the city lies—the oppressive lack of interest and variety in the city itself—the sameness of the people; here are three phenomena to be set down as closely connected.[12]

There were, of course, many local citizens who admired the architecture of their city. Alexander Chapoton, a builder, wrote in the *Detroit Free Press*:

[Detroit] . . . is already conceded to be the most beautiful of American cities, and I think its reputation is deserved. We have a number of most competent architects, thorough masters of their profession, having taste, good judgment, versatility, and enthusiasm. The forms of buildings in Detroit take on greater variety; there is less repetition of styles than in any other city. Take New York, for example. There are blocks and blocks of brownstone, high-stooped dwellings of the same pattern, very pretty patterns, too, but monotonous when you see it repeated hundreds of times. The same way with business structures in New York and many other cities, all follow closely some stereotyped example. Drive about the streets of Detroit and you find the buildings have individuality about them. One differs from another, exhibits some new grace, shows some new idea, and the succession of different forms lends a charm and originality to the whole. Our Detroit architects have not received all the credit which they deserve for their ability and merit.[13]

Not everyone was as happy about the status of domestic architecture as Alex Chapoton. In fact, it seems to have given another critic in the *Free Press* grounds for serious doubts, for he wrote:

The taste for extravagant show which is extending over the whole country takes a very special pleasure in advertising its vanity in the shape of fine homes. The immense outlay, directed by a love of ostentation, and in some instances by a barbaric delight in the veriest tinsel, builds a house as far removed as possible from the idea of a home. Nothing in it indicates the presence of domestic love. The rage in modern domestic architecture is for splendid parlors and saloons that may give entertainment to crowds and glorify a wintry midnight with gaslights. Downright worldliness is the chief end proposed—a good home is a true and genuine home—a home for the blended intellect and heart—not the mocking counterpart of the open world, repeating the glare of the street, the glitter of the concert hall, the gauds of the theatre, but a world to itself and for itself, presenting evermore an image of trust, a hope, a joy better than itself.[14]

Whether one liked it or not, the quickened tempo of life generated by the Industrial Revolution introduced an increasingly materialistic set of values. It was the day of the Horatio Alger success story. Any young country boy could move to the big city; if he displayed the necessary qualities of honesty, thrift, perseverance, and temperance, then fame and fortune knocked at his door. The competition was keen, but the stakes were high. Wealth was the royal road to luxury and culture.

The bucolic life in sylvan glades held no charms for the parvenu. Gregarious and competitive by nature, he directed his energy toward keeping up with the Joneses. This could best be done by building an ostentatious house on a fashionable street. The next step was an extended tour of Europe to fill in the gaps of his education. The new steam vessels had shortened the Atlantic crossing to nine days and made it a pleasure trip instead of an ordeal. A dress fitted at Worth's or a diamond broach selected at Cartier's in Paris assured *Madame* that she had reached the pinnacle of fashion, and a marble copy of Canova's Three Graces or an oil copy of Raphael's Sistine Madonna, brought back from Europe and deposited in the parlor, was a silent testimony of one's refined taste. Amid all this splendor, the breadwinner of the family had to struggle with his own New England conscience, and as likely as not dispensed large sums to his church and his favorite charities. His concern for his fellow man frequently went beyond the mere distribution of largesse; he might give up a remunerative career to enter the arena of politics, emerging in the end as a public-spirited mayor, governor, or senator.

The Search for a New Style

A young lady traveler from Detroit reached Vienna in 1887 at the peak of its imperial grandeur. "This is a beautiful city," she wrote in her diary. "The houses are all massive stone structures with no cheap ornamentations but decorated with statues and carvings of stone. The boulevards are broad and handsome. They say Vienna will soon vie with Paris in beauty and it does almost now." And after visiting the Houses of Parliament there she commented rather wistfully, "We think, after walking so much on marble, it will be hard to come down to common floors again."[15] Overwhelmed by impressions of grandeur and worldliness, American tourists returning from the capitals of Europe would never again be satisfied with the simple surroundings of their youth. Their misfortune was that in seeking to create an atmosphere of elegance at home, more often than not they were satisfied with mere profusion.

Today it seems strange to us, who have traveled through the full gamut of historical revivalism, that it never occurred to the generation of the seventies and eighties to attempt to recreate literally the refinements of European architecture and furnishings. The scarcity of photographs and drawings of actual buildings placed a heavy reliance upon the imaginative faculties of architects whose education was at best rather sketchy. Nevertheless, it was an age of extraordinary vitality in which nothing seemed impossible, and the architects plunged ahead with something of the same adventurous gusto that impelled their industrialist clients to carve an empire from a wilderness. In the seventies Marcus F. Cummings, a New York architect, admitted in his book, *Architectural Details:*

No attempt has been made to illustrate any well-defined style of architecture, for it seems to be folly for us, who live in the nineteenth century, to undertake to transport to this new country any foreign style, which was perfected centuries ago, and which, though eminently fitted for the age in which it flourished, is not well adapted to our wants, and to this age of wood in American architecture. The author has not undertaken to initiate a new style; such a thing may be produced some time in the future, but it is probable that, instead of one American style being produced, we shall have a multitude of styles, each one stamped by the genius and individuality of its author, and each possessing more or less merit.[16]

A self-appointed judge of architectural taste, Martha J. Lamb seems equally nebulous in her opinions. In her book *The Homes of America* published in 1879, she opened the chapter on "The Modern Period" by saying:

Within the present half century domestic architecture has been running a race with the general development and prosperity of America. Countless styles from all climes, with modifications and abbreviations, have been made subservient to the convenience and tastes of a mixed population. Cottages and villas combining the beautiful with the practical and useful in design, and as variously adorned as the idiosyncrasies of the human character, dot the length and breadth of our land. Many of these are in themselves the expression of sentiment, self-respect, and artistic culture.[17]

Architecture had entered a phase of free eclecticism. There was a bewildering number of styles to choose from, namely, French and English Renaissance, Gothic, Romanesque, Byzantine, and even Swiss. They were not followed literally but served merely as points of departure for uninhibited improvization with resultant crudities. More or less diverse elements were selected, modified, and fused into a composite whole. Then, too, the introduction of woodworking machinery, by providing new techniques, was a stimulus to new vocabularies of design. In the rush to provide shelter for the new ranks of moneyed bourgeoisie there was no time to brood over academic subtleties. Individual details were important only in the contribution they made to the total effect, and the only aesthetic demand upon architects was to provide a vaguely scintillating and impressive backdrop for the prosperous merchant in his Prince Albert and opera hat and his wife in her bustle and stays.

A French Accent

"Paris is the most civilized city on earth and is entirely unique and beyond parallel and comparison. London, New York, Berlin, and Vienna may struggle among themselves for priority in the second rank, but Paris stands alone." Thus ran an editorial in the *Detroit Free Press* in 1880.[18] A lover of architecture, Napoleon III had done much to beautify Paris. Under his regime, Baron Haussmann had laid out the splendid boulevard system, Charles Garnier had built the elegant Opera House, and Visconti and Lefuel had made sumptuous additions to the Louvre following seventeenth century precedent. France had risen to new heights of wealth and power, and the world was dazzled by the theatrical court life that surrounded Napoleon III and his beautiful Empress Eugénie.

The lush opulence of the *Nouveau Louvre* was a tantalizing dish for susceptible architects. Even in staid Victorian England, Sir Charles Barry deserted his Gothic and Italian repertories in time to close his career with a French Renaissance town hall in Halifax (1860–62).[19] In America new town halls, posts offices, and courthouses in major cities paid homage to the grandeur of the Second Empire with mansard roofs, superimposed orders, and rustication.

In 1871 James Anderson completed a new Detroit City Hall in his version of *(85)* the current French vogue.[20] The plans were ready in 1861, but the outbreak of the Civil War caused a postponement of the construction, and the cornerstone was not laid until 1868.[21] The material used was cream-colored sandstone quarried near Cleveland. Anderson had had experience in this type of stonework in the Italianate Detroit Post Office and Custom House of 1860, and many details of *(79)*

77

the City Hall stemmed from the earlier building. Apparently Anderson had originally intended the City Hall to be Italianate also, but later made some changes to conform to the French mode. The newspapers of the day referred to the style as Roman, and certainly the portico was clearly sixteenth century Italian. In 1869 while construction was under way, the city aldermen, upon the recommendation of the building committee, voted to change the roof to the mansard type.[22] This feature and the projecting central and corner pavilions gave the building an unmistakably French character. Probably the vermiculations, paired pilasters, and swags were added later to give a further French flourish. However, the arcaded windows in the bays between the pavilions bore an affinity to contemporary commercial structures and were a concession to practicality. To complicate matters further, a Georgian cupola, that indispensable adjunct to American civic structures, was added as a crowning feature. The floors were laid with rolled iron joists and brick arches, the hall floors being covered with alternating black and white marble tiles. The grand staircase was of iron, and in front of the building were two iron fountains.[21]

Such a grandiose edifice demanded architectural sculpture. Detroit's first sculptor, Julius Theodore Melchers, rose to the occasion by providing the base of the cupola with female personifications carved in sandstone of the civic virtues— Justice, Art, Industry, and Commerce. Melchers was born in Soest, Prussia, in 1829. At fifteen he was apprenticed to the sculptor Ministerman. The Revolution of 1848 drove him to Paris where he graduated from the École des Beaux-Arts, but participation in political activities forced him to leave in 1852. He worked as a modeler at the Crystal Palace in London and came to Detroit a year later. At the beginning of his career in Detroit, Melchers was employed as a wood carver and received many church commissions. During the intervals when demands for the nobler forms of art slackened, he found it necessary to turn out an occasional wooden cigar-store Indian. Later in his life he taught a large class of young men in drawing. Among his pupils were several who attained distinction, including the artists Gari Melchers (his son) and Julius Rolshoven, and the architect Albert Kahn.[23]

After the City Hall was completed the four niches on the corner pavilions remained empty for several years. Then Bela Hubbard conceived the idea of filling them with statues of La Salle, Cadillac, Marquette, and Father Richard, and presenting them to the city. He first asked the architect John M. Donaldson to undertake the project. Donaldson, who had previously done some architectural sculpture, at first declined, but upon the insistence of Hubbard consented to do the model for Marquette. For the others he recommended Melchers who modeled the remaining three figures and cut all four in stone.[24]

(382) With the completion of the new City-County Building in 1955, the City Hall was doomed. "We cannot afford the luxury of this inefficient building," said James Holden, a prominent realtor. After a long controversy between those who wanted to save it as a reminder of Detroit's past and those who wanted to make way for 'progress,' the building was finally demolished in 1961. The statues of the early French explorers, after a long exile at Fort Wayne, were rescued by the University of Detroit. Kennedy Square, a landscaped plaza with an underground parking garage below it, occupies the site of the City Hall.

While the civic pride of Bela Hubbard produced Detroit's first example of architectural sculpture, the first example of monumental sculpture was a Civil War memorial. The Soldiers' and Sailors' Monument was formally unveiled in *(85)* 1872 in Cadillac Square opposite the old City Hall. The body of the monument is of granite. Golden bronze figures rise in four tiers to an apex. On the bottom

78

tier are four eagles. On the next tier are four statues representing four United States services: Infantry, Artillery, Cavalry, and Marine. Behind these are bronzed medallions of Lincoln, Grant, Farragut, and Sherman. On the next level are four allegorical figures representing Victory, Union, Emancipation, and History.[25] On the top is a colossal personification of Michigan as a semi-civilized Indian queen menacingly brandishing a sword with her right hand and clutching a shield with the left.[26]

The sculptor of the monument was Randolph Rogers. Although he had spent his boyhood in Ann Arbor, Rogers was trained at the Academy of St. Mark in Florence under Lorenzo Bartolini. In 1852 he established a studio in Rome where he spent most of his life, returning to the United States only on occasional business trips. He did Civil War monuments for several other cities besides Detroit, but his most important commission was the bronze doors for the main entrance of the Capitol in Washington.[27] His popular subjects, of which he did numerous replicas, found their way into many American homes.[28] The Soldiers' and Sailors' Monument in Detroit holds its own in the vast area of swirling traffic that is the Campus Martius of today. Although the figures at the base of the monument seem quaintly Victorian now, the commanding figure of Michigan compares favorably with the best French or American sculpture of its day.

In the seventies French Renaissance architecture took Detroit by storm. Mansard roofs, superimposed orders, broken pediments, and heavy rustication appeared on new buildings in alarming profusion. Ceilings were heightened, windows narrowed and lengthened, and domes attenuated. In 1869 the Detroit Opera House was opened in a glow of gaslight across the Campus Martius from *(86)* the City Hall. Bristling with the trappings of the Second Empire, it was acclaimed by the *Free Press* a "luxurious temple of art."[29] The material was brick, covered with mastic to resemble cut stone. Statues in niches by Julius Melchers represented Tragedy, Comedy, Music, and so on, as expressed by the great masters in each art, such as Shakespeare, Molière, and Beethoven.[30] The interior of the opera house was lavishly decorated by the artist Robert Hopkin.[31] In 1881 the J. L. Hudson Company opened its first store on the ground floor.[32] Remodeled in 1887, the building was completely destroyed by fire in 1897.

The architects of the Opera House were Sheldon Smith and Son. Mortimer L. Smith, the junior member of the firm, was born in Jamestown, New York, and educated at Oberlin and Sandusky. He and his father came to Detroit from Ohio in 1855. They were associated in business together from 1861 to 1868. Upon the death of Sheldon Smith, Mortimer L. Smith continued the practice under his own name.[33] In 1871 he completed the Godfrey Block on Woodward avenue, a long low building with a mansard roof, since demolished.[34]

Wistfully turning his back on his beloved Gothic, Gordon W. Lloyd reluctantly surrendered to the French fashion. His Whitney Opera House, erected in 1875 on the site of the present Federal Building, showed he was ill at ease with his newly acquired vocabulary.[35] Here he had laid out for himself the impossible task of attempting a free adaptation of the Second Empire style to the requirements of a modern structure. Undaunted by the difficulties involved, Lloyd attempted the same treatment of the six-story Newberry and McMillan Building *(87)* of 1879 with scarcely more reassuring results. For many years Detroit's tallest and most elegant office building, it stood on the southeast corner of Griswold and Larned streets. The exterior walls were of brick and cut stone. Unaccustomed to thinking in terms of multi-storied buildings, the architect was inhibited by traditional concepts. He divided the building horizontally by three entablatures. The top story was hidden behind a mansard roof, but received ample illumination through large ornate dormer windows. The narrow central bay with its pediments and crowning pyramidal dome suggested a central pavilion. By opening up the wall surfaces with banks of windows, Lloyd made a necessary concession to utilitarian demands.

The banking interests of Detroit were soon demanding a setting in keeping with the increased importance and prestige of their operations in an expanding economy. In 1876 the Wayne County Savings Bank opened what the *Free Press* *(88)* called "a splendid monument" on the north side of Congress street west of Griswold.[36] William Scott, an architect who had recently arrived from England, thus brought to the streets of Detroit his version of the magnificence of Paris.[37] The exterior was encrusted with elaborately carved stonework. A caryatid and an atlas guarded the entrance, and pairs of red granite columns rose to a polychromatic slate roof penetrated by ornate dormer windows. On the interior *(89)* equally ornate wood carving created an atmosphere of dazzling splendor.

In 1881 the Russell House, which stood on the site of the present National *(106)* Bank Building, was rebuilt on a larger scale with an inevitable mansard roof.[38] Considered "the most complete and elegant hostelry in Michigan," it counted among its more distinguished guests the Prince of Wales and the Grand Duke Alexis of Russia.[39] Already some of the smaller communities of Michigan, which had so recently emerged from a primitive wilderness, were beginning to put on imperial airs. When a disastrous fire wiped out the buildings of Hillsdale College in 1874, the Free Will Baptists called upon the Detroit architects Brush and Smith to replace them. The still-extant Central Hall was an extraordinary exercise in architectural melodrama, its domical clock tower rising one hundred and forty feet among the hills of southern Michigan.[40]

Another Detroit architect, Elijah E. Myers, won the competition for the *(90)* Michigan State Capitol in Lansing. The cornerstone was laid in 1873 and the building was completed in 1878.[41] Born in Philadelphia, Myers learned the trade of carpenter and joiner, spending the evenings studying architecture. In Detroit he became very successful. Not only did he excel in engineering, but he also acquired a broad knowledge of architecture based on an extensive personal library.[42] In the course of his career he built city halls, courthouses, and state capitols in every part of the United States.

The Michigan State Capitol is a blend of Italian and French Renaissance motifs. In comparison with the City Hall in Detroit, there was greater consistency and discipline of design. The State Board of Building Commissioners had no taste for ostentation and insisted that the architect avoid superfluous ornamentation. As a result there is a certain dry mechanical quality that comes as a surprise in an age of prolixity. On the interior the girders, beams, joists, and stairway were made of iron. A central rotunda rises the full height of the building to a tall slender cast-iron dome evoking memories of Mansard's Hôtel des Invalides Chapel in Paris.

A French Accent at Home

For his home the self-made businessman of the seventies wanted none of the melancholy seclusion of the Gothic or Italian villa. The temper of the times was not conducive to genteel meditation or reverie. The telegraph, the telephone, and the steam engine had so accelerated life that the air was charged with a new impatience soon to be felt in architecture. The eye was no longer satisfied with severely geometrical houses. Walls began to bend and billow with wings and bay windows, roofs erupted with dormers and domed towers, and porches were attached to provide the added drama of deep shadows. The first signs of change came in the substitution of French for Italian motifs, for the Franco-American mansion did not stem from French prototypes, but rather from the asymmetrical or symmetrical Italian villa.

In the latter category an early example was the Hazen S. Pingree house built *(92)* in 1871–83 on Woodward avenue between Warren and Farnsworth, now the site of the Rackham Memorial. A mansard roof and a few extra French flourishes were added to what otherwise might have been a cubical Barryesque villa.

If the French influence on the stone exterior of the house was lukewarm, the interior left no doubt as to Mayor Pingree's French taste. Success in the shoe business, which had preceded his political triumphs, enabled him to indulge himself without reservation. In the central hall the visitor was confronted with a tapestry that had belonged to Napoleon Bonaparte, and the First Empire theme was continued in the sitting room. Here could be found mahogany chairs covered with satin damask, draperies of heavy maroon plush, a cabinet of inlaid wood, and a dull ivory and maroon table with a circular marble top. The drawing room paid homage to Louis XV with its Aubusson rug, its gilded chairs covered with Gobelin tapestry, its crystal chandeliers, and its white marble mantels draped in deep rose plush bordered with more Gobelin. Works of art in the room included Bouguereau's Going to the Bath, Schreyer's Returning from the Hunt, and the Lost Pleiad by Randolph Rogers. The mayor's favorite piece, however, was a table with a carved onyx and brass standard and a circular porcelain top depicting Louis XV surrounded by medallions of court beauties.[43]

The David Whitney Jr. house, built in 1870 on Woodward avenue, went *(91)* much further than the Pingree house in discarding the restraints of the Barryesque villa.[44] In spite of its sober dignity, there was an increasing Victorian restlessness; advancing and receding wall surfaces provided a rhythmical cadence, supplemented by a counterpoint of porches and semi-octagonal bay windows. *(161)* This house has been attributed to Mortimer L. Smith.[45]

In 1876 Henry T. Brush, formerly a member of the firm of Brush and Smith, completed a house on West Fort street for Clement Lafferty, a member of an *(95)* old French family.[46] The tower, an element borrowed from the Italianate villa, differentiated it from the Whitney house and represented a further step in the evolution of the symmetrical mansardic type of design. Treated like a central pavilion, the tower was provided with a curved pyramidal roof. The residence of *(93)* Wilhelm Boeing, a lumber baron, carried the formula of the Lafferty house to its logical extreme. Built in 1875 on Woodward avenue, this bold and ornate house was the Detroit equivalent of the Cyrus Hall McCormick house in Chicago and the Charles Crocker house in San Francisco.[47]

The John P. Phillips house, built in 1874 on West Fort street, was perhaps *(94)* the most archeologically correct of any of Detroit's Second Empire mansions.[48] Here the architect went directly to Lefuel's *Pavillon de Flore* at the Louvre for inspiration. Even so, the Parisian prototype, with its superimposed orders, broken pediments, and bull's eye windows, underwent a radical transformation to adapt it to the requirements of the modern dwelling. The above houses have long since disappeared from the Detroit scene.

In 1877 Gordon W. Lloyd built a house for Henry P. Baldwin, a successful *(97)* shoe manufacturer who later became governor.[46] The location on the northwest corner of Fort street and Cass avenue had been the site of a frame house built for Lewis Cass upon his return from his ministerial duties in France in 1843.[49] The Baldwin house represented an attempt to develop a new type of town house, although the paired columns of the portico and the narrow windows with their shrunken pediments still betrayed French influence. The joining of the window caps at the bases to form a novel fret'pattern revealed Lloyd's inventive turn of mind, and the triple tiers of bay windows showed him to be concerned about adequate illumination. In the central entrance hall was a grand staircase; opening off the hall were large high-ceilinged rooms, their walls lined with the governor's collection of paintings. It was here that Governor and Mrs. Baldwin received President and Mrs. Rutherford B. Hayes and General W. T. Sherman.

The exterior walls and the interior load-bearing walls of the house were of brick, while the non-load bearing partitions were of stud frame construction. Inside walls were covered with lath and plaster.[50] The house was torn down in 1943. The smaller yet somewhat similar Traugott Schmidt house, also by Lloyd, still stood on East Jefferson avenue until recently.[50]

(96) To trace the development of the asymmetrical mansardic mansion, it is necessary to turn back to the house of Charles Du Charme, a hardware merchant and later president of the Michigan Stove Company. Located on East Jefferson avenue, it was built in 1869. Clearly its derivation was from the Italian villa of John *(71)* J. Bagley, but the elimination of the gabled wing and the introduction of a mansard roof gave it a definite French flavor. The architect of the Du Charme house was E. Willard Smith.[51] In 1859 Dankmar Adler, who was later the partner of Louis Sullivan, entered Smith's office. It was there that he laid the foundation of his knowledge of his profession. In his autobiography Adler speaks of Smith as "an honor to his profession."[52]

(98) Until its demolition in 1948 the Du Charme house was in good condition and contained some of its original furnishings. In the lofty rooms with their elaborate molded plaster ceilings the aura of Second Empire elegance lingered on. The large hallway was dominated by a grandiose stairway in black walnut and curly maple. An unsupported flight of over twenty steps swept to the landing, from which the stairway continued in two reverse flights. At the end of the long *(99)* parlor was an enormous mirror divided into three sections and framed with rich carving picked out in gold. In it were reflected the dim luster of the ornate brass chandeliers and the sheen of the deep blue brocade valances. In the dining room hunting subjects carved in high relief ornamented the sideboard and chairs.

(100) In 1876 the residence of Philo Parsons, president of the First National Bank, was built on Woodward avenue. Already the asymmetrical mansardic type of house had reached a standardized norm which might be found repeated with variations in dozens of other houses. The architect of the Parsons house was Elijah E. Myers who made an enviable reputation in the field of public build- *(90)* ings.[46] One might have expected something more distinctive to have come from his office.

(112) The Michigan pine land business enabled George O. Robinson to indulge in what the *Free Press* called "the most elaborate structure of the kind within the city limits."[53] Located on the northwest corner of Cass and Ledyard, the Robinson house (1876) was a monument of Victorian ebullience. In the hands of Brush and Smith architecture had become malleable and responsive to the promptings of the imagination. The rigid contours of the asymmetrical Italian villa were submerged under a curious melange of Italian and French elements. The delicate colonettes, the rich window dressings, the flaring eaves with their manifold modillions, and the pagoda-like cupola with its bizarre iron finial, all joined forces to create a strange vision half-way between reality and fantasy.

Apparently ordinary balloon frame construction was not utilized in such an elegant structure, for there was a lining of brick behind the flush siding. On the interior of the house there was an innovation of surprising modernity: the four principal rooms were connected with folding doors so that they could, for all practical purposes, be thrown into one large area.[54] During World War II the Robinson house, looking melancholy and neglected, was finally torn down.

The John S. Newberry house (1875) on East Jefferson avenue was one of *(101)* the great mansions of the period. Newberry was very active in promoting the early industrial development of Detroit. In 1864 he and James McMillan organized the Michigan Car Company to manufacture railroad freight cars. This led to the organization of numerous iron works.[55] Designed by Gordon W. Lloyd, the Newberry house was constructed of brick and was somewhat similar to the Baldwin house except that it was derived from the asymmetrical rather than the symmetrical Italian villa. Italian features were the tower with a Palladian window and the balustrades. French features, reduced to mere vestiges, were the small pediments, the Neo-Grec incised ornament in the stonework, and the rusticated porch columns which, incidentally, were made of wood.

Lloyd was not particularly interested in the use of historical details to create plastic or decorative effects. Rather, he was concerned with providing the Newberry house with modern comforts. Bay windows afforded sunshine and a view of the street, while large rooms connected by broad sliding doors offered ample and flexible space. Following the latest English trend, the center of the house was opened up with a large baronial hall provided with a fireplace. At the landing of the staircase was a Tiffany window set between marble columns. The woodwork of the house left no doubt that Lloyd had fallen under the spell of the Englishman Charles L. Eastlake whose *Hints on Household Taste* was revolutionizing interiors on both sides of the Atlantic. The old-fashioned marble mantels of the Baldwin house gave way to ornate wooden ones decked out with fluted columns, *(102)* carved insets, and narrow shelves for china and bric-a-brac.[56] In the dining room *(103)* there was a built-in sideboard done in a similar style. Such detailed carving was too demanding for the average carpenter, so Lloyd had his designs executed by William Wright, a decorator who had just come from England and was soon to make a name for himself in Detroit.[56] A center of the social life of its period, the Newberry house survived until 1960 when it was razed to make way for urban renewal.

In 1876 a competition was held for the design of the Detroit Waterworks. *(104)* Capturing the Victorian imagination, the design of Joseph E. Sparks easily won over the work submitted by other contestants, including George D. Mason.[57] It is apparent that the architect drew his inspiration from the current vogue for the Franco-Italian villa. The precedent for the adjacent tower, however, may be found in the Oriental minaret. Later doubled in size, the old Waterworks complex on East Jefferson avenue was torn down after World War II.

The Influence of Ruskin

In the late seventies and eighties the simmering potpourri of Victorian design received a new ingredient. Amid the welter of stylistic confusion a voice of authority was needed to clarify the issues and expound fundamental truths. John Ruskin had answered the challenge with an outpouring of magnificent prose that was to captivate a generation of the English-speaking world. In *The Seven Lamps of Architecture* (1849) and *The Stones of Venice* (1853) he brought to light the secrets of architecture that he had discovered, mainly in northern Italy. In his quest for architectural honesty he was aware of the imprudence of attempting in the nineteenth century to slavishly imitate the vaulted structures of the past. A pattern for the multi-storied buildings of the future could be found, he felt, in the superimposed arcades of Venetian Gothic palaces and Pisan Romanesque churches. Here, shimmering in the warm southern sunshine, were the polychromatic stone surfaces and naturalistic carved ornaments that were the basic components of architecture.[58]

Under the influence of Ruskin, architects in England and America were soon opening up their buildings with arcades supported on slender shafts, filling in spandrels and tympanums with carvings, and introducing structural polychromy whenever possible. Perhaps the most conspicuous contribution of Ruskin was the banded arch. He had found the alternate bands of masonry in the Pisan Romanesque much to his liking.[59] "Straight lines are ugly things as lines, but admirable as limits of colored spaces," he explained.[60] As if this were not enough to convince his readers, he even cited rock stratifications in nature as further justification.[61] In 1862 Peter B. Wight brought memories of the splendors of Venice to the streets of New York with his old National Academy of Design, a Ducal Palace in miniature,[62] and in 1876–78 Sturgis and Brigham adorned Copley Square in Boston with the old Museum of Fine Arts, another adaptation of the same Venetian masterpiece.[63]

(107) In Detroit, Julius Hess, an architect who had come from Switzerland in 1872, turned to the Italian Romanesque for inspiration for his St. Mary's Parsonage completed in 1876 on Monroe street east of the church.[64] In the next year he combined with Louis Mendelssohn to build a business block for the Schloss *(109)* brothers on the south side of East Jefferson avenue between Woodward and Bates. Prior to its erection the *Free Press* announced that the "front will present as handsome and rich an appearance as any store in the city." Here the superimposed arcades of the Pisan Romanesque, lending themselves to generous fenestration, were well adapted to a commercial structure. Detached blue granite shafts with carved sandstone capitals supported sandstone arches, while on the ground floor rusticated granite piers divided the shop windows, the remainder of the building having been of brick. On the interior ornamental cast-iron columns supported the floors.[65] This building was torn down recently to make way for the new Civic Center.

In 1883 Mortimer L. Smith and William E. Brown completed the six-story *(105)* Campau Block on the southwest corner of Griswold and Larned streets.[66] On the ground floor there was a Romanesque arcade with polished red granite shafts and blue granite piers. Arches and spandrels were of carved buff sandstone. The *Evening News* was of the opinion that this was the "richest and most magnificent first story front in America."[67] The upper part of the building was of brick, the carved stone window arches receiving different treatment on each floor. Venturing into the realm of aesthetics, the same newspaper noted, "In the ornamentation there is nothing projecting, but everything is reversed; in other words, the form is being taken out of the solid wall instead of being applied to it." This was a notable improvement in the design of commercial buildings, for the projecting Italian Renaissance architraves of earlier usage had been structurally meaningless. On the interior of the building there was an entrance hall resembling a Roman atrium from which one could be spirited to the desired floor by elevator. Of all this splendor nothing remains, for obsolescence at last caught up with the Campau Block and a parking lot is now operated on its site.

In 1879 Gordon W. Lloyd designed a building for Burnham, Stoepel and *(108)* Company, a wholesale dry goods firm, on the southwest corner of Woodward and Jefferson avenues.[68] Never very much at home with the Second Empire style, Lloyd must have welcomed a return to the Gothic. This time, however, it was the Italian Gothic instead of the northern Gothic, for here we find the delicate shafts and finely carved tympanums so extolled by Ruskin. Yet, true to the teachings of his new mentor and his own convictions as well, Lloyd never allowed himself to become subservient to the past, and always hoping to devise a new vocabulary of architecture suited to modern needs, improvised freely. This building, later converted into a hotel, was razed to make way for the new Civic Center. Two other buildings of 1879, to the west in the same block, were so similar in style to the Lloyd building that they were undoubtedly also by him. They were the Allan Shelden and Company wholesale dry goods store and the Board of Trade Building; they also have been demolished.

In 1881 D. M. Ferry and Company, the seed firm, erected a large office and *(110)* warehouse building on the west side of Brush street extending between Lafayette and Monroe. Mortimer L. Smith had submitted plans, but the company preferred the drawings of two young fledgelings, Mason and Rice. As Mason was then only twenty-three years of age, there was some doubt as to the wisdom of entrusting such a large commission to so young a man. However, with the plans laid out before them, Dexter M. Ferry, president of the company, subjected Mason to a thorough questioning until he was convinced that the building would be structurally sound. Heavy white pine floor beams supported on round cast-iron columns were employed throughout the building which was divided into three parts by brick fire walls.[57]

Making the largest business block in town architecturally interesting on the exterior was an unprecedented problem that might have puzzled even Ruskin. He probably would have frowned at the commercial implications, however appropriate, of the floral designs of the cut-stone ornament and would have questioned the use of banded arches made of red and black bricks, yet a warehouse could scarcely be expected to flaunt the stone extravagances of a bank or office building. Waving aside these technicalities, the *Free Press* was thoroughly reassured about Mason and Rice's latest achievement. "The long Brush Street front," it stated, "is ingeniously broken up with center and end pavilions, projecting the general mass of the building and obviating the monotonous effect so common to buildings of this class."[69]

The entire warehouse was provided with an automatic sprinkler system in case of fire. Mason had made a special trip to Boston to study this new device that had just come into use.[57] His efforts were of no avail, however, for on New Year's morning of 1886 the whole building burned to the ground. Floors and walls crashed in a flaming holocaust. Crowds gathered to see the spectacle which, according to a *Free Press* reporter, "was almost terrifying in its grandness."[70] For many days thereafter the air was filled with the odor of smoldering seeds. The origin of the fire is unknown, but one of the factors that prevented it from being brought under control was the presence of empty seed boxes on the top floor which could not adequately be reached by fire hoses.[57] There were broken hose lines and inadequate equipment and water supply.[71] In the following year D. M. Ferry and Company commissioned Gordon W. Lloyd to erect a new *(170)* building which is still standing today.

George D. Mason was later to become one of the outstanding architects in Detroit. He had come to the city with his parents in 1870 from Syracuse, New York. By 1873 he had finished his education in the public schools. His mechanical ingenuity soon brought him a job at G. S. Wormer and Son's Michigan Machinery Depot. Grover Wormer was on the board of the Detroit Lithographic Company when the plates for the diploma of the State Agricultural Society were burned. Recognizing young Mason's ability at drawing, Wormer asked him to design a new diploma, which he did with great aplomb. It was Wormer who gave Mason the idea of being an architect. When the question came up whether to enter Lloyd's office or Smith's, Wormer favored the latter on the grounds that he could design good cornices and Lloyd could not. Mason tried working in Smith's office one summer, but in 1875 he entered the new office of Henry T. Brush, as he thought he had a better chance there. The first nine

(112) months he worked without pay. In Brush's office Mason worked on the detailing

(132) for the George O. Robinson house on Cass avenue and for the old Public Library. He collaborated with Brush in 1876 on the Ransom Gillis house, still

(111) standing (although greatly altered) on the northeast corner of John R. and Alfred streets, in which the influence of Ruskin is apparent. In 1878 Mason joined in partnership with Zachariah Rice, a family friend from Oswego, New York. Their first job was a stable for Thomas Berry of Berry Brothers. Thomas

(82) W. Palmer gave them an office in the Merrill Block and agreed they should have five hundred dollars the first year whether they made anything or not. Palmer was not disappointed, as they made eight hundred dollars. In 1879–80 they built

(106) the Central Market Building in Cadillac Square in the prevalent Ruskinian manner. It was demolished in 1889.[57]

In the meantime Gordon W. Lloyd was welcoming the Ruskin-inspired revival of interest in the Gothic as a sanction to return to his favorite domestic style.

(63) He had learned from his experience with the Sidney D. Miller house the folly of trying to fit a prosperous businessman with a large family and retinue into a snug Gothic villa, for it had been necessary for him to increase the size of the Miller house with addition after addition.[50] When called upon to design a house for

(113) James McMillan, Lloyd knew it was no time for rustic coziness.[68] The large mansion which rose in 1873–80 on the northeast corner of Jefferson avenue and Russell street was characterized by billowing brick walls and bay windows, the better to provide sunshine and view for the many large rooms. The main objective was comfort and convenience. However, there were scalloped Gothic vergeboards, and a small Italian Gothic porch was a succinct yet unmistakable acknowledgement of Ruskin's influence. The McMillan house was occupied by

(311) the University Club from 1913 to 1931, when it was torn down to make way for the existing clubhouse. In the pseudo-Gothic design of Harper Hospital, built on

(115) John R. street in 1883–84 by Elijah E. Myers, one may detect a family resemblance to the McMillan house.[72] Billowing brick walls and bay windows were merely enlarged in scale and arranged in regular rhythmic sequences.

James McMillan was closely associated in business with John S. Newberry.

(87) With him he had formed the Michigan Car Company out of which grew numerous iron works and related industries. He also controlled extensive shipping and railroad interests. It was he who conceived and carried out the Duluth, South Shore and Atlantic Railroad which opened up the Upper Peninsula to settlement. In 1888 he was elected to the United States Senate. Like many other wealthy men of the day, McMillan was an avid art collector and philanthropist.[73]

The residence that Lloyd built for Henry B. Ledyard in 1887 remained until recently on East Jefferson avenue. Again, Gothic details were minimized. No gem architecturally, the house suffered from having been built on too narrow a lot. Perhaps its most interesting feature was the wide variety of wood used for the interior paneling which, according to the *Free Press,* included red oak, cherry, white holly, white maple, and black walnut.[74] Ledyard was successively president and chairman of the board of the Michigan Central Railroad from 1883

(141) until his death in 1921. During his regime the railroad was extended throughout

the state and modernized, the railroad tunnel under the Detroit River to Canada *(264)*
was constructed (1910), and the present station was erected.

In 1875 Lloyd built a house, since demolished, on West Fort street for the *(114)*
enterprising merchant Allan Shelden.[68] In contrast to his lukewarm Gothic domiciles, the Shelden house was aggressively monumental. Cut stone was used with
a lavish hand to contrast with the brick by means of banding and rustication.
Stylistically the house was a curious hybrid. The symmetrical Elizabethan gables
harked back to Lloyd's Dey house of 1862, while the central tower was derived *(68)*
from the mansardic tradition.

Mortimer L. Smith built a residence in 1878 for Joseph Black, a banker and *(118)*
hardware merchant. Located on Woodward avenue at Parsons, it was termed
"modern domestic Gothic" in the *Post and Tribune*. In general mass the house
resembled the Shelden house, but Smith went further than Lloyd in the direction
of Ruskin. There were delicate stone engaged columns and carving in the tympanums, while the tower had acquired a wedge-shaped Gothic roof. The newspaper account informs us that in the hallway the wainscoting was of black
walnut with French walnut veneering, relieved with gilded figures, and that in
the dining room it was of chestnut burl ash inlaid with ebony and gilding, and
the flooring was of maple, cherry, and walnut laid in marquetry. The newspaper
reporter had nothing but praise for the architect who, he maintained, had "furnished special designs for everything therewith—even the cut glass in the door."
"He has superintended every detail of the work," continued the reporter, "and
the beauty and richness of the whole as it stands completed, speak in the highest
terms, not less of his skill as an architect than of his genius as an artist. The
combinations of color and of form and figure in the interior finishing are such as
please the cultivated eye and minister to the cultivated taste."[75]

Mortimer L. Smith was a colorful figure in the artistic life of Victorian
Detroit. Handsome and athletic, he enjoyed fencing and ice skating. An inveterate traveler, he covered the principal countries of Europe and much of the
United States. An artist in his own right, he did landscape paintings of New
England and the Midwest. His *Winter Landscape*, a scene in northern Michigan,
is now at the Detroit Institute of Arts. A panorama of Niagara Falls was perhaps
his most ambitious project.[33] When in Alaska with Clarence Black, the son of
Joseph Black, he did a painting of a glacier. The foot of the glacier, he afterward *(175)*
explained, was as large as the J. L. Hudson store he built in 1891.[76]

Somewhat similar to the Black house is the residence of Lucien S. Moore, a *(119)*
successful lumber dealer. Built in 1885 on Edmund place, the house is still intact
today. Again we find a Gothic tower and fragile colonettes, but here dormer
windows with Renaissance details broke the cornice, and the banded arch became a playful motif in an imaginative and sprightly ensemble. Larger in scale,
yet in the same exuberant vein, is St. Mary's Church of 1885, still standing on the *(116)*
southeast corner of St. Antoine street and Monroe.[77] The architect was Peter
Dederichs, who was born and trained in Germany.[78] From the Pisan Romanesque and the Venetian Renaissance he extracted diverse details which he ingeniously fused together into a composite fabric of great originality.

Gordon W. Lloyd was much less spontaneous in his scheme for the West- *(117)*
minster Presbyterian Church of 1881 which stood, before its demolition, on the
corner of Woodward avenue and Parsons.[79] His inspiration was, no doubt, the
Venetian Gothic of the new Old South Church which Cummings and Sears had
erected in 1877 on Copley Square in Boston, but he added some exotic flourishes
of his own, including banded Saracenic arches, chimneys that looked like mina-
rets, and an awkward tower with a round belfry corbeled out from its shaft.[80]

The Gothic of northern Europe never completely lost its hold upon the imaginations of Detroit church-builders. Two typical late Victorian churches, which are still extant, are Ste. Anne's Church of 1887 on Howard street at Ste. Anne (formerly Nineteenth), designed by Leon Coquard,[81] and the Sweetest Heart of Mary Church of 1893 on Russell street at Canfield, by Spier and Rohns.[82] Brick on the exterior, they display a characteristically restless multiplicity of forms. On the interiors clustered stone piers and ribbed vaults were simulated in wood and plaster. St. Anne's is the oldest parish in Detroit, although this is the eighth structure. In the crypt lie the remains of Father Gabriel Richard and in the chapel are relics from the church he built in 1828.[83]

(122)

(121)

(27)

In this age of the picturesque, even the railroad station was forced to hide behind an assortment of towers, gables, and steep roofs. A dramatic silhouette was imperative at any cost. Sir George Gilbert Scott masked the iron shed of St. Pancras Station (1863–76) in London with a Gothic façade, and Americans were quick to follow his lead.[84] In 1882–83 Cyrus L. W. Eidlitz of New York built the Michigan Central Station in Detroit on the southwest corner of West Jefferson and Third avenues. Medieval German in aspect, it was deprived of its lofty clock tower for many years, and was finally torn down in 1966.

(123)

The Age of Iron

The dreams of Ruskin of an architecture replete with hand-carved stone ornament were bound to founder on the shoals of economic reality. The feverish building activity of the nineteenth century was inimical to laborious craftsmanship, which was obviously impractical in an age of limited budgets and fixed cost estimates, yet it would have been difficult for a generation already wedded to rich surface ornament to forego this predilection overnight.[85] It was James Bogardus of New York who was to resolve the dilemma. In 1848 he built the first complete cast-iron building, his own factory in New York. Sills and columns were bolted together to form a homogeneous whole. Later he erected similar buildings in New York, Philadelphia, Baltimore, Washington, and San Francisco. Iron had served in England and other European countries for beams and columns, but its use on the exteriors of buildings was largely an American phenomenon.[86] Bogardus did not wait for a biographer to extoll his ingenuity. He himself wrote:

It was whilst in Italy, contemplating the rich architectural designs of antiquity that Mr. Bogardus first conceivèd the idea of emulating them in modern times. This was the year 1840; and during his subsequent travels in Europe, he held it constantly in view; and cherished it the more carefully, as he became convinced, by inquiry and personal observation, not only that the idea was original with himself, but that he might thereby become the means of greatly adding to our national wealth, and of establishing a new, a valuable, and a permanent branch of industry.

In addition to its structural advantages, Bogardus pointed out that

. . . another recommendation of cast iron is its happy adaptability of ornament and decoration. Were a single ornament only required, it might perhaps be executed as cheaply in marble or freestone; but where a multiplicity of the same is needed, they can be cast in iron at an expense not to be named in comparison,

even with that of wood; and with this advantage, that they will retain their original fullness and sharpness of outline long after those in stone have decayed and disappeared. Fluted columns and Corinthian capitals, the most elaborate carvings, and the richest designs, which the architects may have dreamed of, but did not dare represent in his plans, may thus be reproduced for little more than the cost of ordinary castings. Ornamental architecture—which with our limited means is apt to be tawdry, because incomplete—thus becomes practicable; and its general introduction would greatly tend to elevate the public taste for the beautiful, and to purify and gratify one of the finest qualities of the human mind.[87]

In England and later in America it became apparent that the Venetian Renaissance palace, because of its generous window areas, was a better model for commercial buildings than the Tuscan palace with its infrequent and fortress-like apertures.[59] The technique of casting iron was ideally suited for reproducing the repetitious columns and arcades of Venetian façades, so it was the work of Sansovino and his confreres that provided the inspiration for the iron fabrications of Bogardus. In Detroit, where the dearth of stone quarries and skilled stone workers had always been a problem, the economic advantage of substituting iron for cut stone was particularly welcome. This aspect of the contribution of Bogardus was more appealing than his structural innovations, for in Michigan there was a plentiful supply of brick and lumber for the underlying structure of commercial buildings. To be sure, round iron columns had been introduced to support wood beams and joists, and iron lintels and mullions were in general use, but in Detroit, at least, the iron façade was purely ornamental. Iron panels were bolted together and attached to conventional brick exterior walls.[50]

Gordon W. Lloyd had earlier experimented in the use of cast stone, so it is not surprising that he readily became interested in the possibilities of cast iron. Bartlett, Hayward and Company's Architectural Iron Works in Baltimore had provided the castings for several of Bogardus's buildings, and it was to this firm that Lloyd turned for assistance in translating his designs into iron.[50] Perhaps his earliest iron front was for C. J. Whitney and Company's music store which he *(124)* built on West Fort street in 1874.[88] The Venetian palace façade, with its rustication, balustrades, and superimposed orders, was the basis for the design; but in his quest for a new architectural language suited to modern usage, Lloyd was much less literal than Bogardus in the adaptation of Venetian motifs. The store was the headquarters of the musical empire of Clark J. Whitney who, at the age of eighteen, had abandoned a lucrative fishery business in the remote Beaver Islands to undertake in Detroit the manufacture of melodeons, pianos, and organs. He was later to own a chain of theaters in Michigan and Ontario, including Whitney's Opera House in Detroit.[89] Of this once thriving empire, nothing remains today.

As the retail trade crept up Woodward avenue, the importance of Jefferson avenue as a wholesale district steadily increased. Francis Palms realized that it *(43)* was an ideal area in which to invest in real estate. With the aid of Lloyd as architect, he built several large stores along Jefferson avenue.[50] As mentioned previously, Lloyd had already erected several commercial buildings on Jefferson avenue in the Ruskinian Gothic and Romanesque styles with ornate stone trim. With cast iron now at his disposal, he launched into the modified Venetian Renaissance in his work for Francis Palms. This included the wholesale clothing store of Heavenrich Brothers (1880),[90] the wholesale dry goods house of Edson, Moore and Company (1881),[91] and the Palms Block (c. 1881).[92] Of these the last *(126)* mentioned survived the longest, but was recently razed to make way for the

(398)   Hotel Pontchartrain. At the turn of the century it was occupied by Crowley Brothers (wholesale dry goods), forerunner of Crowley, Milner and Company.

(125)   The Edson, Moore and Company building, which stood on the southeast corner of Jefferson avenue and Bates, was completely destroyed by fire in 1893.
(139)   The fire started on the fourth and fifth floors where cotton had been kept for packing purposes. The interior of the building burned like timber. In no time at all the four walls enclosed a raging inferno. Fire hoses were of no avail. Finally all the walls went down except the heavily bolted front wall of iron. Although the fire escapes had been approved by building inspectors, seven lives were lost. A building considered to be fireproof was consumed by flames in half an hour.[93]

(127)   Still standing today on the southwest corner of Woodward avenue and State street is Lloyd's Parker Block (1883), now B. Siegel Company. Intended for occupancy by retail stores, it was somewhat more elaborate than Lloyd's other iron-fronted buildings. When first completed the left half was occupied by Mme. Rabaut's children's furnishings store, and on the right was M. S. Smith and Company's jewelry store which the *Free Press* considered the "finest establishment of its kind in the West."[94] Above the door was an unusual timepiece, imported from London, with life-size allegorical figures of Father Time and a smith who chimed the hours on a series of bells with his hammer.[95]

(128)   Mortimer L. Smith turned to the use of cast iron for his Ferry Building (1879) located on the east side of Woodward avenue on the site of the present J. L. Hudson Company store.[96] Erected by Dexter M. Ferry, it was occupied by the Newcomb, Endicott and Company store. Although of Venetian derivation, the building manifested a tendency toward simplification. Piers and spandrels had been so reduced that the front wall was dematerialized into an astonishingly modern grille of glass and metal.

(129)   In 1885 Gordon W. Lloyd built the Grand Circus Building for David Whitney Jr., a lumber baron, on Park street at Woodward avenue.[68] It was somewhat similar to the Ferry Building. Foreseeing the trend of business northward, Whitney bought the property when the area was still residential. In 1914 the building
(215)   was torn down to make way for the present David Whitney Building.

(137)   During the seventies the tradition of cut stonework persisted. A small anonymous store building on West Jefferson avenue, recently torn down, may be cited for its charming yet economical design. Incised Neo-Grec patterns on the window caps and consoles created a lacy Victorian effect. On the ground floor slender cast-iron columns permitted the use of large display windows. The design as a whole revealed a high degree of spontaneous native artistry.

(135)   A very late example of a metal-fronted building is the Detroit Cornice and Slate Company (1897) on St. Antoine street. In this case the entire street front was made of galvanized steel manufactured by the company that still occupies the building. Some of the shapes were made in presses, but much of the delicate simulated carving in the friezes and tympanums was hammered by hand.[97]

(133)   The use of iron for grand architectural effects was not limited to the exteriors of buildings. In the reading room of the Detroit Public Library (1875–77) in Library Park, by Brush and Smith, there was a vast arcaded peristyle of ornate iron columns extending the full height of the building to a skylight in the middle of the roof.[98] Through the arcade on all sides of the room could be seen five stories of book stacks connected by iron catwalks and spiral stairs. The exterior of the brick building was Second Empire in detail. For economic reasons the
(134)   curved pyramidal dome of the original design never materialized, and the engaged columns and broken pediment of the portico were executed in white pine
(132)   instead of stone. George D. Mason, who was then working in Brush's office, did

much of the detailing.[57] The building was replaced by the present Downtown Library in 1932. A reading room somewhat similar to the one in the old library may still be seen in Edmund G. Lind's Peabody Institute in Baltimore (1861).[99]

Iron columns were used dramatically on the interior of Mortimer L. Smith's *(138)* Woodward Avenue Baptist Church (1887), still standing on the southeast corner at Winder.[100] Here the monumental piers, so much a part of the Gothic tradition, have been dissolved in the cavernous void of the interior, and in their place tenuous members of iron rise boldly to support the fanciful Victorian trusses of the roof. L. A. Boileau had used this type of column in his Church of St. Eugène in Paris (1854–55);[101] but there the comparison ends, for the spatial concept of the Detroit church was altogether unique. Galleries on all four sides of the interior, which is a Greek cross in plan, were supported on shorter columns. Supplementing the illumination from large windows with stone tracery are small clerestory windows that interrupt the slope of the roof. The exterior of *(136)* the church is less revolutionary. There is little to differentiate it from one of Lloyd's stone churches except the increased fussiness of detail of the later Victorian Gothic. Unfortunately the tower was removed and the west façade moved back and radically altered when Woodward avenue was widened in 1936.[102]

In the Days of Queen Anne

By 1860 there was a reaction in England against the Gothic and Italian Renaissance styles. Architects were tired of endless masquerading and yearned for simplicity and informality. Careful to avoid the pitfalls of mere copyism, Philip Webb found inspiration in the fifteenth century English farmhouse for the famous Red House he built for William Morris at Bexley Heath in 1859. Norman Shaw launched into free interpretations of the seventeenth century Queen Anne style in a series of town houses he built in London. These dwellings, with their brick walls, tall narrow windows, and Renaissance details, were to give English domestic architecture a new orientation.[103]

In their haste to seize upon the latest architectural vogue from London, American architects overlooked the subtlety and studied casualness of Shaw's manner. For them it meant merely a new vocabulary of ornament to be used in place of Gothic or mansardic motifs. Thus, in its main outlines the American Victorian mansion remained unchanged. In Detroit the new Queen Anne trap- *(139)* pings could be seen in profusion on a house Lloyd built in 1881 for George F. Moore, president of Edson, Moore and Company.[68] In 1890 the house was oc- *(125)* cupied by Dexter M. Ferry and became a repository for his large collection of paintings. Located on the corner of Woodward avenue and Farnsworth, it was torn down in the twenties to make way for the Detroit Institute of Arts. Lloyd *(247)* even resorted to the Queen Anne style for his Police Headquarters (1884) which stood on the present site of the Water Board Building at Bates and Randolph streets.[104] Here he merely enlarged upon and dramatized the motifs found in his domestic work.

In 1885 Lloyd built a residence for General Russell A. Alger on Fort street.[68] *(130)* It resembled his earlier Baldwin house except for the elimination of bay windows *(97)* and a shift from Second Empire to Queen Anne in its decor. A *Detroit News* reporter found the interior of the house "as beautiful as money, refined taste and care and thought can make it." The house was filled with "treasures of art and bric-a-brac gathered from the four quarters of the globe by General Alger and his family."

The hall, which was finished in oak, contained "large chairs and a great chest all of Italian workmanship quaintly inlaid with pearl and silver" and a "settle inlaid with ivory" which General Alger had picked up in Milan. "Upon the wall," observed the reporter, "hang some paintings by Sell, which afford the necessary coloring. They gleam among the somber surroundings like so many jewels. Underneath the arches are large majolica pots filled with palms, and over them swings on one side a strangely wrought iron lamp, found in a Venetian bric-a-brac shop, and on the other some stained glass, which was undoubtedly once a part of a window. Its colors are dull, its design difficult to comprehend. The date is 1530. Further down the hall is a great fireplace with a meditative stag's head placed high up amid its beautiful carving. On the wall is the great Schreyer picture of Bedouins, and a Russian winter scene by Kowalski." The drawing room might well have been called the picture gallery, for its walls were lined with pictures, mostly of the French School.[105]

Alger was another one of those nineteenth century Detroit capitalists who rose from a simple rural background to a high place in the world of business and politics. Quick to sense the opportunities of a rapidly expanding economy, he abandoned the law profession to take an active part in lumbering, building railroads, and developing iron industries and mines. To his business career was added the distinction of being a general in the Civil War and later of becoming the governor of Michigan.[106]

(131) One of the great lumber fortunes of Michigan was founded by Simon J. Murphy. At first operating in Maine, he later moved to Michigan when it became the center of the lumber industry.[107] In 1887 William Scott and Company built a house for Murphy on the corner of Woodward and Putnam where the *(243)* Detroit Public Library now stands.[108] The high roof, steep pediments, and unorthodox use of classical ornament were characteristic of the Queen Anne style.

Art Comes to the Fore

In the late nineteenth century it was a foregone conclusion that every Detroit millionaire should indulge in an art collection, and there was scarcely one of the larger mansions on Fort street or Woodward avenue without its tiers of canvases and its population of marbles and bronzes. According to the standards of today, most of these "treasures of art" would be relegated to the limbo of sentimentality and sheer pictorialism. Nevertheless, in some of the better collections there were many paintings of the Barbizon and Hudson River Schools by artists who are recognized and admired today.

(120) Enthusiasm over art reached such a pitch in Detroit that by 1883 wealthy citizens were subscribing one thousand dollars each to guarantee an Art Loan Exhibition. A lot was rented on the south side of Larned street between Bates and Randolph and a gallery erected.[109] Since the building was only temporary, there was a refreshing lack of any architectural pretension. Modeled after the Philadelphia Centennial Art Annex, it was one story high with walls and partitions of brick. Each room was lighted from above by monitors by day and electric lights at night.[110] Most of the material in the exhibition was borrowed from local collections. In addition to paintings and sculpture, there were displays of prints, textiles, and other artifacts. Besides examples of the American School, there were works of art from all the principal European countries. Among the Detroit artists represented were Lewis and Percy Ives, Robert Hopkin, Gari

Melchers, Julius Rolshoven, Mortimer L. Smith, Seth A. Whipple, and John Mix Stanley.[111]

Besides being both a popular and a financial success, the exhibition was a milestone in Detroit's artistic history. A *Free Press* reporter reflected: "Even those who do not regard it as the very best method of developing and securing permanent art culture in this community gladly welcome it as a means to that end. It is the first serious step, and we trust a long step, toward an artistic education of the community."[110] That the public was well prepared for the exhibition may be deduced from an editorial in the *Detroit Free Press* in 1869, which stated: "Chromo-lithography is rapidly becoming the most popular class of art in this country as well as in Europe, and at the present time chromo copies of many of the finest paintings extant, equal in many respects to the originals, can be obtained for a comparatively nominal sum."[112]

Swiss Coquetry

To the Victorian businessman architecture meant romance, and if he found the Gothic or Renaissance styles too oppressively formal for his taste, he could escape to the equally picturesque but more rustic charm of the Swiss chalet. This style of building had been revived in Germany, France, and even England.[113] As early as 1850 Andrew Jackson Downing was recommending "the genuine Swiss cottage" to his American readers. He felt that this type of dwelling would be most suitable in a wild and romantic landscape, but conceded that it might be permissible in a more subdued setting, if modified accordingly.[114] This was not merely the importation of another eclectic style; for the wooden peasant architecture of Switzerland had a special significance in America, a land of plentiful timber, and its introduction to this country coincided with a preoccupation with the skeletal articulation of the wooden frame. American architects became absorbed with the notion that the expression of wooden structural members—horizontal, vertical, and diagonal—was the key to a new architectural honesty. Along with the fanciful interpretation of Swiss prototypes came a renewed interest in the half-timbered structures of the Middle Ages.[115]

One of the first architects in Detroit to come under the influence of the new theories was Gordon W. Lloyd, as was clearly indicated by the house he built *(140)* for himself at Petite Cote (now La Salle), Ontario, about 1872. Here we find him experimenting with half-timbered construction. So far his acceptance of the Swiss mode seems to have been limited to the small gable trusses filled in with tracery, as the general conformation of his house followed rather closely the pattern of the local vernacular. An architect's own home is usually an interesting commentary on his personal taste, and this house reveals an uncompromising suppression of the historical trappings usually demanded by clients.

There could be no more delightful spot for a dwelling than the peaceful verdant Canadian bank overlooking the majestic Detroit River. The site Lloyd chose for his house was one that had caught his fancy from a boat as it descended the river. It was too inaccessible from his office in town to make daily commuting feasible. Therefore it is understandable that he chose to stay in town all week, returning to Petite Cote only for the weekends. Depending on the season, he would drive a buggy or a cutter to Windsor to catch the ferry to Detroit. Frequently the family would rent a house in the city for the winter.

The life in the country brought with it the delights of gardening, although time and inclination limited the busy architect to the raising of fruits and vegetables. He might have enjoyed literary pursuits, but again the pressing demands of his profession left him little time to read more than the newspapers and magazines of the day. To break the monotony of routine, there were always the outings on Belle Isle, a large island in the Detroit River, where the main attraction was hunting and fishing. The island was quite wild then, since it had not yet been turned into a public park and was inaccessible except by boat. For this reason Lloyd had provided himself with a boathouse at the foot of Bates street. A frequent companion on these camping trips was Frederick J. Stevenson, an English engineer who had come to Detroit to aid in building the railroad to Port Huron. Stevenson was an excellent photographer and made a panoramic view of Detroit from the Canadian shore in 1866.[50]

In those days Belle Isle was owned by the Campau family, who lived in a frame house in the center of the island, which is known today as the Garden Center. The Campaus operated extensive fisheries on the island, and the annual fall picnic which they held at the fishermen's cabin was a fashionable event. Guests swarmed to the island in every imaginable craft from the private boathouses that lined the Detroit River. In 1879 the island was sold to the city and the old way of life there came to an end.[116]

In the middle of the nineteenth century Detroiters discovered the sleepy rural community of Grosse Pointe nearby on the shores of Lake Saint Clair, and recognizing its recreational advantages, set about transforming it into a summer colony. Wealthy businessmen bought up old French ribbon farms along the lake and erected summer cottages there. Every pleasant summer afternoon would see fast teams and turnouts following the narrow dirt road that led from the city through the countryside to this veritable Eden. "The approach by road is not *(144)* unattractive," wrote Theodore P. Hall in 1886. "The blue lake is first seen through a row of poplars, and then with a sharp curve one suddenly emerges upon the shore, and the cool breezes and plashing waters seem doubly invigorating after a long drive."[117]

Perhaps the first man to choose Grosse Pointe as a summer residence was George V. N. Lothrop, a prominent lawyer and later ambassador to Russia. In 1850 he built a cottage on property once owned by Commodore Alexander Grant. Another early cottage was built in 1856 by Colonel Elijah Brush's son Edmund Brush, who had made a fortune by subdividing the old Brush farm in Detroit.

Even if Grosse Pointe could boast no mountains, it did not take long for Gordon W. Lloyd to realize that the broad verandas and jutting balconies of the Swiss idiom were ideally suited to a lake exposure. In 1875 he built twin chalets *(142)* there for John S. Newberry and Senator James McMillan.[118] The porch railings and gable trusses gave him an opportunity to indulge in some lacy jigsaw ornament, with here and there his favorite quatrefoil motif. No one would have *(186)* suspected the erstwhile somber Gothicist capable of such a light-hearted mood.

In front of the Newberry and McMillan cottages was a long dock projecting out into the lake. Their steam yacht *Truant* and Edmund Brush's *Lillie* were always ready to take their owners on a run into the city or an excursion about the lakes, while the *Leila*, owned by a group of residents, was pressed into daily service to and from Detroit. On up the shore from the dock was a steady procession of frame cottages of varying styles, each with its boathouse and strand of sandy beach. Hall has left us a delightful description of the Victorian resort in its heyday:

Under the broad verandas that surround the houses, hammocks are strung, wherein recline aesthetic maidens, or languid gentlemen of leisure, deep in the mysteries of the latest novel, or extracting comfort from a fragrant Havana, as the case may be. In an open space beyond the trees, we catch glimpses of the picturesque costumes of the devotees of lawn tennis, baseball, or croquet.[119]

Among the more charming summer retreats at the Pointe were a pair of *(141)* cottages Lloyd built in 1882 for Henry B. Ledyard and Hugh McMillan, the brother of the senator.[118] The pseudo-Swiss manner was still favored, but here the architect went far beyond his previous Newberry and McMillan houses in the study of massing and construction. There were hipped-back Swiss gables, exposed framing with diagonal braces, and vertical siding. Both houses bore a striking resemblance to the Thomas G. Appleton cottage which Richard Morris Hunt had built at Newport, Rhode Island (1875–76). Probably Lloyd had seen this house illustrated in some architectural magazine and was strongly influenced by it. In *The Homes of America* Martha Lamb described the Appleton house as a "bewildering mass of outcropping fancies, Swiss roofs, overhanging balconies, and novel conceits."[120]

An all-year-round residence in Grosse Pointe belonged to Theodore P. Hall, *(144)* who had married Alexandrine Godfroy of old French lineage. Hall had made a success of the grain business early enough in life to enable him to retire and devote his time to travel, literary pursuits, and the improvement of Tonnancour, as his sixty-three acre estate was called.[121] His house was built by Mortimer L. Smith in 1880. In addition to jigsaw fretwork there were turned posts and ornaments on the porches and gables, giving the house the appearance of a white gingerbread cake. The Swiss boathouse was the scene of gay dancing parties, theatricals, and other evening amusements.[122] Further up the shore on the estate was a rustic grotto that enshrined a statue of Notre Dame de Ste. Claire.[123] According to an old French legend, it was there in the days before Cadillac that a nun sought refuge from the sinister *loup garou* (werewolf).[124]

Before falling too irretrievably under the spell of Victorian Grosse Pointe with its rustic charm and lingering aura of French heritage, it is perhaps advisable to return to Detroit, if only to discover that the Swiss vogue had even penetrated the more fashionable residential areas of the metropolis. The horrors of the Chicago fire of 1871 were too fresh in the memory to permit a total surrender to wood construction, so brick was ingeniously combined with wood.

The Woodward avenue residence Mortimer L. Smith built in 1876 for the *(145)* shoe merchant Richard H. Fyfe was actually a restatement of the traditional *(321)* Victorian house utilizing all the pseudo-Swiss clichés.[45] In comparison with Tonnancour, the details were more refined and the wooden members more skillfully articulated. Gordon W. Lloyd may have been the architect of the John B. Dyar house of 1880 on Alfred street.[125] Worn and weather-beaten, it survived until recently. Projecting gables, incongruous on such a tall narrow façade, created a bizarre effect.

The Swiss style rose to a climax in the Michigan Building at the Centennial *(143)* Exposition of 1876 in Philadelphia. Fantasy and exuberance had been combined to create just the right effect for such a festive event. The pavilion was constructed entirely of wood above the foundations. On the inside the walls and ceilings were paneled, no plaster having been used.[126] On the exterior the decorative quality of the framing members was recognized and used as the basis for a complex overall pattern emphasizing verticals, horizontals, and diagonals. It would perhaps be asking too much of architect Julius Hess to credit such a brilliant *tour de force* entirely to his own imagination, and it is only fair to point out that the Michigan Building was very similar in many respects to the *Chalet de la Commission Imperiale* at the *Exposition Universelle* of 1867 in Paris.[127] Nevertheless, it was very appropriate for the occasion, as the following contemporary description testifies:

On the north side of State Avenue . . . is the very showy structure erected by the State of Michigan. In appearance, elaboration and detail, embellishment and ornamentation, it is as rich as any State structure upon the grounds. The house is Swiss in appearance and decoration, the outlines being broken up by bay-windows, verandas, porches and hanging galleries, with snug little piazzas and much open work. The central tower is an imposing feature, and strikingly illustrative of the most ornate characteristics of the architecture of Switzerland. The coloring is in happy contrast, and the general effect of the exterior is graceful and pleasing. The ground plan shows an area of about 50 x 65 feet. The idea has been to make this building in all respects illustrative of Michigan material and of Michigan workmanship. The brownstone foundation comes from the Marquette quarries; the roofing slate is from Huron Bay, Lake Superior; the wainscoting in the reception-room is of highly-polished alabaster from the Grand Rapids quarries. The office of the governor of Michigan is ornamented with a mantel and side panelings of Michigan marble. The interior finish of other rooms is of native woods and polished marble and alabaster. The floors are laid with hardwoods of various kinds and patterns. The main staircase is spacious and handsome. The doors are of solid walnut and elaborately carved. The fitting up is the finest character. The furniture is of Michigan woods, made by Michigan cabinet-makers. The walls are ornamented with pictures by Michigan artists. "Off Sleeping Bear Point, Lake Michigan," a large and elegant painting by Robert Hopkin, occupies a prominent position. The interior is fitted up with offices, parlors, reception-rooms and other conveniences, and it is expected that the citizens of Michigan visiting the Exhibition will not omit a friendly call at the State headquarters building, and certainly, when they see it, they will all agree that they have something to be proud of.[128]

City Hall, *J. Anderson*,
1; Civil War Monument,
R. Rogers, 1872 (JSC)

Detroit Opera House,
S. & M. L. Smith, 1869
(BHC/JKJ)

(87) Newberry and McMillan Building, *G. W. Lloyd*, 1879 (MB)

(88-89) Wayne County Savings Bank, *W. Scott*, 1876 (BHC/JKJ)

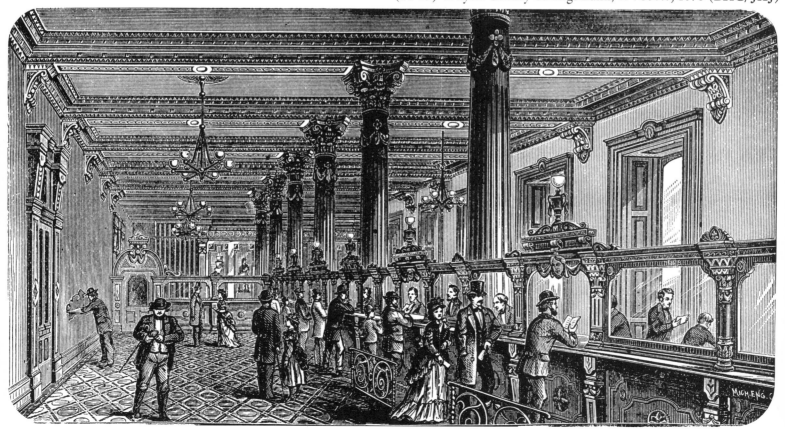

(90) Michigan State Capitol, Lansing, *E. E. Myers*, 1878 (BHC)

(91) David Whitney Jr.
House, *M. L. Smith(?)*
1870 (BHC)

(92) Hazen S. Pingree
House, 1883 (BHC)

(93) Wilhelm Boeing House, 1875 (BHC)

(94) John P. Phillips House, 1874 (BHC)

(95) Clement Lafferty House, *H. T. Brush*, 1876 (BHC)
(96) Charles Du Charme House, *E. W. Smith*, 1869 (MB)

(97) Henry P. Baldwin House,
G. W. Lloyd, 1877 (DN)

(98-99) Charles Du Charme House (ELA)

(100) Philo Parsons House, *E. E. Myers*, 1876 (BHC)

(101-103) John S. Newberry House, *G. W. Lloyd*, 1875 (MB) (JSC) (EI

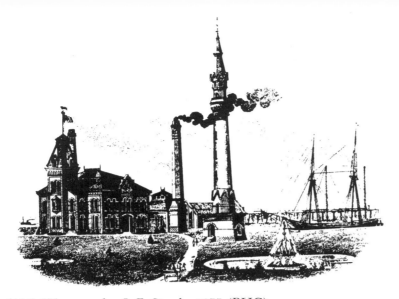

(104) Waterworks, *J. E. Sparks*, 1877 (BHC)

(105) Campau Block, *Smith & Brown*, 1883 (MB)

(106) Central Market Building, *Mason & Rice*, 1880 (BHC/JKJ)

(107) St. Mary's R.C. Parsonage, *J. Hess*, 1876 (JSC)

(108) Burnham, Stoepel & Co., *G. W. Lloyd*, 1879 **(ELA)**

(109) Schloss Brothers Block, *Hess & Mendelssohn*, 1877 **(JSC)**

(110) D. M. Ferry & Co., *Mason & Rice*, 1881 **(FMS/JKJ)**

(111) Ransom Gillis House, *Brush & Mason*, 1876 (MB/DIA)

(112) George O. Robinson House, *Brush & Smith*, 1876 (MB)

(113) James McMillan House, *G. W. Lloyd*, 1880 (BHC)

(114) Allan Shelden House, *G. W. Lloyd*, 1875 (BHC)

(115) Harper Hospital, *E. E. Myers*, 1884 (BHC)

(116) St. Mary's R.C. Church, *P. Dederichs*, 1885 (JSC)

(117) Westminster Presbyterian Church, *Lloyd & Pea...*
1881 (BHC)

(118) Joseph Black House, *M. L. Smith*, 1878 (BHC)

(119) Lucien S. Moore House, 1885 (JSC)

(120) Art Loan Exhibition Building, 1883 (BHC)

(121) Sweetest Heart of Mary R.C. Church, *Spier & Rohns*, 1893 (JSC)

(122) Ste. Anne's R.C. Church, *L. Coquard*, 1887 (C-C/GR)

(123) Michigan Central R.R. Station, *C. L. W. Eidlitz*, 1883 (BHC)

(124) C. J. Whitney & Co., *G. W. Lloyd*, 1874 (BHC)

(125) Edson, Moore & Co., *G. W. Lloyd*, 1881 (BHC)

(126) Palms Block, *G. W. Lloyd*, c. 1881 (ELA)

(127) Parker Block, *G. W. Lloyd*, 1883 (ELA)

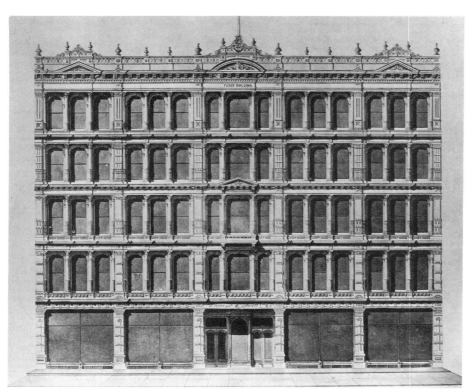

(128) Ferry Building, *M. L. Smith*, 1879 (WHF)

(129) Grand Circus Building, *G. W. Lloyd*, 1885 (BHC/JKJ)

(130) Russell A. Alger House, *G. W. Lloyd*, 1885 (BHC)

(131) Simon J. Murphy House, *W. & J. Scott*, 1887 (BHC)

(132-134) Public Library, *Brush & Smith*, 1877 (MB) (BHC) (GDM

(135) Detroit Cornice & Slate Co., 1897 (JSC)

(136) Woodward Avenue Baptist Church, *M. L. Smith*, 1887 (BHC)

(137) Store Building, c. 1875 (ELA)

(138) Woodward Avenue Baptist Church (ELA)

(139) Moore-Ferry House, *G. W. Lloyd*, 1881 (BHC)

(140) Gordon W. Lloyd House, *G. W. Lloyd*
c. 1872 (MLH/JKJ)

(141) Henry B. Ledyard House, *G. W. Lloyd*,
1882 (BHC)

(142) John S. Newberry House, *G. W. Lloyd*,
1875 (BHC)

(143) Michigan Building, *J. Hess*, 1876 (BHC)

(144) Theodore P. Hall House, *M. L. Smith*, 1880 (FF)

(145) Richard H. Fyfe House, *M. L. Smith*, 1876 (BHC)

5. Searching for Fundamentals

Queen Anne: Second Phase

In the foregoing chapter we have noted the influence of Norman Shaw, the leader of the Queen Anne movement, upon the architecture of Detroit, but this influence was derived largely from Shaw's town houses, which displayed a partiality for Renaissance detail. In the English countryside Shaw preferred to work in the Tudor vein, and this phase of his work was also reflected in American architecture. In fact Shaw used the two styles so freely and interchangeably that both have been rather loosely designated by the term Queen Anne.

The English Commission Building at the Philadelphia Centennial Exposition of 1876 gave the American public their first opportunity to come face to face with an example of Tudor architecture. According to a description in the *Centennial Portfolio*, the building seemed very strange to American eyes and aroused considerable curiosity and interest.[1] By 1877 the *American Architect and Building News* was wholeheartedly endorsing the new style:

The monks and saints and medievalism are banished to the ritualistic churches, while elsewhere reign supreme gods and goddesses, Earthly Paradise and Chaucer and old Kensington, sunflowers, sconces, blue china, turned work instead of notches and chamfers, and above all Japanese screens, fans, stuffs, papers, pictures, bronzes, china.

All this can only truly be thought of as the period of odds and ends, beauty in any form, coziness, comfort, picturesqueness,—in short, the bric-a-brac style.[2]

And by the eighties the Queen Anne style was already well established in the American architectural repertory. In 1886 a thoughtful columnist wrote in the *Detroit Evening Journal:*

The marked improvement which has come over the domestic architecture in Detroit within the past few years has been achieved not in the most expensive houses but in the medium-priced homes. The reason for this is that the houses of millionaires have been built by the older architects who seem to have been incapable of feeling the new impulses that have lately stirred American architecture. These men have stayed in their ruts and have kept on building meaningless masses of brick, while their younger and more enterprising colleagues have broken over the traces and have given us houses that are a credit to the city.

In discussing domestic architecture, it is necessary to establish some general principles to go by. The first thing to be considered always is the outline, which should be simple, harmonious. The different parts of a house must stand well together, and no detail should be allowed to distract attention from the building as a whole. The fault that architects, and especially Detroit architects, most readily fall into is to break up a house with projections and to cut up the roof with all sorts of jogs and jiggles.

After outline comes color. The harmonious arrangement of brick and stone, so as to give a good color effect, is but little understood, or, at least, is but little practiced by the architects of today; but in this direction the best of effects can be obtained. The value of a wide wall space of solid color is a thing to be sought for, not to be shunned. Too often architects are afraid of their walls and so seek to break them with a piece of terra cotta or of carved stone. This is a very great mistake. A building gains solidity and repose—two essentials—by leaving some absolutely plain wall spaces. On the other hand, over ornamentation, no matter how good the material, gives a tawdry effect. It goes without saying that to mark off the individual bricks is an unpardonable offense.

It should be understood that the materials employed should be what they pretend to be. In good building galvanized iron has no place, nor has wood painted to imitate stone. Wood constructions, when used as iron, are entirely allowable. In this connection it may be said that the use of wrought iron crestings, etc., is heartily to be commended, because wrought iron represents thoughtful hand work and is therefore thoroughly artistic in its motive. A principle too little recognized is that of adequate support. To support anything by a column smaller at the base than at the top is to fly in the face of all laws of good construction.[3]

One of the younger Detroit architects stirred by the ferment that was going on in the architectural world was George D. Mason. In 1876 he visited the Philadelphia Centennial Exposition where the English Commission Building could not have escaped his notice.[4] In 1884 he made a tour of Europe to study architecture, recording his impressions in his sketchbook.[5] Shortly after his return Mason was quoted in the *Evening Journal* as follows:

The change in domestic architecture in Detroit began to be felt in all its force about seven years ago. Of course there had been occasional departures from the old style previous to that date, but I speak now of the prevailing designs in

(111) *architecture. About that date the residence of Ransom Gillis, corner of John R. and Alfred Streets, was built. This was a representative design of the new Gothic architecture. This style prevailed for about two years subsequent to the erection of the Gillis residence, and then a tendency toward the Queen Anne and the Colonial began to make itself felt. The last named styles prevail at*

(68) *present in Detroit. The Jefferson Avenue residences of A. H. Dey and T. A.*
(70) *Parker are very good specimens of what is known as English Gothic architecture. They must have been built something like twenty years ago. The Queen Anne is a combination of Gothic and Renaissance bordering mostly upon the latter. The Colonial is what may be termed more of a classic, adapted to modern requirements.*

The tendency in Detroit at present seems to be to overdo the matter in the way of exterior adornment. The ornamentation, being necessarily of wood, is perishable, and the durability of plainer exteriors is consequently lost. I think we are about to drift back to a more solid basis in architecture. Of course the return journey will necessarily be gradual. Brick, terra cotta and stone are always preferable to wood for outside use, and their adoption will do away with much of the work which is used solely for adornment. Wood should be very sparingly used in exterior work.

In the old country you seldom see wood used for outside work. Of course they haven't much of that sort of material, but my observation satisfied me that they wouldn't favor its use under any circumstances. Stucco and mortar are largely used for finishing exteriors in England. In Germany, the classic in architecture prevails exclusively, while in England everything is Gothic. The latter is inclined to be broken up, while the former is severely plain.

Medieval relics furnish the required inspiration for all the best work of the present day. Old things in general are freely drawn upon. Old wrought iron work of the middle ages—old armor came in for a part in the restoration. So you see, after all, in architecture we are only getting back to where the nations of the earth were centuries ago. In this country this state of affairs is not in the least a matter for surprise. We have had to come back from the log cabins and board shanties. We have had to draw upon the old country for everything. We are just beginning to have ideas of our own. It is only quite recently that America has had art schools worthy of the name. The old country still leads us in this regard.

Detroit citizens can afford to build finer homes than those of almost any other city in the entire country. The price of lumber is about one-half cheaper than in eastern cities. Labor is also much more reasonable.[6]

The above statements give every indication that Mason's days of apprenticeship were over. His words seem to bear the weight of a recognized authority on the subject and should prepare us for his eventual rise to the top of his profession. In time he was to become one of Detroit's chief exponents of new architectural trends. As such his interpretation of the Queen Anne style left much to be desired, but it should be remembered that he had only just emerged from the imbroglio of free eclecticism; so, at least for the time being, his understanding of the new approach to architecture was conditioned by his previous thinking habits.

Mason and Rice experimented with the Queen Anne style in Detroit, but certainly their most ambitious project in this style was the Joseph H. Berry *(147)* house of 1882 on Lake Shore road in Grosse Pointe. Unmistakably there were the varied textures, steep roofs, and ornamental chimneys of Shaw's rural medievalism, and a curious medley of borrowed Renaissance details might be traced to Shaw's town houses. Yet one must search in vain for the Shavian discipline and refinement of design, for under the guise of a new style there still persisted the restless whimsicality and overloaded surfaces of the earlier American vernacular.

The Berry house was one of the first substantial all-year-round houses in Grosse Pointe. Every day Berry would drive a spanking pair of horses into town to the Berry Paint and Varnish Company, of which he was president and founder. The fussy and pretentious exterior of the Grosse Pointe mansion gave no clue to the secluded private life of its owner. Saddened by the early death of his wife, Berry shunned the delights of social life and devoted his leisure moments to the upbringing of his daughters. Retiring within the boundaries of his extensive estate, called Edgemere, he became absorbed in the art of landscaping. Formal flower beds, lawns, and unusual varieties of trees and shrubs bordered lagoons fed by the waters of Lake St. Clair. The extensive greenhouses on the place were his pride and delight, for it was there that Berry kept his fabulous collection of orchids.[7] Nothing remains of the Berry house today—it was torn down in 1942—but the many beautiful trees in the neighborhood are a testimony of one man's love for the beauty of nature.

The Romanesque Revival: Churches

In the seventies and eighties a giant loomed on the horizon of the American architectural scene in the person of Henry Hobson Richardson. After graduating from Harvard in the class of 1859, he took up the study of architecture at the École des Beaux-Arts in Paris. One of the first Americans to receive such splendid academic training, he returned to his homeland in 1865. All about him he found architecture in a distressing state of pettiness and indecision. One might have expected him to launch forth on a crusade of French academic dogma, but apparently he must have felt that classicism in America was already a thing of the past. There was something about the Romanesque of southern France that appealed to his sense of honesty and simplicity, for there he found building masses resolved into elemental geometric components and the essential quality of masonry expressed in rough-hewn surfaces and sturdy round arches with deep reveals.[8] Using this style as a point of departure, he was prepared to explore its possibilities in terms of the society in which he lived.

The first monument of the Romanesque Revival in America was Richardson's Trinity Church (1872–77) in Boston. Although the church proper was in the French Romanesque style, the design of the tower was borrowed from the Cathedral of Salamanca in Spain. Stained glass windows were designed by Sir Edward Burne-Jones and John La Farge, and the latter also painted large figure panels. Such a triumph of architecture and allied arts received great acclaim, and soon the church became a model for similar structures throughout the nation.[9]

(149) In Detroit, Mason and Rice rose to the occasion with the First Presbyterian Church (1889) on the northeast corner of Woodward avenue at Edmund place.[10] As at Richardson's Trinity, enormous masonry arches supported the massive tower, but there were certain marked differences from the Boston masterpiece. Rock-faced red sandstone was used instead of granite, the detail was less archeological, and the general outline was much more compact. The nave was shortened so that the plan of the church is actually a Greek cross, the shallow arms of which lent themselves to a concentric arrangement of pews. Thus there is an intimacy altogether lacking in Trinity. When Woodward avenue was widened in 1936 the handsome triple-arched entrance porch with its charming marquetry and stone carving was shifted from the western to the southern façade.

(148) The First Congregational Church (1891) was designed by John Lyman Faxon of Boston.[11] Located on the northeast corner of Woodward and Forest avenues, it closely resembled Richardson's First Baptist Church (1886) in Newton, Massachusetts. Both in general configuration and detail the Detroit church was an improvement over its predecessor. This is not surprising since, according to Henry-Russell Hitchcock, the Newton church was built at a time when Richardson was too busy to supervise all the work that went out of his office.[12] Be that as it may, Faxon showed himself adept in blending elements drawn from the Romanesque and Byzantine of Italy and Dalmatia, and designed an especially handsome tall campanile with slender arcades.

(146) The First Unitarian Church (1890) by Donaldson and Meier, on Woodward at Edmund place, was remarkable for its severely simple design.[13] The gabled front facing Woodward avenue relied for its effectiveness upon the rich texture of the masonry which stood out in contrast to the deep shadow of a starkly plain

Romanesque porch. Penetrating the façade there were three round-arched windows with choice stained glass designed by John La Farge, recalling his earlier work at Trinity in Boston.[14] A small round turret at the front of the church and a square tower at the rear added further interest to this exercise in pure design. Unfortunately the La Farge windows were removed when the building was sold to the Church of Christ,[15] and the porch was disfigured by alterations during the widening of Woodward avenue in 1936.

John M. Donaldson, the senior partner of the firm of Donaldson and Meier, was born in Stirling, Scotland. At the age of two his parents brought him to Detroit where he received his early schooling. Following the trend among architects in the East, he completed his education abroad, studying art and architecture at the Polytechnic and Art Academy in Munich and the École des Beaux-Arts in Paris. Returning to Detroit he became associated with Henry T. Brush for about a year until the latter's death in 1879. In the following year he entered into partnership with Henry J. Meier, whom he had met in Brush's office.[16]

Another firm that added to Detroit's roster of Romanesque Revival churches was Malcomson and Higginbotham. Their little red sandstone Central Christian *(151)* Church (1891) on Cass Park stayed on the side of simplicity.[17] It was probably influenced by Richardson's Brattle Square Church in Boston, but the general effect was quite different. Much of its charm was due to the pure geometry of its massing and the fine quality of its rugged masonry. A series of deeply-cut window and entrance openings provided the principal decorative themes, archeological ornament having been minimized. The structure was recently razed.

The same firm's Cass Avenue Methodist Church (1891) on the northwest *(150)* corner at Selden was somewhat similar, but the masonry is more mechanical and the suggestion of a medieval fortress in the tower strikes a note of spurious picturesqueness.[18] These tendencies became even more exaggerated in their St. Joseph's P. E. Memorial Church (1896) on Woodward at Medbury (Ford freeway), now the R. C. Church of the Holy Rosary.[19] William G. Malcomson and William E. Higginbotham became partners in 1890.[20] They had begun their architectural training in the offices of local architects. While serving in the capacity of consultant architects for the Detroit public school system, they designed many schools, including the Central High School building (1896) at Cass and Hancock, now Old Main of Wayne State University.[21]

The Jefferson Avenue Presbyterian Church between Rivard and Russell *(60)* streets was one of the most popular churches on fashionable East Jefferson. In 1891 Bradford L. Gilbert of New York replaced the earlier Gothic Revival church with a large brick structure with redstone trim. Whatever it lacked in *(153)* magnificence was atoned for in originality. Across the front there was a bank of tall narrow windows with interlacing Romanesque arcades. The lean-to front porch and gabled roof were covered with Spanish tiles, and at one end there was a tall tower with a pyramidal roof. The interior was finished in white mahogany glinted with gold and the yellowish walls were hung with tapestries, producing an unorthodox yet refreshingly cheerful effect.[22]

If economy was necessary for the church itself because of the urgency of *(152)* diverting funds to mission churches, the same stringency was not necessary for the adjoining church house and chapel donated by Mrs. John S. Newberry in *(186)* 1888 in memory of her husband. "I wish to build a chapel for the church," she *(101)* said to the church authorities, "and I do not care about the expense and wish the chapel to be as the congregation desires it."[23] The architect apparently sensed an opportunity to give free rein to his imaginative powers and forthwith proceeded to blend the Romanesque Revival and Art Nouveau styles in an altogether unprecedented manner. The arched entry with its serpentine iron grille brought to mind the contemporaneous work of Antoni Gaudí in Barcelona, while the tall cylindrical tower, adorned by over-scaled angels' heads, seemed to foreshadow the world of surrealism. Today the church proper has been altered beyond recognition for commercial purposes, and church house and chapel have vanished altogether.

The Romanesque Revival: Houses and Clubs

(154) The Bagley Memorial Fountain in the Campus Martius was provided for in the will of John J. Bagley to quench the thirst of Detroiters with "water cold and pure as the coldest mountain stream."[24] It was unveiled in 1887 in its original location in a space south of the City Hall.[25] The designer of the fountain was none other than the great master Henry Hobson Richardson.[26] Nothing could more perfectly illustrate his insistence on the finest materials and workmanship. Fashioned entirely of white granite, it was an adaptation of a small ciborium in St. Mark's Cathedral in Venice. In contrast to the smooth surfaces of the pyramidal canopy, the arch spandrels and the column capitals were richly embellished with crisp foliate carving.

(173)
(155) The Bagley family was also responsible for commissioning Richardson to design the Bagley Memorial Armory of 1886. When John N. Bagley, the son of the governor, built a house in 1889 on the corner of Jefferson and Joseph Campau avenues, Richardson would have been a logical choice as architect, but his death in 1886 made it necessary for the Bagleys to satisfy themselves with the services of a lesser architect. Still in a good state of preservation, the house was built of red brick with brownstone trim. The round bay with a conical roof and the prominent Gothic dormer are characteristically Richardsonian. Particularly noteworthy is the handsome stone Renaissance entrance carved by Julius Melchers. On the interior the living room was finished in English oak, and the dining room in Santo Domingo mahogany. The exquisite mantels in both rooms were also carved by Melchers.[27]

(157) Jefferson avenue, broad and fringed with elms and maples, was a magnificent residential street in the eighties. When Mason and Rice were commissioned to design a store and residence building on the corner of East Jefferson and Rivard street (1883), they were careful to endow it with an elegance in keeping with its surroundings. Above the corner entrance to the store was a round medieval turret with a candle-stopper roof. The turret and the entrance were adorned
(156) with delicate and fanciful reliefs carved in stone.[28] This charming building has since been torn down and the whole of Jefferson avenue has been converted into a sea of tawdry commercialism.

(158) In 1888 Mason and Rice built a house for Charles A. Du Charme on the corner of East Jefferson and Dubois street. Although the design was very free, considerable study was given to massing, details, and materials. Above the porch entrance there was some skillful foliate carving, and Romanesque capitals adorned a second floor window opening.

(159) Similar in style, but on a much grander scale, was the house the same firm built, also in 1888, for Gilbert W. Lee, president of Lee and Cady, a wholesale
(174) grocery firm. Located on John R. street at Ferry avenue, it consisted of a large asymmetrical brick mass with a dominant gabled bay and a subordinate semi-octagonal bay. The window openings, although perhaps too diversified, were nevertheless well organized, and the design as a whole was brought to a climax

by the round-arched *art nouveau* entrance with its intricate carving inspired by   *(160)*
late Gothic motifs. On the interior the rooms on the first floor were finished in
birdseye maple, mahogany, and quartered white oak, and the mantels were done
in Numidian marble, onyx, and mosaic. A large central hall was dominated by an
impressive stairway that led up to a Tiffany stained glass window at the landing.[29] In one of the upstairs bedrooms an unpretentious tile mantel was star-
tlingly modern in its horizontality and lightness of form and color.

In 1890 Mason and Rice built a residence for the lumberman Albert L.   *(164)*
Stephens on the southeast corner of Woodward and Ferry avenues. In general
outline it was similar to the Lee house, but the exterior walls were of red
sandstone instead of brick, and the roof was covered with glazed Spanish tiles
instead of slate. The window openings were congested and the application of
two round turrets with conical roofs only served to increase the confusion.   *(252)*

At this time a promising young architect named Albert Kahn was working in
Mason's office. He had risen to be in charge of designing and had a hand in the
design of the Du Charme, Lee, and Stephens houses. In this work he was
strongly influenced by some domestic architecture he had seen earlier in
Chicago.[30] In 1890 at the age of twenty-one he won the *American Architect*
scholarship of five hundred dollars for study abroad. In Europe his understanding of architecture was considerably broadened. During three months of the trip
he found an ideal mentor and traveling companion in the person of Henry Bacon
Jr., the cultivated architect who was later to design the Lincoln Memorial in
Washington.

The meteoric rise of Albert Kahn from obscure beginnings to world renown
is one of the most phenomenal success stories in the annals of American architecture. The eldest of eight children, he was born in Rhaunen near Germany's Ruhr
basin in 1869 and was educated at the German public schools and gymnasia.
When he was only eleven years old the family emigrated to America, first
settling in Baltimore. In 1884 they moved to Detroit. As a child Kahn displayed a
precocious talent for the piano and entertained the hope of becoming a concert
musician, but upon arrival in Detroit the poverty of his family compelled him to
take any job available.[31] He particularly enjoyed being an office boy and appren-
tice in the architectural firm of John Scott and Company. After about a year he
was discharged because his boss felt he had no aptitude for the work.

Then a miracle happened. The sculptor Julius Melchers found the young boy
in tears after his dismissal and invited him to attend his drawing classes on
Sunday mornings. Soon the pupil was doing so well that Melchers found him a
job in the office of Mason and Rice. From then on his progress was rapid and the
ten years he spent in Mason's office marked the beginning of a brilliant career.[32]

In the meantime Gordon W. Lloyd was trying his hand at the Romanesque
Revival. The mansardic house which David Whitney Jr. had built in 1870   *(91)*
already seemed outmoded. Determined to keep up with the times, the Whitneys
decided to erect a domicile in the new Romanesque style further out Woodward   *(161)*
avenue at Canfield street. Whitney himself made it known that he would be
happy living in a log cabin, but Mrs. Whitney felt otherwise. Begun in 1890, the
house took four years to build. Upon its completion the *Detroit Free Press*
stated: "All the splendid houses which have been erected before and which
adorn the broad avenue of the town are fairly eclipsed and the new home enjoys
the distinction of being the most pretentious modern home in the state and one
of the most elaborate houses in the West." Jasper from South Dakota was the
material selected for the exterior walls. This is one of the hardest kinds of stone
and requires the utmost in time and patience to cut. The *Free Press* was of the

opinion that the Whitney palace would "last as long as is given to houses made by man to endure."[33] Now housing the Visiting Nurse Association, it is still standing on Woodward avenue, but the passage of time has shown that the choice of Lloyd as architect was anything but judicious. Belonging to an earlier generation, he was unable to grasp the aesthetic innovations inherent in the Romanesque Revival. Therefore the restless undulating rhythms of an earlier period were misapplied to a style that more properly demanded static monumental forms.

(162) In marked contrast to the ostentatious luxury of the Whitney house, the Detroit Athletic Club, once its neighbor on Woodward avenue, was a model of functional simplicity. Designed by Joseph V. Gearing, it was built in 1887.[34] The street elevation consisted of a long brick mass with a hipped roof and two projecting bays arranged in a carefully studied asymmetrical composition. To the rear of the building was a balcony overlooking an extensive athletic field *(237)* where a wide variety of sports events took place.[35]

(163) A purely social organization, the Detroit Club, which is still in use, breathes an air of old-fashioned gentility. Designed by Wilson Eyre Jr. of Philadelphia, it was built in 1891 on the northeast corner of Cass at Fort.[36] It is a symmetrical four-story building with a rounded bay at each end of the entrance façade. The exterior was treated with restraint and dignity. On the ground story the walls were faced with rock-faced brownstone and above Roman brick with terra-cotta trim was used. The entrance porch was recessed behind a round arch, and round- and flat-headed Renaissance windows alternate between floors. There is a generous Richardsonian hall with a broad rambling stairway and it has a fluid plan of large connecting rooms. The elegant dining room, with its high ceiling, black walnut paneling, and red brocade curtains, recalls the era of Edward VII.

The work of Wilson Eyre Jr. was a vindication of the benefits to be derived from academic training. It was only in 1866 that the Massachusetts Institute of Technology offered the first course in architecture to the American student; and it was there that Eyre pursued his studies in the late seventies at a time when most American architects relied upon self-education.[37]

The Romanesque Revival: Public Buildings

The Romanesque Revival received such popular acclaim that its appropriateness for every type of building was never questioned. In 1883 Mason and Rice built the old Y.M.C.A. Building on Grand River avenue and Griswold. The only commendable feature was an ornate Norman Romanesque entrance that consisted of a triple arch with richly carved capitals and moldings.[38] Since the building was later converted to commercial use, the entrance has been replaced by store frontage. In 1889 the same firm built the Detroit Business University on East Grand River avenue. The character of the Richardsonian house was carried over into a larger structure with the loss of appropriate scale. To make matters worse, an extra story, not contemplated in the original plans, was added while the building was under construction.[28] Perhaps, from the viewpoint of the architectural historian, it was no misfortune that this building was later demolished.

The railroad station was a better vehicle for the consummation of the Richardsonian ideal than the large institutional building. The external expression of closely interrelated functional elements provided an opportunity for interesting geometrical compositions. In 1888 Mason and Rice completed the stations in Walkerville and Kingsville, Ontario, not far from Detroit. The Walkerville sta-

tion, a long low building, was built of brick. A vertical accent was provided by *(167)*
the observation tower rising above the projecting bay of the stationmaster's
office. In Kingsville rough fieldstone walls endowed the small station with rustic *(166)*
charm. To be sure, there was a lack of restraint in the window openings, but
great skill was shown in the grouping of roof masses and in the alternating
rhythm of projecting and recessed wall surfaces. These stations were outlets for
the Lake Erie, Essex and Detroit River Railway which was owned by the whiskey magnate Hiram Walker. Opened in 1888, the railroad extended from
Windsor to St. Thomas, Ontario, making Detroit and Windsor better markets
for the produce of the Canadian hinterland. It is now a part of the Chesapeake
and Ohio Railway system.[39]

In 1893 the completion of the Union Station on the southwest corner of Fort *(165)*
street at Third in Detroit provided a metropolitan terminus for the Pennsylvania,
Wabash, and Pere Marquette Railroads.[40] The architects James Stewart and
Company of St. Louis created a robust plastic composition dominated by a
massive clock tower at the corner of the building.[41] Romanesque arcades, square-
headed windows, and dormers were effectively combined in the overall scheme.
The interior has been drastically remodeled.[42]

In 1891 Gordon W. Lloyd erected a building for the Detroit College (now *(168)*
Dowling Hall of the University of Detroit) on Jefferson avenue east of SS. Peter
and Paul's. Clarity and order prevailed in the design of the façade, but the three- *(31)*
dimensional quality and the chiaroscuro generally associated with the Romanesque Revival are nowhere in evidence. In the last phase of his work Lloyd seems
to have been unable to strike a balance between the excesses of the Whitney *(161)*
house and the monotony of the Detroit College.

One of the most outstanding monuments of the Romanesque Revival in De- *(169)*
troit was the old Post Office and U. S. Court House which was built in 1890–94
at Fort and Shelby and was replaced by the present Federal Building in 1934.[43]
Designed by James H. Windrim of Philadelphia, it followed in a general way the
pattern established by Richardson in his Allegheny County Buildings erected at
Pittsburgh in 1884–87. It was a symmetrical arcaded building with corner pavilions and a tall slender central tower above the main entrance. Its successor was
built by Derrick and Wetmore.

The Art Loan Exhibition of 1883 was so successful that soon plans were *(120)*
afoot to erect a permanent art gallery. For this purpose public spirited citizens
subscribed $100,000, and the gift of a lot on the corner of Jefferson avenue and
Hastings was accepted. From among fifty-two entries submitted in an architectural competition the design of James Balfour of Hamilton, Ontario, was selected. Incorporated in 1885, the Detroit Museum of Art opened its doors to the *(171)*
public in 1888.[44] To house the arts Balfour created a fortress-like structure of
rugged buff sandstone flanked by two round stair towers with conical roofs. The
formidable aspect of the building was offset by a broad inviting entrance porch
extending between the towers. This was entered through a Romanesque arcade
of five round arches supported on clustered red granite shafts. On the first floor
of the building there was a sculpture gallery, and on the second floor a picture
gallery illuminated by a skylight.[45]

The creation of such a monumental repository of the arts posed the problem
of laying the foundation of a permanent collection. No one was more aware of
this problem and better qualified to solve it than James Edmund Scripps. Born in *(282)*
London, he came to America with his parents at the age of nine. A journalistic
career, which began in Chicago, brought him to Detroit where he became the
founder and owner of the *Detroit News* (1873).[46] Having progressed so far, he *(358)*

133

might have been content to rest on his laurels, but the accumulation of wealth put him in a position to enter another sphere of activity. Years spent in collecting engravings and etchings of old masters had contributed to his knowledge and taste in art. The erection of a new museum in Detroit provided an opportunity for him to realize his fondest hopes.[47] "For several years it has been a favorite idea of mine," he mused, "that Detroit might be made the art center of the West, just as Cincinnati is the acknowledged musical center, and just as Florence is the art and Milan the musical center of Italy."[48] Scripps was no man of idle words. For two years he studied the galleries and probed the art markets of Europe. After spending between $75,000 and $80,000 he returned with a collection of paintings which he presented to the Detroit Museum of Art in 1889.[47] Although he concentrated mainly on Dutch seventeenth century masters, he also acquired works of the Flemish, Italian, and Spanish schools. In 1935 Dr. William R. Valentiner, then director of the Detroit Institute of Arts, was of the opinion that in the greatly enlarged collection of the museum the works of the Scripps collection not only held their own, but in many cases took first place.[49]

Although not as important as the Scripps collection, the Frederick Stearns collection, which was given to the museum in 1890, deserves mention as an example of the widespread interest in Oriental art prevalent at the time. It contained sixteen thousand objects of art from China, Japan, Korea, India, and Persia. Frederick Stearns was the founder of the drug firm which bore his name. Possessed of the leisure and means for travel, he became an inveterate globe-trotter. Following a trip to Japan in 1889, he wrote a series of articles in the *Detroit Free Press* describing the life and customs of Japan.[50]

Through the years purchases and gifts increased the size of the museum's collection, compelling several additions to be made to the building. When Detroit took on its remarkable growth in the early years of the twentieth century, it became apparent that larger and more commodious quarters were desirable. In 1927 the old Detroit Museum of Art was abandoned, later to be demolished, and *(247)* the present Detroit Institute of Arts on Woodward avenue was opened to the public.

The Rise of the Skyscraper

Henry Hobson Richardson was so convinced of the intrinsic merits of the Romanesque that he did not even hesitate to apply it to commercial structures. Going a step further than the superimposed arcades of Ruskin, he introduced giant arcades which enclosed several stories of windows vertically under arches between piers. This permitted greater window areas, since exterior walls were concentrated in widely-spaced narrow piers, and it also provided the exteriors of buildings with great unity and cohesion of design.[51]

The J. J. Bagley Memorial Armory which H. H. Richardson built in Detroit *(173)* in 1886 paralleled the designs of some of his commercial buildings in the East.[52] Plenty of light for deep space was provided by the three bold arches characteristic of his work. The rather trivial treatment of the attic story suggests that he must have relegated some of the detailing to his office force.[53] On the lower floor *(172)* there were social rooms, while on the upper floor there was a drill room for the Light Guard Infantry. This was roofed by a barrel vault supported on laminated wood arches, a surprising feature considering Richardson's alleged indifference to structural innovations. The Bagley Armory was located on the south side of Congress street between Randolph and Bates. On the corner to the east Rogers and MacFarlane, a Detroit firm, erected the Banner Cigar Factory (1888) in the same style.[54] Both these buildings were demolished in 1957 to make way for a Greyhound Bus Lines terminal.

In 1887 Gordon W. Lloyd completed a new warehouse for D. M. Ferry and *(170)* Company on Brush street to replace the one destroyed by fire in the previous *(110)* year.[55] To reduce the fire hazard he employed slow-burning laminated mill construction. This would be prohibitively expensive today, but in those days the supply of lumber from Michigan forests was plentiful. Huge solid white oak posts were used to support pine joists spiked closely together on edge. As additional fire preventives the architect provided fire walls, a sprinkler system, and iron shutters on the alley windows.[56] So far, at least, these precautions have been adequate. In the formalization of the brick exterior of the warehouse, Lloyd was undoubtedly influenced by Richardson's Marshall Field Wholesale Warehouse in Chicago (1885–87), even if he made no attempt to emulate its subtlety of proportion or its titanic monumentality.

Increasing business prompted the J. L. Hudson Company to erect a large new *(175)* eight-story department store on Farmer at Gratiot in 1891. Mortimer L. Smith, the architect, showed that he was abreast of the times by creating a handsome Richardsonian structure in red brick trimmed with brownstone. In order to provide ample daylight there was an extraordinary concentration of wall surface in widely-spaced piers continuing through each story and joined at the top by massive arches. These wide bays also permitted broad display windows on the ground floor. The interior was planned for efficiency and convenience. Four elevators made each floor readily accessible and there were no partitions to impede the circulation of customers throughout the store. The floors were supported by sixteen iron columns which ran in sections from the basement to the roof. These columns and all other interior surfaces were plastered with fireproof adamant and the floors were lined with asbestos paper.[57] It was only a matter of time, however, before this splendid monument of commerce was outgrown and subsequently demolished. Its site is now only a small portion of the area covered by the present J. L. Hudson Company store erected in 1924–29 by Smith, Hinchman and Grylls.

In 1890 Detroit was astir with excitement over the completion of its first *(176)* skyscraper, the Hammond Building which stood on the southeast corner of Fort and Griswold streets. To celebrate the opening a tightrope walker was hired to walk from the roof of the ten story structure to the tower of the City Hall across Fort street.[58] The architect of the Hammond Building was Harry W. J. Edbrooke of Chicago. He had read in the newspaper that George H. Hammond, a wealthy Detroit meat packer, was planning to put up an office block, and noted that Hammond had recently sold his slaughterhouse in Hammond, Indiana, for $750,000. Hoping to share in this bonanza by becoming the architect of the proposed building, he hurried to Detroit. In the meantime Hammond died, but by offering a low bid Edbrooke was able to persuade Mrs. Hammond to give him the job.[4]

The characteristics of modern utilitarian commercial architecture were already apparent in the exterior of the Hammond Building. To be sure, the old canons of proportion were observed in the division of the wall surfaces into base, shaft, and cap, but for all intents and purposes the piers, spandrels, and windows formed a uniform grille of brick and glass. A degree of Romanesque flavor was retained in the solid rock-faced brownstone piers of the ground floor and the carved capitals at the eighth floor level, but the round arch, that essential device of earthbound masonry structures, was banished to the historic past. The main interior division walls on the ground floor were of brick. Above this there were iron columns supporting iron girders. All exposed ironwork was encased by fireproof material, and the wood floor joists were covered with fireproof tile below and concrete mortar above.[59] After many years of service the Hammond

(387) Building was torn down in 1956 to make way for a new building for the National Bank of Detroit.

Although they cannot be classified as skyscrapers, two large buildings which Mason and Rice designed in the nineties deserve more than a passing glance. The old Masonic Temple, which was built on the northeast corner of Lafayette and First streets in 1894, was given a rather monumental Richardsonian exterior in keeping with its institutional character.[60] By then Mason and Rice realized that a formal rather than a picturesque treatment was preferable in adapting the Romanesque style to a large urban structure. The building was fireproof throughout with a steel frame independent of the brick walls, which were self-supporting.[28] Although later enlarged, the old Masonic Temple was eventually

(322) outgrown and demolished. In 1928 George D. Mason completed the present massive building on Cass Park.

Also in 1894 Mason and Rice built the T. W. Palmer Block on the northwest

(174) corner of Cass avenue and Larned. Since this was a warehouse for Lee and Cady, simple mill construction was used. Round cast-iron columns supported wood girders and beams.[61] The exterior of the building was notable for the simplicity of the architectural treatment. There being no necessity for large windows, the architects sought to emphasize the smooth unbroken surface of the bricks, yet monotony was avoided by the careful study devoted to subtle details, such as the gracefully flaring cornice and the molded bricks of the arches and piers. No doubt Mason had learned a lesson of restraint from the last great masonry building in Chicago, Burnham and Root's Monadnock Block (1891).[62]

Chicago again pointed the way with William Le Baron Jenney's Home Insurance Building (1884), the first metal-skeleton skyscraper. Outside and inside walls and floors were supported on the iron frame.[63] In the second Rand McNally Building (1889–90) Burnham and Root were the first to use the all-steel skeleton.[64] The Union Trust Building and the Chamber of Commerce Building, both erected in 1894–95, shared the honor of being the first examples of this type of construction in Detroit.[65] Designed by Donaldson and Meier, the Union Trust

(180) Building was located on the northeast corner of Griswold and Congress streets. The first three floors were faced with granite and the upper floors with gray brick trimmed with terra cotta.[66] The heavy incrustation of Italian Renaissance detail denoted a surrender to the fashionable elegance of McKim, Mead and White, although a trace of the 'Chicago School' manner was still evident in the

(387) rippling bay windows of the central bay.[62] The building was demolished in 1956 preceding the erection of the National Bank of Detroit on the same site.

Similar in style to the Union Trust Building, the Chamber of Commerce

(179) Building (1895) is still standing on the northeast corner of Griswold and State. The architects were Spier and Rohns. William C. Rohns was born in Göttingen, Germany, and received his technical training at the Hanover *Polytechnicum*. Coming to Detroit in 1883, he spent some time in the offices of Gordon W. Lloyd and Elijah E. Myers. In 1884 he formed a partnership with Frederick H. Spier, who had come to Detroit to superintend the construction of the Michigan

(123) Central Station on Third street for architect Eidlitz of New York. Spier and Rohns received many commissions for stations from the Michigan Central and Grand Trunk Railroads. Among these were stations in Ann Arbor, Battle Creek, Niles, Lansing, and Grand Rapids. The firm also designed several buildings in

136

Ann Arbor for the University of Michigan, and St. Thomas's Roman Catholic Church there too. Much of this work reflected Richardson's influence.[67]

Spier and Rohns' Chamber of Commerce Building remained Detroit's tallest skyscraper for only a short while, for in 1896 it was overshadowed by the fourteen-story Majestic Building prominently located at the juncture of Woodward and Michigan avenues overlooking the Campus Martius. The new building was impressive not only in size but also in the luxury of its appointments. The lobby was finished in Italian marble, ornamental iron work, and mosaic, while the office suites were provided with the finest mahogany cabinetwork.[68]

(178)

The architect of the Majestic Building was Daniel H. Burnham of Chicago. Mason and Rice collaborated with Burnham in Detroit and followed his construction drawings.[69] With his usual thoroughness, Mason examined Burnham's Marshall Field Store in Chicago and studied the working drawings for it.[4] Burnham and Root had become famous for the many fine skyscrapers they had erected in Chicago, including the twenty-two story Masonic Temple (1891), reputed to be the tallest building in the world at the time. John W. Root had attempted to evolve from the Romanesque a formula for the expression of the skyscraper. From the ground floor arcade to the attic course he emphasized the soaring quality of the structure by the use of continuous piers uninterrupted by arbitrary horizontal divisions.[70] There was also a shift from the earlier simplicity of the Monadnock Block (1891) to a greater emphasis on antiquarian detail. When Root died in 1891 the firm assumed the name of Daniel H. Burnham and Company. For some time thereafter Burnham continued to follow Root's principles.[71] This was very evident in the design of the Majestic Building. Structurally it was an example of the most advanced techniques of its day. Like the second Rand McNally Building in Chicago (1889), it was faced entirely with terra cotta on the front wall.[72] The foundation was of steel and concrete resting on piles and every portion of the superstructure was covered with fireproof tile.[68]

At last the skyscraper had come of age. American technical ingenuity had made possible the erection of mammoth buildings and, paradoxically, had also minimized the danger of disastrous conflagrations which were for so long the bane of cities. In 1915 a fire caused by defective wiring broke out in a storeroom of the Majestic Building between the roof and the fourteenth floor. It took two hours for the firemen to extinguish it. In spite of their efforts the fire had every chance to make headway, but the fireproofing prevented it. "The fire proved one thing to my complete satisfaction," said one of the owners of the building on the following day. "That one thing is that we have a fireproof building here. . . . People come up to condole with me on my loss, when they should come up here to congratulate me on my discovery."[73]

Recreational Facilities

In the latter half of the nineteenth century great urban parks and residential avenues were introduced in American cities as compensations for chaotic industrialization. Many Americans had seen the magnificent pleasure areas and boulevards which Baron Haussmann had created in Paris under Napoleon III; it was inevitable that these would set an example for American cities.[74] As Detroit grew larger it became apparent that the little parks scattered through the city did not provide adequate breathing space for the populace. Belle Isle in the Detroit River seemed like a logical place for a large recreational area as it was already being invaded by picnickers disgorged by the increasing number of steamers on the river. In 1879, following the request of the city council, the legislature in Lansing passed two bills providing for the construction of Grand boulevard and the purchase of Belle Isle as a public park.

To have built Grand boulevard on land that was already developed would have been prohibitively costly. From the beginning the plan was formulated of laying out a landscaped residential boulevard extending for twelve miles around what was then the periphery of the city. It was intended to serve as a pleasure drive and also to provide connecting links between the main traffic arteries radiating out from the center of the city. In spite of considerable opposition, the project gained momentum through the collective efforts of many men to secure the necessary state legislation and municipal financing. Probably the whole scheme would have foundered had it not been for the generous contribution of *(73)* land and funds by private individuals.[75] It is interesting to note that Bela Hubbard, the pioneer citizen and landscaping enthusiast, was responsible for developing a stretch at the western end of the boulevard with a landscaped strip between the two driveways.[76] In 1889 the eastern end of the boulevard was connected by a bridge to the western end of Belle Isle.

When Belle Isle was first purchased by the city in 1879 it was a wilderness of forest and marsh land. Promptly the park commissioners called upon the distinguished landscape architect Frederick Law Olmsted to improve and beautify it. From coast to coast he had adorned the larger American cities with vast parks which combined the axial or formal style of layout with the naturalistic or informal method. Forthwith he proceeded to draw up a plan for Belle Isle which provided for a central driveway and a canal running across one end of the island. There were many who felt that better arrangements could be devised. Michael J. Dee, a newspaperman, conceived the idea of a series of canals covering the island, the earth taken from them to be used to fill in the sloughs and marshes. Olmsted had intended to use city refuse to fill these depressions. The commissioners were so favorably impressed by Dee's plans that they discarded those of Olmsted, retaining only his concept of a central driveway.[77] John M. Donaldson, the local architect, was then commissioned to bring the work to completion following the pattern suggested by Dee.[78] Belle Isle Park was originally 768 acres; through land reclamation it was increased to 985 acres in 1940.

(244) In 1893 Senator and Mrs. Thomas W. Palmer gave Palmer Park out Woodward avenue to the city. It consisted of 130 acres carved from the 725 acres of the original Palmer estate. In 1895 the Palmers added to this gift a log cabin and the surrounding grounds. This had been their summer residence and was designed by Mrs. Palmer in 1882. The park itself was laid out in 1870 on a mildly undulating wooded tract containing two small lakes.[79] In 1920 the city purchased an additional 147 acres.

The outdoor life which became so popular in Detroit toward the end of the nineteenth century was by no means confined to parks. People were becoming more aware of the marine paradise at their door. The broad Detroit River invited them to escape from the summer heat on its cool, shimmering surface. After visiting the city Captain Willard Glazier wrote in 1883:

The ferry boats of the several lines plying between Detroit and Windsor are the most attractive type. In summer a corps of musicians are engaged for regular trips, and are considered as indispensable to the boat's outfit as the captain or the pilot. Their syren strains entice the lounger at the wharf, and he may ride all day, if he chooses, for the sum of ten cents. Whole families spend the day on the river in this way, taking their dinner in baskets, as they would go to a picnic.

The people of Detroit perhaps inherit the pleasure-loving characteristics of their French ancestors, or at least they do not seem to have their minds exclusively concentrated on the struggle after the almighty dollar.[80]

The location of Detroit on a strait between the upper and lower lakes made it the point of embarkation for a wide variety of lake and river trips. Daily excursion steamers left for the islands in the Detroit and St. Clair Rivers and Lake Erie. The more adventurous could explore the solitudes of Georgian Bay in Lake Huron or savor the delights of Mackinac Island in the Straits of Mackinac.[81] These outings on the water endowed life in Detroit with a special charm until the coming of the automobile all but banished the excursion boat.

The Shingle Style

The Romanesque is essentially an architecture of masonry. Its deep arches and rough surfaces denote a ponderous, stubborn material. In spite of the popularity of the Romanesque in America, it was natural that wood, which had for so long been the principal building material, should continue to be used for the more informal structures. Wood buildings, by their nature, should express lightness and ease of construction. Therefore, in doing this type of work, the architects of the eighties wisely avoided a literal interpretation of the Romanesque, but nevertheless derived from it a sense of picturesque massing, an impatience with superfluous ornament, and a feeling for texture. They soon learned that rich surface effects could be obtained from the use of shingles. These covered not only the roofs, but also the walls, and for the sake of variety were cut in different sizes and shapes and often arranged in patterns.[82]

The shingle style did not spring into being overnight but stemmed from a variety of sources. We have seen the traditional frame building fall prey to Swiss and Queen Anne mannerisms. Then the Romanesque influence prevailed. To complicate matters further, there was later an admixture of colonial details. Obviously the movement would have ended in total confusion if the architects had not from the beginning been consciously striving for greater discipline, simplicity, and originality. From the older elements they were attempting to fuse a new style based on American climate, materials, and living conditions.[83] The shingle style was an answer to the intensified yearning for a more bucolic life, and both in the suburbs and at the resorts Americans were responding to a new architectural vernacular devoid of urban pretensions.

Even H. H. Richardson realized that there were times when it was more appropriate to abandon his Wagnerian orchestration for humbler native melodies. His M. F. Stoughton house of 1882–83 in Cambridge, Massachusetts, was an important contribution to the shingle style. McKim, Mead and White carried the development through a significant phase with the Newport Casino (1879–81) and several private houses in Newport, Rhode Island, and elsewhere. Stanford White and Charles Follen McKim had worked in Richardson's office in the seventies. They were later to become renowned for their contribution to classicist architecture, but at the beginning of their careers they favored a free style as a result of their early association with Richardson.

Repercussions of the work of McKim, Mead and White at Newport were evident in the Belle Isle Casino (1884) designed by Donaldson and Meier.[84] The *(177)* casino was magnificently located at the western end of the island looking down the Detroit River. Verandas were informally arranged on all three floors to take advantage of the view and the breezes. The areas of these verandas diminished and receded progressively, from the broad projecting shelter on the ground floor to the small porch cut into the slope of the roof on the third floor. Finally, to crown the structure, there was a little observation tower, the curved surfaces of which gave an early hint of the plastic possibilities of wood construction. By 1908 the casino was already outgrown and was replaced.[85]

(182)   One of the most attractive early buildings on Belle Isle was a small police station designed by Mason and Rice (1893). The rustic charm of its rough fieldstone and shingled surfaces and the slight suggestion of a Norman farmhouse made it perfectly suited to the naturalistic setting. Here the shingle style betrayed a greater dependence than usual upon Romanesque precedent, as the use of the round masonry arch and engaged columns clearly demonstrates. The motif of the twin towers flanking an arched entry had already been developed on a larger scale by McKim, Mead and White on some of their shingled structures in the East, but to Mason and Rice we are indebted for a particularly happy interpretation of this theme. The continued use of the building as a police station up to the present day is a silent testimony of its architectural merit.

The Detroit Boat Club, founded in 1839, is the oldest river-club in the United States. Originally it was located on the mainland, but in 1891 a new clubhouse was built on the north shore of Belle Isle near the bridge. When this was destroyed by fire in 1893[86] Donaldson and Meier erected a new building in *(181)* the following year.[87] The flexible shingle style lent itself admirably to a structure so specialized in its function. It was a simple rectangular block with a hipped roof and prominent dormers. Boats were stored on the lower floor at the water level. Upstairs there were social rooms giving on a long veranda which looped around towers at the corners of the building. The largest of the towers was surrounded by two more levels of balconies. The whole building served as an excellent grandstand from which to watch boat races on the river. Another disastrous fire destroyed the club house in 1901 and it was then that Alpheus Chittenden was called upon to design the existing fireproof structure.

Today all types of pleasure craft are moored at the dock of the Detroit Boat Club. This often obscures the fact that it was originally founded as a rowing club. In the earliest days four-oared barges were used for racing, but were later supplanted by sleek modern shells. At the turn of the century ten-oared barges were used on occasion for the gay mixed boating parties that typified the leisurely recreational life of the time. On warm summer evenings young swains, their lady friends sitting beside them, would row two miles upstream to the head of the island. Then they would all eat a picnic supper, and join in singing while drifting back to the club in the moonlight.[88]

While Belle Isle was developing as a boating and picnicking center, Grosse Pointe was expanding as a summer colony. Shingled cottages were springing up next to their Swiss and mansardic forerunners. To keep up with the times Sena- *(142)* tor James McMillan and Mrs. John S. Newberry covered their twin Swiss cha- *(186)* lets with shingles, not without first adding towers, heavy arcades, and portecocheres. A shingled cottage of considerable charm was built in Grosse Pointe *(184)* about 1893 for John V. Moran, a member of one of Detroit's oldest French families. It suggested an early New England house with two upper stories included under a steep gabled roof and a lower kitchen ell projecting at the rear. Other features that clearly identified it with the shingle style were the withdrawal of the front porch under the unbroken slope of the roof and the insertion of a small upstairs porch between two dormer windows. Picturesque details included diamonded window panes, a small oriel window at the peak of the gable, and the rather Chinese fretwork of the porch railing. Unfortunately nothing remains of this happy expression of the leisurely life of early Grosse Pointe.

In 1884 the need for a social center in Grosse Pointe was answered by the organization of the Grosse Pointe Club. Two years later a clubhouse designed by   *(185)* William E. Brown was completed overlooking Lake St. Clair.[89] It was a shingled structure of elephantine proportions with prominent gables and a projecting veranda encompassing the first floor. A massive circular tower, rather ingeniously tied in with the rest of the building, offered a broad panorama of the lake from its many windows, but unquestionably the most delightful vantage point from which to view the lake on a hot summer day was the circular belvedere at the top of the tower. This in turn was surmounted by an enormous hovering conical roof which echoed the bold thrust of the gables and finished off the general pyramidal effect of the building as a whole. Although the new clubhouse was the last word in architecture and appointments, it soon became apparent that it was ahead of its time. Grosse Pointe was too inaccessible. The membership of the club was insufficient to support it adequately, so it was forced to close down two years after its completion.

At that time there was no easy way to reach Grosse Pointe. The dirt road from the city was so poorly maintained that in wet weather it was sometimes impassable for horse and buggy. In the eighties a trolley route was extended to Grosse Pointe along Jefferson avenue. About this time the game of golf was becoming popular. By the nineties the trolley transportation was good enough to make it possible for several golf courses to be opened in the area. The Grosse Pointe Club was reorganized under the name of the Country Club of Detroit.   *(214)* The clubhouse was reopened and a golf course laid out nearby.[90]

Detroiters had always been fond of fishing and duck hunting, and one of the favorite locales for these sports was a group of islands known as the Flats in the delta of the St. Clair River. Since time immemorial the river had brought down a wide variety of fish and the nearby marshes were a stopping place for migrating wild fowl in the spring and autumn. By the eighties the Flats could be reached by excursion steamers running twice a day across Lake St. Clair from Detroit and increasing numbers of private yachts offered a more luxurious means of transportation.[91] Hotels, clubs, and summer cottages sprang up on the islands and along the banks of the river, and facilities for tennis, croquet, boating, and bathing were provided. In 1897 a journalist of the *Detroit News-Tribune* rhapsodized over the delights of the Flats:

One's first trip to the Flats is a red-letter day in life's calendar. This Western Venice, rising out of the waters of Lake St. Clair, is a spot where the sights and sounds of the city are lost in the new and more musical sensations; where tired feet and dusty pavements are no more, but where the people float the rough liquid streets, and drifting out into the wider waterways, adjust the sail or dip the oar and, without a thought for slumbrous Italian skies or soft Mediterranean zephyrs, glide into an expanse of blue American waters, and inhale with rapture the bracing breezes.[92]

Such surroundings provided an ideal setting for the Lake St. Clair Fishing and   *(183)* Shooting Club, now known as the Old Club. Built about 1886, it was one of the finest examples of the shingle style in the neighborhood of Detroit. Resting on piles at the edge of the main channel of the St. Clair River, it gave the impression of rising out of the water, its sleek lines and surfaces seeming to borrow the principle of fluidity from the surroundings. The shingles of the long porch roof and of the walls of the building merged imperceptibly in a graceful curve, and banks of windows were arranged in rhythmic sequences. A carefully studied overall abstract design precluded any reliance on historical details. At one end was a polygonal tower that remotely suggested a lighthouse, but its inflated bulk and the merging of its shingled walls and roof made it a new plastic architectural form with a character of its own. At the other end of the asymmetrical composition, opposite the tower, was a lopsided gabled roof whose long slope provided a sheltering termination for the exposed end of the building. Near the middle of the façade, but off-center, was a small projecting bay that echoed the rounded and the angular forms of both the tower and the large gable. Finally, deep shadows were provided by the projecting porch roof on the main floor, by the recesses sharply cut into the main bulk of the building, and by the apertures at the top of the tower. Unfortunately this masterpiece of the shingle style was destroyed by fire in 1924 and was replaced by the existing clubhouse.

(190)

(188)

Hiram Walker, the whiskey magnate, deserves the credit for having made the cool breezes of the northern shore of Lake Erie more accessible to Detroiters during the summer months. In 1889 he opened a magnificent resort hotel near Kingsville, Ontario, about thirty miles from Detroit. The Mettawas Hotel, as it was called, was located on the route of Walker's railroad, so from the beginning there was no problem of transportation. The hotel provided a golf course, tennis courts, and a splendid beach fringed with cedar trees on Lake Erie. An adjacent casino offered facilities for social activities.[92]

Designed by Mason and Rice, the hotel and casino were extraordinary exercises in free design with powerful abstract forms. The gable formed by a gambrel roof was used as a recurrent motif. Derived from colonial sources, it was chosen more for the interesting character of its broken lines than for any historical connotation. The bold juxtaposition of these gables with conical and pyramidal roof forms convincingly demonstrated the plastic possibilities of the shingle style. The precision of the paneling of the central tower and the delicacy of such colonial features as the porch columns and the modified Palladian windows contrasted pleasingly with the rough texture of the shingles.

Although possessed of undeniable originality and distinction, nevertheless the design of both the hotel and the casino brought clearly into focus one rather serious defect of the shingle style. Since it evolved as a highly capricious and individualistic domestic style, it was not ideally suited for large buildings devoted to public use. Its application at Kingsville amounted to an arbitrary imposition of a domestic scale on buildings which, by the nature of their organization, demanded more formal treatment. In spite of these rather academic considerations, the Mettawas was a very attractive hotel, and it is a misfortune that Detroiters and others can no longer enjoy its fine facilities. The buildings burned many years ago and were never rebuilt.

(187)

When Louis Kamper, a young German-American architect, designed the Detroit International Fair and Exposition Pavilion of 1889, he must have realized that the shingle style was inappropriate for such an enormous building. A combination of Gothic and Romanesque in a structure made entirely of wood normally would be unthinkable, but the festive atmosphere of an exposition and its temporary nature permitted a display of fantasy that would have been unwarranted under ordinary circumstances. The main exposition building demanded a picturesque and imposing silhouette, and Kamper found the inspiration for this in the Houses of Parliament in London with their massive towers, turrets, and Gothic roofs.[93] For details, such as entrance arches, arcades, and fenestration, he fell back on the contemporary Romanesque vocabulary. It was only in the long stretches of the building between the towers that a simplified architectural treatment established a link with the shingle style. Certainly the architectural climate of the Detroit exposition corresponded more with the Philadelphia Centennial of 1876 than with the Chicago Columbian Exposition, which at that time had not yet opened its doors to the public.

As Detroit was then a city with a population of only 205,876, it is not surprising that the rather presumptuous title of the exposition concealed the fact that it was little more than a glorified state fair. It was held on a tract of seventy acres at Delray on the Detroit River north of the mouth of the River Rouge. Besides the main exposition buildings there were horse and cattle barns, swine and sheep sheds, a race track, a restaurant, and an art gallery. A dock provided for steamer service to the city. In order to attract more visitors there were balloon ascensions featuring trapeze artists performing in mid-air. The fair turned out to be a great success and was reopened every year for three additional years (1890–92).[94] Considering the size of Detroit at the time, it was an ambitious project reflecting the economic growth of the city.

Among the businessmen who made large fortunes during this prosperous period in the development of Detroit, Charles L. Freer deserves our attention as an outstanding patron of art and architecture. Born in Kingston, New York, he began his industrial career as the auditor for the Eel River Railroad in Indiana. At that time Colonel Frank J. Hecker was the manager of the railroad. When the Wabash Railroad absorbed the Eel River Line in 1878 the positions of auditor and superintendent were dispensed with. Freer and Hecker then came to Detroit. With a few thousand dollars they founded the Peninsular Car Company to manufacture railroad cars; Hecker was the president and Freer the vice president.[95] Later the company merged with the Michigan Car Company, thus forming the Michigan Peninsular Car Company. Hecker became the president of the new concern, Senator James McMillan was the chairman, and Freer and William C. McMillan were managing directors. In 1899 both Freer and Hecker retired, millionaires several times over.[96]

Long before that date, however, Charles Freer began to devote himself to art. In 1888 he met James Abbott McNeill Whistler and they became good friends. Freer was one of the first Americans to collect Whistler's work. He also bought the work of other contemporary American artists, such as Dewing, Hassam, Homer, Melchers, Metcalf, Murphy, Ryder, Sargent, Thayer, Tryon, and Twachtman; but perhaps his most absorbing interest was the acquisition of painting, sculpture, pottery, jade, lacquer, and metal work from China, Japan, India, and the Near East. He traveled to Japan and remote parts of China in quest of treasures. Eventually his collection of Oriental paintings became one of the finest outside Japan.[95]

The discerning eye of Freer was quick to recognize the artistic merits of the *(193)* shingle style. For his own house on Ferry avenue he chose as architect a recognized master of the style, Wilson Eyre Jr. of Philadelphia.[97] Built in 1890 and still standing, the house displayed a sensitivity to line and texture that marked it as one of the most distinguished houses of its period in Detroit. Beginning with a simple rectangular block, the architect applied subtle and meaningful modifications that endowed it with an individual character—the graceful curvature of flaring eaves, the breaking of sweeping horizontals with gables and bay windows, the interpenetration of inner and outer space in the area of the porches—suffusing all with the muted vibrancy of contrasting shingle and limestone surfaces. On the interior the plan assumed a new fluidity. Porches and windows *(194)* established a close relationship between the interior of the house and its sur-

(192) rounding grounds, and an enlarged stairwell removed the customary barrier between the floors. Even in the details a new orientation could be detected: inglenooks with settees and built-in cabinets with fine metalwork locks and hinges betrayed the influence of the Arts and Crafts movement. Yet if there was a reminder of William Morris, it was not without a certain anticipation of Frank Lloyd Wright.[62]

It was inevitable that Freer's house would in time become inadequate to contain his growing collection. In 1904 he sold his horses and carriages, remodeled the stable behind the house to make a private art gallery, and acquired the

(191) famous Peacock Room upon the death of Frederick R. Leyland, the noted English collector in whose London house the room was originally executed (1877).[98] An architect had designed the room to contain Leyland's porcelains and James McNeill Whistler's painting, The Princess from the Land of Porcelain (1864). Whistler did not like the room, so by his hand it underwent a transformation into a beautiful chamber in gold and turquoise blue, with peacocks as the principal decorative motif. The ceiling was finely paneled, and along the walls shelves were built to contain antique porcelains. Freer bought the room and the painting it contained, and installed them in a building specially built for them adjoining his art gallery in Detroit.[95]

A bachelor, Freer had many friends and entertained frequently. His house was staffed with a full retinue of servants, including a chef imported from New York. Many Detroiters enjoyed the rare privilege of a magnificent dinner, an escorted tour of the gallery, or perhaps an informal cup of tea in the Peacock Room. Today the house and art gallery serve an entirely different purpose, as they are the property of the Merrill-Palmer Institute, while the famous collection and the fabulous Peacock Room are housed in the Freer Gallery of Art in Washington, D.C.[99]

The Colonial Revival

After the Civil War the burgeoning industrialization of cities drove increasing numbers of Americans to seek the salubrious atmosphere of seaside resorts during the summer months. There they were confronted with specimens of colonial architecture which inspired them with a nostalgia for the simple life of their ancestors. They were captivated by the informal charm of the rambling interiors with their low ceilings, capacious fireplaces, and winding staircases. Colonial motifs were soon introduced into current architecture along with Queen Anne features. Both these influences were symptomatic of a craving for the old and the picturesque and were eventually to merge in the formation of the shingle style, yet there were still those who favored a more complete resurrection of the colonial style. Patriotic pride was stimulated by the Philadelphia Centennial of 1876 and served to emphasize the symbolic significance of a style that represented a national heritage. Thus it was only a matter of time before the colonial style emerged as a full-fledged revival.

As early as 1872 Charles Follen McKim remodeled an old eighteenth century house in Newport. Since he had been educated at the École des Beaux-Arts in Paris in 1867–70, it is not surprising that he should have evinced an early interest in a classical type of architecture. In 1877 he took a trip through New England with William R. Mead, W. B. Bigelow, and Stanford White to study colonial architecture.[100] In 1878 McKim, Mead and Bigelow formed an architectural firm in New York, White taking the place of Bigelow in 1880. Since White and

McKim had worked together in Richardson's office, at first their work was strongly Richardsonian in character, but in the course of time colonial details appeared with increasing frequency. In 1878 McKim, White, and the sculptor Augustus Saint-Gaudens made a sketching trip through France, and in 1884 White visited Italy and Greece.[101] After this a complete break with the shingle style was inevitable. The firm's H. A. C. Taylor house of 1885–86 in Newport, Rhode Island, was Colonial-Palladian, with emphasis upon axial symmetry.

The Taylor house created widespread reverberations in the American architectural profession. In Detroit, Mason and Rice were clearly influenced by it in their design for the William C. McMillan summer residence of 1888 on Lake *(189)* Shore road in Grosse Pointe. The academic details were identical, but there was a reluctance to accept rigid symmetry. The easy informality of the shingle style persisted in the rambling porch, partly recessed and partly projecting. A contemporary description in the *Detroit Free Press* made this feature seem particularly inviting: "On the veranda, which is shaded by vines, awnings, and Venetian shutters, palms are banked. Chairs and divans covered with loose dull red toned fabrics suggest all manner of easy positions."[102] Later the house was moved to University place to make way for the Truman H. Newberry house. It is still *(331)* standing although altered beyond recognition.[103]

In 1885 the *Detroit Evening Journal* commented, "When a residence is clothed in Colonial architecture, it has a modest, Puritan maiden sort of cast of countenance that is quite refreshing."[104] By the nineties the new style had lost some of its freshness and was beginning to show signs of pedantry. This could have been noted in the Edward H. Parker House (1896) located on Jefferson *(195)* avenue in the fashionable Indian Village district of Detroit. It combined many details borrowed from the early New England houses of Salem, Newburyport, and Portsmouth. The front door was framed with sidelights and a fanlight; there were delicate carvings and slender columns, pilasters, and balusters; and at the top of the hipped roof was a widow's walk. From 1907 until 1921 the house was occupied by Dr. Howard W. Longyear.[105] After World War II it was torn down and replaced by a commercial structure.

Gari Melchers commissioned Donaldson and Meier in 1897 to provide a house *(198)* on Seyburn avenue for his father Julius Melchers, the sculptor.[106] Fortune smiled upon the younger Melchers all his life. He had achieved a national reputation as a painter of murals, portraits, and genre. Educated at the Royal Art Academy in Düsseldorf and the École des Beaux-Arts in Paris, he later maintained studios in Paris and at Egmond-aan-Zee in Holland, where he painted scenes of native life. In 1916 he bought an estate in Virginia where he spent the remainder of his life.[107] Donaldson and Meier did not do very much domestic work, but they made an exception in this case since Donaldson and Julius Melchers were friends and associates, having collaborated on the statues for the niches of the City *(85)* Hall.[84] Gari Melchers brought back some beautiful tiles from Holland for the mantels, and to carry out the theme, Dutch gables and shutters were added to what was otherwise a colonial house.[106] The talent of the elder Melchers found expression in the elaborate carving in the gable of the large central dormer.

Louis Kamper was well prepared to be a protagonist of the Colonial Revival since he had worked in the office of McKim, Mead and White in New York from the time of his arrival in America in 1880 until he moved to Detroit in 1888. He was born in Bliesdalheim, Germany, and studied at the technical school in Rheinpfalz before coming to this country.[108] In 1898 he built a summer residence for Hugo Scherer on Lake Shore road in Grosse Pointe. In his inter- *(196)* pretation of the Colonial Revival there was something of the exuberant baroque theatricality of his native Bavaria. The trim mansions of New England were too restrained for his taste, so he turned instead to the stately plantation houses of the Old South. There he found inspiration for the lofty porticoes of the Scherer house, which provided such generous shelter·from the summer sun. A profusion of curving bay windows and balustrades added a Victorian note and contributed further to the atmosphere of luxurious relaxation. After World War I when the automobile had made Grosse Pointe more accessible, the house was turned into an all-year-round residence.[109] Wisteria vines have clambered up the giant columns of the front and converted it into a leafy bower from which one can gaze at the blue waters of Lake St. Clair.

(197)   In 1902 the David C. Whitney residence by Walter MacFarlane was added to the series of white clapboard Colonial Revival houses that were lining Lake Shore road at the turn of the century.[110] More historically correct than the Scherer house, it bore a certain resemblance to the executive mansion in Washington. Without sacrificing formal emphasis, it was brought into relationship with the naturalistic surroundings by the front verandas and the sunrooms added to each end of the building. The house was torn down in 1956 and the property added to an adjoining estate.

As Grosse Pointe became more elegant, so did other resorts in Michigan, in a large measure due to improved rail and steamship transportation. One of the most popular centers was Mackinac Island in the Straits of Mackinac between Lake Huron and Lake Michigan. It became the summer home of prominent people from Detroit, Chicago, and other cities. "Many of these occupy cottages which, in their appurtenances and appointments are little less than palaces," wrote a visitor in 1893, "and thither are transported for purposes of the summer outing gorgeous equipages, blooded stock, liveried servants and other conveniences afforded wealth."[111]

The island offered many attractions. Facilities for golf, tennis, bathing, and fishing were provided. There were delightful horseback rides or drives in carriages through the pine-scented forests with here and there glimpses of the irregular shore line with its precipitous cliffs and sheltered coves.[112] Those historically minded could visit the ancient fort that loomed above the little town, a grim reminder of the sanguinary days before the ingenuity of man had converted a wilderness into a playground.

(199)   In 1887 the Grand Hotel was erected on a bluff outside the town, its vast piazza commanding a magnificent view across the straits toward distant islands and the mainland.[113] Mason and Rice, the architects, chose a style of architecture that may be classified as Colonial Revival. Actually it followed the pattern of the early nineteenth century hotels of New England and New York State which were situated in the mountains or on the seacoast. A long narrow three-story structure, fronted by a continuous colonnade running its entire height, the building was ideal for a site that commanded a panorama of inspiring natural beauty.[114] Certainly this classical type of architecture, with its uniformity and cohesion, was more appropriate for a large resort hotel than the rather whimsical and domestic shingle style, although it should be noted that the central gables and cupola of the Grand Hotel reveal that the architects had not altogether forgotten this other popular architectural idiom of the period. Even today the hotel maintains its role as the leading hostelry of the area.

(146) First Unitarian Church, *Donaldson & Meier*, 1890 (MB)

(147) Joseph H. Berry House, *Mason & Rice*, 1882 (MB)

(148) First Congregational Church, *J. L. Faxon*, 1891 (JSC)

(149) First Presbyterian Church, *Mason & Rice*, 1889 (MB)

(150) Cass Avenue Methodist Church,
Malcomson & Higginbotham, 1891 (JSC)

(151) Central Christian Church,
Malcomson & Higginbotham, 1891 (JSC)

(152-153) Jefferson Avenue Presbyterian Church
and Chapel, *B. L. Gilbert*, 1888-91
(BHC/JKJ)(DN)

(154) Bagley Memorial Fountain, *H. H. Richardson*, 1887 (BHC)   (155) John N. Bagley House, 1889 (JSC)

(156-157) Store and Residence,
Mason & Rice, 1883 (UW)(BHC)

(158) Charles A. Du Charme House, *Mason & Rice*, 1888 (ELA)

(159-160) Gilbert W. Lee House, *Mason & Rice*, 1888 (ELA)

(161) David Whitney Jr. House, *G. W. Lloyd*, 1894 (MB)
(162) Detroit Athletic Club, *J. V. Gearing*, 1887 (BHC)

(163) Detroit Club, *W. Eyre*, 1891 (BHC)
(164) Albert L. Stephens House, *Mason & Rice*, 1890 (GDM/MB)

(165) Union R.R. Station,
J. Stewart & Co., 1893 (MB)

(166) Kingsville R.R. Station, *Mason & Rice*, 1888 (BHC)

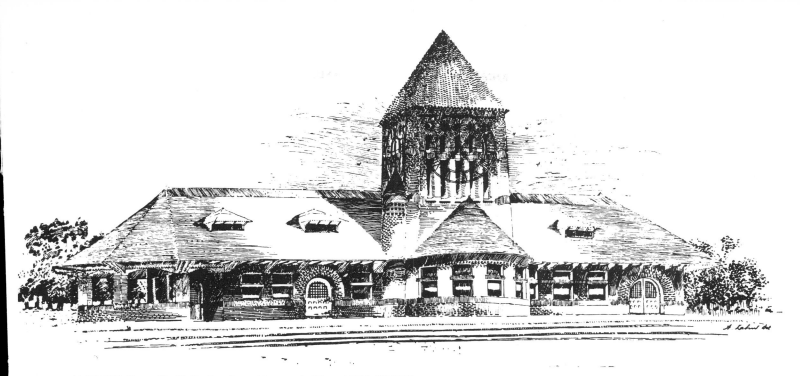

(167) Walkerville R.R. Station, *Mason & Rice*, 1888 (BHC)

(168) Detroit College, *G. W. Lloyd*, 1891 (MB)

(169) Federal Building, *J. H. Windrim*, 1894 (BHC)

(170) D. M. Ferry & Co., *G. W. Lloyd*, 1887 (GDM)

(171) Museum of Art, *J. Balfour*, 1888 (BHC)

(172-173) Bagley Memorial Armory,
H. H. Richardson, 1886 (ELA)

(174) T. W. Palmer Block, *Mason & Rice*, 1894 (ELA)

(175) J. L. Hudson Co., *M. L. Smith*, 1891 (BHC)

(176) Hammond Building,
H. W. J. Edbrooke, 1890 (BHC)

(177) Belle Isle Casino, *Donaldson & Meier*, 1884 (BHC)

(178) Majestic Building, *D. H. Burnham*, 1896 (M

(179) Chamber of Commerce, *Spier & Rohns*, 1895 (BHC)

(180) Union Trust Building,
Donaldson & Meier, 1895 (MB)

(181) Detroit Boat Club, *Donaldson & Meier*, 1894 (BHC)

(182) Belle Isle Police Station, *Mason & Rice*, 1893 (JSC)

(183) Lake St. Clair (Old) Club, c. 1886 (BHC)

(184) John V. Moran House, c. 1893 (BHC)

(185) Grosse Pointe Club, *W. E. Brown*, 1886 (BHC)

(186) John S. Newberry House (remodeled) (BHC)

(187) Exposition Pavilion, *L. Kamper*, 1889 (BHC)

(188) Mettawas Casino, *Mason & Rice*, 1889 (GDM/MB)

(189) William C. McMillan House, *Mason & Rice*, 1888 (GDM/MB)

(190) Mettawas Hotel, *Mason & Rice*, 1889 (GDM/MB)

(191) Peacock Room (by Whistler), 1877 (FGA)
(192-194) Charles L. Freer House, *W. Eyre et al.,*
1890 (BJ/DFP)(ELA)(MPI)

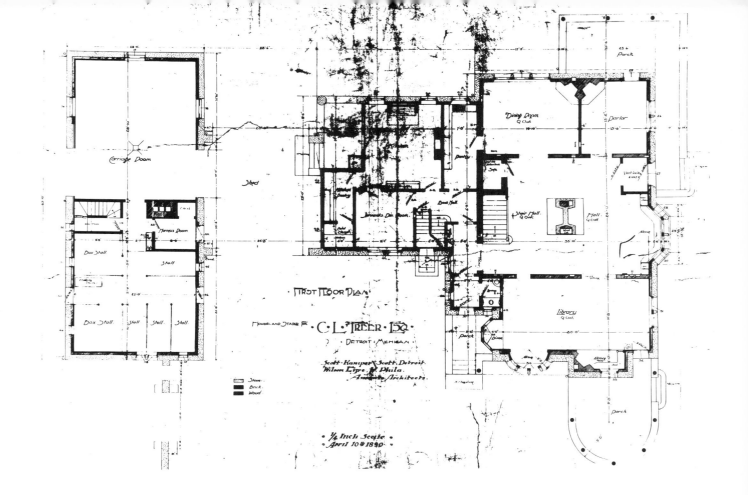

(195) Edward H. Parker House, 1896 (MLP)

(196) Hugo Scherer House, *L. Kamper*, 1898 (HAL)

(197) David C. Whitney House, *Rogers & MacFarlane*, 1902 (MB)

(198) Julius T. Melchers House, *Donaldson & Meier*, 1897 (HHR)

(199) Grand Hotel, Mackinac Island, *Mason & Rice*, 1887 (BHC)

6. The Motor City

The Advent of the Automobile

Shortly after midnight on an early spring morning in 1896 Charles B. King ran the first automobile on the streets of Detroit. Few people were about. He and his assistants trundled the car out of a machine shop on St. Antoine street. They cranked it, and after a few preliminary puffs it started off. Pausing occasionally for minor adjustments, they drove out Jefferson avenue and several blocks up East Grand boulevard before returning. For some time afterwards King continued these secretive nocturnal expeditions. Finally he felt sure enough of his new contrivance to stage a public demonstration on March 6, but such immense crowds gathered that he was compelled to discontinue such runs thereafter. Even on Belle Isle the police did what they could to discourage his endeavors. At that time the horseless carriage was considered dangerous and disturbing, and such men as King were regarded as misguided cranks.[1]

A few months afterwards a friend of King's, a young mechanic named Henry Ford, was ready to launch the machine he had been working on in a brick shed at the rear of his home on Bagley avenue. In the small hours of the morning of June 4 the car was wheeled into the alley behind the shed. Ford's assistant was on hand, ready to ride ahead on his bicycle to warn drivers of horse-drawn vehicles. Ford had no difficulty in starting the engine and was soon steering the car out of the alley and down Grand River avenue. By the time he reached Washington boulevard motor trouble had developed. When the necessary repairs were made he drove back to his shed, thus completing a history-making run. Later, when the car was improved, he drove about town and made several trips to Greenfield and Dearborn.[2]

The renown that later came to Ford has given rise to the popular misconception that he was a mechanical genius. Actually the achievements of King and Ford up to this point were by no means extraordinary. These men were merely demonstrating that they could do in Detroit what Daimler and Benz had done in Europe. In constructing their first cars they were driven by the same wave of enthusiasm that was impelling others to make similar experiments in other parts of the United States. Even a superficial review of early automotive history cannot be made without mentioning the names of the Duryea brothers, Elwood Haynes, Alexander Winton, and Ransom E. Olds. That Ford should have outdistanced these men and achieved an international reputation is due in a large measure to his determination and vision. At a time when the automobile was a plaything for the wealthy few, he foresaw the day when it would be within the reach of the average man. Forging ahead with this objective clearly in mind, he was able to found a vast industrial empire.[3]

The astonishing growth of Detroit in the early years of the twentieth century was a dramatic example of the functioning of the American economy. In a short span of years a local trading emporium developed into the nation's automobile capital. The demands of the new industry were so complex that it was apparent from the beginning that a pooling of talents and resources in a central area was essential. Competition was keen among a score of American cities, but a combination of favorable circumstances ultimately gave Detroit the lead. Michigan at the time surpassed all other states in the manufacture of marine gasoline engines and also led in the output of carriages, buggies, and wheels. Added to this was a long tradition in the production of iron, brass, and copper. In short, all the essential parts of an automobile were readily available.[4]

Such a young and erratic industry naturally posed the problem of raising the necessary capital. Conservative Boston and New York remained timidly aloof, but Detroit capitalists were more adventurous. Inheritors of lumbering and mining millions, they were in a position to understand the advantages of taking risks. There were catastrophic reverses, to be sure, but the general trend was upward. In the vertiginous pyramiding of wealth old fortunes were aggrandized and new ones established.

It was in the automobile industry that mass production received its major impetus. The complex nature of the product and the steadily increasing demand for it called for the utmost in precision, speed, and organization. A new economic frontier had been opened up with opportunities for rapid promotion and an improved standard of living. As the automobile increasingly captured the imagination of the public, the legend of Detroit spread far and wide. Into the city from the hinterland streamed droves of unskilled workers, released by the mechanization of farms and the depletion of timberlands. Skilled workers from the older established industrial centers of Ontario and the East joined the migration.[5] Added to this was a steady influx of recent European immigrants.

In the meantime the population of Detroit grew by leaps and bounds. In 1890 it was 205,876; in 1900, 285,704; in 1910, 465,766; and by 1920 it had reached 993,678. At this time it may well be considered as having passed the million mark if one were to include the population of Highland Park and Hamtramck, cities which had been surrounded by the enlarging metropolis. In 1920 the population of Detroit was twenty-nine percent foreign-born. These citizens hailed from every country in Europe, not to mention Canada. Among this group of new Americans the natives of Canada, Poland, Germany, and Russia predominated.[6]

The New Industrial Architecture

Once it had gained momentum the automobile industry rapidly assumed gigantic proportions. Constantly changing methods of manufacture and ever-expanding production placed unprecedented demands on factory construction. Therefore Detroit was the center for intensive experimentation in industrial architecture in the early years of the twentieth century. This development in turn was to provide the basis for radically altered concepts of architecture as a whole.

Up until the twentieth century factories had been unsightly conglomerations of buildings with little or no intelligent planning. The plant engineer usually was responsible for any additions. In the rare instances when an architect was called upon the work was generally delegated to a junior draftsman. Some progress had been made in the East in the so-called mill buildings erected mainly for the textile industry. Exterior wall surfaces had been reduced to narrow piers which supported heavy timbers, which in turn carried laminated or heavy plank floors. Wood, iron, or steel columns supported interior girders and beams. These well-lighted mill buildings had become the generally accepted type of factory throughout the country.[7]

A good example of this kind of construction was the Piquette avenue plant of *(201)* the Ford Motor Company built in Detroit in 1904. Ever since 1899 Ford had been struggling to establish himself as a manufacturer of automobiles. The erection of a factory ten times the size of a previously leased building left no doubt that he was well on the way to success. The new plant, which occupied a site 402 x 56 feet and was three stories high, gave evidence of careful planning. Ample precautions were taken against fire. Each story was divided into four sections by fire walls and an automatic sprinkler system was provided. The architects were Field, Hinchman and Smith.[8]

The leading industrial architect in Detroit during this period was Albert Kahn. Most of his fellow architects felt that designing a factory was beneath their dignity, but he had no such compunctions. The hardships of his early life had given him a realistic viewpoint which served to emancipate him from the flimsy architectural pedantries of the day. His rational and orderly mind quickly perceived the benefits to be derived from better plant organization. He also recognized the advantages of a healthful and pleasing industrial environment. Endowed with an extraordinary vitality and driven by a restless ambition, he was to lift industrial architecture from the doldrums and endow it with a new distinction. After leaving the office of Mason and Rice in 1895, Kahn formed a partnership with George W. Nettleton and Alexander B. Trowbridge, former fellow draftsmen in Mason's office. This partnership was dissolved in 1897, leaving him to continue the business alone.[9]

The first factory which may definitely be attributed to Kahn was the Boyer Machine Company.[10] Joseph Boyer had invented a pneumatic hammer which he had been manufacturing in St. Louis. Dissatisfied with the warm climate of St. Louis, he moved to Detroit in 1900 and hired Kahn to build a small mill building on Second avenue where he continued his manufacturing operations.[11]

In 1904 Boyer employed Kahn to build a factory for the Burroughs Adding Machine Company on Second avenue. In St. Louis, Boyer had manufactured adding machines for William S. Burroughs, inventor of this boon to the business world and founder of the company that later bore his name. Burroughs died in 1898 and in 1902 Boyer became president of the company. Trade union domination in St. Louis made conditions unfavorable for proper growth, so in 1904 Boyer used his influence to remove the entire concern to Detroit.[12] The new factory on Second avenue was a well-planned building with a saw-tooth roof admitting plenty of light. Some attempt had been made at artistic treatment of the two-story office section at the front, and the neighboring thoroughfares were widened and landscaped. Although no structural advances were as yet discernible, the Burroughs plant was a convincing demonstration that industrial blight was becoming a thing of the past.[13]

In 1903 Henry B. Joy commissioned Albert Kahn to construct a new plant for the Packard Motor Car Company on a forty acre tract on East Grand boulevard. Joy was the son of James F. Joy who, as president of the Michigan Central Railroad, had laced Michigan with a network of railroads in the latter part of the nineteenth century. In the meantime, however, the automobile had appeared on the scene to challenge the older means of transportation. Easily matching his father in zest and enterprise, the younger Joy lost no time in plunging into the infant automobile industry. He had seen a Packard car at the annual automobile show in New York and recognized its merits. This prompted him to visit the factory, the Ohio Automobile Company at Warren, Ohio. The owners were impressed by his ideas on production and distribution, and he soon became general manager and director of the company. At this time Detroit was becoming known as the automobile manufacturing center of America and offered much greater advantages than Warren, Ohio, for the production of the Packard car. Accordingly, Joy moved the plant to Detroit in 1903, succeeded James W. Packard as president of the firm in 1905, and renamed it the Packard Motor Car Company.[14]

The capitalization necessary for the new plant was $500,000. Joy dug into his own pocket for $25,000 and was able to raise the remainder among wealthy relatives and friends. These included his brother Richard Joy, his brothers-in-law John S. and Truman H. Newberry, Philip H. McMillan, son of the senator, Joseph Boyer, Frederick M. and Russell A. Alger Jr., Charles A. Du Charme, and Dexter M. Ferry Jr. Joy employed Albert Kahn as architect for the Packard factory upon the recommendation of Joseph Boyer.[15]

The first large automobile plant in Detroit, the Packard factory was the golden opportunity of Kahn's life and was to determine the future course of his career. The progress that he made may be attributed largely to his ability to satisfy the requirements of his client. The new plant was laid out in the shape of a hollow square with windows on all eight sides. The processes of manufacturing a car were arranged progressively around the square. In 1904 *Motor Age* lauded the "bright, cleanly, and cheerful aspect of the different departments." "It is one of the new style of factories," it pointed out, "that are gradually displacing the old prison work shops, which, especially in cities, and sadly enough, were common in all industries until the last decade. It is most fitting that the automobile industry as the newest great industry of the country should in its new factories add to the strength of the movement toward rational working places."[16]

The success of the Packard commission might easily have made Kahn complacent, but he realized that his biggest problems lay ahead. Conventional mill construction was certainly not ideal for such a large-scaled industry. The necessarily limited distance between columns was objectionable and any span beyond twenty feet required part-steel construction. On top of this, there still remained the danger from fire. Machinery floors soaked with oil were heavy risks in spite of sprinkler systems. The so-called fireproof construction was out of the question because of excessive costs.[7]

Between 1903 and 1905 Kahn built nine buildings for the Packard group, all of mill construction. In the meantime he had become very much interested in a new method of construction then coming into use on both sides of the Atlantic—so-called reinforced concrete. François Hennebique had employed this building method for many kinds of structures in Europe, including mills in Nantes and an apartment house in Paris. In 1903 Auguste Perret built his famous apartment house on the Rue Franklin in Paris.[17] In America, Ernest L. Ransome erected two reinforced concrete factories, one in Beverly, Massachusetts, and one in East Rochester, New York.[18] Earlier he had done some work in California. It took considerable courage to design in concrete in those days, for handbooks were not available and formulas virtually nonexistent.[19] Nevertheless, Kahn was willing to take the risk, and in 1902–03 he and George D. Mason built the Palms

Apartment Building on East Jefferson avenue in Detroit and the Engineering Building at the University of Michigan in Ann Arbor.[7]

Albert Kahn's brother Julius helped to construct the Engineering Building.[20] After earning his B.S. and C.E. degrees at the University of Michigan, Julius Kahn had become a civil engineer for the U.S. Navy and an assistant engineer for the U.S. Engineering Corps.[21] From 1898 to 1900 he was the chief engineer for a group of sulfur mines in Japan. Upon returning to Detroit he became associated with Albert as chief engineer of the firm.[22] Working on the construction of the building in Ann Arbor made him aware of the shortcomings of the empirical method of reinforcement, so he set about designing a system of reinforcement along scientific principles. Up until then concrete beams had failed in shear, the steel remaining intact. If the steel could be caused to fail first in testing, a more precise method of calculation would be possible. Captain John S. Sewall, then in charge of construction for the District of Columbia, had pointed this out in a professional periodical. Therefore, when Julius Kahn substantiated the statement with actual tests, Captain Sewall invited him to Washington, approved of his design, and induced him to accept a contract for supplying his form of reinforcement for a group of buildings called the War College.[7] Although Hennebique and Ransome had used stirrup reinforcements, Kahn was the first to attach the stirrups rigidly to the horizontal tension bars.[18] This was a more scientific method of resisting shearing stresses. Soon the "Kahn system" became established and popular throughout the country.

In order to manufacture the Kahn bar, Julius Kahn organized the Trussed Concrete Steel Company in Detroit in 1903. Later this became the Truscon Steel Company which was eventually absorbed by the Republic Steel Company of Cleveland.[22] Soon after the founding of the original company Julius Kahn and his staff undertook the structural design of two enormous concrete buildings, the Marlborough-Blenheim and the Traymore Hotels in Atlantic City.[7]

Now that his brother had perfected the technique of concrete construction, Albert Kahn realized that this hitherto unreliable material was exactly what he needed to solve his problems in industrial architecture. In 1905 he made history *(202)* by erecting the first reinforced concrete factory in Detroit. It was the tenth unit of the Packard Motor Car Company on the Grand boulevard site.[18] The Trussed Concrete Steel Company prepared the structural design. The two-story building was 60 x 457 feet in plan with an ell 60 x 240 feet at the rear. The entire frame was of concrete. Down the center was a row of columns spaced thirty-two feet *(204)* apart. These supported a longitudinal girder, which in turn supported transverse beams at intervals of sixteen feet. Thus a clear floor space of 32 x 60 feet was left between columns, which was a great advantage for assembling machines. The floor and roof consisted of narrow concrete joists between single rows of hollow terra-cotta tiles. The floors were covered with cement and the ceilings with plaster. Exposed on the exterior, the concrete frame carried low brick outer walls beneath the window areas.[23] The building is still standing today, although *(203)* two stories have been added.

By introducing reinforced concrete in factory design, almost overnight Kahn had eliminated the deficiencies of mill construction. In addition to being fireproof, concrete was stronger and more rigid against vibration, and it also provided more floor space and maximum window areas. On the other hand, structural steel would have been more costly and would have required more time for construction.

According to Kahn himself, the Packard building was the first of its kind in Detroit.[7] Nevertheless, almost simultaneously a building of similar construction was erected for the Cadillac Motor Car Company on Cass avenue at Amsterdam (1905). George D. Mason was the architect and the Trussed Concrete Steel Company supplied the structural design. It, was a three-story structure with a basement, the plan measuring 90 x 300 feet.[23] Only a short time previously most of the original Cadillac plant had been destroyed by fire. It had been built for the Leland-Faulconer Manufacturing Company, producers of marine and automobile motors, machinery, and tools. In 1905 this company and the Cadillac Automobile Company merged to form the Cadillac Motor Car Company.[24] Mason's reinforced concrete building insured against a recurrence of the previous disaster. In fact, it is still standing today, although no longer occupied by the Cadillac Motor Car Company.

The Cadillac and Packard plants were situated on the Michigan Central Belt Line. Looping around the urban core, this railroad served the city's industries.[25] For some time it had been congested, so as early as 1904 a group of businessmen organized a syndicate to build an outer belt line to open up a new area to industrial enterprise.[26] The last section of the line was completed in 1914. Known as the Detroit Terminal Railway, it was acquired by the Michigan Central and Grand Trunk Railways.[27] The route began at a point on the river one mile east of Waterworks Park. Describing a broad arc outside what was then the city limits, it crossed Woodward avenue six miles north of the City Hall and joined the main line of the Michigan Central to the west. Not only did the new route facilitate the interchange of traffic among various railways radiating out of Detroit, but it also provided a central artery for a vast new industrial complex which sprang up on what had formerly been flat farmlands on the fringe of the city. Interspersed between the industrial areas, row upon row of monotonous frame houses were quickly thrown up to accommodate the ever increasing numbers of factory workers.

After the initial success of the reinforced concrete building for the Packard Company, Kahn received a commission for fireproof additions to the Burroughs Adding Machine Company. By then his reputation as Detroit's leading industrial architect was firmly established. When the burgeoning automobile industry created an unprecedented demand for more factories, Kahn was well prepared for the task at hand; almost without exception manufacturers turned to him for architectural assistance. Soon he was covering vast acreages with sprawling stuctures of concrete and glass. The Chalmers plant (1908) on East Jefferson avenue (later sold to the Chrysler Corporation), the Hudson plant (1910) also on East Jefferson, and the Ford Highland Park plant (1909–14) on Woodward avenue occupied key positions on the outer belt line. The Dodge plant (1910–14) in Hamtramck and the Cadillac plant (1921) on Clark street were located on other important railroad lines. Year after year the Kahn office was called upon to expand these factories with additions and branches. In time Kahn's name became synonymous with the new industrial architecture, and his practice became national and later international in scope.

Kahn's most outstanding achievement during the early years of his industrial work was unquestionably the Ford Highland Park plant. The success of this undertaking may be attributed to an unusually happy combination of architect and client. Henry Ford was even more zealous than Henry B. Joy in his search for more efficient methods of production. With skill and imagination Kahn was able to interpret Ford's bold planning concepts in terms of architecture.

Ford had realized that his Piquette and Bellevue plants were inadequate, so as early as 1906 he purchased a sixty-acre tract in suburban Highland Park with the hope of enlarging and consolidating his operations.[28] There he visualized an entire factory under one roof with no division walls and no open courts. It was his idea to locate the main structure along Woodward avenue, thus leaving the remainder of the property for future expansion, unit by unit.[29] Begun in 1909, this building was already producing cars shortly after New Year's Day in 1910. *(200)* With its four stories, its length of 865 feet, and its breadth of 75 feet, it was the largest building under one roof in Michigan.[30] Concrete-slab girder-beam construction was prevalent throughout, although mushroom construction was adopted in later units. Steel sash, which it was then necessary to import from England, was utilized for the first time.[7] The vast expanse of glass, interrupted only by the exposed concrete framework, created a novel effect. Apparently Kahn felt that some type of formal treatment was required to relieve the monotony of the façade. Therefore he faced corner bastions and first floor piers with brick and added the suggestion of a cornice at the roof level. In later practice he was to eliminate these minor concessions to academic tradition.

The original group of buildings was completed in 1914. Centered in front of *(205)* the main building was the monumental power plant with its five tall smokestacks which for so long were a landmark on north Woodward avenue. Nearby and also facing Woodward was the handsome four-story concrete and brick office *(207)* building in which Ford's own office was located. Behind the main building and paralleling it was a one-story machine shop 840 x 140 feet with a saw-tooth roof. Joined together by a skylight-roofed crane-way 860 x 57 feet, the main building and the machine shop functioned as one unit without division walls. This was a realization of Ford's concept of a complete factory under one roof. A foundry 300 x 200 feet obviated dependence on outside sources for steel castings. Thereafter units were continuously added until the plant covered 180 acres.

The story of the Highland Park plant was one of the most brilliant chapters in American industrial history. Here mass production techniques were perfected as never before and here the moving assembly line was first introduced. Such an emphasis upon efficiency led inevitably to the reduction of production costs. That such a consequence was turned to public benefit may be attributed to a social conscience on the part of the management that was peculiarly American. The institution of the five-dollar day in 1914 was an unprecedented demonstration of advanced labor policy, but the most significant contribution of the Ford Motor Company was the impetus it gave to the democratization of the automobile. In so doing it transcended the boundaries of mere business enterprise to become a factor in the transformation of modern life.[31]

In the meantime a vigorous new architecture had risen almost automatically in response to the complex and varied requirements of a large-scaled industry. Yet such an astonishing architectural revolution might never have taken place without the guiding genius of a single man. To an extraordinary degree the necessary imagination, organizational ability, scientific knowledge, and understanding of functional and human needs were combined in the person of Albert Kahn.

The Skyscraper Comes of Age

Just as the emergence of the modern factory may be identified with the growth of the automobile industry in Detroit, so the evolution of the skyscraper was a direct consequence of the commercial development of Chicago. Facilitated by improved building techniques and services, both types of buildings were an expression of the acceleration of American economic life. The old architecture of static masonry had given way to a new modular system of construction based on the steel or concrete skeleton. The subsequent increase in scale brought with it unprecedented problems of planning and design.

In designing the earliest of skyscrapers the architects of Chicago clung persistently to the long-established concept of the 'mercantile palace' and attempted to disguise the unwonted height and bulk of the new giants with traditional architectural forms. It was not until the last decade of the nineteenth century that any serious study was devoted to the aesthetic aspect of the skyscraper. Outstanding among those who contributed to a solution of the problem was the now-famous architect Louis Sullivan. In a series of distinguished architectural monuments he was able to demonstrate convincingly that utilitarianism in itself could be a valid basis for the design of buildings independently of any preconceived academic formulas. In so doing he was able to lead the way out of the chaos of eclecticism toward a new form suitable for the towering commercial structures of the modern city.

In his Wainwright Building (1890–91) in St. Louis a simple external grille of soaring unbroken piers and spandrels frankly and dramatically expressed the underlying structure of the steel frame. The ornamentation, limited to a textural treatment of surfaces, in no way vitiated the structural integrity of the design. His Guaranty Building (1895) in Buffalo utilized red terra cotta on the exterior. First introduced by Burnham and Root, this lightweight material served merely as an external sheathing since the internal skeleton had assumed the load-bearing function. Sullivan's Gage Building (1899) in Chicago went even further in the reduction of the brown terra-cotta exterior to the minimum necessary to provide a casing for the skeleton. This permitted the expansion of the windows into continuous strips. A band of translucent glass was introduced at the top of the windows to reduce the glare.[32]

Throughout the Midwest Sullivan's work was a vital stimulus to the younger generation of architects. In Detroit, Stratton and Baldwin were unmistakably influenced by the Gage Building when they built the J. Sparling and Company *(206)* store on Woodward avenue in 1906. Its clean-cut functional lines make a startling contrast with the cast-iron grandiosity of the old Parker Block directly *(127)* adjacent. Both buildings are now occupied by the B. Siegel Company store.

The firm of Stratton and Baldwin was the first in Michigan to be made up of men trained in American architectural schools.[33] William B. Stratton, a native of Ithaca, New York, acquired his early education in Elmira and received his B.S. in architecture at Cornell University in 1881. Frank C. Baldwin was born at Galesburg, Illinois, attended St. Paul's School, Concord, New Hampshire, and completed a three-year course at the Massachusetts Institute of Technology in 1890. Both men moved to Detroit and became partners in 1893, Baldwin having worked briefly in the office of John Scott. Although trained in design and draftsmanship, Baldwin became the administrator of the firm. The partnership was dissolved in 1911 when Baldwin moved to Fredericksburg, Virginia, and established an office in Washington, D. C. Arthur K. Hyde and D. J. V. Snyder were associated with Stratton during different periods after Baldwin's removal to Washington.[34]

Another Detroit building which recalls the Gage Building is the D. J. Healy *(208)* Company store (1910) on Woodward avenue. Designed by Postle and Mahler of Chicago, it was constructed of reinforced concrete with cream-colored terra-cotta facing.[35] Although the building is Sullivanian in its general aspect, nevertheless the cornice and friezes are Renaissance in character.

The firm of Baxter, O'Dell and Halpin was also influenced by Sullivan in the design for the T. B. Rayl Company building erected in 1915 on the corner of Woodward and Grand River avenues.[36] The red terra-cotta exterior with its rich surface ornament, the slender piers terminating in arcades, and the cavetto cornice harked back to Sullivan's Guaranty Building (1895) in Buffalo. Unfortunately, however, the building has suffered from the demands of modern merchandizing, as the windows of the lower stories have been filled in with tiles.

(210)

The question now arises as to what influence, if any, Sullivan had upon Albert Kahn. Undoubtedly Kahn must have admired the great Chicago master, but he was too independent a thinker ever to be purely imitative. Certainly the same principle of functionalism was operative in the design of Kahn's factories as in the design of Sullivan's office buildings, but this was probably more the result of the demands of enlightened clients than of any outside stimulus. That a rapport existed between the two men is borne out by the fact that early in his career Kahn was actually offered the position of chief draftsman in Sullivan's office. Fortunately for Michigan and the future of industrial architecture, the offer was turned down on the grounds that the pay was insufficient for the support of a family of ten.[37]

Although these two great titans of architecture had much in common, there was also much to differentiate them. Admittedly, Kahn never attained Sullivan's stature as an architectural philosopher, for he was far too busy all his life to be able to devote much time to solitary meditation. Unlike Sullivan, he was not a consistent modernist, as he was forever torn between his admiration of the past and his vision of the future. In the matter of ornament Sullivan characteristically turned for inspiration to the pages of Gray's *Botany*, while Kahn drew on more conventional architectural sources. The many sketches of architectural details which he made on his trip to Europe in 1891 are a testimony of his respect for fine craftsmanship. This antiquarian interest was greatly strengthened by his exposure early in life to such men as Henry Bacon Jr. and George D. Mason. On the other hand, the problems which he faced in industrial architecture demanded direct straightforward solutions which, by their very nature, defied historical precedent. Thus during his entire career he was to oscillate between two poles. Yet, in spite of his prodigious output and the encyclopedic diversity of his styles, there is everywhere a sense of dignity and simplicity tempered by intelligent judgment and sensitivity. To the student of architecture the early years of the twentieth century are perhaps the most interesting period in his career, for it was then that a rationalist impulse originating in his early innovations in industrial architecture was to permeate the entire range of his work.

During his lifetime Kahn did a considerable amount of commercial work in Detroit. His Trussed Concrete Building (1907) was the first office building of concrete construction in the city.[38] Located on the northeast corner of Lafayette boulevard and Wayne, it was an eight-story structure with white brick piers, metal spandrels, and a large overhanging cornice supported on paired brackets. Later known as the Owen Building, it was torn down in 1957 to make way for the widening of Wayne street, which is now an extension of Washington boulevard.[39] It was the headquarters of both Albert and Julius Kahn early in their careers. Although they were the heads of two different organizations, they had one consuming purpose in common, the formulation of a new architecture based on concrete construction. A vivid description of the two brothers, which appeared in the *Detroit News Tribune* at about this time, gives an illuminating insight into their characters and objectives:

Julius, the engineer, is the complement of Albert, the architect. He is quick, restless, eager, while Albert is graceful and well-poised. Julius bears the lines of hard work and encounter with the world. He drives himself as a master does his horse. He broods and studies, he probes and speculates. The restless nature of the man is clearly indicated in his appearance. It would be impossible for him to assume the more rotund, comfortable, artistic, physical poise of Albert. Julius is the doer. It is he, indeed, who has set his name upon the monolithic structures that are now being reared on pillars and beams of concrete.

And all the while, Albert, the artist, admires his brother, "the man who does things." He contemplates the gaunt skeletons reared in concrete by the intrepid Julius, who spans distances with poured beams. Albert pictures them as adorned with lines and forms and colorings. He is trying to do for the new structural exterior what Julius has done for the skeleton.

"So long as the lines of the building indicate that there is behind them a sustaining skeleton, and so long as they do not mask the reality and pretend to be themselves the sustaining material, there is no offense," said Albert Kahn, himself. "We must learn to treat concrete as concrete, but to construct concrete pillars and cornices, concrete walls and buttresses so that they will advertise the fact that they are concrete and so that they will still be beautiful." Nevertheless he was not without his doubts. "It is a trying problem," he confessed. "Concrete presents many discouragements to the architects. Its ugly surfaces and its lack of fine edge make it a difficult material." Then with characteristic Kahn spirit he added: "But it is a great deal more interesting to study the artistic uses for concrete than it is to follow in some old beaten paths. It is difficult, that is why it interests us"[20]

(207) The commission in 1909 to build an office building in front of the Ford Highland Park plant gave Kahn an opportunity to put into practice his theories. The factory and office buildings were of similar concrete construction, but different in architectural treatment. The former, simple and unadorned, was adapted to large-scaled manufacturing; while the latter, more elegantly appointed, was scaled-down to correspond with the more limited spatial requirements of executives and office workers. The façade of the office building was composed of exposed concrete piers with iron spandrels. The end bays were of red brick. Ornament consisted of a frieze of glazed blueish-green tiles below the cornice and bands of similar tiles on the spandrels of the brick bays. There were also ornamental iron railings in front of the windows. Originally the building was only two stories in height, but later two more floors were added.

In 1910 Kahn placed a two-story office building in front of the Hudson Motor Car Company on East Jefferson avenue. The exterior surface was of stucco with green glazed tiles framing the entrance and forming decorative accents on the walls.[41] In 1931 the building was lengthened and covered with limestone veneer.

Exposed concrete or stucco may have been satisfactory for an extensive industrial site, but when faced with the problem of the office building in downtown Detroit, Kahn preferred a more finished surface. White glazed terra cotta was his choice for the Grinnell Building (1908) on Woodward avenue. The similarity of the material to classic white stone led him to favor Renaissance ornamental motifs. Iron spandrels and window railings, however, followed the pattern of those previously noted on the Ford office building. White terra cotta

(216) piers and iron spandrels were again featured on the Woodward Building (1915) located on the southwest corner of Woodward avenue and Clifford street. Here

Kahn made evident a tendency toward bold transparency and an increasing restraint and delicacy of detail.

In 1910 Kahn built the former Ford Sales Office, now known as the Boulevard Building, on the northeast corner of Woodward and Grand boulevard. Originally the building was only half its present height, but in 1913 four stories were added.[42] The entire exterior was faced with white glazed terra cotta. Ornament having been reduced to the minimum, piers and spandrels amounted to little more than a uniform casing for the concrete frame. Thus the purely functional ideal was approximated. Possibly because of its association with the automobile industry, this building seemed to be linked with Kahn's industrial work wherein the modular unit was the common denominator. One may look even further for an analogy with the order, precision, and mechanical repetition of the industrial system itself. When the glazed terra cotta began to deteriorate recently, the building was resurfaced with stone in horizontal bands, thereby completely altering its appearance. *(211)*

It would be tempting to draw a comparison between the Boulevard Building and Sullivan's Carson, Pirie and Scott Store (1904) in Chicago, but one must turn to the Finsterwald Building (1919) on the northwest corner of Washington boulevard and Michigan avenue for more recognizable Sullivanian characteristics. Here corner piers were enlarged to give definition to the outline of the building, and the pairing of windows was abandoned in favor of a uniform treatment. Piers were buff-colored brick with matching terra-cotta spandrels and frieze. In contrast to the botanical ornament of Sullivan, Kahn chose a more architectonic diaper pattern for the terra-cotta work. *(209)*

In spite of certain similarities in their styles, it is well to remember that Kahn, as an industrial architect, was accustomed to working with concrete, whereas Sullivan's experience in commercial work had been entirely with steel. In buildings over eight stories high concrete was not only impractical but uneconomical. Kahn showed his versatility by changing over to steel construction in his taller buildings. An example is the ten-story former Free Press Building (1911–13) on Lafayette boulevard.[43] For many years known as the Transportation Building, it has recently been renamed the Canadian National and Grand Trunk Building. The design of the white terra-cotta façade conformed to Sullivan's concept of vertical continuity, even though details were derived from Gothic and Renaissance sources. By 1914 Kahn was building the eighteen-story Kresge Building, now the Kales Building, on the northeast corner of Adams avenue and Park street. Faced with white brick, it is simpler and more straightforward in design than the former Free Press Building.

During this period some of the most important commissions in Detroit fell to the Chicagoan, Daniel H. Burnham; for, although Kahn was the acknowledged authority in the field of industrial architecture, Burnham's prestige as a designer of skyscrapers was difficult to challenge. Not only was he the head of a firm that could boast of probably the largest architectural practice in the United States, but he had also been chief consulting architect at the Chicago World's Fair of 1893.[44] Then, too, Detroiters could scarcely forget that he was the architect of one of the city's most imposing commercial monuments, the Majestic Building. *(178)*

Burnham's eighteen-story Ford Building, erected in 1909 on the northwest corner of Griswold and Congress streets, made it clear that he had irrevocably renounced the Romanesque. That he was already affected by the wave of classicism from the East was indicated by a few minor classical details. By and large, however, he followed the Chicago tradition by expressing the steel frame with the clean sharp lines of the white terra-cotta facing. *(213)*

(212)

(215)

Soon therafter Burnham designed two more somewhat similar office buildings in Detroit. Classical detail is slightly more in evidence in the Dime Building of 1910.[45] Located on the northwest corner of Griswold and Fort streets, it was U-shaped above the lower stories for the admission of light. The David Whitney Building (1915) on Grand Circus Park was intended for doctors and dentists. Corridors face an inside court, thus permitting an outside exposure for all offices. The Italian Renaissance provided motifs for the architectural ornament on the exterior.

This increasingly archeological detail was an indication of the decline of the impact of the Chicago school in Detroit. Further evidence of this tendency may be noted in the recurrence of literal Gothic motifs in the Real Estate Exchange Building (1918), now the Cadillac Square Building, on Cadillac Square. Louis Kamper, the architect, was undoubtedly influenced by Cass Gilbert's Woolworth Tower (1911–13) in New York, but in comparison to the carefully studied integration of design of the New York mammoth, the application of Gothic ornament by Kamper seems superficial and misapplied.

The last of the larger skyscrapers to retain something of the membranous exterior and simplicity of outline inherited from Chicago was the forty-story Barlum Tower (1927), now called the Cadillac Tower, also on Cadillac Square. Although they used some diluted Gothic details, architects Bonnah and Chaffee of Detroit relied upon color for the main decorative effect, the top five stories being sheathed in gold terra cotta in contrast to the white terra cotta of the lower stories.

But to speak only of the important office buildings of this period in Detroit is to overlook a large number of excellent smaller commercial buildings which, because of the limitations of time and space, must remain unnoticed. It should be pointed out, however, that much of their merit stems from the influence of the Chicago school. Mostly of white brick or terra cotta, they may be easily recognized by their generous window areas and functional simplicity. But regardless of size or importance, the commercial buildings of this era have stood the test of time, and their adaptability to modern usage is as good a proof as any that almost fifty years ago American commercial architecture had come of age.

The Halls of Learning

It may be recalled that one of Albert Kahn's first experiments with reinforced concrete was the Engineering Building (1902) in Ann Arbor. In the second decade of the century he was called upon to design several more buildings for the University of Michigan. By then he had already become one of the leading practitioners in concrete with a great wealth of experience behind him. The quiet landscaped setting of the campus, far removed from the bustle of commerce, was the ideal milieu in which to bring to fruition his ideas concerning the aesthetic treatment of the new concrete architecture.

In 1912 Kahn went on a vacation trip in Europe. As usual he carried his sketch pad with him and recorded anything that happened to appeal to him visually. On this trip he seemed to have been particularly attracted by the beautiful brickwork of the old palaces of Siena and Bologna, for he made detailed annotations on the margins of his sketches as to the size and placement of the bricks. Although most of his studies were done in pencil, the arcade of San Stefano in Bologna inspired him to do a watercolor rendering. Only thus could he capture the subtle patina of the reddish-brown brick ornamented with insets of terra cotta.[46] This warm, mellow surface quality was precisely what he needed to humanize the raw concrete skeletons of his buildings.

His experiences at Bologna proved invaluable when designing the brickwork of the Hill Auditorium in Ann Arbor (1913).[47] A rich veneer of brick and tile *(218)* provided a contrasting frame for the monumental stone colonnade of the entrance façade. Here classical formality prevailed, but not without a considerable freedom in the handling of details. On the east side of the building Kahn went a *(219)* step further in the abandonment of orthodoxy, for in the treatment of the tiers of vertical windows separated by brick piers there was already a suggestion of Sullivan and Frank Lloyd Wright. On the interior a parabolic plan with the speaker's stand at the focal point assured the maximum in acoustical advantages.

Because of its highly specialized function, the Hill Auditorium stands out as an anomaly in the chronology of Kahn's work, but his Natural Science Building *(221)* (1916) signalized a return to the more familiar modular unit system noted earlier in his industrial and commercial practice. After all, the concrete skeleton with its dematerialized walls was admirably suited to almost any type of working space. There is thus a distinct family resemblance between the Natural Science Building and the Ford office building in Highland Park, or even the Ford Highland *(207)* Park plant itself. Of course Kahn was not insensible to the difference in charac- *(200)* ter between an industrial site and a university campus. Accordingly, the concrete frame, so openly exposed in Highland Park, in Ann Arbor retreated behind exquisitely patterned brick with stone and terra-cotta trim.

Functional simplicity was again the keynote of Kahn's General Library *(220)* (1919).[48] Here a colored terra-cotta frieze and medallions in the spandrels provided accents against the fine brickwork. It is interesting to compare this building with the Widener Library (1913–14) at Harvard University by Horace Trumbauer. Absent is the oppressive ostentation of Trumbauer's Corinthian colonnade across the façade and his grand staircase on the interior. Kahn's one concession to the prevailing taste for Renaissance splendor is the coffered barrel vault in the main reading room. In the two lunettes formed by this vault there are murals by Gari Melchers, The Arts of Peace and The Arts of War.

These three buildings by Kahn for the University of Michigan were products of one of his most creative periods. It is a tribute to him that even today they are outstanding for their usefulness, simplicity, dignity, and charm. Without being imitative, he was able to combine various elements from the past and present and forge them into a living architecture.

The Rationalization of Domestic Architecture

That Albert Kahn was a man of conviction is borne out by an amusing anecdote concerning the provision of a doll's house for his daughter Lydia. None of these miniature dwellings on the market at the time conformed to his idea of simple straightforward architecture purged of extraneous anachronisms. Therefore he was not satisfied until one was specially made that suited his taste and consequently would not lead his daughter astray in the formation of hers.[49] Such scruples over a doll's house were indicative of Kahn's renewed interest in domestic architecture. Since a sense of rational order and restraint was manifest in his industrial and commercial work, it is not surprising that he should have found in the Georgian or Colonial style a suitable point of departure for his residential work. As the relatively smaller scale of houses obviated the use of steel or concrete frames, the brick wall assumed its traditional role as a bearing member. Concrete, however, was still used for floor construction.

A growing suburban movement in Detroit offered unprecedented opportunities for a fresh approach toward the design of houses. The newly-perfected automobile, bringing with it improved highways, permitted businessmen to seek out permanent home sites in verdant landscapes far from the din of the city. Grosse Pointe was a popular choice because of its magnificent waterfront on Lake St. Clair. In 1903–04 Jefferson avenue was paved from the Waterworks in Detroit to Fisher road in Grosse Pointe. This was all that was needed to facilitate the gradual but inevitable conversion of an isolated summer resort into a thriving suburb.

(214)
(185) The increasing importance of the local Country Club of Detroit as the social center of the Grosse Pointe community necessitated the erection of a new brick clubhouse in 1907 on the original site on the lake south of Lake Shore road.[50] Considerable perspicacity was shown in the selection of Kahn as architect, for no one but a man of his imaginative endowments could have responded so admirably to the beauty of the surroundings. Without indulging in the pretentious or the falsely picturesque, he was able to combine monumental simplicity with informal charm.

The clubhouse was approached from Lake Shore road on the north by a driveway that skirted a broad stretch of lawn. The massive brick structure was flanked at each end by projecting bays, while at the center was an ample porte-cochere. At the western end of the building a recessed porch overlooked the tennis courts. Facing the lake on the south, a covered glass-enclosed veranda extended the full length of the building. This was interrupted at the center by a two-story portico with brick piers. Although the general character and details of the clubhouse were vaguely colonial, a suggestion of the shingle style persisted in the interplay of projecting and recessed verandas and in the treatment of the hipped roof and dormers. The sudden accessibility of Grosse Pointe caused such a rise in land values that only four years after the completion of the clubhouse
(303) the adjoining golf course had to be moved further out to its present location. In 1926 a new clubhouse was built next to the relocated golf course. The old
(279) building was demolished and in 1934 Mrs. Horace E. Dodge built her present house on the site.

Although Kahn's country club was not, strictly speaking, an example of domestic architecture, nevertheless it was closely related in style to some of the houses he was building at the time. His preoccupation with vast industrial projects left him little time for residential work, but he was willing to accede to the demands of his major clients to create a setting for their private lives. In 1910 he
(224) built a house for Henry B. Joy on Lake Shore road in Grosse Pointe. Here unaffected simplicity and livability were combined to produce a very modern effect. Ample fenestration permitted all the principal rooms to take full advantage of the magnificent southern exposure toward the lake. This was especially true of the glass-enclosed sun room in the west wing. The horizontal lines and the mild reference to Georgian precedent harked back to the country club, but the increasing regimentation of larger and more uniform window openings suggested an analogy to Kahn's industrial and commercial work. This homogeneity of building types represented a very early manifestation of the integration of architectural expression in Detroit.

The design of the Joy house reflected the personality of its owner. In the life of Henry B. Joy there were no artificial barriers but a harmonious balance between business activities and personal interests. Progress and civic betterment were the goals toward which he strove. The development of the Packard Motor Car Company, of which he became president, was largely the result of his enterprise, and it was he who employed Albert Kahn in 1905 to build the first *(202)* reinforced concrete factory in Detroit. Just as his father James F. Joy had promoted the westward expansion of the railroad, so the younger Joy was a leader in the movement to span the continent with an improved highway. As first president of the Lincoln Highway Association, organized in 1913, he made seven trips across the country seeking the ideal route.[51]

The atmosphere of the ranch which Joy built near Mt. Clemens on Lake St. Clair recalled the hearty outdoor life he had enjoyed so much in the Far West.[52] There he established a bird sanctuary. His interest in the newly-perfected radio prompted him to become an amateur radio broadcaster.[53] By this means he could keep in touch with his office in Detroit whether he was at his ranch or on his yacht gliding through the St. Lawrence River to his summer home at Watch Hill, Rhode Island.[54] In her own way Mrs. Helen Joy also was a remarkable person. The daughter of John S. Newberry, she followed in the footsteps of her parents in tirelessly pleading the cause of innumerable civic organizations. Outliving her husband by more than two decades, the lively white-haired lady, even in her eighties, was a familiar sight driving her 1914 electric automobile around Grosse Pointe. On longer trips to the city in her Packard limousine she kept herself busy at a desk which she had installed in the car.[55] Her death in 1958 marked the passing of an era.

In 1912 Kahn built a house on Lake Shore road for Senator McMillan's son *(223)* Philip H. McMillan, a director of the Packard Motor Car Company and its largest stockholder.[56] Gone was the expansiveness of the Joy house. Windows assumed their normal Georgian proportions and on the ground floor conventional French doors opened on a broad terrace overlooking the lake. Hollow tile faced with stucco replaced brick on the exterior walls. All was serenity and understatement, saved from monotony by a muted note of classicism introduced by a denticulated cornice, a stringcourse breaking the wall surface, and a Doric peristyle surrounding the sun porch.[57] It was evident that Kahn's domestic architecture had acquired a certain polish without sacrificing its basic rationality.

The Fremont Woodruff house (1917) by George D. Mason is somewhat *(217)* similar to the McMillan house. Located on Jefferson avenue in Grosse Pointe, it also overlooks the lake. Both houses were built of hollow tile faced with stucco, but here the roofing was gray slate instead of red tile. A parallelism has been noted already between the industrial architecture of Mason and Kahn, and here a similar approach may be noted in their domestic work.

The automobile, in addition to facilitating suburban life, also was the means of escape to the remote countryside where weekend retreats doubled as summer cottages. Albert Kahn himself was among the first in Detroit to enjoy this type of nomadic existence. In 1916–17 he built a little frame house for his family on *(222)* Walnut Lake in Oakland County north of Detroit. In Grosse Pointe he had succeeded in opening up houses to the sunshine and the outdoors. Now the light frame construction of a more or less temporary dwelling permitted him to go even further in this direction. One summer, when visiting their daughter at a summer camp in Massachusetts, the Kahns stayed at the Weldon Hotel in Greenfield. Their room was located in a recent top floor addition which took advantage of the summer breezes by means of a continuous band of windows. This arrangement pleased Kahn so much that he was determined to incorporate it in his new summer home.[49] In doing this he provided two floors surrounded by continuous casement windows. The effect of horizontality thus achieved was further emphasized by two lateral screened porches extending out into the landscape. In the final analysis he reached the same point with the wood frame that he had with the concrete frame in his factories. In the reduction of wall surfaces to a minimum he achieved the ultimate realization of a structure almost totally enclosed in glass in modular units. Thereby he created what was doubtless the most advanced residential design of his career.

It is not difficult to detect in the house at Walnut Lake certain characteristics of the Prairie style, that indigenous expression of domestic life that had been evolved in the environs of Chicago. The flattening out of the roof to conform to the lines of the terrain, the unbroken horizontal sweep of the windows, and the intimate communication between the house and its surroundings—all held forth the promise that Kahn was ready to embark on a new phase of his career that would establish a link between his work and a movement that was to revolutionize the concept of the American home. As subsequent residences that Kahn designed clearly indicate, this was not the case. His reverence for traditional domestic architecture was so deep-rooted that he felt that adventurous experimentation should be confined to such relatively inconsequential work as the cottage at Walnut Lake. Detroit architects as a whole were not receptive to the Prairie style, and Kahn was no exception. Furthermore, he had chosen industrial leaders as clients, and these men were more inclined to emulate their Eastern counterparts by surrounding themselves with the splendors of bygone days. It was not likely that he would again have the opportunity of building a house for a man as progressive in his concept of home environment as Henry B. Joy. Thus inevitably the path led toward an increasing antiquarianism.

At this point it is well to remember that Kahn was primarily an industrial architect. In the perspective of time it is becoming apparent that he did for the factory what Sullivan did for the skyscraper and what Frank Lloyd Wright did for the private residence. Yet, unlike the work of the two Chicagoans, his factories were not the product of a mystical philosophy. Rather, they seemed to spring into being, like some gigantic natural phenomena, as a direct response to the pressing demands of a relentlessly expanding economy.

Even the egocentric Wright recognized the importance of Kahn's achievement. In 1953 when Lydia Kahn Winston was attending an exhibition of Wright's work at the Guggenheim Museum in New York, she recognized the great master himself among the visitors. Introducing herself she explained that she was the daughter of his friend, the late Albert Kahn. With the look of an ancient seer making a pronouncement, Frank Lloyd Wright declared, "He was a great man."[49]

(200) Ford Highland Park Plant, *A. Kahn*, 1909 (AKA)

(201) Ford Piquette Avenue Plant, *Field, Hinchman & Smith*, 1904 (FMC)

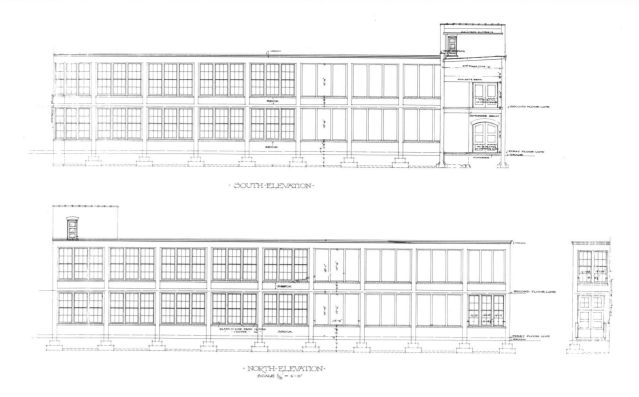

· SOUTH · ELEVATION ·

· NORTH · ELEVATION ·
SCALE ⅛" = 1'-0"

(202-204) Packard Building No. 10, *A. Kahn*, 1905 (AKA)

(204) Packard Building No. 10

(205) Ford Highland Park Plant, *A. Kahn*, 1909-14 (AKA)

(206) J. Sparling & Co., *Stratton & Baldwin*, 1906 (DIA)

(207) Ford Highland Park Plant Offices,
A. Kahn, 1909 (HAL)

(208) D. J. Healy Co., *Postle & Mahler*,
1910 (MB)

(209) Finsterwald Building,
A. Kahn, 1919 (MB)

(210) T. B. Rayl Co., *Baxter,*
O'Dell & Halpin, 1915 (MB)

(211) Boulevard Building, *A. Kahn*, 1913 (MB)

(212) Dime Building, *D. H. Burnham*, 1910 (MB)

(213) Ford Building, *D. H. Burnham*, 1909 (MB)

(214) Country Club of Detroit, *A. Kahn*, 1907 (BHC/SL)

(215) David Whitney Building, *D. H. Burnham*, 1915 (MB)   (216) Woodward Building, *A. Kahn*, 1915 (MB)

(217) Fremont Woodruff House, *G. D. Mason*, 1917 (FD)

(222) Albert Kahn House, *A. Kahn*, 1917 (AKA)

(221) Natural Science Building, *A. Kahn*, 1916 (HAL)

(223) Philip H. McMillan House, *A. Kahn*, 1912 (A

(224) Henry B. Joy House, *A. Kahn*, 1910 (MB)

7. The Renaissance
and Classicism

Academic Eclecticism

If H. H. Richardson and Louis Sullivan did not feel that the classicism to which they had been exposed at the École des Beaux-Arts was appropriate for the United States, their views were not necessarily shared by the many American architectural students who flocked to the French seat of learning in the latter part of the nineteenth century. This renewed contact with Europe brought with it a feeling of frustration over the raw brutality of the American scene, and kindled a missionary zeal to counteract it with the canons of a tradition that had met the test of time. There had been entirely too much freedom and improvisation in American architecture, they felt, and it could well afford a greater discipline of plan and an insistence on more accurate historical detail. Richard Morris Hunt and Charles Follen McKim, both products of Beaux-Arts training, and Stanford White, who became McKim's partner, were the leaders of a movement to bring about an American Renaissance.

Architectural schools had multiplied in America, beginning in 1866 with the Department of Architecture at the Massachusetts Institute of Technology. These schools, offspring of the École des Beaux-Arts, turned out an increasing number of youthful classicists.[1] The architect's traditional sketching tour of Europe assumed a new importance now that detailing became more literally imitative, and whenever sketchbooks were found wanting, recourse could be had to the libraries of illustrated books which became the necessary concomitants of every architectural office.

Now that America was tied together by railroads, the profits from industry and the exploitation of natural resources were mounting at an astonishing rate. In those taxless days individual annual incomes frequently ran into millions.[2] Not burdened by the accumulative exertions of their forebears, sons and grandsons of founders of family fortunes had more leisure to think about outlets for their affluence. It was the heyday of conspicuous consumption. Matters of taste became paramount, for it was all too obvious that there was room for improvement. Photographs and increased travel had made American millionaires more aware of the man-made grandeur of Europe, and soon French châteaux and Italian palaces were throwing into shadow the rows of dreary brownstone fronts in New York and crowding out the earlier frame cottages at Newport. To employ Hunt or McKim, Mead and White as architects was not only a guarantee of the best in quality, but it was also the surest route to social recognition.

Reform spread from exteriors to interiors. No one was more voluble than Edith Wharton in espousing the new cause. Sounding the doom of the cluttered Victorian interior, she extolled the virtues of the laws of harmony and proportion as practiced by the architect-decorators of old.[3] Stanford White, perhaps more than any other architect, was able to live up to her ideals. He was fortunate in having clients who were able to indulge his taste for lavish interiors. In order to furnish their houses he was accustomed to make periodic European raids, bringing home carved doorways, mantels, furniture, rugs, and tapestries. When reproached for his depredations, he vindicated himself by maintaining dominant nations had always plundered works of art from their predecessors.

Creating an aristocratic background for businessmen was too much of a temptation for most architects of the period and they found themselves little by little taking on the elegant mode of living of their clients. Stanford White was no exception. His house in New York was replete with drawing room, music room, and picture gallery, all furnished in the ornate manner of the Italian Renaissance. He could even boast of a country estate on Long Island.[4] It was a world designed for the cultivated gentleman in which an artistic indiscretion was as much a heresy as a social blunder. To console social conscience Edith Wharton observed, "Every good moulding, every carefully studied detail, exacted by those who can afford to indulge their taste, will in time find its way to the carpenter-built cottage. Once the right precedent is established, it costs less to follow than to oppose it."[5]

The premise having been agreed upon that archeological verisimilitude was *sine qua non*, architects were left no choice but to follow out the full gamut of elegant styles. Italian, French, and English Renaissance designs enjoyed a prolonged vogue. The World's Columbian Exposition of 1893 at Chicago did much to encourage a return to ancient Roman sources. Even the Tudor and Gothic were exploited with renewed vigor and enthusiasm. From coast to coast America was becoming a veritable museum of spurious antiquities. This is not to deny, however, that some architects were extraordinarily dexterous in adapting their buildings to contemporary needs and that some were even able to rise to the heights of consummate artistry.

Be that as it may, the passage of time brought a growing awareness of the negative aspects of the American Renaissance, not the least of which was the temporary eclipse into which it put the pioneering efforts of such men as Louis Sullivan and Frank Lloyd Wright. Toward the end of his life Sullivan was a defeated and embittered man. The American Renaissance had been his Waterloo. In his autobiography, written in 1922, he mercilessly vilified the existing status of the architectural profession:

All sense of reality has gone. In its place has come deep-seated illusions, hallucinations, absence of papillary reaction to light, absence of knee-action—symptoms all of progressive cerebral meningitis: The blanketing of the brain. Thus architecture died in the land of the free and the home of the brave—in a land declaring its fervid democracy, its inventiveness, its resourcefulness, its unique daring, enterprise and progress. Thus did the virus of a culture, snobbish and alien to the land, perform its work of disintegration; and thus ever works the pallid academic mind, denying the real, exalting the fictitious and the false, incapable of adjusting itself to the flow of living things; to the reality and the pathos of man's follies, to the valiant hope that ever causes him to aspire, and again to aspire; that never lifts a hand in aid because it cannot; that turns its back upon man because that is its tradition; a culture lost in ghostly mésalliance *with abstractions, when what the world needs is courage, common sense and human sympathy, and a moral standard that is plain, valid and livable.*

The damage wrought by the World's Fair will last for half a century from its date, if not longer. It has penetrated deep into the constitution of the American mind, effecting there lesions significant of dementia.[6]

The Italian Renaissance: Public and Commercial Buildings

In writing a biography of Charles Follen McKim, Charles Moore seems to have been unaware that the American Renaissance was anything but a glorious achievement. Having been one of its most active though less renowned supporters and having been closely associated with its leading protagonists, he could scarcely have thought otherwise. He states in the biography:

It was no mere worship of architectural forms, however beautiful in themselves, that sent Charles McKim back to the Italian Renaissance. It was rather because that particular architecture best expressed the things of the intellect and the imagination, and, above all, "the ethical qualities of which the Renaissance was a consummate type." It represented good order and proportion and balance, and those eternal verities that are the very essence of beauty—the qualities that make for good living and right thinking, and that produce the permanent satisfaction of life.[7]

The classicizing tendency of McKim, Mead and White began to be apparent during the period of their preoccupation with the Colonial Revival, but it is understandable that this provincial ramification of classicism could not be the ultimate goal.[8] In their search for the best models they became convinced that Italian architecture of the sixteenth century was the supreme manifestation of the ideal. The firm's first creation in the new manner was the Villard house (1885) in New York, which was an adaptation of a Roman palace.[9] Boston followed suit with a commission for the Boston Public Library in 1887. In New York one triumph followed another—the Herald Building (1894), the University Club (1899), the Morgan Library and the Tiffany Building (1906). A resurrection of sixteenth century Rome, Florence, and Venice in New York gave it a splendor that it had never known before. Soon the rest of the continent, which had so recently wrested itself from the wilderness, was demanding the architectural sophistries of an ancient civilization.

In Detroit, George D. Mason, always so eager to keep abreast of the times, lost no time in declaring his allegiance to the new revival. It was a moment when his architectural library proved invaluable; but what was even more pertinent, considering his somewhat limited education, was his ability to surround himself in his office with a group of very talented young architects who were well versed in the new vocabulary—William Reed-Hill, George Nettleton, and Alexander B. Trowbridge—the last-mentioned having been educated at Cornell University and the École des Beaux-Arts.[10]

Mason was fortunate in having as one of his principal clients Hiram Walker, the owner of the distillery that bore his name, for he was a man responsive to the beauties both of nature and of architecture. The industrial and agricultural empire which he had carved out of the Canadian shore opposite Detroit was already studded with masterpieces by Mason in the Romanesque style or its more rustic counterpart, the shingle style. Walker had the good taste to choose

(48) for his personal abode the fine Greek Revival house on Fort street in Detroit which had formerly belonged to Oliver Newberry. When he found the cares of business too oppressive, he could board his yacht the *Pastime* and sail for Peche Island, his mile-long insular retreat at the head of the Detroit River, where he could contemplate the vast network of canals which made the island into a latter-day Venice.[11]

(225) Such a predilection for marine life quite naturally led the manufacturer to select as a site for the offices of Hiram Walker and Sons a sloping riverbank in Walkerville that commanded a splendid view of Detroit and Belle Isle across the river. As his architect, Mason had no difficulty in persuading him that the location was ideal for an impressive monument in the Italian manner. The building was completed in 1892. The slope of the land left room for two extra stories on the side facing the river.[12] Here there was generous fenestration. The one-story façade toward the street demanded a more formal treatment and gave Mason an opportunity to recapture the somber dignity of the Palazzo Pandolfini in Florence with its rusticated entrance, balustrades, and alternating angular and segmental pediments above the windows.

(86) The destruction by fire of the Detroit Opera House in 1897 was a challenge to the architects of the city. Mason visualized a handsome Italian Renaissance building taking the place of the former structure on the Campus Martius. Nettleton, Kahn, and Trowbridge had left him in 1895 to set up an office of their own, so the task of evolving a design rested entirely upon his shoulders. Determined to receive the commission, he sought out the owner of the property, William B. Clark, who was then living in Colorado Springs. There he engaged a hotel room, improvised a drafting board, and set about making drawings. Favorably impressed by the results, Clark hired Mason as the architect of the new opera *(226)* house.[10] Like the offices of Hiram Walker and Sons, it was faced with brick and terra cotta. Employing Italian Renaissance details, Mason was able to give the façade a certain formal dignity in spite of the many shops and offices that it was necessary to incorporate in the building. Later the entire structure was converted into a department store which was demolished in 1966.

Like Mason, John Scott, the son of architect William Scott, fell under the spell of Italy. A native of Ipswich, England, he was thoroughly trained for professional practice before arriving in this country in the seventies. With his younger brother Arthur, he opened an office in Detroit under the firm name of John Scott and Company and for many years carried on an active practice in the city.[13] At the peak of his career William Reed-Hill, who was trained at the Boston Technical School, became his associate.[14]

(227) Scott was assigned the task of designing the Wayne County Building erected in 1896–1902 at the eastern end of Cadillac Square. Cost does not seem to have been a consideration. At the time it was unquestionably the most sumptuous building in Michigan and it remains today an outstanding monument of the 'Age of Elegance.' The cold Florentine restraint of the Hiram Walker and Sons offices gave way to a rather florid Roman Baroque. The ground and first floors were constructed of rusticated granite, while the upper three stories and tower were of Ohio sandstone. The main entrance was emphasized by a Corinthian portico approached by a broad flight of steps. The lofty square tower, enriched by a Corinthian colonnade, was terminated with a small cupola. The interior is aglow with every variety of imported and domestic marble.

It was an age in which the sister arts of architecture were receiving enthusiastic encouragement. This was reflected in the sculptural ornamentation of the Wayne County Building. Above and flanking the portico were placed two

heroic bronze quadrigas symbolizing Progress, the work of J. Massey Rhind of *(228)*
New York. At the four corners of the tower colonnade parapet were installed
single bronze figures representing Law, Commerce, Agriculture, and Mechan-
ics.[15] The pediment of the portico was decorated with a carved stone relief by
Edward Wagner of Detroit depicting eponymous "Mad Anthony" Wayne con-
ferring with the Indians. Born in Germany, Wagner had come to Detroit at an
early age, became a pupil of Julius Melchers, and later completed his studies in
New York.[16]

In 1897 John Scott designed the handsome Wayne County Jail, now demol- *(230)*
ished, on the corner of Clinton and Beaubien streets.[17] The fortress-like palaces
of Florence, denoting to Scott a sense of confinement, provided the basis for the
external treatment. In those plush days even the lives of prisoners were dignified
with fine stonework and careful architectural detail.

Banks have always been among the most substantial buildings in Detroit,
symbolizing the importance of economic life in the community. At a time when
matters of taste received so much consideration, the erection of an important
bank demanded the best architectural talents available. Built in 1900, the Peoples *(229)*
State Bank bears the distinction of being the only building in Detroit by the
famous firm of McKim, Mead and White. Located at the southeast corner of
Fort and Shelby streets, it now houses the Manufacturers National Bank of
Detroit. Stanford White's son tells us that his father took a leading part in its
creation.[18] Certainly it is not difficult to detect in the exquisite refinement of its
details and proportions the handiwork of the most gifted and fastidious of the
partners. Although faced with white marble inside and out, the broad arcades of
the windows admit plenty of light, and the restrained rationality of its design
makes it, even today, ideally suited for its purpose.

Donaldson and Meier, as associate architects, were responsible for the faithful
execution of the plans prepared by McKim, Mead and White for the bank.[19]
Having been trained at the École des Beaux-Arts, John M. Donaldson was in
familiar territory. However, during that period the bulk of the work of his firm
was different in character. The success of their Union Trust Building (1894–95) *(180)*
had established them as the leading skyscraper architects in Detroit. This led to
the commission for the original thirteen-story Penobscot Building (1905) on
Fort street and a later twenty-four story addition on Congress street (1916). As
might be expected, these buildings were overlaid with Italian Renaissance detail.

The ten-story Pontchartrain Hotel by George D. Mason received similar *(232)*
external treatment. Erected in 1907 to replace the old Russell House, it was *(106)*
located on the southeast corner of Cadillac Square and Woodward avenue. The
lower three floors were rusticated and the entrances were flanked by rusticated
Italianate columns. Above this the main mass of the building was too severely
plain to suit the prevailing taste. Accordingly, when five stories were added
above the cornice in 1916, a mansard roof with ornate dormers was superimposed.[20] Structurally the building differed from the work of Donaldson and
Meier, the Kahn system of reinforced concrete having been used throughout.[21]

Upon its completion the hotel assumed an important role in the social life of
the city. Gala events took place in the glow of Tiffany lighting fixtures amid a
forest of potted palms. But more important in the annals of civic history were
the fabulous financial transactions that transpired there.[22] The leaders of the
burgeoning automobile industry needed a common meeting ground where they
could make business contacts and exchange ideas. The bar of the hotel suited
their needs to perfection and they made it an important focal point of the
automotive world.[23] The history of the Hotel Pontchartrain, although brilliant,

was destined to be brief. Modern ideas were rapidly changing the concept of the American hotel. With less than four hundred guest rooms and only half of them with baths, the Pontchartrain soon became obsolete. In 1920 the property was *(266)* sold to the First National Bank and subsequently the hotel was razed to make way for a new bank building.[22]

When Ellsworth M. Statler, the owner of the Statler chain of hotels, decided *(231)* to build in Detroit, he was astute enough to realize that the fashionable retail business was moving uptown. Consequently he located his new hotel at Grand *(71)* Circus Park and Washington boulevard on the site of the old Bagley homestead. Designed by George B. Post of New York, it was opened in 1914. The eighteen-story building was efficiently planned. There were eight hundred guest rooms, each with a bath.[24] The subtle Italian architectural details with their strong Adam influence gave the hotel an atmosphere of *haut luxe*. A new standard of excellence for hotels was established in Detroit, hastening the decline of the old Pontchartrain.

George B. Post had been a pupil of Richard Morris Hunt. This in itself would have been a sufficient recommendation, but since then his career had been highlighted by such memorable landmarks as Cornelius Vanderbilt's French château on Fifth avenue in New York and the important Manufactures and Liberal Arts Building at the Chicago World's Fair of 1893. The Statler Hotel in Detroit proved that his abilities had not declined.

Long before the Statler Hotel had added its impressive bulk to the Detroit skyline, J. Burgess Book Jr. was dreaming of making Washington boulevard the exclusive shopping district of Detroit. He and his younger brothers Herbert and Frank were born in the old Cadillac Hotel on the site of the present Sheraton-Cadillac Hotel. At the turn of the century Washington boulevard was already deteriorating as a residential street. Down the center of it was a landscaped mall which the Book boys used as a playground. Early in life J. B. Book Jr., foreseeing the upward trend of property values in the area, visualized an avenue comparable to Fifth avenue in New York or Michigan avenue in Chicago. After an education at the Detroit University School he traveled extensively in Europe. Everywhere he went he made a point of stuying the principal thoroughfares and individual buildings.

Young Book was no mere idle daydreamer. His maternal grandfather Francis *(43)* Palms had been one of the wealthiest men in Detroit. The family interest in Washington boulevard began when Palms bought a lot on the corner of Washington boulevard and Grand River avenue in 1886. Upon the death of his father in 1916 J. B. Book Jr. became administrator of the Book estate. It was then that he seriously began to devote himself to the realization of his ambitious plans. His brothers Herbert and Frank were of inestimable value in assisting him. In time the Book interests were to control sixty percent of the frontage on Washington boulevard.

Book found in Louis Kamper an architect who was entirely sympathetic to his ideas. Kamper, too, had journeyed about Europe studying the architectural monuments of the past. In America he saw the opportunity to impart to the new skyscraper the beauty of these masterpieces insofar as it could be adapted to commercial use. The development of Washington boulevard was a project of *(235)* unparalleled magnitude, and it is to Kamper's credit that he was able to visualize the undertaking in the grand manner and to design each part to fit into the whole scheme.[25]

The first product of the collaboration of Kamper and the Book brothers was *(236)* the thirteen-story Book Building (1917).[26] This is a simple but handsome stone-faced building with Italian details. A curious feature of the design was a series of twelve nude caryatids supporting the cornice. After the Book Building came the twenty-one story Washington Boulevard Building of somewhat similar character. However, here brick took the place of stone in a wall surface that was ostensibly a more candid expression of the steel skeleton, and continuous piers afforded greater vertical emphasis.

Unquestionably the most ambitious Book undertaking was the mammoth *(233)* Book-Cadillac Hotel (1924) with twelve hundred rooms, each with a bath. Kamper had made a study of hotels in New York, Chicago, and Atlantic City. In the exterior treatment there was a certain similarity to Post's Statler Hotel, but the general effect was heavier with greater surface plasticity. The lobby and ballroom floors, comprising four stories in all, were adorned with Corinthian pilasters and columns following the pattern of the later palaces of the central provinces of Italy. This formed a monumental base from which rose twenty-three stories of guest rooms. Of these, the first sixteen stories were treated as a very simple shaft with regularly spaced windows, subdivided horizontally by molded belt-courses. The windows of the three stories above the shaft were grouped vertically between Ionic pilasters and engaged columns, recalling the great loggias so often placed at the top of large Italian palaces. This colonnade supported two stories embodied in the cornice, above which were four two-story pavilions with terraced roofs.

The interior of the hotel gave Kamper an opportunity to indulge his taste for lavish splendor. "I like it varm," he said with a trace of Bavarian accent. The entrance stairway and lobby were in the Venetian style. The walls were of beautifully colored *brèche violette* marble trimmed with either yellow Siena or white Alabama marble. The ceiling was composed of intricate panels decorated in subdued colors on a ground of gold leaf. The main restaurant continued the Venetian theme. It was an enormous vaulted room with arched walls covered with richly diversified wood paneling, murals, gilded moldings, and sculptural ornament. The chandeliers were of bronze hung with white and colored crystals, while the drapes were of red brocade. The grand ballroom shifted to the more delicate mood of the Florentine Renaissance with classical decorations in cream, rose, and gold. From the ceiling hung two gorgeous chandeliers each containing more than a ton of crystal.[27]

Today all is changed. The public has no inclination to be dazzled. All the rooms except the ballroom have been remodeled. The walls and ceilings, which entailed so much workmanship and expense, have been covered with sleek modern surfaces. Even the proud name of Book has disappeared, for under new management the hotel is now known as the Sheraton-Cadillac.

After the success of the Book-Cadillac the Book brothers were not satisfied to rest on their laurels. The boom of the twenties had precipitated tremendous building activity and soaring skyscrapers were transforming the skyline of Detroit. Now all that was needed to round out the handsome grouping of commercial structures on Washington boulevard was a tower of impressive height. Louis Kamper was able to satisfy the Books with his design for the thirty-six story *(234)* Book Tower. The site chosen was the original lot purchased by Francis Palms on the southwest corner of Washington boulevard and Grand River avenue directly adjacent to the Book Building. Completed in 1926, the Book Tower was one of the shining stars in the Book firmament.

This is not to say that it deserved any special commendation for its architectural merits. On the contrary, it seems that Kamper's involvement with the Italian Renaissance had ill-prepared him to cope with the aesthetic problems of the skyscraper. Apparently the theories of Sullivan, Burnham and Root, or even Raymond Hood had made little impression on him. Like many nineteenth century architects, he was embarrassed by the sheer verticality of the tall building. Accordingly he decided to relieve the vast expanse of wall surface of the Book Tower with horizontal bands of Italian Renaissance ornamentation, greatly enlarged so as to be visible from the ground.[25] In so doing he failed to realize the effectiveness of the design of a skyscraper lies more in its mass than in its detail.

The next commission Kamper received from the Book family was for the twenty-two story Industrial Bank Building on the northeast corner of Washington boulevard and Grand River. By then Kamper seems to have fallen more in line with contemporary thinking in skyscraper design. Ornamentation was reduced and simplified, and a vertical emphasis was achieved by using continuous piers. A tapering effect was created at the top of the building by a series of minor setbacks. The crowning achievement of the Book estate was to have been a second Book Tower on the northwest corner of Washington boulevard and State street. Rising seventy stories into the air, it would have dwarfed every other structure in Detroit. Studies for it reveal a minimization of ornament, soaring lines, and a tapering termination. Not only had Kamper caught up with the times in his conception of the skyscraper, but he was even challenging the tallest towers of Manhattan. Such giantism, however, proved to be merely a symptom of the overconfidence of the times, for the financial crisis of 1929 prevented this colossal monument from ever becoming a reality.

We have seen how Mason, Scott, and Kamper became devotees of the Italian Renaissance style and applied it to public and commercial buildings. Albert Kahn had been exposed to this style in Mason's office. On a trip to Italy in 1912 he made many detailed sketches of the palaces of Florence and Rome.[28] Their restrained and disciplined design must have appealed to his logical mind. His study of these buildings was to bear fruit when he was asked to design a new building for the Detroit Athletic Club in the downtown area. Henry B. Joy, *(237)* president of the Packard Motor Car Company, set out, as he declared, "to get the men of the automobile industry out of the saloons on Woodward avenue;"[29] and it was largely through his efforts that the monumental limestone edifice took form on the quiet tree-shaded extremity of the Madison avenue mall not far from Woodward avenue. When the club opened in 1915 it immediately became the meeting place of the automobile industry elite.[23]

Italian palaces had proved to be satisfactory archetypes for men's clubs ever since Sir Charles Barry dignified Pall Mall in London with two such buildings almost a century earlier. In New York at the turn of the century McKim, Mead and White had found the same architectural formula well calculated to create an atmosphere of masculine prestige and importance for meetings in the upper echelons of the city's financial world. For the citadel of Detroit's automobile aristocracy Kahn turned to Renaissance Rome for inspiration. The Palazzo Borghese provided him with a model for the portico of the D.A.C., and the arcaded loggia with its delicate Corinthian pilasters in the courtyard of the Palazzo Farnese gave him an idea as to how to treat the large windows of the main dining room on the fourth floor. For the interior he provided handsome carved stone mantels and fine coffered ceilings.

By again borrowing details from Italian palaces Kahn was able to give his *(238)* Police Headquarters (1923) an appearance which suggested order and authority.[30] However, this nine-story structure on Beaubien street, occupying the site *(230)* of Scott's Wayne County Jail, was more modern in design than its predecessor.

214

Italian details, strictly architectonic in nature, were skillfully blended with modern pier-and-spandrel wall construction.

In the same year he built the Police Headquarters, Kahn had the opportunity to build the little jewel-like Clements Library in Ann Arbor which was a much closer approximation of the true spirit of the Italian Renaissance. He is credited with making the statement that he desired most of all to be known as the architect of this building.[31] The library was given to the University of Michigan by William L. Clements of Bay City to house his distinguished collection of rare Americana. There is, of course, an obvious parallel to the Morgan Library (1906) in New York by McKim, Mead and White, but actually the building bears a closer resemblance to the same firm's Butler Institute of American Art (1919) in Youngstown, Ohio. The design of the latter was derived from Vignola's charming little casino in the gardens of the Palazzo Farnese at Caprarola. Kahn admired the original structure in Italy and photographed it on one of his numerous trips abroad.[28] The façade consists of a triple-arched loggia flanked by two narrow bays. This simple scheme, so refined in its understatement of detail, seemed to Kahn singularly appropriate for the library he was called upon to design in Ann Arbor.

(239)

Kahn completed the vast General Motors Building on West Grand boulevard between Cass and Second avenues in Detroit in 1922.[32] Although only fifteen stories high, it was then the second largest building in capacity in the world after the Equitable Building in New York. The site chosen for the building was in the geographical center of the city, removed from the congested downtown area near the river. Since there was plenty of room to spread out, there was no necessity for reaching to the skies, and provision could be made for ample lighting and circulation of air. Hence four massive cross-wings were arranged so as to form large open courts.

(240)

At first glance there appears to be little relationship between the Clements Library and the General Motors Building, but a closer study reveals a striking similarity between their entrance loggias with their triple arches and groined vaults. At the General Motors Building this arch motif was continued around three sides of the building in a continuous arcade which serves as display windows for automobile show rooms. Above this arcade was a shaft consisting of stone piers and spandrels forming a uniform system of windows. Above the shaft an attic was suggested by a colonnade of the Corinthian order crowned by an ample cornice. On the interior the walls and floors of the lobbies and corridors were faced with marble, and the ceilings were richly decorated in colors and old gold in the style of the Italian Renaissance.

(241)

In spite of historical details, there is a distinct relationship between the General Motors Building and Kahn's industrial work. It, too, was an enormous project of great complexity carefully organized and unified. Arbitrary aesthetic concepts were not superimposed, for the exterior frankly expressed the arrangement and purposes of the interior. The chief architectural interest of the building lies in the masterly handling of units of majestic size. Here, as well as in the fenestration, the principle of mechanical repetition so closely associated with mass production was made evident. Kahn, however, was not satisfied. He tried to humanize the building and give it a sense of scale by the introduction of traditional materials and details. In this he showed intelligent restraint. Even though he could not lose sight of the past, the General Motors Building nevertheless leaves no doubt as to Kahn's ability to cope with the architectural problems of his day.[33]

The City Beautiful

For all the make-believe histrionics of the Chicago World's Fair of 1893, it was a convincing demonstration of the unification of the arts. Ever since the days of the Greek Revival, Romanticism had plunged American cities into a chaos of competitive individualism. Industrialization and urban expansion had played havoc with the doctrines of architecture and city planning advocated by George Washington and Thomas Jefferson. Then, after an interim of half a century, the teachings of the École des Beaux-Arts revived the classic ideal. The exposition at Chicago provided an opportunity for a dramatic realization of this ideal on a comprehensive scale. Once again architects, sculptors, painters, city planners, and landscape architects collaborated for a common objective. The 'White City' that rose upon the shores of Lake Michigan set a new standard of urban beauty that was to have an incalculable effect upon the development of the American city.

Under the supervision of Daniel H. Burnham as director of works the best artistic talent of America was summoned to Chicago. Frederick Law Olmsted and his son prepared the landscape setting for the fair. With the exception of Sullivan's famous Transportation Building, all the principal pavilions adhered to the rules of architecture laid down by the Greeks and Romans and later followed by the Italians during the Renaissance. At the head of the Court of Honor, Richard M. Hunt reared his impressive Administration Building with its gilded octagonal dome, and nearby McKim, Mead and White erected their massive Agricultural Hall. On the buildings and in the plazas and esplanades a whole population of statuary sprang into being. On the central dome of the Agricultural Hall, Augustus Saint-Gaudens' bronze Diana was gracefully poised, while above the triumphal arch at the center of the Peristyle rode French and Potter's Columbus quadriga, recalling the Brandenburg gate in Berlin. Frederick MacMonnies was entrusted with the design of the central fountain at the fair, which consisted of a barge of state filled with symbolic figures. Above all, at the end of the Grand Basin loomed a sixty-foot colossus by Daniel Chester French, the gilded Statue of the Republic.[34]

Even Charles Eliot Norton, the fastidious professor of fine arts at Harvard, was moved by such splendor. After visiting Chicago he wrote a friend that he considered the fair on the whole "a great promise, even a great pledge," although he later admitted that "not one of those great façades was an expression of the plan, construction, or purpose of the building behind it."[35] Daniel H. Burnham was not troubled by such reservations. This vision of an Augustan age had inspired him with dreams of the future. He was already planning schemes for the permanent beautification of Chicago. "When a citizen is made to feel the beauty of nature," he reflected, "when he is lifted up by her to any degree above the usual life of his thoughts and feelings, the state of which he is a part is benefited thereby. A very high purpose will be served if the lake shore be restored to the people and made beautiful for them." Burnham's motivations were not purely aesthetic, however. He lamented that so many of the well-to-do were running off to Cairo, Athens, the Riviera, Paris, or Vienna, and queried:

Does anyone grown rich in the mines, the forests or the plains of our country come here to live, or even linger for the sake of pleasure? Does he not pass through our city, remaining only as long as he is compelled to, so that we get the benefit neither of his money nor of his presence among us? What would be the effect upon our prosperity if the town were so delightful that most of the men who grow independent financially in the Mississippi valley, or west of it, were to come to Chicago to live? Should we not without delay do something competent to beautify and make our city attractive for ourselves, and especially for these desirable visitors?

Burnham's first study of Chicago appeared in 1896, but it was not until 1909 that he completed the Chicago plan with the assistance of Edward H. Bennett. There were radial streets converging at strategic points, as in Baron Haussmann's plan of Paris, but Burnham and Bennett surpassed Haussmann in their comprehension of the city as a whole, for their plan included an outer belt of parks and parkways.[36]

The City Beautiful movement, which originated at the Chicago World's Fair, also produced significant results in Washington. At the centennial celebration in 1900 of the removal of the seat of government to the District of Columbia, the American Institute of Architects protested against the prevailing practice of disregarding Major L'Enfant's original plan of the city.[37] With the legislative assistance of Senator James McMillan of Michigan, the A.I.A. secured the appointment of a commission consisting of Daniel H. Burnham, Charles F. McKim, Augustus Saint-Gaudens, and Frederick Law Olmsted Jr. Known as the McMillan Park Commission of 1901, it undertook the modernization and extension of the L'Enfant plan.[38] This included a coordinating system of outlying parks and boulevards providing for the entire District of Columbia.[37]

In the course of time there was scarcely a large city in the country that was not affected by the prevailing zeal for civic improvement. In Detroit Mayor Philip Breitmeyer was instrumental in founding a City Plan Commission in 1910.[39] Its first president Charles Moore was well prepared for his post.[40] As political secretary to Senator McMillan, he had helped carry through the extension of the L'Enfant plan in Washington.[41] One of the first endeavors of the new commission was to invite Daniel H. Burnham and Edward H. Bennett of Chicago to make a tour of Detroit. In the company of the mayor and other city officials they were shown the Detroit riverfront from the deck of a steamer hired for the purpose.[42] The Plan Commission then engaged Bennett to make a preliminary plan of Detroit, which was completed in 1915.

In the downtown section of Detroit there were still remnants of Judge *(17)* Woodward's plan of 1807, so French in its geometric precision. Woodward had envisioned broad avenues and plazas adorned by public buildings, fountains, and statues.[43] He had planned for a city of 50,000, but since then the population had reached 700,000. In the interim little had been done in the way of city planning, notable exceptions being the development of Belle Isle, Palmer Park, and Grand Boulevard. Like Woodward, Bennett was now faced with the task of doing a comprehensive plan for the entire city and, in so doing, he was able to revive his predecessor's dream of an elegant metropolis. In his plan Bennett suggested an ideal treatment of Cadillac Square. There would be a civic center at Grand Circus Park and a center of arts and letters on Woodward avenue between Warren and Kirby. At the intersection of Woodward avenue and Grand boulevard there would be a grand plaza, and also a plaza in front of the Michigan *(264)* Central Station.

Detroit was well suited for planning in the French tradition. In no other American city except Washington were there such convenient diagonal thoroughfares as Michigan, Gratiot, Fort, and Grand River. Bennett planned an additional diagonal from the Michigan Central Station to the new center of arts and letters, and another diagonal from there to the Belle Isle bridge. Included in his studies was a sketch for a new bridge to Belle Isle by Cass Gilbert. Surrounding the city he outlined a system of parks and outer boulevards, while along the riverfront he proposed a continuous park extending from Lake Erie to Lake St. Clair. Although many of his schemes failed to materialize, nevertheless Bennett's plan laid the groundwork for what are today many of the city's most desirable facilities. These include the Cultural Center on Woodward avenue, Outer Drive, Roosevelt Park, Rouge Park, the Detroit Zoological Park, and the Huron-Clinton Parkway.[44]

Monuments

"The city must fail to attain the commonest standards of civic art, if there be not conscious decorative effort," states Charles M. Robinson in his book on civic art of 1903. He pointed out that there had long been cities where "fountains bubbled in the squares, chiselled heroes were enthroned as masters of the scene, commemorative arches stood at focal points, and bridges were the stateliest parts of urban highways."[45] Swept along by a new sense of civic pride, Detroiters eagerly erected monuments to honor their forgotten heroes. Bronze statues began to fill the parks and open spaces. General Alexander Macomb, hero of the War of 1812, assumed a proud stance in his long military cloak and cocked hat, at the head of Washington boulevard; General Alpheus S. Williams, who had distinguished himself in the Civil War, took up a position astride his faithful steed at the main intersection on Belle Isle; Stevens T. Mason, Michigan's first governor, returned to preside over Capitol Park, site of the old State Capitol; while amid the trees of Grand Circus Park appeared Daniel Chester French's female personification of Michigan to remind the passerby of the political and military achievements of General Russell A. Alger.[46]

(244)   Even grander memorials than statues could be erected by those who were prepared to finance them. When Lizzie Merrill Palmer, the wife of Senator Thomas W. Palmer, decided to honor her father, the lumberman Charles Merrill, with a fountain, she asked Carrère and Hastings, one of New York's most distinguished architectural firms, to prepare the designs. The dedication cere-
(72)   mony in 1901 provided Senator Palmer with an opportunity to launch into a dissertation on the historic fountains of Europe. "As men were crowded into great cities and denied the frequent sight of the contact with water in agitation or repose," explained the senator, "a craving for it, as a feature of the landscape, has led to construction of artificial lakes, cascades and fountains to cool the air, please the eye and soothe the ear, as well as supply the physical wants of the people."[47] Centrally located in front of the Detroit Opera House on the Campus Martius, the Merrill Fountain was a magnificent white marble structure in the Italian Renaissance style. A small recessed fountain flanked by balustrades formed the background for two large basins animated by a series of jets. Later the fountain was moved to a more idyllic setting in Palmer Park.

(242)   When Chauncey Hurlbut, a member of the Board of Water Commissioners, left a bequest for beautifying Waterworks Park on East Jefferson avenue, the decision was made to honor him with the Hurlbut Memorial Gate. Erected in 1894 at the foot of Cadillac boulevard, it followed the prevailing taste of the day for formal and stately entrances to parks. Designed in the most florid baroque style by Brede and Mueller, it has the appearance of a triumphal arch raised upon a rusticated base and crowned by a slender dome.[48] A grand staircase ascends to a terrace above the central gate. It should come as no surprise that the architects of such an ingenious if somewhat pretentious monument were men of

training and experience. Born in Copenhagen, Denmark, Herman A. Brede was brought to Detroit as an infant by his parents. After graduating from the public schools, he studied architecture under James Anderson, having worked on plans of the old City Hall. Gustave A. Mueller was born in Dresden, Germany. He came to America as a young student and served his apprenticeship in engineering with the French in their unsuccessful attempt to build the Panama Canal.[49]

The passion for monuments in Detroit reached its apogee in a movement to erect a vast memorial to celebrate the two hundredth anniversary of the founding of the city, but like so many of the most ambitious projects, its realization was more difficult than had been anticipated. The "Bi-Centennial Memorial" was to have been built on land reclaimed from the river at the lower end of Belle Isle Park. A Doric column twenty-four feet in diameter was to rise two hundred and twenty feet from the water while surrounded by groups of sculpture in the water, all situated in a court formed by a marble colonnade one thousand and five hundred feet long. This colonnade was to contain statues of Cadillac and others notable in the history of Detroit. Above the colonnade on the land side there was to be an artificial lake fed by decorative fountains. Facing the lake on each side were to be an aquarium and a horticultural building. From the top of the central column visitors would have been able to obtain a magnificent view of the Detroit River, Lake St. Clair, Lake Erie, and the surrounding country, while a torch flashing fire at intervals would have marked it unmistakably at night. *(245)*

There was about the Bicentennial Memorial project a lingering aura of the Chicago World's Fair. Many of the nationally-known artists who had helped to create the "Dream City" on the shores of Lake Michigan were invited to participate in the Detroit enterprise. The concept of the unification of the arts persisted. Stanford White was the architect, Augustus Saint-Gaudens and Frederick MacMonnies were chosen as sculptors, and Tryon and Dewing were selected as painters. Behind the venture were many of Detroit's leading patrons of art, including Charles L. Freer, James McMillan, Russell A. Alger, and Frank J. Hecker.[50] A campaign was started to raise one million dollars for the monument, but somehow it failed to capture the imagination of the public sufficiently to make it economically feasible and like a golden dream it faded in the cold light of reality.

For a while, at least, it seemed as if the scheme for the artistic treatment of the foot of Belle Isle was destined for oblivion, but then the unexpected happened. Detroiters, who had envisioned an impressive memorial to honor the city's great, winced when they heard that in its place a monument would be erected in memory of James Scott, a man who had the reputation for being a vindictive scurrilous misanthrope. During a long life he had made shrewd investments in downtown real estate. His enemies were legion, for he seemed to delight in feuds, law suits, and practical jokes. The greatest practical joke of all came at the end of his life, for his will provided that his sizable fortune was to be used to erect a fountain on Belle Isle to be called the James Scott Fountain. *(246)* Pulpits thundered in protest against perpetuating the memory of such a man, but the cause of civic beautification won out in the end. The fountain was completed in 1925, fifteen years after the death of the donor. In the meantime the value of his legacy had increased from $350,000 to around a million.[51]

The Bicentennial Memorial looked well on paper, but it is perhaps fortunate that future generations were spared the impact of its rather overpowering pretentiousness. Certainly the Scott Fountain fitted more gracefully into the landscape. The final designs by Cass Gilbert were chosen in a nation-wide competition by a carefully-picked group of judges which included Daniel Chester

French, the sculptor, Frederick Law Olmstead, the landscape architect, and Charles A. Platt and Robert S. Peabody, architects. The entire lower end of Belle Isle was reconstructed to serve as a setting for the fountain which rises from the central basin in a series of white marble bowls or receptacles to a central column of water forty feet high. Supplementing this are myriad jets which form a symmetrical mass of water. Placed as inconspicuously as possible at the base of the fountain is a life-size seated figure in bronze of James Scott by Herbert Adams.[52]

The Art Center

In his plan of Detroit of 1915, Edward H. Bennett provided for a center of arts and letters. Designed to meet the needs of a greatly magnified population, a new public library and an art museum were to complement one another across Woodward avenue between Warren and Kirby. In the same year a competition for the design of the Detroit Public Library was won by Cass Gilbert, a man whose background gave every assurance that Detroit would possess a library worthy of the ideals of the American Renaissance. After studying at the Massachusetts Institute of Technology, he had exposed himself to the architectural wonders of England, France, and Italy. Upon his return from Europe, he worked in the office of McKim, Mead and White before establishing his own practice. Already to his credit were such well-known structures as the Minnesota State Capitol, the Woolworth Building in New York, and the Central Public Library in St. Louis.[53]

Gilbert believed that a library was not only a repository for books but a symbol of the cultural life of the community. "It would be as improper," he maintained, "to house a library in a building that was 'illiterate' in its architecture, as to fill it with books written in an illiterate manner. A library should create an environment of scholarship and refinement; it fails of its purpose as an educative factor if it is other than a beautiful building." In view of his experience with McKim, Mead and White, it was perhaps inevitable that Gilbert should have found the embodiment of his philosophy in the Italian Renaissance and should have chosen as a suitable prototype for the Detroit Public Library their Boston Public Library of 1887. However, whereas McKim followed the rather stern fifteenth century manner of Alberti, Gilbert preferred to adopt the more mellow sixteenth century elegance of Sangallo, Peruzzi, Brunelleschi, and Sansovino. No mere imitator, he chose to synthesize the productions of these men in a creation that was his own, that is insofar as the standards of his day permitted. In order to prepare himself better for the task at hand he set out once more for Italy to refresh his memory of the great monuments so dear to his heart.[54]

(243) The fruit of his labors was a building, dedicated in 1921, that set a new standard of magnificence for Detroit.[55] Set back from Woodward avenue with an approach of terraces, the white marble façade was a model of carefully studied proportion and detail. The first floor, serving as a base, consisted of a delicately rusticated wall pierced by molded openings and capped by a belt course. On the second floor the bold arches of the loggia provided a measure of plasticity to the otherwise flat surface of the building. Framing these arches were fluted Ionic pilasters supporting an entablature. Above this was a frieze broken by small windows and adorned with panels in low relief representing the signs of the zodiac. Inside two rows of Doric columns in white marble led to the grand

staircase. The general sobriety of the design was relieved by a richly coffered ceiling in the sixteenth century Italian style. Above the staircase was a barrel vault treated in a manner resembling the Raphael arabesques in the Vatican. On the walls were murals by Edwin H. Blashfield representing great authors, musicians, and artists. In the delivery room on the second floor were murals by Gari Melchers depicting events in the early history of Detroit.[56]

In 1927, six years after the completion of the Detroit Public Library, the Detroit Institute of Arts opened its doors to the public.[57] Located across Woodward from the library, it rivaled its sister institution in its white marble splendor. The Arts Commission had been formed in 1919 to take over the control of the old Detroit Museum of Art in the name of the city. As first president of the commission, Ralph Harman Booth was the driving force in bringing to completion Detroit's new repository of the arts.[58] Booth secured the services of Paul Philippe Cret as architect for this monumental undertaking. This was to be the nucleus of an enlarged institute ranking with the best in the country.[59]

(247)

(330)

Born and educated in Lyons, France, Cret graduated in 1901 from the École des Beaux-Arts in Paris. Two years later he arrived in the United States to accept a position as professor of design at the University of Pennsylvania. In 1907 he resigned to launch his own career. Before commencing his work in Detroit he had already designed the Pan-American Union Building in Washington and the Central Public Library in Indianapolis.[60] As a Philadelphian he seems to have found the still-standing art gallery of the Philadelphia Centennial of 1876 satisfactory as a point of departure for his Detroit museum.[61] Following the general outlines of this exposition building, he designed a large one-story structure in a modification of the Italian Renaissance style. The central bay was treated like a Roman triumphal arch, the entrance being formed by three arches springing from Ionic columns. Bronze copies of famous statues relieved the classic simplicity of the façade. Michelangelo's Slave and Donatello's St. George found new homes in niches on the walls, while on either side of the broad flight of steps leading to the entrance, Antoine Coysevox's River God and Philippe Magnier's Nymph and Cupid, both at Versailles, gaze demurely at the passing traffic on Woodward.

The architectural principles which Cret had absorbed at the École des Beaux-Arts became particularly apparent on the interior of the museum, for there he showed himself to be a master in the organization of the plan, the manipulation of space, and the attention to detail. Along the main axis of the building are three central rooms. First there is the handsome entrance foyer with its Ionic columns and arches. This opens directly upon an impressive concourse or great hall with its lofty Pompeian-style ceiling and tapestry-lined walls. Beyond through an archway is an enclosed court dominated by an imposing loggia and enlivened by a refreshing fountain.

Leading off this central axis are the exhibition galleries. Weary of the scientifically planned nineteenth century museums, Cret sought to recapture some of the charm of the European museums that were originally old residences. Instead of monotonously uniform galleries with neutral backgrounds, he planned a series of 'period rooms.' Arranged in historical order and grouped around courts, these rooms provided appropriate architectural settings for related examples of paintings, furniture, and objects of art. In some instances original interiors were installed. Except in the temporary exhibition galleries, skylights were avoided and a more natural lighting effect was created by the use of windows.[62]

A good measure of credit for the arrangement of the period rooms at the Institute of Arts must go to Dr. William R. Valentiner, the eminent connoisseur of art called in by Ralph H. Booth during the planning stage of the building.[63] He had been trained at the museum in The Hague, and later was associated with Dr. Wilhelm Bode at the Kaiser Friedrich Museum in Berlin.[64] When he consented to become the director of the new museum in Detroit, its future was assured. To be sure, James E. Scripps had laid the foundation of the museum collection in the nineteenth century, but it was not until the twentieth century that the golden age of art patronage began. Under the tutelage of Dr. Valentiner and his successor Dr. Edgar P. Richardson, Detroit was to acquire a collection of the first magnitude.

The habit of collecting in Detroit was greatly accelerated by the unprecedented prosperity of the automotive industry. In a mechanized world the work of art became a mark of distinction. Latter-day Medicis vied with one another in the magnificence of their houses which became veritable museums recalling the glories of past ages. The most public-spirited collectors presented works of art to the Institute of Arts which became in many respects a synthesis of the eclectic taste of the day; through the combined efforts of many donors a comprehensive survey of the world's art could be enjoyed by the public at large. "It is such things that make a city great," observed Ralph H. Booth, "not mere bigness or simply usefulness in production."[65]

In more ways than one Detroiters can be proud of their Cultural Center. Architecturally the Institute of Arts and the Public Library are outstanding examples of public buildings in the academic style. Together they form a civic unit exemplifying a notable achievement of the City Beautiful movement.

The Italian Renaissance: Residences

Detailing in the style of the Italian Renaissance began to appear on Detroit residences as early as 1889, for it was then that Mason and Rice completed a house on Trumbull avenue for George Gough Booth who was later to become an outstanding patron of the arts. Although the gables revealed the influence of the architecture of the Netherlands, the carved entrance with its frolicking cherubs imparted the warm radiance of the Italian Renaissance. In 1895 Mason and Rice built a house on Ferry avenue for Watson M. Freer, the brother of Charles L. Freer.[12] At that time Albert Kahn was working in the office of Mason and Rice, and the Freer house was the first building he helped to design after returning from a two-year sojourn in Europe on a fellowship provided by the *American Architect.* The Italian Renaissance details incorporated in the design of the house were an indication of the early impact of the work of Alberti and Bramante upon the youthful architect.

But it was not until the J. Harrington Walker house was erected in 1895 on the corner of Jefferson and Joseph Campau avenues that the Italian Renaissance style could be said to have made more than a cursory appearance in domestic architecture. It signalized a return to formality after the vagaries of the Victorian era. The glass doors with their iron grilles and lace curtains provided a typical note of Edwardian elegance.

In 1914 when the lumberman Albert L. Stephens decided to abandon his turreted Romanesque abode on Woodward avenue in favor of a more cheerful Italian villa on Jefferson avenue in the fashionable Indian Village district, he chose as his architect George D. Mason. By then Mason was already a full-fledged devotee of the Italian Renaissance. By no means a purist, he improvised freely with ornamental details which contrasted with smooth limestone wall

(249)

(369)

(250)

(193)

(251)

(164)

(252)

222

surfaces. Triple-arched loggias took advantage of the impressive site overlooking the Detroit River opposite Belle Isle. Later the house was owned by Edsel B. Ford and was eventually torn down.

As early as 1911 James B. Book Jr. joined the migration to the Indian Village *(253)* where Louis Kamper provided him with a distinguished residence on the north side of Jefferson at Burns avenue. Book had traveled extensively in Europe and shared his architect's notions of urbane living. Kamper had worked in the office of McKim, Mead and White in New York in the eighties and was fully imbued with the Italian spirit.[66] In the early years of the century McKim, Mead and White were ennobling New York with great domestic establishments based on the Italian palaces of the sixteenth century.[67] The Book house followed this tradition. Balustraded steps led to a handsome arched entrance flanked by engaged Corinthian columns, while Corinthian pilasters rose the full height of the building to an entablature surmounted by a balustrade. The interior was notable for its exquisitely carved marble mantels, marble floors, and ornately molded plaster walls and ceilings.

Later Book was to employ Kamper in the transformation of Washington *(235)* boulevard from a declining residential street to an elegant metropolitan thoroughfare. It is not difficult to discern in the Book house the architectural basis *(233)* for the mammoth Book-Cadillac Hotel of 1924 on Washington boulevard. Kamper's own residence on Iroquois avenue in the Indian Village (c. 1910) *(255)* followed very much the same pattern as the Book house. However, there were superimposed orders instead of continuous pilasters, and the attic story was contained under a hipped roof covered with tiles.

In 1917 when Kamper was engaged to design a house on Jefferson avenue in *(248)* Grosse Pointe for Murray W. Sales, his thoughts turned to the rural Italian villa with its characteristic raised central portion known as the *altana*. Breaking away from strict academic discipline, he opened up the house toward the terrace and lawn with French doors and large Georgian windows. The present owner James Gibson, an architect, appreciates the elegance of the interior with its fine woodwork and mantels.

One of the most dedicated votaries of the Italian Renaissance, John Scott is chiefly remembered for the Roman magnificence of his Wayne County Building *(227)* in Detroit. When he received an important commission to provide a residence for Dr. Harry N. Torrey on Lake Shore road in Grosse Pointe, he rose to the *(254)* occasion with a full-blown Palladian palace. Completed in 1913, it recalled Marble House which Richard Morris Hunt had built for William K. Vanderbilt twenty years earlier in Newport, Rhode Island.[68] To be sure, Scott was not Hunt's peer in the mastery of detail. The two-story Corinthian portico seemed to be unrelated to the general design because its entablature did not continue around the house. Like so many of the Newport villas, the Torrey house was a formal drawing-board exercise in the Beaux-Arts tradition. The beautiful setting was merely a backdrop for an imposing façade. An attempt was made to establish a closer relationship to the surroundings by means of two rather incongruous terminal loggias which looked like afterthoughts. In front of the house were formal Italian gardens with balustraded terraces, hedges, and fountains, while at the rear was an irregular lagoon surrounded by a wooded area. The demolition of the house in 1960 effaced one of Grosse Pointe's most notable souvenirs of Edwardian grandeur.

The Torrey garden was a manifestation of the renewed interest in landscaping which had been activated by the suburban movement. In accordance with the general academic trend, gardens followed the patterns established in Renaissance Europe. For the first time Americans took up country living in the grand manner. No one did more to promote this way of life than Charles A. Platt of New York. Starting his career with the idea of becoming an artist, he studied at the École des Beaux-Arts in Paris. In 1892 he took a trip to Italy with his brother, a landscape architect, to study Renaissance gardens. Two years later his book *Italian Gardens* appeared. "From the Renaissance builders," one of his biographers wrote, "he has learned the lesson that 'villa' connotes a house and gardens, derived as a unity for the enjoyment and comfort of the owner."[69] When he returned to America, Platt began designing gardens for his friends at Augustus Saint-Gaudens' artists' colony in Cornish, New Hampshire. Soon his services were in demand everywhere. His experience with gardens and their decorative structures led to his undertaking the design of houses and estates treated as an integrated whole.[70]

(256) In 1902 Platt was asked to do a garden for the exclusive Yondotega Club located on Jefferson avenue in the downtown Detroit area. It was surrounded by walls and contained a pergola and a handsome wall fountain. In 1959 when the club and its gardens were demolished and a new clubhouse was built further out Jefferson avenue, the fountain was saved and moved to the new location.

(257) Soon Platt was designing a series of estates in Grosse Pointe. One of his most important commissions was a house on Lake Shore road for Russell A. Alger, the son of General Alger.[71] Built in 1910, it was situated on one of the highest pieces of ground along the lake shore and the natural variation in ground levels was taken advantage of to produce the most charming landscape effects. Extending from one of the lateral loggias, a pergola originally tied the house to its surroundings and served as a dividing line between the formal gardens to the north and the abrupt slope toward the lake on the south.

(259) The house itself reflected a change of mood. The rigid formality of the previous era gave way to a restrained elegance and easy refinement. There was a contrast between the vertical emphasis of the entrance façade with its exquisite doorway and pediment details in stone and iron, and the horizontal sweep of the (258) lake façade where a series of French doors and iron balconies permitted the maximum enjoyment of the commanding view. In every way Platt so subtly and so tastefully adapted the Italian Renaissance ideal to local conditions that his houses almost seemed indigenous. "By nature and training a traditionalist," said an admiring chronicler, "Platt has transcended tradition by his individuality and charm."[69] The beauty of the Alger house may now be enjoyed by Grosse Pointers as a whole, for it is now the Grosse Pointe War Memorial, a commu- (345) nity center, as a result of the generosity of Mrs. Alger. A new auditorium blends architecturally with the original house; unfortunately, however, it blocks the view of the lake from the garden.

Albert Kahn was a great admirer of the work of Charles Platt. With self-effacing modesty he actually had recommended Platt to the Algers as an architect for their house. The residence which Kahn built for Goodloe Edgar soon (261) afterwards on Lake Shore road is similar in many ways to the Alger house. However, it is simpler and smaller. The terrace is higher above the level of the lake and is more intimately related to the living quarters.

In 1911 Henry D. Shelden built an Italian mansion on Lake Shore road. The (263) architect was Arthur Heun of Chicago who designed several large houses in Lake Forest. It was a freer interpretation of the Italian villa than the Alger house. Deeplands, as the Shelden estate was known, consisted of some eighty acres. The house could be seen from the road at the end of a long grass *allée* bordered with woodland. The exterior walls were faced with grayish yellow bricks and the roof tiles were green. French doors opened upon an inviting terrace flanked by projecting bays. The entrance, approached by a driveway, was at the rear of the house. Soon after World War II, Deeplands was demolished and the property subdivided.

In the restless twenties the desire for formal grandeur subsided and architects began their frenetic search for the romantic and picturesque. One of the most prolific and versatile architects of the period in Grosse Pointe was Hugh T. Keyes whose Charles A. Dean house of 1924 on Lewiston road displayed a *(260)* predilection for colorful detail and at the same time a fine sense of overall design. Located on one of the few sloping sites in the area and surrounded by giant oak trees, this rambling Italian villa with its red tile roof evoked memories of rural Tuscany. The long axis of the house was built on two different levels. There is a handsome living room with a high-beamed ceiling and a fireplace framed by twisted baroque columns and surmounted by a sculptured Madonna in a niche. In the library a medieval corner-fireplace with a conical hood was featured. Other picturesque details were used, such as wrought iron railings and balconies, and colorful tiles on the stairs. The skillful way these details were incorporated in the overall design added to the picturesque ensemble and prevented them from being mere stage accessories. The romantic atmosphere was further enhanced by the varying scale of the rooms and the pleasing way in which they opened up through French doors on intimate gardens or stretches of lawn.

The romanticism of the twenties came to a climax with the Grosse Pointe Yacht Club of 1927. Architect Guy Lowell of Boston created a Mediterranean *(262)* mood with cream-colored stucco walls and red tile roofs. Rising out of the waters of Lake St. Clair on a man-made island is a vision of Venice replete with a campanile, Gothic window tracery, and an arcaded loggia overlooking the lake. On the interior a grand stairway leads to the lounge which was adorned with a Renaissance mantel and wrought iron chandeliers from Italy. Fourteen windows provide marine views from an octagonal dining room, from the ceiling of which was suspended an Italian chandelier in leaded red, amber, and green glass. A central fountain group by Wheeler Williams, known as The Rhythm of the Waves, was based on the famous Dance of the Three Graces as posed by the late Isadora Duncan and her pupils.

Classicism

The Chicago World's Fair of 1893 had an even more profound effect upon American architecture than upon city planning. Its magnificence and serenity seemed like an antidote for the current architectural chaos and it promised a revival of a language of form which had early been identified with the ideals of the republic. At the annual dinner of the American Institute of Architects in Washington in 1905, Nicholas Murray Butler, the president of Columbia University, sounded the clarion call for a return to classicism. He admitted our debt to the architectural genius of England and France, but insisted that "back of all we go, and must always go to the eternal well-springs that were fed by Greece and Rome." "It was given to them to create the highest standards of excellence alike in architecture, in sculpture and in letters," he maintained, "and to those standards it has been the effort of all intelligence ever since to conform."[72]

Even McKim, Mead and White cooled in their ardor for the Italian Renaissance. The moment had arrived for them to impart to New York something of the grandeur of Imperial Rome. The Pantheon of Hadrian served as the basis for their Columbia University Library (1896), while their Pennsylvania Station (1906–10) brought memories of the Baths of Caracalla. Travelers, who for so long had associated railroad stations with noise and soot, were given a welcome befitting a great city for the first time.

Warren and Wetmore also resorted to a vast vaulted concourse for New York's Grand Central Station (1903–12), but with somewhat less archeology and more efficiency. In 1913 the same architects, in collaboration with Reed and *(264)* Stem, completed the Michigan Central Station overlooking Roosevelt Park in Detroit. Here the Roman magnificence of the waiting room section—with its columns, arches, and gables—contrasts with the sixteen-story connecting office building directly behind it. This was an early example of functional expression in a railroad station.[73]

New York set the pace for another Detroit building in the classical tradition. *(265)* Albert Kahn's Detroit Trust Company of 1915 (now the Detroit Bank and Trust Company) on the southwest corner of Fort and Shelby streets followed closely McKim, Mead and White's Knickerbocker Trust Company (1904) in New York. Lavish Corinthian columns and pilasters were intended to give the impression of wealth, permanence, and security, at the same time permitting generous fenestration.[74] In 1926 the building was widened one hundred feet to the west, *(392)* and in 1966 it was completely modernized.

Kahn's twenty-four story National Bank Building (1922) on Woodward at *(266)* Cadillac Square is more typical of his work. The simple grid-like treatment of *(240)* the stone veneer covering the steel frame recalls his General Motors Building, although here the emphasis of the details is classical rather than Renaissance. The Corinthian pillars between the large windows of the banking rooms on the second floor were patterned as nearly as possible after the columns of the Tem- *(387)* ple of Castor and Pollux in the Roman Forum.[75]

In the twenties there was a reaction against the modernity of Kahn's earlier buildings at the University of Michigan in Ann Arbor. The board of regents was *(221)* of the opinion that his Natural Science Building (1916) was too commercial-looking. When they engaged him to design Angell Hall (1925) they pleaded for a return to more academic standards.[76] Only three years earlier Henry Bacon had completed the Lincoln Memorial in Washington, a temple-like Doric structure. It is more than likely that Kahn's admiration for the work of his friend and early *(268)* mentor was responsible for the imposing portico of Angell Hall with its eight massive Doric columns.

One of the most attractive buildings of the classical persuasion in the Detroit *(267)* area is the McGregor Public Library on Woodward avenue in Highland Park. Completed in 1926, it was designed by Edward L. Tilton and Alfred M. Githens in association with Marcus R. Burrowes and Frank Eurich Jr. The limestone exterior was ornamented with a series of fluted pilasters and a cornice with a polychrome terra-cotta frieze.[77] The main entrance was placed in a coffered alcove flanked by Ionic columns. An unusual feature was the location of the book stacks in the basement, thus making the entire main floor available for public use.[78]

To be sure, classicism had some effect upon domestic architecture during this period, but its impact was much milder than it had been in the early nineteenth century. In 1926 George D. Mason built a house on Lake Shore road in Grosse *(270)* Pointe for Harley G. Higbie. The Doric columns and entablature framing the front door added a classical touch to a house of the Georgian tradition which was also distinguished by a carefully studied arrangement of window openings.

226

The French Renaissance

French architecture had been popular in America ever since the days of Napoleon III, but it was not until Richard Morris Hunt finished his studies at the École des Beaux-Arts in Paris that any American architect could rightfully be said to understand this complex language of form. It was not difficult for Hunt to persuade the merchant princes of New York that they deserved something better than drab brownstone houses and before long he was providing the Vanderbilts and the Astors with appropriate settings for their lavish balls. In one château after another he brought to upper Fifth avenue the grandeur of the days of Francis I.[79]

The newly revived style spread quickly to Chicago where millionaires began ensconcing themselves in sumptuous châteaux along Prairie avenue and Drexel boulevard.[80] Even in Detroit where the tempo of life was more leisurely and the social rivalries less keen, the taste for French magnificence became apparent. In 1890 the glistening white limestone towers and steep gray slate roofs of Colonel Frank J. Hecker's new mansion rose on the edge of the city at the northeast *(272)* corner of Woodward and Ferry avenues. Designed in the style of the Early French Renaissance, it followed the general outlines of the Château de Chenonceaux near Tours. The beautifully carved stone details struck a new note of sophistication in Detroit. Clearly architect Louis Kamper had benefited from his training in the office of McKim, Mead and White in New York. It should be mentioned, however, that John Scott and his brother Arthur also worked with Kamper in the construction of the house under the firm name of Scott, Kamper and Scott.

Notwithstanding the sixteenth century aspect of the Hecker house, its floor *(271)* plan retained certain Victorian characteristics. At the center was a colonnaded reception hall from which a grand staircase rose to a stained glass window at the landing.[81] William Wright and Company of Detroit did the fine cabinetwork. The hall was paneled in white oak, the oval dining room in mahogany, and the *(273)* library in English oak with matched graining. In cheerful contrast the adjoining *(274)* parlor and music room were finished in white and gold.[82] The fireplaces were done in Egyptian Nubian marble and onyx, while the vestibule was wainscoted in Italian Siena marble. The Hecker house was ideal for the many gala parties which were given there. When the great doors were rolled back the entire first floor became an immense ballroom. Couples waltzed slowly and gracefully over the parquet floors. One of the most colorful occasions there was the reception held in 1898 after the marriage of Colonel Hecker's daughter Louise to Guyla Hope Joseph de Szilassy of Vienna.[83] The groom was dressed in the brilliant uniform of the Austrian army. According to a newspaper account, "It consisted of a white satin undercoat, tucked and frogged and trimmed with gold braid. Hanging over the left shoulder was a rich coat of blue velvet trimmed with mink. Tight fitting red trousers and patent leather Hessian boots, spangled with gold tassels hanging from them, completed the uniform."[84]

Behind all these gay festivities loomed the distinguished figure of Colonel Hecker himself. With his regular features, high forehead, and Van Dyck beard, he was the image of Napoleon III. A veteran of the Civil War and the Spanish American War, he had come to Detroit in the railroad business and ended by amassing a fortune in the manufacture of railroad cars. He had helped to organize the Peninsular Car Company of which he became president.[85] Associated with him in this company as vice president was Charles L. Freer, the noted

(193) connoisseur of art who was a close personal friend. For many years they lived next door to each other on Ferry avenue. Today the Freer house is part of the Merrill-Palmer Institute and the Hecker house is occupied by the Smiley Brothers Music Company.

(269) The William Livingstone house of 1893 on Eliot street is convincing evidence that the architects Mason and Rice were as happy with the French Renaissance style as they had been with the other popular styles. Actually, young Albert Kahn, who was working in their office at the time, was responsible for the design of the house. He had sketched the châteaux of the Loire two years earlier on a European tour, which accounted for his skill in designing the details of the stonework, later executed by Julius Melchers.[86] As a conscientious follower of architectural periodicals, Kahn was no doubt familiar with the C. A. Whittier house in Boston by McKim, Mead and White, which may have suggested the general treatment of the Livingstone house.[87]

French architecture continued to be popular in the twentieth century, but the movement to the suburbs and the preoccupation with landscaping exercised a mollifying influence. Elegance superseded magnificence. The picturesque medieval roofs and formidable towers of the sixteenth century gave way to the horizontality and greater classical emphasis of the eighteenth century.

(259) Charles A. Platt had proved himself to be a master in evoking the spirit of the Italian Baroque in his Russell A. Alger house of 1910 on Lake St. Clair in Grosse Pointe. Three years later he was equally successful in capturing the essence of
(275) the French Baroque in the house he built for Mrs. Henry Stephens further out Lake Shore road.[88] Henry Stephens, who died in 1910, had been a member of one of Michigan's lumbering and mining families.[89] More restrained than the Alger house, the Stephens house achieved its distinction through simplicity of design and refinement of detail. On the lake side French doors open upon a broad terrace. The Flemish bonded brick of the walls were accented with stone trim and a graceful iron balcony on the central axis. At the west end of the house the
(276) driveway enters a charming entrance court which serves as a setting for the handsome doorway with its exquisite stone details and ornate wrought-iron work. At the rear of the house there was originally a glazed loggia overlooking the garden, but this was later enclosed and filled with antique French paneling by present owner Ernest Kanzler.

Continuing in the same tradition as Charles A. Platt, Bryant Fleming combined the professions of architecture and landscape architecture. He was respon-
(277) sible for both house and garden on the Wesson Seyburn estate on Jefferson avenue in Grosse Pointe (1924). A product of the Cornell University School of Architecture, he carried on his practice in Wyoming, New York, where he received commissions to design residences and country estates throughout the Midwest.[90] Scion of an old Detroit family, Seyburn had married Winifred Dodge, the daughter of John F. Dodge. The Seyburn property was one of those narrow strips of land stretching back from the lake which are so characteristic in Grosse Pointe, deriving their shape from the ribbon farms of the early settlers. The architect ingeniously utilized this area in creating a French house and gardens. The house was located near the lake and was approached by a long straight driveway which passed first through a wooded area and then through a tunnel-like *allée* of sycamore trees with a high wall on each side. To the right were formal gardens where clipped fruit trees, gravel walks, geometric flower beds, and statuary captured the flavor of eighteenth century France.

The elegant yet restrained façade of the house faced a cobblestone courtyard at the end of the driveway. Patterned after a French château of the eighteenth century, it exhibited a fine feeling for detail and texture. The formal stone portico enclosing graceful curved steps stood out against the gray brick of the main mass of the house with its lighter gray window architraves. Also the balustrades surmounting the portico and at the base of the ground floor windows contrasted pleasingly with the fragile wrought-iron railing of the entrance steps. On the less formal lake side of the house French doors opening upon a broad *(278)* terrace took advantage of the lake exposure. The Seyburn house was elegant and at the same time livable. Architecture and landscaping merged in a unified design. Painstaking refinement and adherence to the period created an old-world charm and authenticity which was augmented by the incorporation of genuine antiques as architectural features and motifs.

For those not prepared to indulge in an establishment on the scale of the Seyburn estate, the French *manoir* satisfied the increasing desire for the intimate and picturesque without sacrificing the essential French spirit. In his Edwin H. Brown residence of 1926 on Lake court in Grosse Pointe, architect Robert O. *(281)* Derrick combined mansard roofs and French fenestration with a characteristic round tower to produce the desired effect. The next year Wallace Frost, in his Julian P. Bowen house on Jefferson avenue in Grosse Pointe, created a more *(280)* rustic atmosphere with steep roofs, small windows, and the rough textures of slate and stone. The masses of the roofs, gables, and tower were resolved into a dramatic plastic composition, marred only by too great a diversification and *(324)* scattering of window openings.

Anna Thompson Dodge, the widow of Horace E. Dodge of automobile fame and one of the nation's wealthiest women, could afford to ignore the trend toward simplicity. Her Louis XV château built in 1934 on Lake Shore road is un- *(279)* questionably Grosse Pointe's most regal residence. Inspired by the work of the great eighteenth century master Jacques Ange Gabriel, Philadelphia architect Horace Trumbauer strove for monumental splendor. Somewhat belatedly he attempted to recapture the luster of the 'Gilded Age,' for no less than twenty years earlier he had built an almost identical though somewhat smaller palace for A. Hamilton Rice at Newport,[91] and in 1916 he had built one of America's most sumptuous houses for Edward T. Stotesbury at Chestnut Hill, Pennsylvania.[92]

Mrs. Dodge's dreams of grandeur were tinged with the illusion of history. Steeped in the lore of the past, she spoke of the crowned heads of Europe with the same knowing regard as if they were her neighbors.[93] In a portrait in her library Sir Gerald Kelly depicted her in the elaborate costume of the court of Versailles.[94] Early in her life her husband gave her pearls that had belonged to Catherine the Great and later she was to acquire a piano once owned by Louis XV.[95] Much of the decor of Rose Terrace, as the Dodge abode is called, was retrieved by Sir Joseph Duveen from the imperial palaces of Russia. There are French inlaid furniture, Beauvais tapestry chairs, four cases of Sèvres porcelains, and paintings by Boucher, Gainsborough, and Van Dyck. The late Dr. William R. Valentiner, when director of the Detroit Institute of Arts, "unhesitatingly proclaimed the completed collection at least the equal of any French eighteenth century art ensemble in the world."[96]

No French château would be complete without a garden. To lay out hers, Mrs. Dodge employed Ellen Shipman of New York. To the west of the house is a formal French garden edged with boxwood and adorned with antique marble statues. In the background is a fountain. Adjoining this is a formal flower garden containing beds edged with wisteria trees and fruit trees, from which two flights of stairs lead down to the rose garden. Beyond lies the swimming pool, and beyond that the sweep of Lake St. Clair.[97]

(225) Hiram Walker & Sons Offices, *Mason & Rice*, 1892 (HAL)

(226) Detroit Opera House, *G. D. Mason*, 1898 (BHC)

(228) Progress (by Rhind) (HHR)

(229) Peoples State Bank, *McKim, Mead & White*, 1900 (HHR)

(230) Wayne County Jail, *J. & A. Scott*, 1897 (MB)

(231) Statler Hotel, *G. B. Post*, 1914 (BHC)

(232) Pontchartrain Hotel, *G. D. Mason*, 1907-16 (BHC)

(234) Book Tower, *L. Kamper*, 1926 (MB)

(233) Book-Cadillac Hotel, *L. Kamper*, 1924 (BHC)

(235) Washington Boulevard project,
L. Kamper (LK)

(236) Book Building, *L. Kamper*, 1917 (BHC)

(237) Detroit Athletic Club, *A. Kahn*, 1915 (MB)

(238) Police Headquarters, *A. Kahn*, 1923 (BHC)

(239) William L. Clements Library, *A. Kahn*, 1923 (AKA)

(242) Hurlbut Memorial Gate,
Brede & Mueller, 1894 (BHC)

(243) Detroit Public Library, *C. Gilbert*, 1921 (MB)

(244) Merrill Fountain, *Carrère & Hastings*, 1901 (BHC)

(245) Bicentennial Memorial project, *S. White*, 1900 (BHC)

(246) James Scott Fountain, *C. Gilbert*, 1925 (BHC)

(247) Detroit Institute of Arts, *P. P. Cret et al.*, 1927 (CHE/JKJ)

(248) Murray W. Sales House, *L. Kamper*, 1917 (LK/SL)

(249) George G. Booth House, *Mason & Rice*, 1889 (BHC/JKJ)

(250) Watson M. Freer House, *Mason & Rice*, 1895 (GDM/MB)

(251) J. Harrington Walker House, 1895 (BHC)

(252) Albert L. Stephens House, *G. D. Mason*, 1914 (HAL)

(253) James B. Book Jr. House, *L. Kamper*, 1911 (AS)

(254) Harry N. Torrey House, *J. & A. Scott*, 1913 (MB)

(255) Louis Kamper House, *L. Kamper*, c. 1910 (AS)

(256) Yondotega Club Fountain, *C. A. Platt*, 1902 (HHR)

(257-259) Russell A. Alger House, *C. A. Platt*, 1910 (MB)(HHR)

(260) Charles A. Dean House, *H. T. Keyes*, 1924 (MB)

(261) C. Goodloe Edgar House, *A. Kahn*, c. 1910 (HAL)

(262) Grosse Pointe Yacht Club, *G. Lowell*, 1927 (JPM)

(263) Henry D. Shelden House, *A. Heun*, 1911 (GPH/JKJ)

(264) Michigan Central R.R. Station, *Warren & Wetmore et al.*, 1913 (BHC)

(265) Detroit Trust Co., *A. Kahn*, 1915 (BHC)

(266) National Bank Building, *A. Kahn*, 1922 (MB)

(267) McGregor Public Library, *Tilton & Githens et al.*, 1926 (BHC)

(268) Angell Hall, *A. Kahn*, 1925 (AKA)

(269) William Livingstone House, *Mason & Rice*, 1893 (ELA)

(270) Harley G. Higbie House, *G. D. Mason*, 1926 (MB)

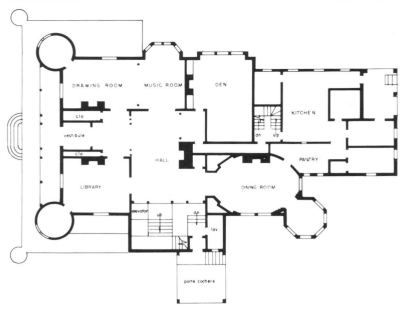

(271-274) Frank J. Hecker House, *Scott, Kamper & Scott,*
1890 (ELA) (BHC/JKJ)

(275-276) Mrs. Henry Stephens House, *C. A. Platt*, 1913 (HHR)

(277-278) Wesson Seyburn House, *B. Fleming*, 1924 (MB)

(279) Rose Terrace, *H. Trumbauer*, 1934 (DN)

(280) Julian P. Bowen House, *W. Frost*, 1927 (MB)

(281) Edwin H. Brown House, *R. O. Derrick*, 1926 (MB)

8. The Lure of the Middle Ages

The Arts and Crafts Movement

One of the salient triumphs of the reign of Queen Victoria was the Great Exhibition of 1851 in London. Here the nations of the world were invited to exhibit their manufactured goods. The size of the buildings and the quantity of the products were impressive, but discerning people realized that the aesthetic quality of the objects displayed left much to be desired.[1] One of those most keenly aware of this deficiency was William Morris. The machine, he felt, had obliterated taste. The charm of useful objects was created by the imagination of the craftsman. Therefore it was necessary to return to the handicraft methods of the medieval guilds.

In 1859 Philip Webb designed the Red House for Morris near London. It was a milestone in the history of modern building. Reacting against the superficiality of Victorian architecture, Webb returned to the sources of native tradition, relying for his effects upon simple massing, color, and materials. All the furnishings and decoration for the house were designed by Morris and Webb since they were unable to find anything suitable on the market.[2]

In 1861 the firm of Morris, Marshall, Faulkner and Company started business in London as fine art workmen in painting, carving, furniture, and metals. Their building contained a small kiln in the basement for firing glass and tiles. On the first floor were an office and showroom, and on the third floor a studio. Webb designed articles for domestic purposes, while Brown, Rossetti, and Burne-Jones painted tiles and made cartoons for stained glass windows. Morris worked at a variety of tasks and in addition was general manager. The firm was dissolved in 1874 and thereafter Morris started his own manufactory at Merton Abbey. There, with the assistance of many of his previous collaborators, he specialized in textiles, carpets and tapestries. In 1890 he established the Kelmscott Press where he devoted much of his talent to the design of books.[3]

Continental Europeans were too preoccupied with the Art Nouveau to be concerned with the Arts and Crafts movement. In the meantime, however, it was gaining ground in the United States. In 1897 the Boston Society of Arts and Crafts was established, and by 1907 there were twenty-three similar organizations in the United States. In 1904 the first exhibition of handicrafts in Detroit was held at the Detroit Museum of Art, followed by a second one in 1905 which *(171)* led to the founding of the Detroit Society of Arts and Crafts in 1906.[4] By a combination of circumstances Detroit was an extraordinarily fertile field for the new movement. A burgeoning industrial center, it had attracted many active and creative minds that were receptive to new ideas. Leading architects, artists, and businessmen rallied to the cause. In many cases ties of blood with England helped to generate enthusiasm for a phenomenon that was essentially British.

The first president of the Detroit Society of Arts and Crafts was George *(249)* Gough Booth. The guiding spirit during its formative years, he had been ideally prepared for the task at hand. Born in Toronto, Canada, he was brought to Detroit by his parents in 1881. His grandfather and great-grandfather had been coppersmiths in the Kentish town of Cranbrook in England.[5] Under these circumstances it is not surprising that early in his career he should have become the proprietor of an ornamental-iron works in Detroit. Then an event occurred that was to alter the course of his life: in 1887 he married Ellen Scripps, the daughter *(282)* of James E. Scripps, founder of the *Detroit News.* At the suggestion of Scripps he sold his prospering foundry and entered the field of journalism as business *(358)* manager of the *News;* after Scripps's death in 1906 Booth became president.[6] All during his long career as a newspaper publisher, however, he was to retain a profound interest in sound craftsmanship.

The phase of William Morris's work which seems first to have attracted Booth was the Kelmscott Press. He had early acquired a copy of the *Kelmscott Chaucer.* In 1900 he established a private press known as the Cranbrook Press on the top floor of the *Detroit News* building. There, during the course of two years, he published a series of books that bore a close resemblance to those designed by Morris.[7]

The first vice president of the Society of Arts and Crafts and head of its *(290)* executive committee was the architect William B. Stratton. He had designed and made furniture for the arts and crafts exhibitions at the Museum of Art in 1904 and 1905.[8] Active on the executive committee were Mary Chase Perry and Horace James Caulkins, founders of Detroit's Pewabic Pottery Company. Born in Hancock, Michigan, Miss Perry had studied to be a sculptor at the Cincinnati Art Academy, but her fondness for color caused her to shift into the field of ceramics. In Detroit she joined forces with Caulkins, who was a clay specialist. They first experimented with ceramics in a stable on John R. street.

In 1907 Caulkins and Miss Perry employed their friend William B. Stratton *(297)* to build the Pewabic pottery works on East Jefferson near Cadillac boulevard. There, in a revolutionary new oil-burning kiln developed by Caulkins, Miss Perry created the brilliant glazes and interesting shapes in clay that won her national acclaim. Over a long span of years the Pewabic Pottery Company provided tiles for some of Detroit's outstanding buildings, including the Institute of Arts, the Public Library, and St. Paul's Cathedral.[9] Their common interest in the arts and crafts led to the marriage of Miss Perry and Stratton in 1918. Her tiles added charm and character to many of his buildings.

The second president of the Society of Arts and Crafts was Frank C. Bald- *(289)* win, an architectural partner of Stratton. In 1911 he resigned and H. J. Maxwell Grylls became president. A native of England, Grylls had come to America in 1881 at the age of sixteen. After experience in several Detroit architectural offices, he became a partner in the firm of Smith, Hinchman and Grylls in 1906.[10]

When the Society of Arts and Crafts was founded in 1906 it rented space for exhibitions and sales on Farmer street. This soon proved to be inadequate and members began looking for new quarters. Stratton and Grylls saw possibilities in an abandoned stable on Witherell street at Adams avenue. With a little ingenuity and imagination they were able to convert it into a charming new center for the society's activities. A balcony around the lofty exhibition room provided extra display space and a fireplace with a tile mantel contributed by Miss Perry afforded an inviting focal point. Even these quarters were soon outgrown. Then George Booth came forward with a generous proposition: he offered to donate a piece of property he owned on Watson street provided the other members would raise the money to erect a new building. He further stipulated that if this could be done within three weeks, he would build a row of craftsmen's workshops on the east end of the building. "It is my belief," he asserted, "that this Society is the strongest art influence we can count upon to bring about a permanent change in the ideals of this city. Under its leadership we can imagine these shops filled with craftsmen and works of art springing up under their hands."

Booth's enthusiasm was infectious. Pledges poured in and the quota was filled almost immediately. Stratton and Grylls were assigned the task of drawing up the plans. By 1916 the society was able to celebrate its tenth anniversary in its new headquarters. "The new building of the Society is not only the most com- *(299)* plete of its kind in the country; it is altogether unique in that it brings together salesrooms, galleries, workshops, and a complete theater," wrote Sheldon Cheney in the *American Magazine of Art*.[23]

Soon after the opening the place was humming with activity. In addition to displaying articles for sale, a series of exhibitions was held as a basis for guidance and comparison in setting standards. Exhibitions of the crafts of England, America, France, Denmark, and Sweden did much to raise the general level of public taste. The shops were used by individual craftsmen for making furniture, wood carvings, and jewelry. One room served as an office for Sam Hume, the director of the little theater, and in another Sheldon Cheney carried on his work as editor of *Theatre Arts Magazine*.

In 1919 the theater was discontinued as the board decided it was not the function of the Society of Arts and Crafts to run one. Having served its purpose, the salesroom was closed in 1931: the kind of wares it sold had become available at the better stores. In 1926 the Art School was founded. As enrollment increased it took over space formerly occupied by the theater. Gradually the emphasis of the society shifted from sales and exhibits to the training of art *(415)* students, which is its principal objective today.[11]

The Tudor Style Revived

Just as Morris had brought about a revolution in design in England in the latter half of the nineteenth century, so Philip Webb and Norman Shaw led the way toward a new concept of architecture. Dissatisfied with the prevalent architectural education, they reexamined the traditional rural dwelling to gain insight into the everyday problems of building.[12] The English Domestic Revival, as this movement in English architecture between 1860 and 1900 was called, was founded upon the principles of structural integrity. One of the best expressions of these principles was Philip Webb's Red House. Too often, however, architects lost sight of the objectives of the movement. Even Shaw was too easily satisfied with mere stylistic evocation as his Tudor-style manor houses clearly demonstrated. H. H. Richardson's Watts Sherman house (1874) in Newport, Rhode Island, was an adaptation of the Shavian manor house. It started a new American architectural trend which was reinforced by the British buildings at the Philadelphia Centennial of 1876.[13]

The first example of the Tudor style in Detroit was the James E. Scripps house of 1891. This was more the product of the personal convictions and background of the owner than of any prevailing trend. In 1879, six years after

(358) founding the *Detroit News*, Scripps had built a small nondescript house on Trumbull near Grand River avenue. Subsequent study and travel in Europe convinced him of the artistic shortcomings of American architecture. Although a man of broad erudition, his strongest ties were with his native England. Deeply religious by nature, he closely supervised and financed the construction of Trin-

(314) ity Church (1892) across the street from his residence. The style of architecture was English Gothic.

When Scripps decided to expand his residence to make room for his growing

(282) collection of art, it was natural for him to think in terms of Tudor Gothic. Mason and Rice were able to accommodate him with a soaring English baronial castle composed of crenelated walls dominated by an octagonal tower. The details, such as the oriel window on the tower, were evidence of Scripps's taste for fine workmanship. The crowning glory of the house was the library added

(284) on the north side by Albert Kahn in 1898. It served as the repository for a collection of rare and scholarly books which are now cherished treasures of the Detroit Public Library.

Perfectionist that he was, Scripps insisted upon authenticity in the Gothic

(283) architecture of his library. Modeled after the chapter house at Westminster Abbey, it contained a fine stone vault. The ribs of the vault branched out from a

(285) single clustered pier at the center towards the external buttresses between which there were narrow lancet windows. After Scripps's death the entire library structure was moved across Trumbull avenue and joined to the former George

(249) G. Booth house to form the Scripps Branch Library. The Scripps house proper became the property of the Daughters of Divine Charity.[14] Long abandoned, the Scripps art gallery and library building was finally razed in 1967.

The Tudor manor house attained a wide popularity in the twentieth century. It is essentially a rural type of dwelling and seemed appropriate in the rural areas that were becoming inhabited as a result of the suburban movement. Albert Kahn's work on the Scripps library first interested him in English medieval architecture. He greatly admired the Tudor domestic vernacular and during the course of his life designed a number of houses in this style. As he became more involved in industrial and commercial work, however, there was little time left for residences. The few that he produced were for the executives of the firms that employed him.

One of Kahn's earliest Tudor houses was commissioned in 1905 by Charles

(286) M. Swift, a prominent attorney. It was located on Jefferson avenue in Grosse Pointe overlooking Lake St. Clair and was faced in gray random ashlar.[15] For a time the house was occupied by the late Horace E. Dodge Jr. In 1906 Kahn did a

(288) residence in Walkerville, Ontario, for Edward C. Walker, the son of Hiram Walker. Here, in contrast to the Swift house, there was a deliberate attempt to evoke the past. Gables with carved bargeboards, leaded windows, and fine stone-work contrasting with half-timbered areas created a medieval effect. Walkerville is now part of Windsor and today the mansion houses a public library and the Willistead Art Gallery.

Somewhat in the same vein was the James Hamilton house (1902) on Jeffer-

(287) son avenue in the Indian Village district of Detroit. Designed by Stratton and Baldwin, it reflected Norman Shaw's rural manor houses. The William B. Strat-

(290) ton house (1895) by the same architects was more reminiscent of Shaw's town houses, although its heavy masonry walls gave it a rustic character. This was the

(305) first of three houses Stratton built for himself. Located on West Warren avenue,

it later served as the office of the president of Wayne State University and his staff until its recent demolition.

In 1916 the firm of Smith, Hinchman and Grylls gave the north side of Grand Circus Park a distinctly medieval flavor with the half-timbered Woman's Exchange.[16] The profusion of gables and the bay windows jutting out, one above the other, remind one of an old English inn.   *(291)*

The Cottage Style

The second generation of architects of the English Domestic Revival became impatient with the cumbersome trappings of medievalism. Charles F. A. Voysey and others led the way toward the solution of the problems of the modern dwelling by a further simplification and rationalization of plan and design. Incorporating the best features of indigenous rural architecture in their houses, they strove to adapt their interiors to the requirements of modern living. In response to this new freedom of planning the exteriors became more plastic and fluid. A new sense of abstract design was apparent in the grouping of the masses and roof forms, the concentration of window areas, and the use of broad wall surfaces to emphasize the color and texture of various building materials. With the development of this informal and intimate 'Cottage Style,' English domestic architecture advanced a step further toward the reality of the present.[17]

In the first quarter of the twentieth century the influence of the cottage style became apparent in the work of leading Detroit architects. Most of these men were members of the Society of Arts and Crafts and took a keen interest in the creative arts of England. William B. Stratton and Frank C. Baldwin were among the first Detroit architects to respond to the new trend. This was shown in their design for Baldwin's own house (1908) on Jefferson avenue in Grosse Pointe.[18]   *(289)*
To be sure, there were still echoes of Shaw and Webb, but the simple stucco walls and organic planning bespoke a new freedom and independence. Sweeping lines and sparse fenestration on the entrance side created a picturesque rustic effect. The more formal Renaissance treatment of the lake side had the advantage of opening up the principal rooms toward the lake with numerous windows at regular intervals. In the twenties Dr. Frederick T. Murphy, a later owner of the estate, had Robert O. Derrick add a large baronial two-story library on the west end of the house. Taking the place of an earlier veranda, a broad garden terrace provided a view of the lake across a lawn studded with ancient apple trees. After the death of Mrs. Murphy in 1956 the property was sold to William Clay Ford. Left unoccupied, the house was destroyed by fire in 1960.[19]

Next door to the Baldwin house Stratton and Baldwin built a residence the same year (1908) for Frederick M. Alger, the son of General Alger.[20] On the   *(293)*
entrance side the house resembled a low rambling English farmhouse. On the central bay there was a hipped-back gable and an oriel window hovered above the front entrance. The walls were faced with stucco with only a slight trace of half-timbered work and the roof was sheathed in copper which time gave a verdigris coloration. One of the most admirable characteristics of the cottage style was its dedication to the enjoyment of living. Nowhere could this be more apparent than on the lake side of the Alger house. Here a continuous series of rooms savored the delights of the waterfront through banks of windows and French doors that opened upon a terrace extending the full length of the house. The phrasing of these doors and of the dormers set in the gambrel roof provided a subtle counterpoint against the broad horizontals of the design as a whole.

(292) On the interior as well as the exterior the Alger house manifested more progressive tendencies than the Baldwin house. Plain unornamented paneling took the place of ornate Elizabethan strap-work. Following in the tradition of the Arts and Crafts movement, Stratton designed much of the furniture for both houses. The product of a vigorous and creative imagination, the Alger house was considerably ahead of its time in its frank functionalism. Its originality and charm were unique and it is unfortunate that it was recently demolished.

(294) Architects Trowbridge and Ackerman also took advantage of the flexibility of the cottage style in their design for a villa on the lake. In 1909 they built the L. Stephen Trowbridge house on Jefferson avenue in Grosse Pointe. Sharp gables stood out against the steep gray slate roof, while rhythmically grouped windows formed a pattern on the rough-textured stucco walls. In contrast to the Alger house, however, the main floor and the terrace were raised up off the ground. This insured a more commanding view of the lake, at the same time avoiding drainage problems in the basement which was above ground level. From 1906 to 1921 Alexander B. Trowbridge was the senior partner in the firm of Trowbridge and Ackerman in New York. A native of Detroit, he was the brother of L. Stephen Trowbridge. After graduation from Cornell in 1890 he studied at the École des Beaux-Arts in Paris.[21] For a brief period he worked in the office of George D. Mason and later was a partner of Albert Kahn before moving to New York.

(297) When Stratton and Baldwin built the Pewabic pottery works in 1907 on East Jefferson avenue in Detroit they could hardly have been expected to think in terms of a factory for mass production. The suggestion of an English cottage with its steep medieval roof and cozy appearance provided the right atmosphere for a small-scaled handicraft industry, and at the same time connoted historical associations appropriate for a project motivated by the ideals of the Arts and Crafts movement. A grouping together of windows assured ample illumination, but monotony was avoided by a playful use of different types of windows and textures of materials and also by an alternation of advancing and receding wall planes.

(299) In 1911 Frank C. Baldwin moved to Virginia after eighteen years of partnership with William B. Stratton, during the latter part of which he was the administrative member of the firm.[18] Five years later Stratton collaborated with Maxwell Grylls in a new building for the Society of Arts and Crafts on Watson street (1916).[22] More than any of Stratton's other buildings, it approximated the work done by Voysey and his contemporaries in England. The flowing lines of the roof, the stucco walls and chimney, and the free grouping of the windows were combined in an overall plastic unity in which the interest derived more from the subtlety of details than from any historical allusion. Sheldon Cheney recorded his impressions of it in the *American Magazine of Art:*

In the design of this unusual structure, the architects . . . succeeded in interpreting the spirit of the organization to a remarkable degree. The building is neither an attempt at 'the monumental' as seen in most art buildings, nor an imitation of the Continental 'new art' abomination. It has, if I may venture a somewhat clumsy metaphor, a 'hand-made' look. It is neither over-refined nor over-rough. In short it has the atmosphere of craftsmanship about it.

The style of architecture may have been inspired by something developed somewhere between England and Italy—just where no one seems to be sure. At any rate, there is a suggestion of English cottage architecture somewhere, and certainly a Spanish or Italian feeling in the court, and (to be perfectly neutral) some vague reflection of clean-cut German craftsmanship in the design of the galleries. . . .

The exterior walls are of yellow-brown stucco with windows leaded in small panes. The roof is of red tile. Chimney pots of brilliant blue, green and yellow Pewabic pottery add life to the color scheme. The structure is U-shaped in arrangement, with the two-storied main building forming one side of the letter, and the line of the low one-story shops forming the other. Between is a little flagged court, one of the most attractive features of the whole design.

One steps from the street directly into the main salesroom. The interior of this is finished in wood, stained a dull gray-brown. An immense open fireplace, trimmed with Pewabic tile, adds a decorative note to one wall. The second important salesroom, or gallery, is upstairs. These two rooms, despite their un-usual size, are comfortably filled by the cases containing the permanent exhibits of crafts work. When special exhibitions are held, the doors between the sales-rooms and the auditorium can be folded back, and both the main auditorium floor and the galleries above added to the display space. The auditorium was designed with this particular purpose in mind, and the floor, instead of having the usual uniform slope, is in three levels, one above the other. It is in the auditorium that one sees the decorative scheme of the building executed, under the direction of Mrs. Sidney Corbett Jr., at its best. The walls are of orange-brown rough plaster. The newel-posts terminating the railing around the lower level, and the posts in the gallery railings, are touched with brilliant bits of red, yellow and black. The chairs are painted in six different colors—a successful bit of departure from tradition, which does much to save the hall from the usual look of somberness and bareness. . . .

It is the workshops, perhaps, that form the most unique feature of the build-ing. There are eight of these grouped in the eastern wing of the building, seven of which face the open court. Each shop has its individual lighting system and water and power connections. The leaded glass windows and the stained wood of the side walls add a decorative touch in each room, but the rough face brick front and rear walls are reminders that these are craftsmen's quarters, and not studios of the bow-tie variety.[23]

Among those who were active in supporting the Society of Arts and Crafts was Albert Kahn, a founding member. Its standards of simplicity and good taste appealed to him. For the same reason he was attracted by the cottage style, but the extravagant taste of his wealthy clients was not conducive to development in this direction. No such hindrance existed when he built his own house at the *(295)* southeast corner of Mack avenue and John R. in 1906. Here the oppressive souvenirs of the Middle Ages had all but vanished to expose the clean surfaces of a house adapted to modern living. Windows were grouped according to the internal needs of the plan yet were adjusted to form a part of a carefully studied overall design. Contrasting materials on different floor levels provided a horizon-tal emphasis, which was broken by the vertical grouping of the bay windows and other minor accents. Today this interesting house belongs to the Detroit Urban League.

In 1909 George Gough Booth engaged Kahn to build a residence in Bloom- *(296)* field Hills north of Detroit.[24] He had bought an estate there in 1904 and called it Cranbrook after his ancestral home in England. As the leader of the Arts and Crafts movement in Detroit, Booth naturally favored the cottage style. Kahn's own house afforded the point of departure for the large rambling mansion that took form on an eminence overlooking the rolling wooded terrain of Bloomfield

(298) Hills. Little by little the original farm lands of the estate were transformed into a carefully landscaped preserve. Under Booth's close personal supervision extensive gardens were laid out, trees planted, and an artificial lake created. In time others discovered the rustic beauty of Bloomfield Hills and it became one of Detroit's most desirable residential suburbs.

(301) Booth provided for the religious needs of the growing community by building a little place of worship known as the Meeting House at the edge of the Cranbrook estate in 1918.[25] He had always been deeply interested in architecture ever since he had been an office boy in an architect's office in Toronto before coming to Detroit. The Meeting House was the product of his own imagination.[26] Resembling a picturesque English farmhouse, it was built of stone rubble and half-timbered work with a steep roof and casement windows. The furnishings came from the workshops of the Society of Arts and Crafts.[27] In 1922 a day school for small children was opened in the Meeting House. This was the beginning of the Brookside School. As enrollment increased it became necessary to enlarge the facilities. An additional structure, harmonizing with the old, was built from the plans of Marcus Burrowes, and in 1929 Booth's son Henry S. Booth served as the architect for still another addition.[28]

(300) In the meantime George D. Mason was trying his hand at the cottage style. His Edwin S. George house (1923) on Long Lake road in Bloomfield Hills displayed the increasing tendency toward theatricality characteristic of the twenties. The rough slate roof with its sagging ridge, the clustered gables, and the flowing roof lines gave it the pastoral character of the English countryside. At the same time the restraint and skill with which diverse elements were combined in a harmonious whole made it an outstanding example of its type. It is *(320)* now a church house for the Kirk-in-the-Hills.

(302) The flexibility and rustic charm of the cottage style made it suitable for country clubs. In 1917 Albert Kahn designed the Detroit Golf Club on Hamilton road in Detroit. Fine brickwork, banks of windows, and an interesting treatment of roof masses combined to make a pleasing and original design. In the twenties Kahn succumbed to the cult of the picturesque. In 1923 he built the new Country Club of Detroit in Grosse Pointe near the golf course. A newspaper columnist in the *Detroit Free Press* classified it as an example of "the English Cottage Style." He referred to the "rough reddish brick and irregular slate roof." "All over the clubhouse artistic details are to be noted," he wrote. "Window flower boxes, the small leaded panes of the windows, the gables and dormers, the rough-hewn timber beams, and even the wrought iron weathervane, a golfer against the rising sun, fit perfectly into the picturesque whole."[29]

(303) In 1925 the building was reduced to ruins by a disastrous fire of unknown origin. Only the servants' wing was left intact.[30] Thereupon the firm of Smith, Hinchman and Grylls was employed to rebuild the clubhouse. They resumed in very much the same style of architecture, but the plans and details were different. Notwithstanding its storybook romanticism, the design was tastefully executed. The rambling plan, large rooms, long connecting gallery, and broad window areas made a cheerful and pleasant gathering place for social activities.

(305) William B. Stratton was not immune to the romanticism of the twenties, but for him it was a means of personal expression. His own house on Three Mile drive in Grosse Pointe, which was completed in 1927, was the final fruition of his architectural credo.[31] In the face of the mounting antiquarianism of the period he returned to the basic essentials of the Arts and Crafts movement, yet with a fresh interpretation that was his own. In 1918 he had married Mary Chase Perry, the ceramist. Together they worked out many of the details. In view of

her profession it is not surprising that their travels should have led them to Mexico and Spain, and there they absorbed the Spanish atmosphere which later permeated their house.

To say that the house was typically Spanish would be underrating Stratton's mastery of pure aesthetics and minimizing his feeling for form, color, and texture. It was a multi-leveled structure with numerous bays and balconies. There were windows everywhere to catch the sun and breezes or to look down into some hidden garden spot shut in by vine-clad walls. Yet, in spite of all this *(304)* seeming confusion, there was an underlying harmony and a strong sense of plastic composition, and over all was suffused the warm glow of the variegated brown and beige tones of brick and tile. On the interior colorful Pewabic tiles adorned the fireplaces and the bathrooms. The ceilings were low and heavily beamed, and the floors were made of time-weathered oak. On the second floor the ceilings followed the slope of the beamed roof rafters. In the library the concrete remained exposed as it left the forms.[32] Here Stratton revealed himself as an artist searching for expressive materials. If sometimes he followed paths that led to the past, it was only in order to discover secrets that would lead to a more vital architecture in the future.

The Tudor Dream

The boom of the twenties brought with it a tremendous surge of building activity. Architectural styles multiplied in bewildering confusion. Americans had been exposed to distant lands and remote times in the motion pictures, and now they were demanding something of this exoticism in their daily surroundings. There were some who still yearned for the grandeur of Renaissance Italy and France, but the general trend was toward the quaintly picturesque. In this category the Tudor style became the popular favorite. The rugged business leaders of the day, largely of Anglo-Saxon origin, identified it with the stirring chivalrous world of their ancestors. At the same time its massive walls, cavernous interiors, and heraldic devices conveyed a message of awesome masculine dignity and prestige.

In the headlong pursuit of the picturesque the principles of the Arts and Crafts movement were easily forgotten, leaving behind the hard core of medievalism. A revival of authentic Tudor architecture required the most painstaking study and research in order to achieve just the right appearance of antiquity and haphazard irregularity. The reproduction of ornate late Gothic stonework was in itself a major undertaking. Undaunted by such obstacles, architects and clients united in an earnest endeavor to recapture the glories of the past. The economic climate was conducive to the realization of the most extravagant dreams, of which the most socially acceptable was the 'Tudor Dream.'

The fabulous automotive fortunes of Detroit gave birth to some of the city's most overwhelming demonstrations of architectural virtuosity. In the magnificence of their domiciles few could hope to rival the Dodge family. When John F. Dodge decided to build a house on Lake Shore road in Grosse Pointe, no *(306)* expenditure of time or money was considered too great to assure the maximum in quality. The walls were to be of solid stone. Granite was shipped in from quarries in Weymouth, Massachusetts. From Scotland came one hundred and ten stone-cutters chosen because of their work on Andrew Carnegie's Skibo Castle. Some of them worked for days, even weeks, on a single piece of granite. The mansion was to contain one hundred and ten rooms and twenty-four baths. In the basement there was to be a ballroom and a swimming pool. Since John Dodge was a lover of flowers, formal gardens and a greenhouse were to contain rare specimens gathered from all over the world. A small artificial peninsula was built, which was to lead to a private dock for the splendid Dodge yacht.

Then in 1920, as the work was nearing completion, John Dodge unexpectedly died. For twenty years the house stood unfinished and neglected. Finally in 1941 it was torn down and the property subdivided.[33] The architects of this ill-fated abode were Smith, Hinchman and Grylls. Fred L. Smith, the president of the firm, represented the third generation of the Smith family to follow the architectural profession. He received his training in the office of his father Mortimer L. Smith, the son of Sheldon Smith.[34] Theodore H. Hinchman Jr., a consulting engineer educated at the University of Michigan, was the treasurer of the firm. H. J. Maxwell Grylls was the vice president. A native of England, he had begun his architectural career in Detroit in the offices of William E. Brown and later John Scott and Company.[10]

Matilda R. Dodge, the widow of John F. Dodge, did not give up the idea of a grand mansion. In 1925 she married Alfred G. Wilson. Fond of country life, they acquired Meadow Brook, a fourteen hundred acre estate near Rochester, Michigan. Then they spent a year in Europe searching for inspiration for their future home. With them went William E. Kapp, head of the design department of Smith, Hinchman and Grylls. They stayed in London for seven weeks, each day motoring out to some ancient manor house to gather ideas. Kapp was able to obtain measured drawings of much of what they saw from the Royal Institute of British Architects or the Victoria and Albert Museum.[35] When they returned *(307)* Kapp started work on the drawings. By 1929 the sprawling baronial mansion was completed in the quiet hills near Rochester.[36]

The main source of inspiration was Compton Wynyates, the great sixteenth century Tudor manor house in Warwickshire. This was particularly evident in the entrance bay with its battlements and Tudor arch surmounted by a three-light mullioned window. It was also evident in the lofty twisted chimney-stacks and the charming mingling of stone, brick, and half-timber work on the exterior walls. The focal point of the vast interior was the spectacular two-story ballroom which could be seen through the stone arches of the broad entrance hall. The staircase leading from the hall was a masterpiece of carving and design.[37] The heraldic stained glass windows, the ornate carved pipe organ, and some of the hand-rubbed paneling were moved to Rochester from the uncompleted house in Grosse Pointe. The vast rooms and halls were filled with opulent furniture, paintings, and tapestries.[38] Through the mullioned windows there were glimpses of formal gardens stretching out toward the distant meadows.

A woman of broad humanitarian interests, Mrs. Wilson was a patron of opera and music, and for years was actively interested in the Salvation Army. In 1957 the Wilsons gave their estate to Michigan State University.

The English experiences of William E. Kapp proved to be invaluable when *(311)* he undertook the design of the University Club (1931) on behalf of Smith, Hinchman and Grylls. The entry of the club on Russell street off Jefferson avenue was a brick version of the entrance bay of Compton Wynyates. The stair hall with its lantern was an adaptation of a stairway in one of the finest of the great houses of England—Knole in Kent.

It was the heyday of the 'Collegiate Gothic,' when Yale and Princeton were abandoning their colonial heritage to return to the cloistered medieval atmosphere of Oxford and Cambridge. As an organization of university graduates, it seemed appropriate for the University Club to do likewise. This effect was obtained with beamed ceilings, leaded glass, and the hand-worn appearance of the interior woodwork. Even the exterior bricks were reproductions of the handmade brick of Cambridge. Many years later Kapp defended his work at the University Club. "The Tudors in Merrie England," he maintained, "had developed what was probably the most flexible planning, the most honest exterior, and the freest use of materials of any of the architectural styles." He was of the opinion that "any interested layman" could "read the internal space designations on the exterior of the building and note the freedom in size, spacing, and relation of the wall openings which the Tudor style provides."[39]

In the meantime architect Robert O. Derrick was turning aside from his charmingly intimate French and Colonial vernacular to enter the grander world of the Tudor. Examples of his work in this style are the Richard H. Webber (1925) and the J. Bell Moran (1929) houses in Grosse Pointe. These paved the way for one of the most impressive mansions there, the Standish Backus house *(309)* (1934) on Lake Shore road. Backus succeeded his father-in-law Joseph Boyer as president of the Burroughs Adding Machine Company. If he had not been a businessman, he would have liked to be an architect. He owned an extensive architectural library and had made a study of the Elizabethan and Tudor styles. The work on his house was therefore a matter of great personal interest to him.

Since Backus was a friend of Ralph Adams Cram, the renowned Gothicist of Boston, he asked Derrick if he would mind submitting the plans of the house to Cram for suggestions and criticisms. Derrick took the drawings to Boston and was pleased when Cram complimented him highly on his design and gave it his complete approval without any suggestions or criticisms.[40]

A long straight driveway, separated from the lawn by a hedge of clipped yew, led from Lake Shore road to a forecourt in front of the Backus house. The entrance façade struck a note of rugged grandeur with its massive stone walls, picturesque gables, and ornately carved entry. The rear of the house was less theatrical. Here rows of mullioned windows overlooked an inviting terrace and *(308)* the garden beyond. Fletcher Steel of Boston, the landscape architect, worked in close cooperation with the architect to create a beautiful setting for the house. Sweeping lawns were bordered by clumps of box bushes and rows of clipped European linden and beech trees. Opposite the house there was a charming fountain ornamented with baroque sculpture. All this has vanished now, for the house was torn down in 1966 and the property is being subdivided.

Among those in Detroit who admired the Tudor style there were some who favored its simpler rural phases in preference to the grandiose architecture of the great mansions. In view of his liking for the simplicities of the Colonial period, it is understandable that Henry Ford should have been attracted by the unaffected charm of the medieval dwellings of rural England. In supervising the far-flung operations of his vast automotive empire, Ford frequently visited the British Isles. Whenever he went there he managed to spend a few days in the Cotswold district of which he was particularly fond. Invariably he stayed at the Lygon Arms, an ancient hostelry in the tiny village of Broadway in Worcestershire. There he used to enjoy talking with the inn's proprietor S. B. Russell who was an authority on local antiquities.

H. F. Morton, engineer in charge of the plant at the Ford Motor Company of England, frequently accompanied Ford on his trips to the Cotswolds where he would drive him around the secluded byways of the unspoiled countryside. Later in a biographical sketch of Ford, Morton noted: "He was much taken with the distinctive architecture which is a feature of these parts, where local stone seems to be the only visible material of construction, and where stone roof tiles, stone dormers and stone mullions all blend beautifully together and form a most attractive and mellow combination which improves with the passage of time."[41]

(346) When Henry Ford saw something that interested him, his acquisitive instincts were aroused, for at that time he was building Greenfield Village in Dearborn, Michigan, a collection of buildings assembled from various parts of the country to illustrate the American way of life from the handicraft period to the machine age.[42] A Cotswold cottage, he felt, would demonstrate the way in which our forefathers lived before they migrated to America.[43] Morton was instructed to find and purchase a modest building with as many characteristic local features as possible. It was then to be taken down, packed, and shipped to Dearborn. In the little village of Lower Chedworth he found a shepherd's cot-*(310)* tage that met all the requirements. Miraculously, it was for sale.

Cox Howman, a local builder well versed in the lore of Worcestershire, was placed in charge of dismantling and shipping the cottage to America. He sent two of his workmen over to aid in the reconstruction.[44] By 1931 the job was completed and fires were again burning in the blackened hearths. Everything had been done to make the place look as authentic as possible. S. B. Russell was consulted on the furnishings and equipment. The original stone garden wall was reinstalled,[45] genuine Cotswold sheep were placed on the lawn to graze, and doves were put in the dove cotes, but for some reason the latter refused to remain in their new homes.[46]

Henry Ford's son Edsel spent some time with his father in the Cotswold country and he too was attracted by the local architecture. He was still under its *(312)* spell when he built his own house in Grosse Pointe in 1927.[47] In later years, when the house was unsuccessfully offered for sale, a descriptive brochure stated:

When Mr. and Mrs. Ford decided to build this Lake Shore residence, they proceeded to carry out two basic ideas. They wanted a modest and picturesque home—not a palace or fortress—and they wanted its architecture to reproduce faithfully the beautiful and practical Cotswold houses of Worcestershire, . . .

The Fords made many visits to the Cotswold district; they engaged in considerable research on the history and construction of Cotswold houses; and then secured the services of the late Albert Kahn, architect, to design and build the home which they enjoyed for so many years, until the death of Mr. Ford in 1943.

Mr. Kahn went abroad for further study of the quaint Cotswold structures, and to make sketches and photographs of a myriad of details. He had noticed that many of the larger houses of this type consisted of an original building to which additions had been built through the years and centuries, resulting in that characteristic rambling appearance.

The residence is faced with Briar Hill sandstone. The stones for the roof of this home were imported from England; and expert British workmen were also brought in to split the stones and to lay them on the roof in authentic Cotswold manner. A proportion of old stones from demolished buildings were mixed with the new stones to obtain the desired weathered effect—just one instance of the infinite detail employed by Mr. and Mrs. Ford to achieve their purpose. This is further illustrated by the entire stairway of weathered oak, huge fireplaces, paneling and other materials—some, hundreds of years old, brought over from England in their entirety and painstakingly reassembled in this home.

The same thoughtful skill was employed in creating an appropriate setting for the home [by Jens Jensen of Chicago, the landscape architect]. Almost every conceivable element for gracious living is present on the grounds—formal ter-

raced gardens . . . a swimming pool, not the conventional type, but of graceful contours, and which cascades into a lily pond. Thence into Lake St. Clair. A deep lagoon, connecting the Boat House at one end with a dock near the home at the other end . . . trees of many species and shrubbery in profusion . . . a vegetable garden of considerable size and productivity.[48]

Somewhat similar to the Ford residence was the great mansion which Albert Kahn built two years later on Lake Shore road in Grosse Pointe for Alvan Macauley, president of the Packard Motor Car Company.[49] The Macauleys were also partial to the Cotswold vernacular and in preparation for the building of their house they spent many weeks in Broadway, Worcestershire, studying the local architecture. They, too, stayed at the Lygon Arms, and at the antique shop adjoining this inn they acquired many of the fine English antiques that were later to adorn their house.[50] *(313)*

Less rambling and secluded than the Ford establishment, the Macauley house stands proudly in the open amid sweeping stretches of greensward which provide a splendid setting for its architectural masses and give it the air of a great landed estate. The landscape architect Edward A. Eichstaedt avoided any suggestion of artificial restraint or stylization in the landscaping. Utilizing the natural characteristics of the terrain as a keynote, he emphasized broad unhampered areas bordered with native trees and shrubs. A terrace of generous dimensions provided a view across the lawn toward the lake.

The massing and proportions of the house were carefully studied and a pleasing effect was secured by a subtle variety of details and a contrast in textures. The excellent quality of the masonry was assured by the employment of Scotsmen with years of experience, supervised by a Cotswold foreman. The skilled woodcarving of the distinguished interior was executed under the direction of the Hayden Company of New York. In the living room which occupies an entire wing there is paneling that combines the medieval linenfold motif with later Renaissance ornament. The dining room is George I in style.[51]

The prosperity of the twenties manifested itself in Grosse Pointe not only in the great mansions, but also in many houses of less awesome proportions, some of which displayed fine workmanship and competent design. Into this category falls the Julian H. Harris house on Windmill Point drive which was designed by William B. Stratton (1925). It is surprising to find this architect in such a conservative mood, considering his usual independence of thought, but even Stratton sometimes had to make concessions to his clients. Although employing traditional details and materials, he reduced the Tudor style to its simplest terms. Banks of windows in undulating bays took advantage of the lake view. By avoiding the purely picturesque and allowing some leeway for personal interpretation, Stratton created a house of considerable charm. *(315)*

Two other Tudor houses in Grosse Pointe which deserve mention for their excellence in design are the William P. Harris house (1925) also on Windmill Point drive, and the Howard F. Smith house on Provençal road. The former was designed by Hugh T. Keyes and the latter by Raymond Carey. Reflecting the ebullience and the overconfidence of the era, the Tudor style reached the peak of its popularity in the twenties. However, it was an extravagant type of architecture that was difficult to reproduce. For every well-designed house there were many shoddy caricatures. The depression of the thirties put an end to these febrile fabrications. Tired of over-theatrical clichés and gloomy interiors, suburbanites turned with relief to the more cheerful and less costly simplicity of the Colonial.

The Gothic Quest

The academic orientation which took place in American architecture at the turn of the century inevitably made its mark upon religious architecture. The Gothic had been popular ever since the beginning of the nineteenth century, but it had never been accurately reproduced. Americans returning from Europe blushed at the gingerbread monstrosities that passed for churches in their own country. With greater knowledge and means at their disposal, architects could now make amends for past indiscretions.

One of the most knowledgeable connoisseurs of art and architecture of his day in Detroit, newspaper publisher James E. Scripps deplored the prevailing level of Victorian taste. By giving the Detroit Museum of Art its first old masters he had appreciably raised the standards of the pictorial arts in his city. *(282)* His own Tudor mansion was a visible protest against the vagaries of the Victorian domicile. Scripps built Trinity Church at his own expense to provide for more than the religious needs of the community. According to his own words he hoped it would "stimulate, if possible, in church architecture a return to the older and more truly artistic forms."[52]

Located on the southwest corner of Trumbull and Myrtle, Trinity Episcopal *(314)* Church was completed in 1892 by Mason and Rice.[53] The style of architecture was Gothic as it was developed in southern England in the late fourteenth century. Scripps had engaged an English architect to visit the churches of this area and make careful drawings of details. From the mass of material forwarded to Detroit, Mason and Rice incorporated many features in their design of the new church. Cruciform in plan, the building was constructed of solid masonry with a massive tower at the crossing. The nave was separated from the aisles by arcades in the traditional fashion. The tracery in the windows was archeologically correct and fine carved stone ornament added to the medieval flavor.

In the meantime two young architects in the East were becoming the national leaders in the movement to reform church architecture. The Romanesque Revival had fallen into disrepute because of the shortcomings of H. H. Richardson's successors. Entering the vacuum thus created, Ralph Adams Cram and Bertram Grosvenor Goodhue picked up the broken threads of the Gothic tradition and breathed new life into it.[54] A medievalist to the core, Cram spread the gospel in speeches and writings. It was not difficult to convince church communicants, regardless of their denomination, that the Gothic lent dignity to their liturgies, and as the leading exponents of this style the firm of Cram, Goodhue and Ferguson received commissions far and wide across the nation.

New York is indebted to them for a truly splendid edifice, St. Thomas's Church of 1906, which brought to Fifth avenue the lofty turrets and lacy stonework of the Flamboyant Gothic of France.[55] In 1911 they built St. Paul's Epis- *(316)* copal Cathedral on Woodward avenue at Hancock in Detroit.[56] The façade with its rose window flanked by jutting buttresses recalled St. Thomas's, but the main body of the church was English Gothic of the fourteenth and fifteenth centuries. The architects planned to place a tower over the crossing, but this was never added. Conseqeuntly, the soaring lines of the building fail to reach a climax and the overall effect falls short of expectations. However, this in no way detracts from the very fine interior with its rows of massive columns and graceful lancet windows.[57]

It is significant that Cram and Goodhue differed in their approach toward architecture. Relying upon archeological verisimilitude, Cram strove to demonstrate the continuity of tradition in Christian culture; while Goodhue, endowed with a more creative imagination, saw each problem from a purely aesthetic point of view. After years of collaboration it became apparent that if they were to reach their full stature individually, they must separate; so their partnership was dissolved in 1913.[58] In the span of years that remained until Goodhue's death in 1924 he scored many triumphs. One of his last commissions was Christ Church *(317)* Cranbrook (Episcopal) in Bloomfield Hills.[59] His death came in the early stages of the work, but the building was completed by his associates in 1928.

In 1918 George G. Booth had established the Meeting House which became *(301)* the center for the religious, educational, and civic life of early Bloomfield Hills. With the growth of population this had expanded into the various educational institutions of the Cranbrook Foundation, his great philanthropic project. Christ Church Cranbrook was his response to the need for a larger and more adequate religious center for all the institutions and the community at large.[60]

As the leader of the Arts and Crafts movement in Detroit, Booth saw in Christ Church Cranbrook an opportunity for a synthesis of the arts and crafts combined to serve religion. The graceful stone structure, a modern adaptation of English Gothic, was adorned by the work of many master artists and craftsmen. Katherine McEwen, a founding member of the Society of Arts and Crafts, painted a fresco in the chancel. Woodcarving was done by John Kirchmayer, a native of Oberammergau, Germany, whose work was exhibited at the Society of Arts and Crafts in 1917. Arthur Neville Kirk, a silversmith at the Cranbrook Academy of Art, created the altar-cross and the sacramental vessels. Other examples of fine craftsmanship are the statues by Lee Lawrie on the buttresses, and the stained glass windows by Nicola d'Ascenzo and James H. Hogan.[61]

The unmistakable influence of Cram and Goodhue is apparent in many of the churches in the Detroit area. The most ambitious of these is the Roman Catholic mother church, the Cathedral of the Most Blessed Sacrament on Woodward *(318)* avenue at Belmont. An example of full-blown Norman Gothic, it was designed by Henry A. Walsh of Cleveland and completed in 1915. The twin towers of the façade dominate the vast cruciform structure. The entrance bay is distinguished by a handsome portal surmounted by a rose window and a carved stone screen connecting the towers. A slender lead spire rises from the roof. On the interior stone groined vaults and tall clerestory windows filled with tracery create an imposing effect.[62]

Of the smaller Neo-Gothic churches, one might choose at random the Jefferson Avenue Presbyterian Church (1925) as a typical example. Here medieval *(319)* motifs were employed with considerable freedom. Architects Smith, Hinchman and Grylls sacrificed orthodoxy in order to create a picturesque grouping of masses of rugged masonry with exaggerated deep reveals. The development of the Gothic in the Detroit area came to a brilliant culmination in 1958 with the completion of the Kirk-in-the-Hills, a Presbyterian church in Bloomfield Hills. It *(320)* was the product of the imagination of architect Wirt C. Rowland, a gifted designer who had delved deeply into the theory of architecture.

Rowland was born and educated in Clinton, Michigan. Graduate work at Harvard occupied him from 1900 to 1902.[63] There his interest in the Gothic was aroused by an inspired professor whose specialty was medieval architecture. This interest was further cultivated by subsequent travel and study in Europe. With such a background the budding architect was well prepared for Cram's *Gothic Quest* and *Substance of Gothic*. While he found these books immensely stimulating, he was not in total agreement with their author's point of view. He felt that Cram overemphasized the part that religion and philosophy played in medieval architecture, and that in the final analysis architecture was primarily an expression of the resolution of natural forces.[64]

In Detroit Rowland's talents were in great demand and in the course of his

(354)
(357)
career he was employed by many of the leading architectural firms. He is perhaps best known for his designs of the Penobscot and Guardian Buildings. In this work he attempted to evolve a new idiom of design appropriate for the skyscraper.

Work slackened for Rowland in the lean years of the thirties, as it did for most of his countrymen. During this period he busied himself with odd jobs. Among other things he designed an iron gate for Colonel Edwin S. George, a businessman who had invested heavily in Detroit real estate. Colonel George lived on a large estate in Bloomfield Hills. A devout Presbyterian, he dreamed of erecting a beautiful church on his property that would serve the community. Rowland was receptive to this idea. His interest in the Gothic was rekindled and he made a series of studies for the project.[65] Then World War II intervened. A year after the armistice Rowland died. Colonel George then employed the firm of George D. Mason to complete the task. In the twenties they had built his *(300)* residence, which later was to serve as a church house. Work on the church was begun in 1951; it was completed in 1958. In the meantime Colonel George died in 1951 and his remains were placed in the crypt.[66]

The Kirk-in-the-Hills was a distillation of Rowland's Gothic predilections. Although he admired the cold, brilliant, structural logic of the medieval French cathedrals, he was more attracted by English Gothic because of the greater warmth and individuality of its small characteristic details. He also preferred the English façades because they were generally uncomplicated by towers and hence were more expressive of the nave and aisles. The tower, he felt, was most effective when treated as a separate unit. He recognized the importance of stained glass in the total Gothic concept and marveled at the mystical luminosity afforded by the windows of medieval churches.[67]

Rowland found inspiration for the Kirk-in-the-Hills in the ruins of Melrose Abbey in Scotland.[68] Here was a subtle blend of the Decorated and Perpendicular English Gothic styles with a pronounced French influence.[69] Rising once again in its pristine glory above the verdure of Bloomfield Hills, the reincarnation of the ancient abbey is a testimony of the final triumph of Rowland in his lifelong Gothic quest.

Secular Gothic

(321)
(145)
Cass Gilbert's Woolworth Building (1913) in New York established a precedent for Gothic commercial architecture. Fyfe's Shoe Store in Detroit, built in 1919, continued that tradition in a fourteen-story structure.[70] Designed by Smith, Hinchman and Grylls, this handsome building with soaring vertical lines and deep window reveals stands as a landmark at the head of the busy thoroughfares that converge at Grand Circus Park.

(322)
The Masons chose the Gothic style for their vast Masonic Temple (1928) on Cass Park. "The spirit and tradition of the Knights Templars was unquestionably Romanesque or Gothic," said the architect of the building, George D. Mason, "and operative Masonry, having its origin in the guilds in Europe, had the tradition of the great cathedrals, of which Masons were the builders." "The hard and fast demands of the plan prevented any great freedom in the handling of the masses," he went on to say. "Yet it was felt that the skyline and bold reveals would give the structure the proper character."[71] For such a complex building the Gothic style was more flexible than the Classical or Renaissance would have been. The structure contains ballrooms, banquet halls, and an auditorium seating 5,000 for grand operas and symphonic orchestras.

(282) James E. Scripps House, *Mason & Rice*, 1891 (JSC)

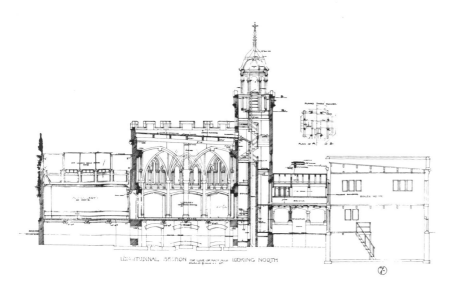

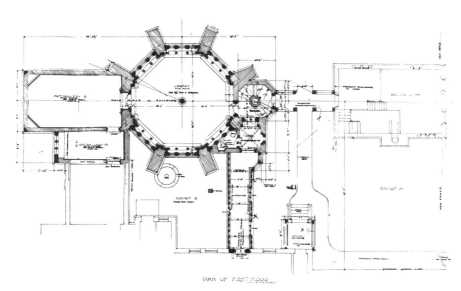

(283-285) Scripps Library, *A. Kahn*, 1898 (DIA/JKJ)

(286) Charles M. Swift House, *A. Kahn*, 1905 (MB)

(287) James Hamilton House,
Stratton & Baldwin, 1902 (DIA)

(288) Willistead, *A. Kahn*, 1906 (JS

(289) Frank C. Baldwin House,
Stratton & Baldwin, 1908 (DIA/S

(290) William B. Stratton
House, *Stratton & Baldwin*,
1895 (HAL)

(291) Woman's Exchange,
Smith, Hinchman & Grylls,
1916 (BHC/JKJ)

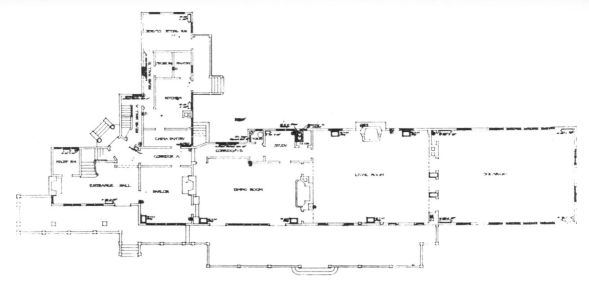

(292-293) Frederick M. Alger House, *Stratton & Baldwin*, 1908 (W-A)(MB)

(294) L. Stephen Trowbridge House, *Trowbridge & Ackerman*, 1909 (MB)

(295) Albert Kahn House, *A. Kahn*, 1906 (JSC)

(296) Cranbrook House, *A. Kahn*, 1909 (HAL)

(297) Pewabic Pottery Co.,
Stratton & Baldwin, 1907 (DIA

(298) Cranbrook House
and Grounds (CI)

(299) Society of Arts and Crafts, *Stratton & Grylls*, 1916 (AS)

(300) Edwin S. George House, *G. D. Mason*, 1923 (GDM/JKJ)

(301) Cranbrook Meeting House,
G. G. Booth, 1918 (CI)

(302) Detroit Golf Club, *A. Kahn*,
1917 (H-B)

(303) Country Club of Detroit,
Smith, Hinchman & Grylls, 1926 (GPF

(304-305) William B. Stratton House, *W. B. Stratton*, 1927 (DIA)

(306) John F. Dodge House, *Smith, Hinchman & Grylls*, 1920 (DFP)

(307) Meadow Brook Hall, *Smith, Hinchman & Grylls*, 1929 (L-A)

(308-309) Standish Backus House, *R. O. Derrick*, 1934 (MB)

(310) Cotswold Cottage in Greenfield Village (HFM)

(311) University Club, *Smith, Hinchman & Grylls*, 1931 (HAL)

(312) Edsel B. Ford House, *A. Kahn*, 1927 (DN)

(313) Alvan Macauley House, *A. Kahn*, 1929 (MB)

(314) Trinity P.E. Church, *Mason & Rice*, 1892 (JSC)

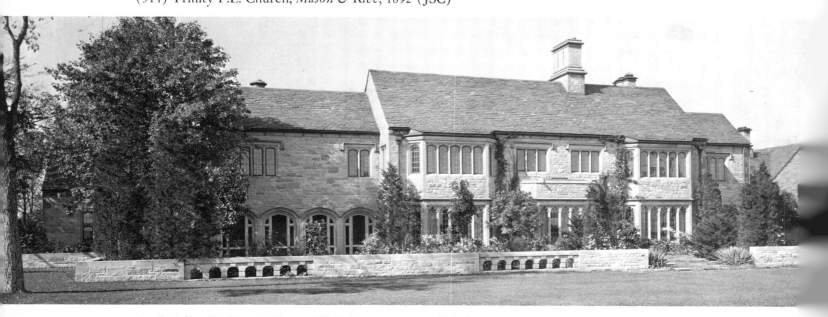

(315) Julian H. Harris House, *W. B. Stratton*, 1925 (DIA)

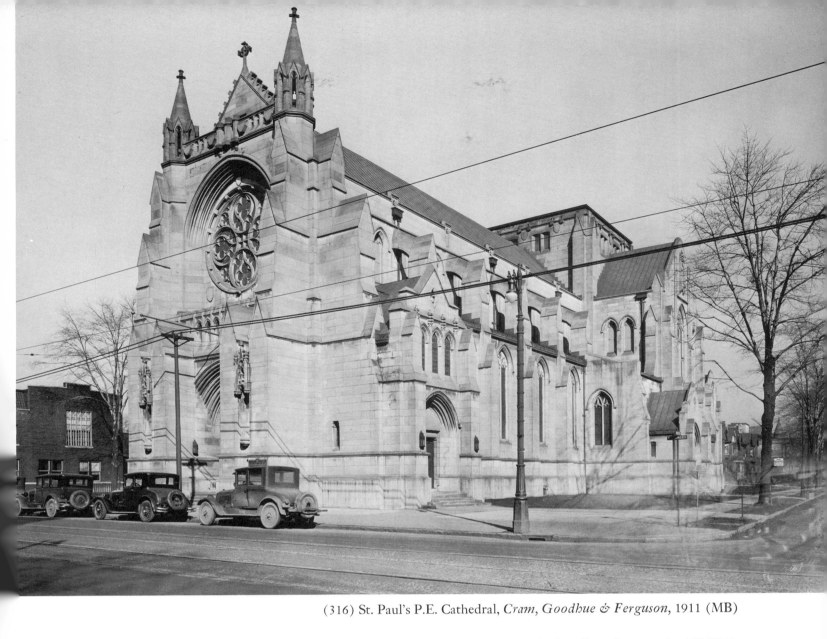

(316) St. Paul's P.E. Cathedral, *Cram, Goodhue & Ferguson*, 1911 (MB)

(317) Christ P.E. Church Cranbrook, *B. G. Goodhue Assoc.*, 1928 (CI/HC)

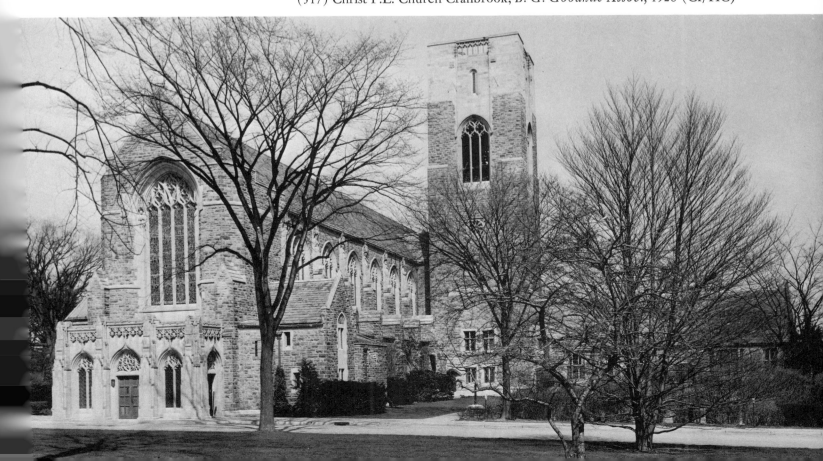

(318) Blessed Sacrament R.C. Cathedral, *H. A. Walsh*, 1915 (MB)

(319) Jefferson Avenue Presbyterian Church, *Smith, Hinchman & Grylls*, 1925 (DIA/JKJ)

(320) Kirk-in-the-Hills, *Rowland & Mason*, 1958 (BK)

(321) R. H. Fyfe's Shoe Store, *Smith, Hinchman & Grylls,* 1919 (BHC/JKJ)

(322) Masonic Temple, *G. D. Mason,* 1928 (BHC/JKJ)

9. The English Renaissance

The Early English Renaissance

A century after its inception in Italy the Renaissance movement appeared in England. Early English Renaissance architecture, which followed the Tudor, was a transitional style. At first medieval features predominated with only a superficial application of classical motifs. Gradually, as the Roman models became better known, the disciplined regularity of classical columns and entablatures supplanted the quaint irregularity of medieval forms.[1]

In the twentieth century American eclectic architects who found the Tudor style too ponderous welcomed the lighter and more graceful ornament of the Early English Renaissance. It was this style that George D. Mason used for the Lemuel W. Bowen house (1912) on the west side of Woodward avenue between *(324)* Kirby and Ferry in Detroit. It was closely related to the Italian and Early French Renaissance work in which he had already proved himself adept. Mason first planned to build an Italian house, but the taste of the client, who was treasurer and general manager of D. M. Ferry and Company, changed after a trip *(170)* to England, and only the rather square shape of the house remained as a token of the architect's original intention.[2] The entrance porch, carried up as a tower with a jutting oriel window, was grouped with flanking bay windows to form the main feature of the façade. The fine stonework of this central panel stands out against the brick of the main body of the house with its steep roofs and gables. The Bowen house is now part of the Art Centre Hospital.

In 1912 Albert Kahn built a large red sandstone mansion for Horace E. *(323)* Dodge on Jefferson avenue in Grosse Pointe. It bore a certain resemblance to the house next door which he had built earlier for Charles M. Swift, but the details *(286)* were Early English Renaissance instead of Tudor and the design was better articulated. Banks of large mullioned windows took advantage of the commanding view across Lake St. Clair, as did a classical porch with Tuscan columns and a balustrade. Between the house and the lake was a formal garden. From a balustraded upper terrace a broad flight of steps descended to a lower level which bordered the lake. There the fabulous Dodge yacht the *Delphine* was moored to a dock.

Rose Terrace, as the place was called, was the fulfillment of the dreams of Horace Dodge. Behind the public image of the industrial titan who had built up a vast automotive empire, there was a lover of home life, music, and the delights of yachting. When at home he would sit for hours at the great pipe organ playing for his own entertainment or that of his friends. Whenever he desired, his yacht would waft him out across the blue waters that he loved. The climax of his marine adventures was to have been a cruise around the world, but his untimely death in 1920 prevented him from carrying out this plan.[3] In 1927 Dodge's widow married actor Hugh Dillman. Shortly thereafter they bought the *(214)* property of the Country Club of Detroit just east of Rose Terrace. The club-house and the old Dodge mansion were torn down, and the sites were combined *(279)* and relandscaped to provide a setting for the new Rose Terrace that rose on the shores of Lake St. Clair like some vision of the splendors of the court of Louis XV. When not traveling the Dillmans divided their time between their Grosse Pointe mansion and their Palm Beach palace Playa Riente. In 1949 they were divorced and Mrs. Dillman resumed her former name of Mrs. Horace E. Dodge.[4]

A few years after Albert Kahn had built the first Rose Terrace for Horace Dodge in the Early English Renaissance style, architect Albert H. Spahr of Pittsburgh was busy erecting three impressive mansions in a similar style farther out Lake Shore road in Grosse Pointe. More derivative than the work of Mason or Kahn, they relied more heavily upon English precedent. The Elmer D. Speck *(325)* house (1914) was a picturesque half-timbered structure that still clung persist- *(326)* ently to medieval Tudor traditions. More classical in spirit were the Joseph B. *(327)* Schlotman (1915) and Emory L. Ford (1916) houses. The Ford and Speck houses were demolished in the fifties.

No kin of Henry Ford, Emory Ford and his sisters Mmes. Speck and Schlot-man were grandchildren of Captain John B. Ford of Pittsburgh, founder of the Pittsburgh Plate Glass Company and the Michigan Alkali Company at Wyan-dotte. For many years Emory Ford was president of the latter company.[5] The Pittsburgh origin of the family no doubt accounts for their choice of an archi-tect from that city. A third sister Mrs. Harry N. Torrey, however, selected *(254)* Detroit architect John Scott to design her Italian Renaissance palace.

In 1915 the New York firm of Trowbridge and Ackerman built a house in *(329)* Grosse Pointe for Dexter M. Ferry Jr., president of D. M. Ferry and Company, *(170)* the seed firm, and son of its founder. Responsive to the beauties of nature, Ferry had acquired acreage between Jefferson avenue and the lake. He admired the *(331)* way in which Trowbridge and Ackerman had adapted the Truman H. New-berry house to its lake site and consequently selected them as architects for his own home.[6] The Newberry house was too formal for his tastes, so the architects *(294)* returned to something of the simplicity of their earlier Stephen Trowbridge house. Although the Ferry house may be classified as Early English Renaissance in style, historical details were minimized and the freedom of design and plan revealed a kinship to the English Domestic Revival in its later phase.

One of the many charming features of the house was the long straight elm-*(328)* bordered driveway at the end of which could be glimpsed the entrance wing with its handsome Renaissance doorway. The pinkish-red brick of the driveway picked up the red of the tile roof which in turn contrasted with the white stucco walls. Here the architects used color and texture for their own value rather than for any antiquarian connotation.

Since the property was almost the same level as the lake, it was necessary to build the basement of the house above ground to avoid trouble with ground water. Therefore the driveway was graded up to the first floor entrance and terminated in a walled forecourt which was accessible from the sides by means of short flights of steps.[7] On the lake side of the house the principal rooms opened through a series of French doors upon a broad inviting terrace which was flanked by two bays containing glazed loggias. Below this terrace was a secondary terrace, and beyond a vast expanse of lawn where enormous ancient elms and maples framed an enchanting view of the lake. At the side of the house was a formal garden. The landscaping for the entire estate was originally done by Walter Pitkin Jr. of Cleveland, but later work was done by Mrs. Ellen Shipman. After Ferry's death in 1959 the house was torn down and the property subdivided.

In the twenties the architecture of Grosse Pointe was characterized by an increasing antiquarianism and a striving for dramatic effects. This was ostensively demonstrated by the Ralph Harman Booth house on Washington road *(330)* which was designed by Marcus R. Burrowes of Detroit in 1924. The Early English Renaissance façade with its steep medieval roofs and gables seemed to serve as a backdrop for a stage set, the focal point of which was the stone entrance with its twisted baroque columns. But this was only a prelude to what lay in store for the visitor privileged to enter the house in its heyday, for Ralph H. Booth, brother of George G. Booth and president of Booth Newspapers, was one of the great collectors and patrons of art in Detroit.[8] As president of the Arts Commission he presided over the art life of Detroit during one of its most expansive periods.[9] Perhaps more than any other single individual, he was respon- *(247)* sible for the construction of the Detroit Institute of Arts in 1922–27.[10]

The Booth house itself was a veritable museum in the tradition established in the East by Frick, Widener, and Mellon. The paneling in the dining room came from Hamilton Palace in Scotland, while that in the library came from Standish Hall in England. In the living room seventeenth century Florentine brocatelle made a rich background for paintings by Bellini, Boltraffio, and Cranach. More contemporary tastes were rewarded in the music room with a superlative collection of French Impressionist and Post-Impressionist canvases.[11]

As one after another of the business and civic leaders of Detroit built their great mansions in Grosse Pointe, the time came when Henry Ford, the greatest magnate of them all, decided to do likewise. A man of such fame and fortune was constantly being pursued by a stream of favor seekers. If he was to enjoy any kind of private life, it was necessary to insulate himself in extensive grounds protected by fences. He purchased a large piece of property on Gaukler Point on Lake St. Clair. Plans were under way for a house and landscaping when suddenly he became alarmed that he might be expected to participate in the organized community life. He did not really care for the artificial social life of Grosse Pointe, so it was not too difficult for him to drop the idea of living there.

As early as 1908 he had begun acquiring a vast tract along the River Rouge near Dearborn. The heavily wooded terrain provided a natural sanctuary for birds and game. In 1909 he built a cottage there that served as a retreat from the pressures of a busy life. In time it became apparent that this was the ideal spot for his future home, affording privacy and at the same time proximity to the River Rouge plant soon to rise nearby.[12]

Albert Kahn almost invariably designed the residences for his major clients. Since he had built all the Ford factories, he would have been the logical choice of architect for the Ford residence. Although his factories were strictly functional, he was inclined to cater to the extravagant and anachronistic tastes of his clients in his domestic work. Ford shrank from the idea of living like other wealthy men and this perhaps explains why he chose an architect of the Chicago 'Prairie School' for his own home. The younger generation of Chicago architects, led by Frank Lloyd Wright, had cast aside the mantle of history and emerged with a simple unaffected type of dwelling, organic in plan and design. To Hermann von Holst, a young unknown, belongs the distinction of being placed in charge of Wright's office in 1909 when the latter ran off to Europe with the wife of one of his clients.[13] Perhaps it would be jumping to conclusions to assume that Ford discriminated against Wright, but the fact remains that in 1913 von Holst began construction on Fair Lane, Ford's future home.

All would have gone well if difficulties with contractors and suppliers had not developed.[14] Ford became dissatisfied with the original architects and engaged William H. Van Tine of Pittsburgh who took over both construction and landscape gardening.[15] Van Tine's principal qualification was his supervisory ability.[16] He dealt directly with manufacturers, thus eliminating contractors.[17] In Pittsburgh Van Tine was known as an interior decorator rather than an architect.[18] It is unfortunate, therefore, that he took the liberty of completely altering von Holst's design.[19] Completed in 1915, the house is a massive nondescript structure, Victorian in character, with only slight traces of Chicago influence.

(332)

In view of Van Tine's background, emphasis upon the interior woodwork at Fair Lane was to be expected. Ford's desire for the simple life notwithstanding, the interior resembled a Grosse Pointe mansion. The entrance hall was dominated by a magnificent hand-carved oak staircase in the Early English Renaissance style. Of interest in the music room was an ornate Italian walnut and marble fireplace. The living room and the music room were both paneled in walnut, while the dining room was done in mahogany with furniture of matching wood.

The estate as a whole was over two thousand acres. Ford's special projects were farming operations, a power plant, a laboratory, and a garage, while Mrs. Clara Bryant Ford's interests lay in the extensive gardens, greenhouses, and orchards. Over one hundred deer roamed in the wooded areas and peacocks strutted on the lawns. Thousands of bird houses and feeding stations made the place a paradise for birds.[14]

The Georgian

In seventeenth century England the introduction of full-flown Italian Renaissance architecture by such men as Inigo Jones and Christopher Wren succeeded in effacing the last vestiges of medievalism. In the eighteenth century this formal type of architecture was modified to suit local taste, thus giving rise to the Georgian style. Changing social conditions during the nineteenth century resulted in a breaking away from tradition in architecture and a restless exploitation of past styles.[20] It was not until late in the nineteenth century that Norman Shaw rediscovered the intrinsic merits of the Georgian style. His adoption of it, following his success with the Queen Anne style, started a fashion that reached its climax in the twentieth century. According to Nikolaus Pevsner, "Shaw's house at No. 170 Queen's Gate, London, comes as close to the spirit of the new century as one could come without actually breaking with the past."[21]

After the introduction of French and Italian Renaissance architecture in America at the end of the nineteenth century, the analogous Georgian style was adopted as an alternative. Its derivative, the American Colonial, which had been popularized earlier, flourished with renewed vigor. Originally inspiration had come mainly from New England prototypes, but increasingly architects began to emulate the more monumental Southern Colonial.

Charles A. Platt of New York turned from the magnificence of his beloved Italian Renaissance architecture to the more restrained elegance of the Georgian. One of his finest houses in this style was the John T. Pratt house at Glen Cove, Long Island. It should be noted, however, that he still retained certain Italian elements, such as the broad terrace with its pergola and flanking loggias.[22] Trowbridge and Ackerman, also of New York, were undoubtedly influenced by this design when they built the Truman H. Newberry residence in Grosse Pointe. *(331)* Son of John S. Newberry, Truman Newberry was a man of many business *(101)* interests who had been secretary of the navy in Theodore Roosevelt's administration and was later to be senator from Michigan.[23] The Newberrys built their new house in 1914 on Lake Shore road upon returning from Washington.

Like the Pratt house in Glen Cove, the Newberry house was a large brick Georgian structure with a broad terrace and twin loggias, but the general treatment was more formal. The loggias were made an integral part of the building by being incorporated in two-story wings, and a double staircase and balustrade were features of the terrace. Since the Newberrys were fond of the water, ample windows took advantage of the fine view of the lake. Opening on the terrace at the center was a lofty Venetian door surmounted by urns, cornucopias, and a crowning cartouche. The sun shone through the glass door and glinted on the crystal and amethyst lusters of an enormous chandelier that hung in the middle of a two-story hall. In order not to interfere with the view of the lake, access to the house was at the rear. A driveway passed the north end of the house and made a generous loop in front of the main entrance wing. Here, above a recessed porch, pediments and window frames were ornamented with ornate stone carving.

On the interior of the house, according to a contemporary account, care was taken "to secure the impression of the antique without anywhere endeavoring to imitate." Adjoining the two-story hall was a stair hall with an impressive grand staircase. The downstairs rooms were paneled in butternut, Italian walnut, and California redwood. The floors were laid in teak. Most of the rooms were in the Georgian style, but for the sake of variety the music room at the south end of the house was in the Italian Renaissance style. Adjacent to the music room was the music court, a panel of turf enclosed by a pergola and balustrades.[24] The Newberrys often invited their friends to hear concerts there. On one memorable summer evening the entire Detroit Symphony Orchestra performed there in a dream-like setting. The moon rose across the lake and shone through the trees on the velvet lawns and on the pergola hung with white and purple wisteria.

The numerous gardens on the Newberry estate were a source of constant delight to Harriet Newberry. Each season brought its round of colorful blooms. In the early spring wild flowers made their appearance in the rock garden. In June the borders of the driveway and the wooded area adjoining the music court were ablaze with rhododendrons, azaleas, and dogwood. In summer the formal garden was a mass of bloom and the rose garden was at its height. Fall was the season for the chrysanthemums nurtured in the greenhouse; it was the occasion for the Newberrys' annual chrysanthemum show to which they invited their friends. These flowers were placed throughout the house and brought to each room a glow of rich autumnal coloration. If the weather was fair they were also displayed on the terrace overlooking the lake.[25]

It can readily be seen that the Truman Newberry house was far more than a conventional example of Georgian architecture. In the beauty of its proportions and the subtle poetry of its design it was a true masterpiece. With the assistance of the landscape architect Walter Pitkin Jr., Trowbridge and Ackerman had created a synthesis of architecture and landscaping in the best Platt tradition. One of the tragedies of American civilization is that some of the choice examples of architecture of the past cannot withstand the pressure of modern economic forces. The site upon which the Newberry mansion stood had once been occupied by the family's summer cottage and was inherited by Newberry from his father.[24] In the years that ensued land values in Grosse Pointe soared, and rising taxes and wages for domestic help made the maintenance costs prohibitive. In 1950, five years after Newberry's death, his house was torn down and the property subdivided.[26] A world of beauty and elegance vanished, never to return.

(142)

In 1911 Albert Kahn received an important commission to do a residence for John S. Newberry, brother of Truman H. Newberry, on Lake Shore road. Like Trowbridge, Kahn was a great admirer of the work of Charles Platt. In general conception the John Newberry house resembled a French house which Platt had recently completed in Connecticut.[27] The task of designing the house was largely the responsibility of Ernest Wilby, who from 1903 to 1918 was a Kahn associate.[28] Born in Yorkshire, England, Wilby received his early schooling in Canada, but returned to England to complete his education at Wesley College, Harrogate. He brought to his work an extraordinary combination of practicality and artistic insight.

(333)

Far too advanced in his thinking to be a mere imitator, Wilby subtly blended disparate elements into a harmonious whole. Using the utmost restraint throughout, he relied for his effect more upon beauty of proportion and fine workmanship than upon any antiquarian evocation. "It has always seemed to me," said Wilby in later years, "that the mental approach to architecture is even more important than the material one, if we regard architecture as the most noble and most expressive of all the arts."[29] In the John Newberry house he created a timeless symbol of the dignity and refinement of formal living.

There seems to have been little retained of the original French design except the steep roof with its flaring eaves and the handsome stone doorway with its restrained carving and overhanging balcony of crisp wrought iron, but these two features were precisely what was needed to give poignancy to a façade of almost unrelieved understatement. The use of sash windows instead of casements established a preponderantly Georgian character which, however, was somewhat dissipated by the white stucco walls and red tile roof. In the final analysis the great distinction of the façade was attributable to the complete mastery of scale and the fine expression of the formal organization of the plan in the variation of external wall planes.

On the interior the first floor rooms were impressive in scale. At the center of the house was a large manorial hall which opened upon the terrace to the north. Adjoining this was the stair well with a handsome Jacobean staircase. The living room to the west originally contained an Italian Renaissance fireplace, but this was later replaced by an antique Georgian fireplace which Mrs. Newberry acquired in England. The dining room to the east was paneled in walnut in the Georgian style with wall carvings in the manner of Grinling Gibbons. The floors of the principal rooms were laid in teak.[30]

For ten years Edith Stanton Newberry was president of the Detroit Symphony Society to which she gave generously of her time and resources.[31] The Newberry house was often the scene of formal dinners for luminaries of the musical world; Ossip Gabrilowitsch and Bruno Walter were frequent guests. Another of Mrs. Newberry's absorbing interests was gardening and she won many prizes for her flower arrangements. Mrs. Ellen Shipman of New York was the landscape architect for the Newberry estate. On two different occasions the formal garden provided a colorful setting for the outdoor weddings of friends of the family.[30] When the cold weather set in the greenhouse supplied flowers for the house. One of the most beautiful periods was the late winter when the various rooms were filled with masses of vivid azaleas and cyclamens.

When Mrs. Newberry died in 1956 a world of beauty was doomed. High taxes and maintenance costs made such a large establishment untenable. The house was torn down and the property subdivided. With the demise of the two Newberry houses, Lake Shore road lost much of its true distinction. Notwithstanding this irreparable loss, there are many fine examples of Georgian architecture remaining in Grosse Pointe. In fact, it has been one of the most continuously popular styles from the turn of the century to the present. To be sure, the boom of the twenties precipitated a brief but brilliant display of extravagant and exotic architecture, but the depression and its aftermath necessitated a return to the sober practicality of the Georgian. Deeply rooted in the American tradition, it carried with it a certain prestige value associated with the British inheritance. To the quiet shady streets of Grosse Pointe it lent an air of conservative good taste.

It was perhaps no coincidence that the first Detroit architect to work in the academic Georgian tradition was a gentleman of the old school, Alpheus W. Chittenden. Scion of one of Detroit's older families, he could number among his ancestors General Charles Larned, who distinguished himself in the War of 1812, and General Alpheus Williams, who added luster to Michigan's record in the Civil War. Young Chittenden had the foresight to reinforce a natural refinement of taste with a thorough training at the Massachusetts Institute of Technology and the *Hochschule* in Berlin. He began practicing in Detroit before the turn of the century and in 1903 joined Charles Kotting, a native of the Netherlands, to form the firm of Chittenden and Kotting.[32]

They were responsible for the John B. Ford Jr. residence (1904) on Jefferson avenue in the Indian Village district of Detroit. Here the exterior walls were faced with stone instead of the usual brick with stone trim. A loggia and a balustraded terrace in the Italian manner overlooked the Detroit River. When the Indian Village began to deteriorate as a residential area the house was moved to its present location on Windmill Point drive in Grosse Pointe. In 1913 the same firm built a residence for Frank W. Hubbard on Jefferson avenue in *(334)* Grosse Pointe. Academic in style, it recalls the mansions of Colonial Maryland.

Somewhat more rambling and informal was the colonial house Chittenden and Kotting built in 1914 for J. Brooks Nichols on Lake Shore road in Grosse Pointe. In the twenties when the house was occupied by Burt E. Taylor, a realtor, the grounds were improved with imaginative landscaping under the direction of Bryant Fleming. The focal point of the garden was a two-story octagonal pavilion which served as a teahouse and also provided dressing rooms for the swimming pool. This building was connected to the terrace of the main house by a graceful bridge. The last owner of the house was Henry Ford II, who occupied the premises until 1959. The house was later demolished and the property subdivided.

One of Chittenden's most imposing mansions was built for his brother-in-law William T. Barbour, who had followed in his father's footsteps as president of the Detroit Stove Works. The Barbour country residence was dramatically situated on the crest of a hill near Woodward avenue in Bloomfield Hills. A central bay with brick pilasters and a segmental pediment gave the house a formal emphasis, yet at the same time generous fenestration took advantage of the fine view of the surrounding countryside.

(335)
Like the Barbour family, the Dwyer family had long been identified with the manufacture of stoves, one of Detroit's older industries. In 1909 John M. Dwyer, then secretary of the Peninsular Stove Company, engaged Raymond Carey to build a fine Georgian mansion on Jefferson avenue in Grosse Pointe. It is doubtful if he could have chosen an architect more suited by temperament and background to work in the Georgian manner, for Carey was a conservative Englishman who first saw the light of day in Bath, the famous English spa immortalized in Sheridan's play *The School for Scandal*. One of the greatest ensembles of Georgian architecture still in existence, no town could have been better calculated to endow a young architect with the true spirit of eighteenth century England. Having received his training before coming to this country, Carey designed several of Grosse Pointe's finer Georgian houses. After World War II he returned to England and is now practicing on the Isle of Man.[33] The preeminence of Carey's work owes much to the care with which he executed details. The Dwyer house is noteworthy for its semi-circular colonnaded porch and handsome pediment above the central bay. In later years when the Dwyer estate was subdivided and bisected by Lakeland avenue, the house was moved to a smaller lot on the new street.[34]

(336)
The prosperous twenties saw one great house after another completed in Grosse Pointe. In 1927 Roy D. Chapin, president of the Hudson Motor Car Company, commissioned John Russell Pope to erect a stately Georgian mansion on Lake Shore road. Twenty years later, in reviewing the changing tastes in American architecture, critic Henry-Russell Hitchcock Jr. singled out the house as symptomatic of a prevailing trend. It prompted him to generalize:

The liking for formality persisted in the twenties, finding expression in a monumental colonial usually called Georgian. Virginian as well as English models provided specific prototypes, traditional craftsmanship was emulated, and the impression sought was one of dignity rather than splendour. Fine eighteenth century furniture easily grouped made interiors comfortable as well as handsome.[35]

For such an ambitious undertaking the Chapins chose an architect of national reputation. Pope had been trained at the École des Beaux-Arts in Paris.[36] In New York he numbered among his clients Ogden Mills and Mrs. W. K. Vanderbilt.[37] His Scottish Rite Temple in Washington had established him as a leader among the classicists, a position which his later National Gallery of Art and Jefferson Memorial helped to maintain. After his death in 1937 he was remembered as an "amiable and elegant gentleman," who seems to have been not in the least "affected by the style variously called Functionalism, Modernism, Internationalism, whose father was Frank Lloyd Wright, whose grandfather was Sullivan."[38]

(333)
Mrs. Chapin greatly admired the John S. Newberry house and consequently it served as a model for the Chapin house, at least in the general plan. In the hands of Pope, however, the architectural treatment was entirely different; conventional academicism took the place of the free and creative spirit that had marked the earlier house. The Georgian repertory of column, pilaster, and pediment, which had been so discreetly suppressed on the Newberry house, reappeared with all its strongly eighteenth century flavor. The year 1956 saw still another interpretation of the original plan, for it was then that Henry Ford II bought the house following the death of Mrs. Chapin. An ardent Francophile, Anne McDonnell Ford was fond of French eighteenth century decorative arts.

The interior of the house was then remodeled to provide a suitable background for her exquisite French antiques. Impressionist and Post-Impressionist paintings added a modern poignancy to the ensemble.[39]

Originally Bryant Fleming laid out the garden for Mrs. Chapin. Its 600-year-old yew hedges were imported from England.[40] The focal point of the garden was an authentic eighteenth century English doorway with engaged columns and a pediment. With characteristic ingenuity Fleming used this as a wall fountain and water trickled down over rocks where the door had formerly been.

The nostalgia for the past prevalent in the twenties found architectural expression in a variety of ways, running the gamut from grandeur to quaintness. When W. Ledyard Mitchell, a vice president of the Chrysler Corporation, contemplated building a house in Grosse Pointe, his thoughts turned to his old colonial summer residence in East Hampton, Long Island. The Mitchell house on *(337)* Ridge road, designed by Robert O. Derrick in 1926, captured some of the charm of the older building with its low rambling lines, simplified classical details, and weathered shingles. A native of Buffalo, New York, Derrick had been educated at Yale and Columbia. He began his architectural career in the office of Murphy and Dana in New York, but after World War I he moved to Detroit and established his own practice. Bronson V. Gamber, a graduate of the University of Pennsylvania and the Drexel Institute, was an associate for several years.[41]

In 1925 Derrick built a house for Sidney T. Miller Jr. on Provençal road in *(340)* Grosse Pointe. Partly painted brick and partly shingled, it resembled a quaint old New England dwelling. Its picturesque irregularity gave the impression that generation after generation of thrifty Yankees had added to or modified its snug exterior.[42] Derrick imparted some of the intimate charm of the domestic colonial to his Grosse Pointe Club of 1927 with its white painted brick, numerous gables, and broad terraces overlooking Lake St. Clair.[43] His Punch and Judy theater and adjoining shops took on the character of eighteenth century Boston or some provincial English town. That Derrick was well versed in the more formal urban Georgian idiom is attested by his Hannan Memorial Y.M.C.A. (1927) and his *(338)* Jennings Memorial Hospital (1930), both on East Jefferson avenue in Detroit. These finely detailed brick buildings were designed with stone basement stories. Engaged columns, pilasters, pediments, and iron balconies adorn the upper stories.

For many years architect William B. Stratton had been attracted by the straightforward simplicity of the English cottage style. In at least one instance he seems to have been trying to express the same qualities in the colonial style. His Edward S. Bennett house of 1932 on Country Club lane in Grosse Pointe resur- *(339)* rected the massive walls and picturesque gables of the Pennsylvania Colonial. Tall brick chimneys and brick quoins contrasted with the stucco wall surfaces, and a broad recessed doorway with a fanlight and side windows provided an inviting entrance to this gracious and informal residence.[44]

The depression and the subsequent increasing taxation had a sobering effect upon architecture in the thirties. Gone were the dreams of grandeur. Weary of the restless search for novelty, Grosse Pointers fell back upon the discreet elegance of the academic Georgian. Robert O. Derrick forgot his caprices with the American vernacular and designed the soberly dignified F. Caldwell Walker *(341)* house on Vendome road in 1931. This massive brick structure was marked by a strong classical emphasis. There is a stone entrance porch with Ionic columns. Other classical features include urns in niches, blind arches, a balustraded parapet, and decorative carved stone panels.[45]

It was during this period that Raymond Carey produced two of his finest

(342)   creations in Grosse Pointe. The George M. Holley house (1934) on Provençal road is notable for its handsome details. Corinthian pilasters and a columned entrance with a curved pediment adorn the façade, the surface of which is broken by bow windows. On the interior there is a free-standing spiral staircase.

(343)   The Gilbert B. Pingree house (1931) on Voltaire place evokes souvenirs of the Old South. Rising proudly between twin dependencies, the central unit of the house was dignified by a lofty portico with paired Ionic columns.[46]

Charles A. Platt of New York had designed the great Italian villa on Lake
(259)   Shore road for Russell A. Alger in 1910. After Alger's death in 1934, Mrs. Alger built a smaller house for herself on Provençal road. Once again Platt was her
(345)   architect. The time for Italian magnificence had passed, but the Southern Colonial still gave him an opportunity to express his feeling for restrained elegance. He placed a portico with Tuscan columns on the entrance side of the house and a similar one at the rear. The formal garden, with its clipped yew hedges and accents of garden sculpture, was laid out by Mrs. Ellen Shipman. Beyond the garden was a swimming pool, at the head of which was a classical pavilion.[47]

Architect Hugh T. Keyes built several Georgian houses in Grosse Pointe in the thirties. He was born in Trenton, Michigan, studied architecture at Harvard, and until World War I worked in Albert Kahn's office. After two years in the navy, Keyes opened his own office in Detroit.[48] One of his finest houses was
(344)   commissioned in 1934 by Emory W. Clark, president of the First National Bank of Detroit. It is now owned by Benson Ford, son of Edsel Ford. Set in the midst of beautifully landscaped grounds on Lake Shore road, it has the appearance of some venerable English country seat. A gravel driveway loops around to a stone entrance porch with Corinthian columns. The bow-fronted wings on each side of the façade, with their delicate iron window guards, give the house a late eighteenth century character foreshadowing the Regency style.

Falling unequivocally into the Regency category is the John Lord Booth
(347)   house of 1941 on Provençal road. The architect Frank Miles created a pleasing effect with terminal bow-fronted wings and a trellised iron entrance porch. A large hallway with a spiral staircase at one end faces the garden in back of the house.[49] In 1949 John L. Pottle built another somewhat similar house on Lake
(330)   Shore road for John L. Booth, son of Ralph H. Booth.

Since World War II the colonial style has become so popular in Grosse Pointe that other historic styles of architecture have been almost forgotten. A new species has appeared, the ranch house catering to those who prefer to live on one floor. Even this latter-day arrival has been subjected to colonial influence. Always a conservative community, Grosse Pointe is gradually becoming the victim of conformity. It is the era of the medium-sized house there. One by one the great mansions, relics of a vanishing way of life, are being demolished, and the property on which they stood is being subdivided. The velvet lawns and towering trees, so like a continuous park, are being replaced by rows of undistinguished regimented houses on a grid-iron street pattern.

But it will be a long time before the old charm of the community completely disappears. Even if worse comes to worst, the incomparable frontage on Lake St. Clair will still be a major attraction. In 1932 Lake Shore road was made into a parkway, skillfully landscaped by Mrs. Ellen Shipman, where the motorist is confronted with an ever-changing panorama of great beauty in every season of the year. In the winter there is the silent majesty of a crystalline world of ice and snow, and in the summer there is the spectacle of pleasure craft skimming over the water's surface and freighters bound for unknown ports disappearing over the blue horizon.

306

The Ford Museum and Greenfield Village

A craze for early American antiques, which reached its peak in the twenties, went hand in hand with the revival of interest in colonial architecture. New Englanders ransacked their attics for Sandwich glass, pewter mugs, banjo clocks, and Bennington ware. Everywhere antique shops did a thriving business.

As Henry Ford grew older he began to sentimentalize about the past. A man who had devoted so much of his energy to molding the present and the future at last had time to reflect. What he found in antique shops brought back memories of his youth and made him realize what drastic changes had taken place during his lifetime. The more he saw, the more he bought. Before long he was acquiring whole collections by the gross, entire shops. In the back of his mind he was evolving a plan. He hoped to build up a collection that would illustrate the evolution of American civilization by means of its tools, its utensils, and its ornaments.[50] At about this time a chance encounter helped Ford crystallize his ideas. Once when he was crossing the Atlantic, architect Robert O. Derrick happened to be a passenger on the same ship. As fellow Detroiters they were drawn together. In the course of the conversation they discussed collecting Americana. Impressed by Derrick's knowledge and understanding of the subject, Ford later engaged him to erect a museum in Dearborn to house the vast Ford collections.[51]

Completed in 1929, the Henry Ford Museum is a large structure, 450 x 800 *(346)* feet in area. Incorporated in the Georgian façade are full-scale reproductions of Independence Hall, Congress Hall, and the old City Hall in Philadelphia. Harvard handmade red brick, Cold Springs gray granite, a blue-gray Georgian marble, and soapstone were used in order to reproduce exactly the appearance of the originals. Whatever one's reservations may be about such literal replicas, it cannot be denied that they provide an appropriate setting for the fine colonial furniture, china, silverware, and glassware displays which occupy the front rooms of the museum.

The large exhibition hall at the rear of the building is more contemporary in spirit. It is one immense room broken only by columns and illuminated by steel and glass monitors.[52] Here the colonial handicraft period is left behind and one enters the machine age. Row upon row of agricultural implements, carriages, machines, locomotives, and automobiles trace the evolution of the industrial arts in agriculture, manufacture, and transportation.

In order to complete the picture of American life of yesterday, Ford built Greenfield Village as a supplement to the museum. Grouped around a colonial chapel on a 'village green' are buildings of historic interest, actually moved from *(310)* their original sites. Of particular significance is the laboratory from Menlo Park, New Jersey, where Edison invented the incandescent light. Other points of interest are the courthouse where Lincoln practiced law and the bicycle shop where the Wright brothers worked on their first airplane. Old-fashioned mills, stores, and dwellings, maintained as they were several generations ago, recapture the flavor of an earlier America.[53]

(323) Horace E. Dodge House, *A. Kahn*, 1912 (DFP)
(324) Lemuel W. Bowen House, *G. D. Mason*, 1912 (HAL)

(325) Elmer D. Speck House, *A. H. Spahr*, 1914 (MB)

(326) Joseph B. Schlotman House, *A. H. Spahr*, 1915 (MB)
(327) Emory L. Ford House, *A. H. Spahr*, 1916 (EMF/JKJ)

(328-329) Dexter M. Ferry Jr. House, *Trowbridge & Ackerman*, 1915 (MB)

(330) Ralph H. Booth House, *M. R. Burrowes*, 1924 (MB)

(331) Truman H. Newberry House, *Trowbridge & Ackerman*, 1914 (DIA/SL)
(332) Fair Lane, *W. H. Van Tine*, 1915 (FMC)

(333) John S. Newberry House, *A. Kahn*, 1911 (MB)

(334) Frank W. Hubbard House, *Chittenden & Kotting*, 1913 (HAL)

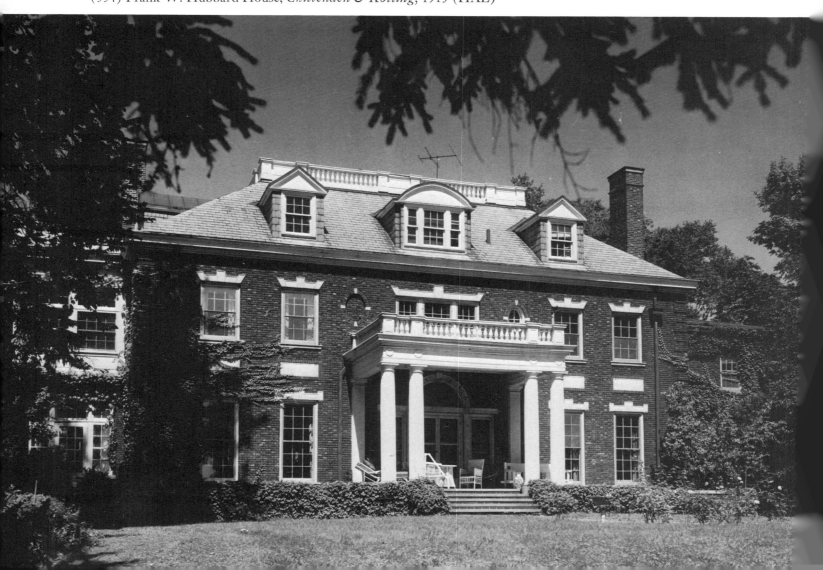

(335) John M. Dwyer House, *R. Carey*, 1909 (HAL)

(336) Roy D. Chapin House, *J. R. Pope*, 1927 (DN)

(337) W. Ledyard Mitchell House, *R. O. Derrick*, 1926 (MB)

(338) Hannan Memorial Y.M.C.A., *R. O. Derrick*, 1927 (HAL)

(339) Edward S. Bennett House, *W. B. Stratton*, 1932 (HAL)

(340) Sidney T. Miller Jr. House, *R. O. Derrick*, 1925 (HAL)

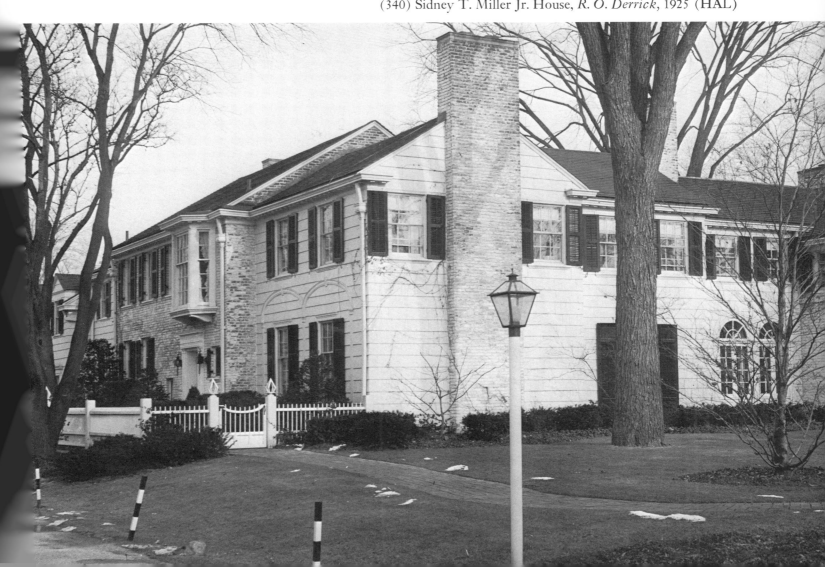

(341) F. Caldwell Walker House, *R. O. Derrick*, 1931 (HAL)

(342) George M. Holley House, *R. Carey*, 1934 (HAL)

(343) Gilbert B. Pingree House, *R. Carey*, 1931 (MB)

(344) Emory W. Clark House, *H. T. Keyes*, 1934 (MB)

(345) Mrs. Russell A. Alger House, *C. A. Platt*, 1934 (HHR)

(347) John L. Booth House, *F. Miles*, 1941 (M

6) Henry Ford Museum, *R. O. Derrick*, 1929 (HFM)

10. Breaking with the Past

The Movie Palace

Lafayette boulevard and its purlieus have long been intimately connected with the amusement life of Detroit. Back in 1875 the Whitney Opera House began its eminently successful span of theatrical life. When its site was sold for a government post office in 1890, Whitney built the Garrick Theater on Griswold street at the head of Lafayette boulevard.[1] Soon thereafter the old Unitarian Church *(45)* across from the post office was transformed into the Folly Theater. Adding further to such a profanation, its fine Greek Revival portico was masked by a shabby theater front of uninspired design.[2]

Theater architecture in Detroit took a turn for the better with the completion in 1914 of the Orpheum Theater, later known as the Shubert. Designed by Smith, Hinchman and Grylls, it was a handsome building faced with tapestry brick and trimmed with Renaissance details in cream terra cotta.[3] In 1925 the interior was completely remodeled in the grand manner by its owner Edward D. Stair, the publisher of the *Detroit Free Press*.[4] In 1926 he bought the Board of Commerce Building, which had been built in 1913. Stores were installed on the ground floor, three stories were added, and the refurbished auditorium became the Cass Theater.[5]

The rise of the motion picture industry added a new dimension to the entertainment world of Detroit. The first movie theater in the city, the Casino, opened on Monroe avenue in 1905. Soon rival houses were providing it with lively competition.[6] The prospects were bright for this new form of amusement, for reduced production costs would enable it to reach a larger audience than the legitimate theater. To meet this new demand it was necessary to build larger theaters.

Since the turn of the century retail trade had been pushing steadily up Woodward avenue and over into Washington boulevard. Clearly the ideal location for movie theaters was in the midst of the new shopping area that had sprung up around Grand Circus Park. Located directly on the park, the Madison and Adams Theaters were opened in 1916 and 1917. These buildings resembled the traditional legitimate theaters but were larger in seating capacity.

No architect in Detroit did more to promote the development of the movie theater than C. Howard Crane. Born in Hartford, Connecticut, he came to Detroit in 1904. Until 1909 he worked in the offices of Albert Kahn and Smith, Hinchman and Grylls. After that experience he organized his own office specializing in theater buildings. By the end of his career he had completed some two hundred and fifty in the United States and Canada. One of his earliest triumphs in Detroit was Orchestra Hall on Woodward at Parsons. A building of dignified Renaissance design, it served the Detroit Symphony Orchestra from 1919 to 1939. It was the Madison Theater, however, that established his reputation as a designer of movie theaters.[7]

By the twenties the motion picture had become an indispensable part of the life of the average American. The movie theater had become the citadel of refuge from the humdrum routine of daily living. The gilded carving, the crystal chandeliers, and the mirrors that had heretofore been the exclusive property of the very rich now belonged to anyone who could forfeit fifty cents or so for an admission ticket. In short, the movie theater became the movie palace.

The broad avenues radiating out from Grand Circus Park were soon lined with these palaces, each competing in architectural grandeur and in the bewitchment of their stage and screen offerings. The Capitol Theater (1922) on Broadway and the State Theater (1925) on Woodward were the products of C. Howard Crane. Their lobbies, resplendent with imported marble columns and staircases, served merely as preludes to the glories that lay beyond. It was still the day of the silent film. The mighty Wurlitzer organs thundered when the hero led the cavalry charges and warbled when he won the hand of the heroine.

Similar entertainment could be found along Bagley avenue. Heretofore a somnolent residential backwater, the street had been made an extension of the commercial and theatrical district by the erection of the Michigan Theater (1925) and the United Artists Theater (1928). The architects of the former were C. W. and George L. Rapp of Chicago. They built theaters all over the country, but it is doubtful if any of them were more opulent than the Michigan.[8]

"It is beyond the human dreams of loveliness," rhapsodized a writer in the *Detroit Free Press* at the time of the opening. "Entering it, you pass into another world," he continued. "Your spirit rises and soars along the climbing pillars and mirrored walls that ascend five stories to the dome ceiling of the great lobby. It becomes gay and light under the spell of the warm coloring that plays across the heavily carved and ornamented walls as myriads of unseen lights steal out from mysteriously hidden coves to illumine the interior with romantic sundown colors."[9]

Prolific architects, the Rapp brothers did not limit themselves to the design of theaters alone.[10] An example of their work in another architectural category may be found in the Detroit Leland Hotel erected on the corner of Cass and Bagley avenues in 1927. Located on the edge of the new shopping and theatrical district, it added seven hundred and twenty rooms to the already ample reservoir of accommodations for the out-of-town visitor. Both the exterior and the interior of the building followed the Italian Renaissance style.[11]

As the mounting crescendo of economic activity of the twenties neared the resounding finale of 1929, architecture burst the bonds of traditional Renaissance forms in the restless search for the picturesque and the bizarre. It was in the make-believe atmosphere of the movie palace that exotic architecture came to its fullest fruition. In the design of his United Artists Theater, C. Howard Crane abandoned the marble halls of Versailles and turned to Spain for inspiration. Colored lights filtered down from perforations in the domed ceiling of the auditorium to bathe Gothic architectural fantasies in a romantic luminosity. According to a contemporary account:

The effect of stone work is splendidly achieved on the walls themselves and the panels of mellowed stone, treated in dull polychrome, picked out with old gold, reds and blues, and grayed-off primary colors, and the intricately carved wall corbels and the tracery screens of the side walls and proscenium give an indescribable air of an ancient Castilian edifice.[12]

The crowning achievement of Crane's career in Detroit was the Fox Theater *(350)* on Woodward avenue. Seating over five thousand people, it outdistanced all other movie palaces in the city in the magnitude of its proportions. The vast auditorium, unobstructed by columns, was ·a marvel of engineering, but the aspect that elicited the most unbridled panegyrics from the press at the time of the opening in 1928 was the fantastic magnificence of the decor. A columnist for the *Free Press* wrote:

Few specimens of architectural splendor, either ancient or modern, surpass the new Fox Theater. Temples to gods and palaces for kings, through long years were the only outlets for architectural dreamings—until the significance of art in daily life became manifest and pervaded the buildings of intimate use.

This tendency, entering the field of motion picture exhibition, has resulted in the creation of palatial buildings, an outstanding example of which is the Fox, newest addition to the William Fox circuit of theaters reaching from coast to coast.

The theater itself is a wonderland of continental treasure, embracing, as it does, the salient features of Burmese, Hindu, Persian, Indian, and Chinese architecture all deftly blended into an ultra-modern American adaptation of the Hindu temples of old. This radical departure in theater design, the first of its kind in the world, will reverberate around the architectural world.[13]

Another writer waxed even more eloquent: "There is a sweep and a flourish, a fullness and a splendid promise to the whole conception of the new Fox that is awe-inspiring. One feels that he is in the midst of nobility, treading among treasures of the mind and of the subtler senses, as ancient and immortal as the exquisite Hindu art that has been modernized in the new drama-temple."[14]

In the afterglow of such fervent eulogies it is perhaps only fair to point out that the architects of movie palaces invariably called to their assistance professional theater decorators, and C. Howard Crane was no exception. Twenty artists worked for months on the clay models of ornamental details that were later reproduced in plaster in the Fox Theater. The contract was handled by the Lennox-Haldeman Company of Cleveland, and the Chicago office of the Interstate Decorating Company of Rockford, Illinois, was responsible for executing all the decorations and color effects throughout the building.[13] Even today the overall effect is dazzling. A host of strange deities, basilisks, chimeras, butterflies, peacocks, and lions is immobilized in the architectural decoration, and the chandeliers and walls gleam with clusters of glass jewels.[15]

Detroit moviegoers had scarcely finished gaping with astonishment at the wonders of the Fox Theater when they were enjoined to enter an even stranger shrine dedicated to the art of the motion picture. An integral part of Albert Kahn's vast Fisher Building at Grand and Second boulevards, the Fisher Theater *(348)* opened its door to the public in the fall of 1928. The Chicago firm of Graven and Mayger designed the interior which was described as follows:

The architecture and decoration of pre-historic Central America have formed the basis of the theater decoration adopted for the Fisher Theater. The charac-

teristic heavy lines are preserved. The motifs are copied. The resplendent deluge of brilliant hue, red, vermilion, yellow, and similar full tones has been cascaded over plaster and stone forms that again depict the motifs of a thousand years ago in their curious stilted combinations, rococo elaborateness, and lavish profusion. . . . The effect is dignified, brilliant, not garish. It carries to Detroit the atmosphere given by a semi-barbaric people of advanced civilization to their temples and palaces, the majesty of their mystic gods and the power of their caciques.[16]

The Fisher Theater was the last of the great movie palaces to be built in Detroit. These great temples of amusement were the product of the prosperity and ebullience of the period that immediately preceded the great depression. In subsequent years the development of neighborhood theaters, talkies, and television changed the conception of entertainment. In 1961 the Fisher Theater was completely remodeled and modernized by the Fisher brothers who had originally built the Fisher Building. Thanks to their enterprise and civic pride, it became the most elegant and luxurious legitimate theater ever seen in Detroit. Thus an old era had ended and a new one begun.

The Development of the Monumental Skyscraper

When the final history of the world's architecture is written, there is little doubt that the skyscraper will rank as America's foremost contribution. Spawned in the chaos of Chicago's loop, it was the product of that city's phenomenal growth during the latter years of the nineteenth century. In the twentieth century the overpowering predominance of New York in the financial life of the nation enabled it to assume the leadership in the development of the skyscraper. Shortly after the turn of the century the New York office buildings began to far exceed their Chicago counterparts in height. Aesthetically, however, they lagged behind. Trained in the eclectic tradition and oblivious to the teachings of Louis Sullivan, New York architects were inclined to apply old rules of thumb to the new architectural phenomenon they found in their midst. The Singer Building (1908) terminated its forty-seven stories with a bulging Beaux-Arts confection, while the Metropolitan Life Building (1909) hid behind an exterior that had been borrowed from the Campanile in Venice.

The first New York architect to develop a rationale for the design of the skyscraper was Cass Gilbert. His fifty-two story Woolworth Building (1913) was perhaps the most aesthetically satisfying of the early mammoths and for many years dominated the skyline of lower Manhattan. In later years Gilbert recalled the principles that underlay his design of the Woolworth Tower:

Height was a stated element of the problem. Steel structure was the only practicable means by which that height could be obtained. I therefore accepted these facts and emphasized them in design. The height was emphasized not only by the dominance of the vertical lines, but by repeated insistence upon them by minor verticals, and resolving these again and again into minor subdivisions of a decorative sort, as was done in the architecture of the fifteenth century.[17]

As skyscrapers shot up higher and higher, a new problem arose which had not been foreseen in the days of Sullivan. Streets were becoming narrow abysses thrown into perpetual gloom. Gilbert had had the good sense to place a setback tower on the Woolworth Building. This not only admitted more light to the streets but also produced a pleasing aesthetic effect. Not all architects, however, were blessed with such prudence. It therefore became necessary for New York City to establish a zoning ordinance in 1916, thereby determining the height and area of buildings in relationsihp to the width of the streets. This required the use of setbacks. It is doubtful if any other legal regulation could have had a more drastic effect upon the design of the skyscraper.[18] The old conception of base, shaft, and cap became a thing of the past, and from then on the tall office building had much in common with the ancient Babylonian ziggurat.

The *Chicago Tribune* competition of 1922 served to focus attention upon the design problems of the skyscraper. In view of Chicago's priority in this field, it is ironical that the first prize was won by two New Yorkers, John Mead Howells and Raymond M. Hood. Completed in 1924, their Tribune Tower did little more than perpetuate Gilbert's Gothicism. Emphatic vertical piers terminated in flying buttresses which were joined to an octagonal tower that recalled the famed Butter Tower of the Cathedral of Rouen in France.

Far more significant was the design that won the second prize. It was the *(349)* creation of Eliel Saarinen of Finland whose reputation was already well established in Europe. Turning his back on historical precedent, he visualized a bold soaring tower with discreet setbacks. Although the design was never realized, it was to have an incalculable effect upon the future evolution of the American skyscraper. In Chicago the aging Sullivan proclaimed it "a voice resonant and rich, ringing amidst the wealth and joy of life." "In utterance sublime and melodious," he rhapsodized, "it prophesies a time to come and not so far away when we shall escape the bondage and the mania of fixed ideas. It goes freely in advance, and, with the steel frame as a thesis, displays a high science of design such as the world up to this day had neither known nor surmised. . . . Rising from the earth . . . it ascends in beauty lofty and serene, until its lovely crest seems at one with the sky."[19]

The influence of Saarinen is clearly discernible in the design by Raymond M. Hood of the American Radiator Building (1924) in New York. This may be noted in the unbroken main shaft of the building and in its silhouette of gracefully tapering setbacks. The rather striking coloration, however, may be attributed to the client's desire to attract attention for promotional purposes. The black brick veneer and gleaming gold details seem to express that desire for exotic splendor so characteristic of the twenties. In contrast to the movie palace, however, the skyscraper was at last breaking away from literal stylistic derivation. Both in design and color it was manifesting new expressive tendencies.[20]

Perhaps no one in New York at this time foresaw the possibilities inherent in the zoning ordinance better than the artist Hugh Ferriss. He perceived in it an unparalleled opportunity for plastic expression. Early in the twenties he published a series of his imaginative renderings of the skyscraper of the future. He realized that the old type of cubic building placed in rows along streets lost its identity and presented to the spectator only one of its façades. On the other hand, the new type of building with setbacks exposed all four sides to view and consequently possessed individuality. He recognized that the spatial envelope required by the zoning ordinance was pyramidal in character. In the pyramid Ferriss found a "sense of vertical axis and the obvious apex or summit, both of which are lacking in the cube." "The effect of all this," he concluded, "is to give back to architecture a dimension which, in crowded metropolitan streets at least, had been lost. With the return of the third dimension, architecture seems to resume possession of a lost glory."[21]

The New York Telephone Building (1926) by McKenzie, Voorhees and

Gmelin was one of the first skyscrapers that emphasized the bold plastic treatment suggested by Ferriss. Its tower and supporting masses created a monumental three-dimensional composition of imposing proportions. The designer Ralph Walker evolved a system of ornament that owed much to Sullivan. "Our civilization is intense, swift, and very complex," wrote Walker, "and the traditional styles no longer can express our life except as a basis of taste from which to look forward with a spirit of experiment and discovery; a spirit that is not satisfied unless seeking the unknown."[22]

Ralph Walker became a partner in the firm of Voorhees, Gmelin and Walker in 1926 upon the death of McKenzie.[23] Their crag-like Western Union Telegraph Building was completed on lower Manhattan in 1930. Here an attempt was made to explore the ornamental possibilities of brick. The shades of color of the brick were graduated from deep rose at the base of the building to pinkish orange at the top.[24] Abandoning the round arch, which is so closely identified with traditional masonry construction, Walker adopted the flat arch and the notched or stepped arch, which he apparently thought were more in keeping with modern architecture. Walker's greatest triumph was the fifty-story Irving Trust Company which was completed in 1930 at the head of Wall street. Its graceful telescopic silhouette and rippling stone walls proclaimed that the skyscraper had acquired a new beauty that was characteristically its own. "It is the skyscraper," wrote Walker, "that is pointing the way, that is showing the possibilities of creating a style more nearly expressive of our time."[25]

The feverish building activity prior to the great depression brought higher and higher towers to Manhattan, culminating in the eighty-four story Empire State Building (1932). Making up for lost time, Chicago produced a whole family of new giants that dwarfed its previous skyline. On the plains and in the valleys, cities large and small acquired the jagged outlines that have become such a characteristic feature of the American landscape.

The Monumental Skyscraper in Detroit

After New York and Chicago, Detroit took third place nationally in building operations during the twenties.[26] Sumptuous new public buildings, hotels, and movie palaces gave the city an air of lush prosperity, but the most ambitious new architectural endeavors were the towering skyscrapers that transformed the downtown skyline.

A lion's share of all this building activity fell to the firm of Smith, Hinchman and Grylls, and from their drafting boards came Renaissance public buildings, Gothic churches, Tudor mansions and clubs, and modern skyscrapers. During this period William E. Kapp was head of the architectural department of the firm, and to him was allotted the task of planning the layout of many of the buildings. With him worked several competent designers. One of the most talented of these was Wirt C. Rowland, who was responsible for determining the physical aspect of many of the firm's most important buildings.[27] Rowland had been steeped in architectural history at Harvard. Fundamentally he was a Gothicist; but, like many of his contemporaries, he believed that the Gothic should be adapted to modern usage. This he was able to demonstrate in the design of the Jefferson Avenue Presbyterian Church of 1925. The buttressed pylons, the canopied niches, and the molded arches with their deep reveals were part of an extensive Gothic vocabulary then commonly applied to all types of buildings.

(320)

(319)

In the same year Smith, Hinchman and Grylls built the Bankers Trust Building (1925) on the southwest corner of Congress and Shelby streets. The firm of York and Sawyer had started the vogue for Romanesque banks with the Bowery Savings Bank on Forty-second street in New York.[27] The Bankers Trust in Detroit, now occupied by Merrill Lynch, Pierce, Fenner and Smith, is a two-story structure in the Italian Romanesque style. An arcade of massive round arches provides excellent lighting for the main banking room on the ground floor, while the second floor containing offices is faced by a smaller arcade with engaged columns. The use of terra cotta on the exterior of the building permitted Rowland to create a rich effect by imitating ornate stone carving. On either side of the arched corner entrance are marble columns supporting seated lions with shields. *(353)*

But the time had come to leave behind traditional earthbound architecture. With the economy expanding at an unprecedented rate, the demand for office space was critical. Towering office buildings were converting Griswold street, Detroit's Wall street, into a veritable canyon. In the short span of four years Smith, Hinchman and Grylls were to complete three of Detroit's tallest skyscrapers: the Buhl, Penobscot, and Union Trust Buildings.

As the firm's most experienced designer, Rowland was entrusted with the aesthetic concept of these three buildings.[28] The first of them, the twenty-six story Buhl Building, was completed in 1925 on the southwest corner of Griswold and Congress streets. It should be remembered that at this time Rowland was also designing a Gothic church and a Romanesque bank, so it is not surprising that motifs from these two projects should have crept into the design of the Buhl Building.[27] By and large the general treatment was Gothic, but the entrance details were Romanesque. An effect of heavy medieval masonry was achieved by the use of random sizes of terra-cotta blocks on the exterior walls. For all its rampant archeology, however, the Buhl Building did manifest some progressive tendencies. The cruciform plan with four wings projecting from a central core solved the problem of providing light and air for the lower stories. This was an improvement over Burnham's earlier Ford and Dime Buildings which depended upon light courts. Then, too, the abandonment of the classical cornice made possible a stronger vertical emphasis in keeping with the increased height of the newer buildings. *(351)*

Three years later the forty-seven story Penobscot Building (1928) was completed on the southwest corner of Griswold and Fort streets. In the meantime Rowland had been absorbing some of the new aesthetic theories about the skyscraper. He began to wonder why architectural verticality was invariably associated with the Gothic. "It is quite this attitude that makes some of us see in the high office building a Gothic opportunity," he reflected, "instead of taking a fresh start with so many means at hand to solve this much disputed problem in a direct and scientific way. This would seem to preclude art." "But the greatest art of the past," he concluded, "has gone hand in hand with science in the expression of human thought, however unconsciously—as in the case of the Greek or [the] French Gothic."[29] *(354)*

In conceiving the design of the Penobscot Building, Rowland was searching for a new idiom for the skyscraper. In contrast to the Buhl Building, it is devoid of archeological details. Its simple limestone mass, H-shaped in plan, rises unbroken to the thirtieth floor. Here a series of setbacks ascend in a masterly cubistic composition to the apex, which is terminated by a slender steel aircraft beacon. Dominating the Detroit skyline with its towering bulk, the Penobscot

Building was a significant achievement. Emancipated from the shackles of historical styles, it was a bold statement in the language of its day. It is well to remember, however, that Rowland was a man steeped in traditional architecture and was still thinking in terms of heavy masonry masses. It was left for the next generation to develop a new style of architecture aesthetically expressive of steel frame construction.

The Buhl Building was built on property held by the Buhl family for three generations.[30] Christian H. Buhl had built the original Buhl Block on the same site in 1868–87.[31] He had made a fortune in the hat and cap trade, the fur trade, and later the hardware business.[32] The Penobscot Building was built by the sons *(131)* of Simon J. Murphy whose name was inseparably woven with the early lumber industry in Michigan. He had built the original Penobscot Building in 1904, naming it after the river in Maine on whose banks he had laid the foundations for success in life.[33]

(357) The next commission received by Smith, Hinchman and Grylls was for an office building for the Union Trust Company. The Buhl and Penobscot Buildings were sober dignified structures intended primarily to provide office space for top echelon business and professional men. On the other hand, the Union Trust Building was to be the headquarters of a concern that hoped to establish cordial relations with the public by means of warm and colorful architecture.[34] Frank W. Blair, the president of the Union Trust Company, was an energetic public-spirited man. Never afraid of new ideas, he was one of the first bankers in the country to lend support to commercial aviation.[35] In the meantime Wirt Rowland had been developing further his theories of modern commercial architecture, and he realized that the opportune moment had come to bring them to fruition. He submitted a colored sketch of the proposed building to Blair and it met with immediate approval.[27]

The plans for the building called for a thirty-six story structure. On the main floor would be a large banking room and lobby, while the numerous floors above would be devoted to office space. Provision was made for public elevators at the north end of the building and for private elevators for the use of the trust company at the south end. The disposition of the plan immediately suggested to Rowland a huge cathedral with a high tower at the north, a nave and aisles extending to the south, and terminated by an apse or small octagonal tower. He was reminded that the highest cathedral nave in the world (in Beauvais, France) was only half as high as the proposed building. He wondered how such a tall and narrow structure could be given an appearance of stability, since the necessity for window space precluded the use of piers as large as those at Beauvais. This problem he solved by the use of alternate solid and open bays on the vast expanse of wall surface.

Although Rowland was still guided by precedent in his concept of architectural masses, he was already convinced of the unsuitability of Gothic or Classical detail for the skyscraper. The decision to use brick veneer for the Union Trust Building suggested to him that this material might be the key to an entirely new system of decoration. Combined with glazed tile and polychrome terra cotta, it offered unlimited possibilities of color, texture, and form. Color was desirable because it could be comprehended so easily. "We no longer live in a leisurely age," Rowland reflected, "nor do we move on streets from which it is possible to contemplate and enjoy minute sculptural detail. What we see we must see quickly in passing, and the impression must be immediate, strong and complete. Color has this vital power."[36]

Completed in 1929, the Union Trust Building, now the Guardian Building, is *(357)* a vast slab-like structure extending between Congress and Larned streets on Griswold. On the lower surface of the building Mankato stone of a rich buff tone was used. Above the seventh floor is a band of patterned terra cotta in green, buff, cream, and vermilion. The main portion of the building was faced with tan-orange brick. Above this is a series of setback parapets trimmed with orange and white terra cotta readily visible at a distance. At the top of the north tower is a polygonal crowning feature decorated with a fretwork of burnished gold. When the building was first completed beams of moving colored lights radiated from this point at night.

One of the most unusual architectural features of the Union-Guardian Building was the use of the stepped or notched arch. This was suggested by the natural way of piling brick without adding any curved or molded forms. The stepped form, in addition to serving as an arch, provided, with various modifications, the principal motif for the decorative scheme of the entire building. Above the Griswold street entrance are three notched arches supporting a recessed semi-dome decorated with glazed tiles of Pewabic pottery. The barrel-vaulted ceiling of the lobby was enlivened with gaily-colored tiles of Rookwood pottery, as were the stepped vaults of the elevator alcoves. At the extremity of each alcove glow the rich colors of stained glass windows, and inserts of opaque glass stand out sharply on the Monel metal elevator doors. From the lobby the lofty barrel vault of the banking room with its massive piers may be glimpsed through a Monel metal grille. No wonder the Guardian Building, when first opened, was hailed as a "Cathedral of Finance."[37]

Today the Guardian Building looms above Detroit like some strange enigmatic presence, a curious blend of the artistic currents of its day. The influence of early twentieth century Dutch architecture is apparent in the fine brickwork, and there are reminders as well of the skyscraper designs of Ralph Walker and Raymond Hood in New York. Certainly the Arts and Crafts movement and the Paris Exposition of Decorative Arts of 1925 left their mark upon the decorative scheme. Everywhere the gaily colored patterns and rich materials are redolent of the ebullient twenties. Their very multiplicity, however, tends to create confusion and redundancy. In the final analysis the building as a whole lacks cohesion, and consequently it cannot be regarded as expressive of its period in the best sense.

By contrast, the thirty-seven story David Stott Building is more restrained in *(352)* design. Built by Donaldson and Meier in 1929, it towers above Capitol Park at the southeast corner of Griswold and State streets. A shaft of tan-orange brick rises from a reddish granite base to the twenty-third story where it is broken by a series of discreet setbacks. The parapets at each setback are ornamented with terra cotta which is graduated in tone from deep tan at the lowest level to buff at the top.[38]

When the David Stott Building was first erected the *Detroit Free Press* classified it as "American in architecture," and noted that it had not been "copied after the great buildings of any city, or country, or period."[39] Hugh Ferriss, the recognized authority on the aesthetics of the skyscraper, compared the David Stott Building to Hood's American Radiator Building (1924) in New York and other similar structures, and observed:

A species of tower-buildings—rather than an assortment of individual towers— seems to be appearing on the contemporary architectural scene; yet, despite their individual differences, it is apparent that they constitute, on the whole, a single architectural species. Their community lies perhaps in some similarity of proportion, or silhouette, or vertical movement, or organic structure. In any case, there is a clear indication that we are in the presence of something more momentous than a sporadic individual; this uprising is one of truly great proportions![40]

At last the skyscraper had been crystallized into a generic type. Perhaps, more than any other man, it was Eliel Saarinen who had given it a definitive form. Although his study for the Chicago Tribune Tower was never realized, its influence is apparent in the design of the David Stott Building and scores of other buildings across the nation.

The Later Commercial Architecture of Albert Kahn

Although Albert Kahn is best known for his sprawling industrial complexes, he was also to leave his mark upon the skyline of Detroit. A man who had made such revolutionary advances in factory construction might be expected to come forward with some interesting solutions for the skyscraper. His earliest commercial buildings were auspicious in that they showed that he had absorbed the teachings of Louis Sullivan, but Kahn was too much of an eclectic to carry the evolutionary trend any further. He regarded his factories as purely utilitarian exercises, but he felt that the tall building was too prominent a feature of the urban ensemble to be treated in such a matter-of-fact way.

Kahn's encyclopedic mind was a storehouse of knowledge of architecture, past and present. He had seen much at first hand in Europe and America, and he would systematically fill in the gaps by consulting books and periodicals in his own architectural library. When working on the design of a factory he would attack the problems of mass production directly, thereby creating magnificent specimens of functional architecture. On the other hand, when working on more monumental types of buildings he was more inclined to fall back upon his knowledge of the past. It was then that the avid pioneer became the self-conscious scholar attempting to extract from the past the guiding principles for the future. As Kahn became older he became more conservative in his outlook, even expressing doubts as to the validity of the modern movement.

"Is all that has proven of merit in the past to be abandoned and replaced with crude vagaries?" he queried. "Must the grotesque be substituted for the beautiful? To the dyed-in-the-wool modernist, the work of the past is a closed book to be forgotten and never to be referred to. But is progress in architecture or any art not to be sought as is progress in science or any other field? Are basic principles, developed through unending experiment and thoroughly proved, to be done away with, untried forms to take their place? Is all that the past has taught us to go for naught?" And he concluded, "Our ultra-moderns would have it so, but their hypothesis is unsound."[41]

(358) In 1916 Kahn built the three-story Detroit News Building at Lafayette and Second boulevards. With it he established the character of much of his later commercial work. Strictly speaking it is an industrial plant, but its location near the commercial hub of the city and the nature of the newspaper industry demanded that it be given a more formal architectural treatment than the average factory. George G. Booth, the president of the *News*, closely supervised the design of the building. According to a contemporary account, Booth "was determined that the new home of the *News* should possess the dignity of style, chastity

of spirit, and substantiality appropriate to an institution which is aware of its intimate association with the welfare of the individual and the state."[42]

Steeped in the Arts and Crafts movement and the English Domestic Revival, *(296)* Booth could hardly be expected to favor the box-like office buildings with terra-cotta veneer then popular. Something essentially modern but with medieval overtones was more to his liking. Kahn found the answer in the solid-looking commercial buildings that had given German cities such an air of prosperity before World War I. "During the past fifty years," he wrote, "there has been a general revival of good taste, keener interest in and appreciation of all the arts. Germany led the van in cutting away from the debased in vogue. In the work of Messel, we see perhaps the first serious abandonment of prevalent tradition and establishment of a new type of work expressive of the modern trend."[43] In the heavy stone arches, piers, and mullions of the Detroit News Building, there is something of the character of Messel's Wertheim Department Store in Berlin.

Ernest Wilby, who was a Kahn associate from 1903 to 1918, played an important part in the design of the *News* building.[44] He had also worked on the *(200)* Ford Highland Park plant.[45] Both buildings were of reinforced concrete construction and both emphasized efficiency of production. Their main difference lay in their exterior treatment. The functional simplicity of the earlier plant heralded a new age of architecture, whereas the monumentality of the later plant bowed deferentially to tradition. The massive corner pylons were about the only features that both buildings had in common.

In 1923 Kahn built a new headquarters for the *Detroit Free Press* on Lafay- *(356)* ette boulevard between Cass and Washington. Since rental space was included in the building, it was of necessity larger than the *News* building. Hence steel construction was preferable to the bulkier reinforced concrete, but the same use of monumental limestone on the exterior was continued. A new element may be noted, however, in the massing of the building in a central thirteen-story tower with lower six-story wings. Here the influence of the setback regulations recently established in New York is apparent.

In general Kahn deplored the individualistic towers that were rising in New York. He objected to their excessive height and lack of relation to one another. Buildings of abnormal height might be effective at focal points, but when crowded together they resulted in a "reign of terror." "Everyone is trying something different," he complained. "Instead of adhering to a type fairly successful and improving upon it, bedlam reigns." Amid this chaos, however, he was able to find individual examples that met with his approval. Walker's New York Telephone Building he found "excellent in composition and skyline."[46]

No doubt his own Maccabees Building in Detroit was influenced by Walker's *(355)* masterpiece. Located on Woodward avenue at Putnam, it was completed in 1927. Its fourteen-story tower and subordinate masses flanking open courts created an imposing three-dimensional composition. In comparison with the New York Telephone Building, however, it seems compact, since the tower has been flattened into a slab-like element.

Kahn greatly admired Saarinen's design for the Chicago Tribune Tower. It *(349)* must have represented to him the logical evolution of the skyscraper. In time he began applying Saarinen-inspired motifs to some of his smaller structures, such as *(360)* his Kresge Administration Building on Cass Park (1927) and his Detroit Times Building on Times Square Park (1929). In both he used discreet setbacks, piers extending above parapets, and vertical accents between piers.

Kahn's greatest opportunity in commercial architecture came when he was *(359)* commissioned to do the Fisher Building (1928).[47] The seven Fisher brothers had made a fortune by providing bodies for the thriving automobile industry.[48] Pioneers in their field, they were responsible for developing the closed body which transformed the nascent automobile from a pleasure vehicle into the indispensable utility which we know today.[16]

The Fishers were determined to make Detroit their home and to use their wealth in furthering the progress of the city. They dreamed of a magnificent office and shopping complex. With this in mind they tried to acquire a downtown block on Woodward avenue but ran into difficulty assembling separate parcels of land. In order to obtain a sufficiently large piece of property they finally settled upon a block three miles from the heart of the city on Grand boulevard near its intersection with Woodward avenue. Here they envisioned the New Center, a secondary business district that would relieve the congestion of the downtown area and at the same time be more accessible to the suburbs. *(240)* Across Grand boulevard from the site loomed the giant General Motors Building which had already introduced a considerable amount of business activity into the area. They planned to build three units, the first and foremost of which was to be the Fisher Building.[49]

Since Albert Kahn viewed with alarm much that went under the name of modern architecture, he was determined to proceed with caution in the design of his new project. In his opinion Le Corbusier, Gropius, and Mendelsohn had gone too far in their glorification of steel and glass. He recognized that the modern skyscraper deserved an exterior treatment expressive of its structure, but he was wary of any indulgence in the strange or the bizarre, both of which he felt were too often mistaken for originality. In a periodical of the day he wrote:

There is a certain appeal to many in what is strange and what seems new to them. In architecture to be worthy of a title there must ever be dignity and good taste, neither acrobatics nor wild orgies. The architect's responsibility is indeed great and should prove a deterrent in erecting structures which at best are but an experiment, often proving a failure. We architects may build in our own back yard anything as ugly and curious as we please, but we have no right to do this for clients who rely on us to create that which will withstand the test of time. Nor have we the right to impose the ugly though different upon the community.[50]

The design of the Fisher Building was a reaction against the so-called 'packing case' type of building, which was considered devoid of interest in the flamboyant twenties.[51] The problem of handling great façades with a multiplicity of windows was solved by breaking the planes into panels by recession of the wall surfaces. Vertical emphasis was achieved by grouping windows in pairs and trios in these panels, and by introducing continuous piers. The transition from the eleven-story wings of the Fisher Building to the twenty-eight story tower was gracefully accomplished by a series of setbacks that produced a tapering effect. The first three stories of the building were faced with pinkish gray granite and the remainder was done in white marble.[16]

It was inevitable that such an overpowering masonry mass, with its strong vertical emphasis and soaring silhouette, should have suggested the Gothic. Although the first studies indicated a flat roof, there was an irresistible temptation to crown the building with a steep pyramidal roof characteristic of Gothic structures. This was ultimately done, not without a weakening effect upon the design as a whole. There was, of course, a precedent for such a feature in Cass Gilbert's generally admired designs for the Woolworth and New York Life Insurance Buildings. In fact, a comparison between the latter and the Fisher Building reveals striking similarities in overall concept. It is to Kahn's credit that he eliminated Gilbert's archeological Gothic detail, but he was too preoccupied with images of the past to be able to make a crisp, clear statement in contemporary commercial architecture.

"It is notable how seldom a sloping roof appears in any of the outstanding new buildings," observed Sheldon Cheney, one of the most astute architectural critics of the 'Golden Age of the Skyscraper.' "The immense New York Life Insurance Building has just been all but ruined by one, and the monumental Fisher Building in Detroit is similarly softened, anticlimaxed. The boldness of the block forms is so much an asset, so clearly an appropriate machine-like element, that the sloping roof can only serve to weaken the effect—if not to make the whole as ridiculous as a naked man under a hat."[52]

Perhaps the general Gothic conformation of the Fisher Building was too sober to make allowance for the pagan splendors to which the Fisher brothers aspired. This may explain why there was a change to the Roman style on the ground floor. The general tone was set by the heroic round arch at the entrance and the round arches that frame the shop windows along the streets. This is but scant preparation, however, for the magnificence of the interior where a vast arcade, extending from one end of the building to the other, provides access to the rear of the shops. Upon the walls gleam forty different varieties of marble that would dazzle even the most jaded Roman emperor. *(359)*

Considering the Fisher brothers' taste in materials, they could hardly be expected to be satisfied with ordinary architectural ornament. Previously Albert Kahn had adorned his buildings with traditional statuary and Classical or Renaissance details. Although he still believed in adhering to the "basic principles" of architecture, he was nevertheless attempting to evolve from historical forms a new architecture adapted to modern life. Concurrently he was searching for new decorative motifs. An early supporter of the English Arts and Crafts movement, he followed with interest the related movements in other countries. It was a time when artists were reacting against academic stereotypes and attempting to come closer to the wellsprings of artistic production by examining their native artistic heritage.

In 1927 George G. Booth had commissioned Eliel Saarinen to build the Cranbrook School in Bloomfield Hills. Among the artists working on the school was Géza Maróti of Budapest. In his work he had developed an individual manner based on the Magyar tradition of Hungary. Using stylized patterns and brilliant colors, he made sculpture and painting the willing servants of architecture. Kahn found what he was looking for in the work of Maróti and engaged him to design a comprehensive decorative scheme for the Fisher Building. An impressive feature of this scheme is the main entrance arch which was ornamented with granite carvings in relief. On the interior the barrel vault of the arcade was decorated with colorful frescoes and mosaics in stylized designs. Also noteworthy are the bronze plaques in low relief on the walls and the richly embossed bronze elevator doors.[16] *(370)*

In 1931 Kahn completed the New Center Building on Second avenue at the northeast corner of Lothrop. The second of the three units originally contemplated by the Fisher brothers, it is a ten-story office building conforming in style to the nearby Fisher Building. In 1950 plans were ready to construct the eleven-story Brothers Building on the corner of Grand boulevard and Second avenue facing the Fisher Building. This would have been the third unit of the New Center group, but it was never built because of governmental restrictions on material and labor during the Korean War.[53]

The Later Industrial Architecture of Albert Kahn

In the final analysis the industrial architecture of Albert Kahn proved to be his greatest achievement. In this work he felt free to abandon the canons of traditional practice and to concentrate upon purely utilitarian considerations. Step by step he evolved a new concept of the factory. His innovations proved to be so salutary in their broader implications that they provided a vital stimulus to the development of modern architecture as a whole.

In considering the industrial work of Kahn, the importance of the role of the client should not be underestimated. In fact, it is no secret that much of Henry Ford's thinking lay behind some of Kahn's most brilliant successes. For years Ford had made a practice of scrupulously supervising the manufacturing processes at his plants. Understandably, he was aware of the importance of architecture in overall efficiency. It was he who conceived the idea of combining all the operations under one roof at the Highland Park plant, and at the River Rouge plant he insisted upon abandoning the old concept of the multi-storied factory in favor of a continuous flow of work on one level. Not the least of his concerns was the personal comfort of the workers, and he made sure that adequate provision was made for heating, lighting, and ventilating.[54]

Kahn had experimented with the one-story plant in Detroit as early as 1904. His Burroughs Adding Machine Company plant of that year was structurally very advanced for its day. Still standing on Second avenue, it is a one-story building with saw-tooth monitors on steel trusses supported on iron columns.

Later, when reinforced concrete became popular, Kahn shifted to multi-storied reinforced concrete structures. An outstanding example of this type of *(200)* construction was the main building of the Ford Highland Park plant of 1909. Here large expanses of steel sash were introduced for the first time in this country. It is interesting to note, however, that the machine shop at Highland Park was a one-story structure with saw-tooth monitors similar to the earlier Burroughs plant. It was parallel to the main building and connected to it by an open craneway.[55]

After building many multi-storied factories Ford became convinced that they were inefficient because of the time wasted transporting materials by elevator. He had the courage to scrap many of his older buildings and to substitute new buildings one story high with wider column spacings. Still he was not satisfied. He had demonstrated the importance of the flow of the assembly line, but he recognized that it was necessary for the manufacturer to obtain a greater control over the supply of materials. Irked by the threat of shortages, high prices, and strikes, he envisioned a vast super-plant that would be self-sufficient.[56]

In 1915 he acquired 2,000 acres in a remote farm area near Detroit along the lower reaches of the River Rouge. No one would have suspected that this property held any promise for the future, but Ford saw it as an ideal location for his super-plant. Far from the congestion of the city, there was plenty of room to spread out. Rail transportation was adequate, and the sluggish River Rouge could be deepened and converted into a harbor.

Developments at the River Rouge took an unexpected turn when Ford was assigned the task of manufacturing Eagle boats during World War I. In those days shipbuilding was an outdoor affair, but Ford thought the work would go faster inside. He planned an expansion of the assembly line methods developed at Highland Park. This called for unprecedented scale in construction and Kahn *(362)* rose to the occasion with a half-mile long structure known as Building B. Wasting no time on architectural niceties, he employed a steel frame with broad spans and walls that were unbroken expanses of glass. Completed in 1917, Building B made architectural history. It is still in use.

After the war Building B was remodeled to adapt it to the manufacture of automobiles and tractors. In 1919 and 1920 the coke ovens and blast furnaces were completed, and in 1921 the power plant was added. The High Line running along the slip became part of a network of twenty-four miles of railroad tracks that serviced the buildings.[57] In short, the River Rouge plant was well on the way to becoming the great autonomous industrial complex that has earned it the reputation of being one of the marvels of twentieth century America.

(361)

Like Building B at the Rouge, the original Lincoln plant in Detroit owed its origin to wartime production. In 1917 Henry M. Leland and his son Wilfred C. Leland formed the Lincoln Motor Company to manufacture Liberty engines. George D. Mason was the architect for the plant at West Warren and Livernois avenues. Wartime shortages of steel and concrete necessitated a reversion to old-time mill construction with brick walls and wood sashes. In 1919 the plant was retooled for automobile manufacture and the first Lincoln was produced in 1920. Long a champion of the inexpensive car, Ford now saw his opportunity to expand his scope to include the manufacture of a luxury car. In 1922 he purchased the Lincoln Motor Company from the Lelands. Albert Kahn expanded the plant with a concrete building and later added more modern buildings of steel construction with saw-tooth monitors.[58] In 1955 the manufacture of Lincolns was shifted to a new factory at Wayne, Michigan, and the old buildings were acquired by the Detroit Edison Company for a service center.

While Ford was expanding his empire, his supremacy in the automotive world was challenged by another giant, William C. Durant of Flint. What Durant lacked in mechanical ingenuity he more than made up for in business acumen. Grandson of Henry H. Crapo, a wealthy lumber operator, he had early acquired control of the Buick Company in Flint. In a highly competitive industry he understood the importance of sound financing and perceived the advantages of merging.[59] In 1908 he organized the General Motors Company, the forerunner of the General Motors Corporation. Starting with Buick, he went on to acquire the Oldsmobile, Oakland, Cadillac, and Chevrolet companies. Along with these he acquired many parts and accessories companies.[60]

The General Motors Corporation is not as closely identified with the Detroit area as the Ford Motor Company, since its principal factories are distributed among other cities of southeastern Michigan. The Oldsmobile plant is in Lansing, the Pontiac plant in Pontiac, and Buicks and Chevrolets are made at Flint. Only Cadillac production is concentrated in Detroit.

The original Cadillac factory was located between Cass and Second avenues at Amsterdam. In 1920 Durant was succeeded as president of the General Motors Corporation by Pierre S. du Pont, representing new interests in the control of the firm, and a new main Cadillac plant was built on Clark street near Michigan avenue. The du Pont Engineering Company of Wilmington, Delaware, was responsible for its design and construction.[61] It was a large complex of four-story concrete buildings with open courts. Since fine craftsmanship rather than fast turnover was emphasized in the manufacture of the Cadillac, the more efficient one-story factory was not considered essential. With increased production, however, a one-story building was later added by Albert Kahn. It is of steel construction with monitors. Kahn also built the administration and engineering buildings.[62]

Although Kahn was the principal developer of the modern automobile plant, many other architects and engineers contributed to its evolution. The Maxwell

337

Motor Company plant on Oakland avenue in Highland Park was an early example of the one-story factory with monitors. One could find there "whole rooms full of automatic machines with an average, of only one man to seven or eight machines."[63] One of the original buildings is still in use as a road test garage for the Chrysler Highland Park plant. Built in 1909, it was designed by Morris Grabowsky, architect, and John A. Kreis, engineer.[64] It is a long concrete structure with a central clerestory. The concrete members are reminiscent of earlier timber construction, and the sashes are of wood. In 1917 and 1919 Kahn added some one-story steel buildings with saw-tooth monitors.[62]

The Maxwell organization dated back to 1904 when Jonathan D. Maxwell and Benjamin Briscoe formed the Maxwell-Briscoe Manufacturing Company to make two-cylinder cars. Maxwell was in charge of engineering and manufacturing while Briscoe handled promotion, sales, and finance. In 1910 Briscoe combined the business with several other automobile companies to form the United States Motor Company. Following reorganization in 1913 this became the Maxwell Motor Company. In 1917 facilities were expanded by leasing part of the East Jefferson avenue plant of the Chalmers Motor Company which Kahn had built in 1907.[65] In 1920 automobile production came to a standstill and Walter P. Chrysler was called in to assist in the reorganization of the ailing Maxwell Motor Company. In 1921 he formed the Maxwell Motor Corporation and in 1925 the company was further reorganized to become the Chrysler Corporation.[66]

Beginning life as a railroad mechanic, Chrysler had risen to be president of the Buick Motor Company and vice president of General Motors before taking over the reins of the Chrysler Corporation.[67] As its chief executive he ushered in a new period of growth and expansion, and soon it was to rival Ford and General Motors as one of the 'Big Three.'

In 1924 the first Chrysler car was produced in the old Chalmers plant which became the Chrysler assembly plant. In 1925 Kahn added a modern assembly building, a two-story structure of steel construction with clerestories.[62] The American Body Corporation plant across Jefferson avenue was acquired in 1927, and in the same year the manufacture of the Maxwell was abandoned.[68] When the Chrysler Corporation was formed the old Maxwell plant became the Chrysler Highland Park plant. In 1926 Kahn built a large one-story addition of structural steel with a saw-tooth roof.[69] Two years later he built the engineering building on Oakland avenue.

The Plymouth Motor Corporation was set up as a division of the Chrysler Corporation in 1928. This provided Kahn with the opportunity to build a completely modern factory unencumbered by obsolete structures. Located on Lynch road at Mt. Elliott avenue, the vast Plymouth plant, all on one level, is one-half mile long. Daylight is provided by various types of monitors and there are twelve and one-half miles of conveyor systems. The assembly line is the longest in the industry.[70]

Also in 1928 the De Soto Division of the Chrysler Corporation was organized and the first car to bear that name was brought out in the East Jefferson avenue plant. In 1936 the Chrysler Corporation acquired the former La Salle plant at the intersection of Wyoming and Michigan avenues, and the manufacture of the De Soto was continued there.[58] Originally built for the Saxon Motor Car Company,[71] the old factory was revamped and a new press shop was constructed by Albert Kahn. Widely acclaimed for the striking simplicity of its design, the De Soto press shop consisted of a huge glass cage suspended from trusses. "Conservatives may rebel at the application of architectural criteria to such structures," wrote George Nelson, "but the fact remains that it is precisely in such buildings

(365)

(363)

that modern architecture has reached its most complete expression."[72] Since De Soto production has been discontinued, the Chrysler Corporation now utilizes the Wyoming plant for glass fabrication and packaging for overseas export.

When the Chrysler Corporation purchased the Dodge Brothers Corporation in 1928 it took over the great Dodge plant in Hamtramck. In order to produce Dodge trucks Albert Kahn built the Chrysler half-ton truck plant in 1937 on Mound road north of Detroit in Warren. The roof design was unique. To provide better natural illumination, monitors hang down below the roof level instead of projecting above it. Kahn triumphed again with the export building.[73] *(364)* Transparent and immaterial-looking, it surpassed the De Soto press shop in the crisp inventiveness of its design.

While Chrysler was spreading out and diversifying in Detroit, Ford was concentrating his efforts on the River Rouge plant. As part of his plan to make it *(361)* a self-sufficient industrial city, he was determined to expand and modernize its steel production. He saw that Detroit was the logical center for a booming steel industry, since it stood half-way between the iron mines of the North and the coal fields of the South, with excellent water transportation right to its door.

In 1925 Albert Kahn enlarged the steel-manufacturing facilities at the Rouge plant with the motor, the pressed steel, and the spring and upset buildings.[74] They are gigantic steel structures with glass walls and enormous monitors. In 1938 he added the mammoth press shop. It is one of the largest industrial buildings ever erected, being a third of a mile in length. An unusual feature is an elevated level for the presses, so designed to permit the use of conveyors on the ground level.[75]

By the twenties Kahn's fame as an industrial architect had spread around the globe. Not only did he build factories in scores of American cities, but he also received commissions from countries scattered over five continents. One of his most extraordinary commissions came in 1928, for it was then that the Soviet government requested him to undertake a tremendous program of industrial expansion. There was no one in Russia at the time capable of organizing a construction project of such magnitude. All told, Kahn built 531 factories for the Russians, including the famous tractor plant at Stalingrad. His task was made even harder by the necessity of training 4,000 Soviet engineers to continue the program.[76]

The outbreak of war in 1939 brought new labors for Kahn. Two of his outstanding war plants in the Detroit area were the Chrysler tank arsenal on Van *(367)* Dyke road in Warren and the Ford Motor Company's Willow Run bomber plant near Ypsilanti. The tank arsenal was begun early in 1940 and turned out its first tanks in six months. Consisting of a huge glass cage three blocks long, it followed the precedent set by Building B at the Rouge plant in World War I and continued in the De Soto press shop and the Chrysler half-ton truck plant.

Built in 1941–43, the Willow Run bomber plant represented a new wartime *(366)* concept of industrial architecture. Because of the increasing menace of air attack, it became necessary to prepare for the blackout. Consequently, the production areas at Willow Run were artificially lighted, thereby reversing Kahn's practice of providing maximum daylight. Only the areas next to the outside walls, which contained the offices and utilities, received natural lighting. The bomber plant was also adapted to a new kind of airplane manufacture. Up until World War II airplanes had been produced by relatively slow handmade methods. Henry Ford proceeded to make them by the mass production techniques developed in the automobile industry. As at River Rouge, the bomber plant was designed to receive raw material at one end and to turn out the finished product at the other.[77] It was no ordinary operation. Sprawling over seventy acres of flat Michigan terrain, the new factory proved to be the largest ever built. The assembly line extended the full length of the building for 3,000 feet; as the planes advanced, sub-assemblies on either side provided the essential parts.[78]

Once again Henry Ford triumphed. Even in his advanced years he was able to visualize the possibilities of the future. At Willow Run, as at Highland Park and River Rouge, he had transformed his revolutionary ideas into reality, and society as a whole was thereby greatly benefited. Perhaps more than any other man, Kahn had helped to bring Ford's ideas to fruition. The bomber plant was the last big project upon which they worked together. In addition to the bomber plant, Kahn built many of the nation's major war plants across the continent. In time the strain of so much work took its toll upon him: Albert Kahn died in 1942 at the age of seventy-two. Five years later Henry Ford died at the age of eighty-four.

Honored here and abroad, Kahn had lived to be the 'No. 1' industrial architect of the age of mass production. How much his industrial architecture influenced other types of architecture remains a matter of conjecture. But it stands to reason that people who had become used to working in his cheerful, spacious, and efficient factories would soon demand similar conditions in their schools, their stores, and their homes.

"The modern course of industry is turning our cities inside out," wrote George Miehls, a later president of Albert Kahn Associates. "The decentralized factory is surrounding itself with houses built along the one-story lines of the plant itself. Nearby is the modern supermarket where production-line selling is on a one-floor basis. The one-story school is there, too, with horizontal communication. All these are offspring of the modern factory."[54]

Cranbrook

While Albert Kahn was forging a new industrial architecture in Detroit, Eliel Saarinen, newly arrived from Finland, was pointing the way toward modernity in institutional buildings. In 1926 he was commissioned by newspaper publisher George G. Booth to build an educational complex on his estate in Bloomfield Hills. In 1927 the Cranbrook Foundation was organized, and by 1943 the buildings were completed for its four institutions, which were to become important factors in the cultural life of the area.

(349)   Saarinen had come to the United States after having won the second prize in the *Chicago Tribune* competition in 1922. Already a man of mature years, he left behind him a distinguished practice in Europe. He had first seen the light of day in 1873 in a small rural town in Finland. One of six children, he was the son of a Lutheran pastor. After finishing high school, he went on to Helsinki to study architecture at the Polytechnic Institute.[79]

In Finland, as elsewhere, the rapid expansion of cities and the introduction of machine-made products had played havoc with architectural design. Fundamental principles were buried under a welter of superficial styles. Saarinen joined the ranks of the rebels in Helsinki. "Architecture has gone astray," he protested. "Something has to be done about it; now is the time to do things." While still a student he joined two classmates to form the architectural firm of Gesellius, Lindgren and Saarinen. In their search for expressive form they returned to the nature of the material and tried to treat it simply and honestly. They learned much by studying early structures built in a period when honesty prevailed in the use of materials.[80]

The three young architects illustrated their theories by building a studio-home in the forest not far from Helsinki (1902). They called it Hvittrask, a name derived from the lake near which it stood. It was made of granite and timber, materials close at hand, and had steep red tile roofs. Although it owed much to tradition, it was nevertheless well adapted to modern usage. Of the three architects in the firm, Saarinen was the most creative. His concept of design reached beyond architecture to encompass all the crafts. It was he who designed the furniture at Hvittrask. Gradually his firm gathered a staff of artisans to create the furnishings for their buildings. One of their most important commissions during this period was for the National Museum in Helsinki.

In 1903 Loja Gesellius, the sister of Saarinen's partner, joined the colony at Hvittrask where she executed commissions for sculpture and interior decoration. She and Saarinen found they held similar views on art and life, and it was not long before they took the vows of marriage. Hvittrask was their home for many years and it was there that their talented children Eero and Pipsan were born.[81]

The partnership with Herman Gesellius was dissolved in 1907, Armas Lindgren having withdrawn earlier. This left Saarinen free to develop an independent philosophy of architecture. Discarding conventional formulas, he returned to nature to discover the underlying principles of design. In 1904 he won the competition for the railroad station in Helsinki. Completed in 1914, it was to bring him lasting fame. In a day when most railroad stations were hiding behind pompous historical façades, it was conspicuous for the handsome simplicity of its design. In 1908 he won the competition for the Finnish Parliament House, but this was never built because of political suppression. During this period he was also active in many city planning projects in Finland, Estonia, and Hungary.[82]

After World War I times were difficult, so for lack of steady work Saarinen entered many competitions. His efforts were rewarded by winning the second prize in the *Chicago Tribune* competition in 1922. After the deprivations of Finland, America seemed like a land of promise. He set out with his family to visit the city that had placed such confidence in his abilities.[83] He could hardly have guessed that in the New World fate would bring him one of the greatest opportunities of his life.

While in Chicago he was invited to be a guest professor at the School of Architecture of the University of Michigan. During his two-year stay at the university in Ann Arbor he became acquainted with student Henry S. Booth, the son of newspaper publisher George G. Booth. Recognizing the abilities of the Finnish designer, young Booth introduced him to his father. The two older men found much in common. Early in his career Saarinen had become very much interested in the Finnish crafts and was later influenced by the German *Jugendstil,* while Booth had been the founder of the Society of Arts and Crafts *(299)* in Detroit.

A pioneer in the suburban development of Bloomfield Hills, Booth had built *(301)* the Cranbrook Meeting House in 1918 to serve as a church and school. As the community grew, he foresaw the need for expanded educational and religious facilities. In view of his deep interest in the arts it was natural that he should have considered education in the arts an essential part of the overall needs. He could think of no better setting for an educational center than the beautifully landscaped acres of his own estate. In Saarinen he found a man admirably qualified to help him materialize his ideas. Soon the two started working together on plans that eventually were to produce the four Cranbrook institutions.[84]

At first Booth intended to convert his substantial farm buildings into a boys' school, but it soon became apparent that it would be easier to start from scratch. Saarinen then drew plans for a larger school, more or less following the lines of

(370) the original farm buildings.[85] Booth approved and work was begun on Cranbrook School. Opened in 1927, the school consists of a number of brick buildings with steep red tile roofs grouped around courts.[86] An individualistic treatment of stone ornament and brickwork suggests that Saarinen was searching for a new idiom, but the general character of the work still owed much to Scandinavian tradition.

(298)

(317) All during Booth's life he was inspired by the ideals of the Arts and Crafts movement. When the Society of Arts and Crafts established their headquarters in Detroit in 1906, it was he who provided the craftsmen's workshops.[87] When he built his own residence in Bloomfield Hills, architects, craftsmen, and artists were given an opportunity to work together in the true spirit of William Morris.[88] Christ Church Cranbrook, the Gothic house of worship that Booth built in 1928, was an even more ambitious example of artistic collaboration. When Saarinen began working for Booth, he continued this tradition of artistic collaboration but translated it into more modern terms. At Cranbrook School the

(359) sculptural ornamentation was done by Géza Maróti, a Hungarian sculptor Saarinen had known in Europe. The quadrangle was enhanced with bronze sculptures by Paul Manship and Carl Milles, and the buildings were adorned with wrought-iron work by Oscar Bach.[89]

Immediately after the completion of the boys' school, plans for Cranbrook Art Academy were developed. The first group of buildings completed was similar in style to the school. Here space was provided for administrative offices, an art museum, a library, arts and crafts studios, and living quarters for students. In 1932 Saarinen was appointed president of the art academy. He planned to have artists of the highest ability live at Cranbrook and execute their work there. The experience of students working in their own studios would be enriched by contact with these master-artists. He established weaving studios under Loja Saarinen and Marianne Strengell, a department of painting under Zoltan Sepeshy and Wallace Mitchell, and a ceramics department headed by Maija Grotell. A design shop was set up under Charles Eames and Eero Saarinen, and a metalworking department under Harry Bertoia. Finally he founded a post-graduate department of architecture and city-planning over which Saarinen himself presided. This enabled serious students of architecture from all over the world to benefit from his broad experience and background.

In 1929 Carl Milles, the eminent Swedish sculptor, visited the Cranbrook community and was asked to become the resident sculptor and director of the department of sculpture at the academy. Saarinen built a residence for him, and also a studio where he executed many important commissions. Numerous examples of Milles's work now adorn the buildings and the grounds at Cranbrook.[90] The house which Saarinen built for himself and his family in 1929 illustrated his concern about every aspect of design. Following the practice begun earlier at Hvittrask, he designed all the interiors and the furniture, while Loja Saarinen designed and wove all the fabrics and rugs.[91]

(368) At about this time George Booth was contemplating building Kingswood School for girls. He was so pleased with the results of the artistic collaboration on the Saarinen house that he suggested that the new school be designed by the architect with the assistance of his family. A site was chosen at the edge of a small lake with a wooded hill in the background. Perhaps it was the beauty of the setting that inspired Saarinen to apply to his design the principles he had found in nature. "The plant grows from the seed," he observed. "The characteristics of its form lie concealed in the potential power of the seed. The soil gives it strength to grow, and the outer influences decide its shape in the environment."

Completed in 1931, Kingswood School seemed almost like a product of nature.[92] The horizontal building masses conformed to the sweep of the shore land, while the copper roofs and pinkish-tan brick and stone blended in with the natural surroundings. Dormitory and work areas were skillfully coordinated around a series of intimate courtyards. The interior was a synthesis of line and texture created by the family of the architect. Loja Saarinen designed the rugs and fabrics, aided by a corps of weavers. The remaining interior appointments were completed by the talented Saarinen children; Eero designed the furniture, while Pipsan decorated the auditorium and the ballroom.

With Kingswood, Saarinen sounded a new note of simplicity. Abandoning the traces of eclecticism so prevalent at Cranbrook, he reached a level of mature expression in accord with his new surroundings.[93] To be sure, the influence of Frank Lloyd Wright is apparent in the banks of windows, the intersecting planes, and the overhanging eaves. Nevertheless, Kingswood bears the earmarks of an individuality that was distinctly his own. Saarinen's later buildings were even simpler in detail than Kingswood, depending more for their effect upon line and mass. Wyandotte brick, which he first used at Kingswood, appealed to him in color and texture, and he chose this brick for all his subsequent work, frequently combining it with Mankato stone trim.

The year 1933 saw the completion of the Cranbrook Institute of Science.[94] Its simple straightforward lines are reflected in a pool animated by playful Triton figures by Carl Milles. Several more buildings were added to the art academy in the period immediately preceding World War II. These included a women's dormitory, studios for the department of painting, and additional housing for faculty and students.[95] In 1943 Saarinen completed the final building of the art *(369)* academy, the art museum and library. Its severely plain walls and monumental portico serve as a background for major fountains by Carl Milles.[96]

In 1939 Saarinen founded the firm of Saarinen, Swanson and Saarinen, in partnership with his son Eero and his son-in-law J. Robert F. Swanson. The former had graduated from the Yale School of Architecture in 1934, the latter from the School of Architecture of the University of Michigan in 1925.[97] Outstanding examples of the work of the firm are the Kleinhans Music Hall, Buffalo, New York; the Crow Island School, Winnetka, Illinois; and the Tabernacle Church of Christ, Columbus, Indiana. A new three-dimensional quality clearly differentiates these buildings from the earlier ones at Cranbrook, and they have received wide acclaim for the excellence of their design.

In 1950 the elder Saarinen died at the age of seventy-seven. His work seems conservative now, but it is well to remember that when he came to America in 1922 architects were steeped in the past. He helped to break the spell of the past and to point the way toward the future. More radical technical and aesthetic innovations were under way in Europe, and their impact was soon to be felt on the architects of the next generation.

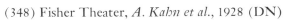

(349) Chicago Tribune Tower project, *Eliel Saarinen*, 1922 (PSS)

(348) Fisher Theater, *A. Kahn et al.*, 1928 (DN)

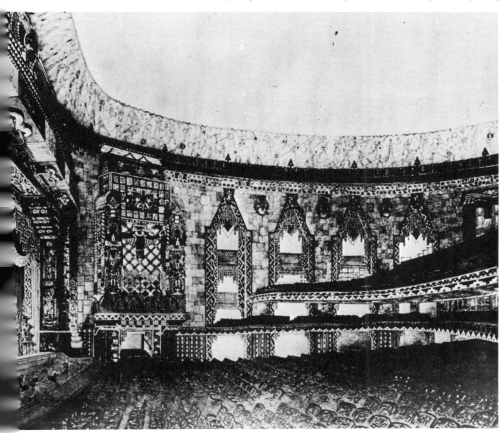

(350) Fox Theater, *C. H. Crane et al.*, 1928 (DN)

(351) Buhl Building, *Smith, Hinchman & Grylls*, 1925 (MB)   (352) David Stott Building, *Donaldson & Meier*, 1929 (MB)
(353) Bankers Trust Co., *Smith, Hinchman & Grylls*, 1925 (SHG)

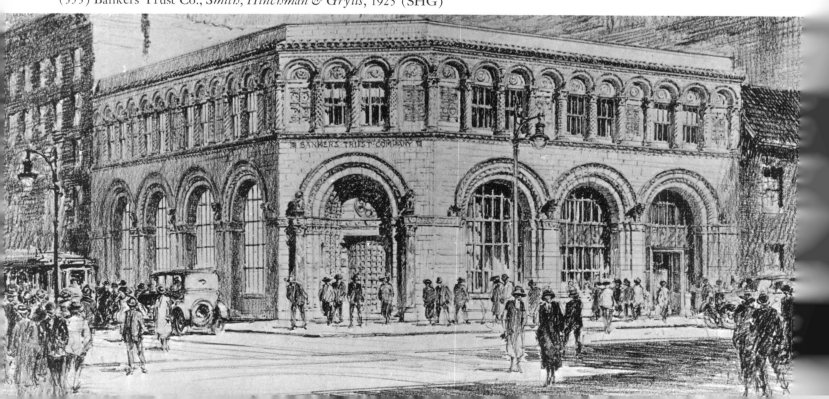

(354) Penobscot Building,
Smith, Hinchman & Grylls,
1928 (L-A)

(355) Maccabees Building, *A. Kahn*, 1927 (H-B)

(356) Detroit Free Press, *A. Kahn*, 1923 (H-B)

(357) Guardian Building, *Smith, Hinchman & Grylls*, 1929 (L-A)

(358) Detroit News, *A. Kahn*, 1916 (MB)

(359) Fisher Building, *A. Kahn*, 1928 (MB)

(360) Kresge Administration Building, *A. Kahn*, 1927 (H-B)

(361-362) Ford River Rouge Plant, *A. Kahn*, 1917-38 (FMC)

(362) Building B, 1917

(363) Chrysler-De Soto Press Shop, *A. Kahn*, 1936 (H-B)

(364) Chrysler-Dodge Half-Ton Truck Plant, *A. Kahn*, 1937 (H-B)

(365) Maxwell Highland Park Plant,
Grabowsky & Kreis, 1909 (CC)

(366) Ford Willow Run Bomber Plant,
A. Kahn, 1943 (FMC)

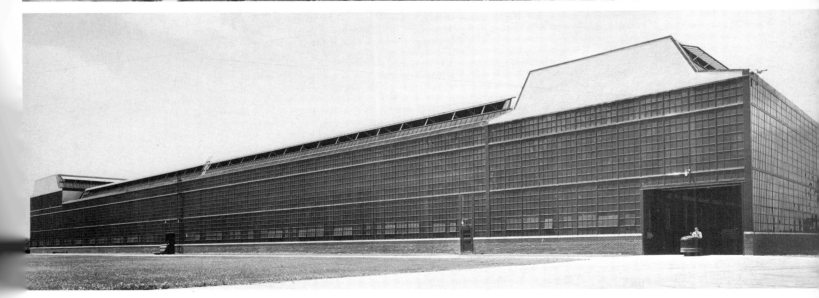

(367) Chrysler Tank Arsenal,
A. Kahn, 1940 (H-B)

(368) Kingswood School, *Eliel Saarinen*, 1931 (HC)

(369) Cranbrook Academy of Art, *Eliel Saarinen*, 1943 (CI)

(370) Cranbrook School, *Eliel Saarinen*, 1927 (HC)

11. The Modern Metropolis

Shifting Population

"I wouldn't say that Detroit was the most beautiful city of my trip," wrote Guido Piovene, the Milanese journalist, after a comprehensive tour of America in 1952. "Except for a certain number of large buildings in the center," he went on to say, "Detroit is casual, improvised, like an encampment: a conglomeration of worn out wooden houses, stores, warehouses, and in the vast outlying districts some roadside lodgings called motels, of which there are hundreds of thousands in America. In all this confusion there are great gashes everywhere which recall our cities after bombardment."[1]

To be sure, years of building stagnation during the depression and World War II had done nothing to improve the appearance of a city that had grown with a minimum of control in architecture and planning. During the war all the building activity had been concentrated in the vast plants that sprang up on the periphery of the city, but this did nothing to relieve the rampant blight and obsolescence that steadily gnawed away at the central core. Even the residential areas that had once been most desirable began to show signs of deterioration.

In former times the suburbs had been reserved for the very rich, but now that the automobile had become a universal possession, the ubiquitous realtor was anxious to accommodate all but the very poor. The time was ripe for the greatest mass exodus that Detroit had ever known. In the decade from 1950 to 1960 the city proper declined in population from 1,849,568 to 1,678,613. On the other hand, there was an increase of 750,000 people during the same period in the three-county metropolitan area. Recent figures show the five-county Detroit region now has a record 4,176,000 people.

All through its later history Detroit has attracted a steady influx of immigrants. In the early nineteenth century it was a magnet for those lured from the eastern seaboard by the promise of the West. Then came the invasion of Europeans which reached a high-water mark in the early twentieth century with the development of the automobile industry. After World War II, however, prosperity in Europe caused this flow to dwindle to a mere trickle. In its place came wave after wave of impoverished Southerners, mostly Negroes from the Deep South, but including white families from the Kentucky and Tennessee hill countries. From 1940 to 1960 the Negro population of Detroit rose from nine percent to twenty-nine percent of the total. The Negroes in the city had long been concentrated in the area directly east of Woodward avenue, but with increasing numbers, they spread out in all directions.

The Master Plan

(16) Up until recently not much in the way of planning had ever been done in Detroit. In 1805 Judge Woodward envisioned a magnificent plan with broad avenues radiating out from focal points. A small portion of this plan was carried out, giving the central business district a spaciousness unique among American cities, but the remainder of the street plan of the city was allowed to develop helter-skelter according to the whims of individual subdividers.

In 1830 Governor Lewis Cass had the foresight to lay out military roads following old Indian trails. These radial roads—Fort, Michigan, Grand River, Woodward, and Gratiot—begin in downtown Detroit and extend to outstate points in all directions. Today these form the backbone of Detroit's street system and carry an enormous volume of traffic. In 1883–87 Grand boulevard was laid out skirting the extant city limits. This boulevard, the five military roads, and (17) the remnants of the Governor and Judges Plan, as the Woodward plan was called, formed the basis of the arterial street system.

With the coming of the automobile industry in the twentieth century Detroit experienced a rapid growth. As congestion increased it became apparent that a more systematic control of expansion was required. Under these pressures the Detroit City Plan Commission came into existence in 1919 with specific duties and powers under a new city charter.

While the city had grown, its parks had remained stationary. Recognizing this deficiency, citizens voted in 1919 for a sizable expenditure to be made for the development of a parks and playgrounds system. Earlier studies made by Edward H. Bennett in 1915 greatly facilitated this work. He had recommended a series of parks connected by driveways and his plan was the basis for Rouge Park and Outer drive. In 1924 a master plan of thoroughfares provided for a system of superhighways, intermediate roads, and major streets in an area within twenty miles of the hub of the city. This plan was responsible for the widening of all the major highways.

The depression of the thirties caused a delay in public construction. In the meantime the heart of the city was threatened by blight and obsolescence. In order to reverse the downward trend drastic action was imperative. Heretofore all plans for Detroit had dealt with only one aspect of the physical development of the city. Under the circumstances, Mayor Edward J. Jeffries Jr. recognized the need for a more comprehensive plan. In 1941 he requested the City Plan Commission to prepare a master plan to guide the future growth and public improvements for the city as a whole.

The resultant plan indicated the use of areas for residential, industrial, or commercial purposes. The city was divided into 150 neighborhoods with appropriate locations of schools, libraries, playgrounds, and fire and police stations. The specific types of buildings allowed on each lot were designated in the zoning ordinance which had become effective in 1940. Some of the older parts of the city had become so completely antiquated that entire neighborhoods needed to be cleared and rebuilt. These areas were shown in the master plan. Under the General Housing Act of 1949 the federal government would pay part of the cost of buying the land which would then either be sold to private developers or be taken over by the city for public use.

The master plan also provided for parks, playgrounds, and playfields. The meadows and woodlands of the open countryside, which had long been within easy reach of Detroiters, were now being encroached upon by urban sprawl. The valleys of the Huron and Clinton Rivers form a belt of natural recreational facilities within a convenient radius of the city, yet outside its jurisdiction. If this area was to be preserved for future generations, a way must be found to save it. In 1939 an enabling act of the state legislature permitted the citizens of the five southeastern counties to vote for the creation of the Huron-Clinton Metropolitan Authority. This agency was empowered to develop and maintain recreational facilities in the metropolitan area and to make them accessible by means of parkways and connecting drives. This project included the development of the St. Clair Metropolitan Beach on Lake St. Clair.

In Detroit itself the magnificent river front offers unlimited recreational possibilities. The thousands who daily enjoy Belle Isle are a living testimony of the wisdom displayed by a previous generation in securing this great park for the city. On the other hand, the smaller parks that line the riverbank, although adequate for an earlier Detroit, do not meet the needs of the teeming population of today. Therefore the master plan recommended increasing these recreational areas and linking them together with a Detroit River drive. It is unfortunate that ineradicable industrial installations preclude an ideal solution of the problem, but there is still hope that some day Detroit will have a river front of which it can be proud.

In the meantime a more pressing problem demanded an immediate solution. As traffic in Detroit increased, congestion became intolerable. A street system inherited from the days of horse-drawn vehicles was inadequate for present-day needs. In the twenties and thirties major thoroughfares had been widened, but this merely served to intensify congestion. A traffic survey made in 1937 revealed a lack of east-west arteries. This stemmed from the fact that the early French ribbon farms running back from the river had blocked the extension of streets parallel to the river.

One of the worst traffic bottlenecks in the metropolitan area was in Highland *(365)* Park in the vicinity of the Chrysler plant. In the early years of World War II the Wayne County Road Commission built the Davison freeway across Highland Park as a demonstration of the kind of highway needed in Detroit. Depressed from twelve to seventeen feet below ground level, the roadway provided space for three lanes of traffic in each direction with a dividing strip in the middle. Cross streets were carried on bridges and access was limited. Also during World War II a surface freeway was built from the western city limits to the *(366)* Willow Run bomber plant near Ypsilanti.

In 1943 Mayor Jeffries' Street Improvement Committee proposed a system of freeways for Detroit. A plan prepared by the Wayne County Road Commission was approved by the Common Council and incorporated in the master plan. Financing was guaranteed by city, county, and state officials, later to be supplemented by federal aid. Immediately after World War II construction was begun *(371)* on a network of freeways, now mostly completed.

The John Lodge and Chrysler freeways are the principal north-and-south arteries leading from the downtown district to the northern suburbs, while the Edsel Ford freeway provides a route for crosstown traffic. These and other depressed highways are linked to a system of surface freeways extending over the entire state of Michigan. Thus in a few short years the driving habits of millions were revolutionized. Liberated at last from the tyranny of the stoplight, Detroiters could take pride in one of the nation's most efficient freeway systems. The suburbs were drawn closer to the city, and the downtown district, which had been threatened by strangulation, showed signs of renewed vitality.

Since the most crucial problem in Detroit was the traffic congestion, priority was given to the construction of freeways. Elaborate studies were made in the

(380)

(418)

(415)

(411)

(405)

(409)

master plan for other projects, but the progress has been comparatively slow. Perhaps the most striking achievement since World War II is the Civic Center on the river at the foot of Woodward avenue. Here buildings were planned around a plaza or open park-like square facing the river. Already the Veterans' Memorial Building, the City-County Building, the Ford Auditorium, and Cobo Hall have been completed.

The additions of new wings to both the Detroit Public Library and the Detroit Institute of Arts mark the beginning of an expansion of the Cultural Center. To the west of the library, the campus of Wayne State University is being developed and many fine new buildings have been completed, and there are plans for a complex of other museums and a center for the performing arts to be located in a park-like setting east of the art museum. Between the Cultural Center and the downtown district a vast no man's land has been cleared for a Medical Center east of Woodward avenue. Already a few buildings have been constructed, but much lies ahead.

Detroit's first major experiment in residential redevelopment has proved to be exemplary. The area just east of the downtown district had long been a depressed slum. One hundred and thirty acres were cleared in 1952, and parcels of land were sold to private developers. An attempt was made to provide attractive midtown living quarters which would lure the middle-income population back from the suburbs. Known as Lafayette Park, the project already contains several high-rise apartments interspersed with town houses. Plans are under way for three more residential developments to be called Elmwood Park, Forest Park, and University City.

Several areas within the city limits of Detroit have been earmarked for industrial redevelopment. The first of these to materialize is the West Side industrial project. A seventy-seven acre tract was acquired in a slum area known as Corktown, directly west of the downtown district. Demolition began in 1959. Parcels of land were sold to private firms for light industry or office buildings related to industry. Developments planned for the future are the Southwest industrial project, the North industrial project, and Research Park West.

Constantly revised and modernized, the master plan serves as an outline for a revitalized city. Charles A. Blessing, director of the Detroit City Plan Commission, envisions "an environment in which each building, each project, and each neighborhood becomes an element in a consciously contrived total concept for the new city."[2]

The General Motors Technical Center

The new Detroit that emerged after World War II was clearly not the place for the romantic architectural styles of bygone eras. It was the city that had created the automobile by means of modern design and technology, and the hour was at hand for it to fashion a new environment by the same means. It was appropriate that the first manifestation of the new order was a magnificent reassertion of the primacy of the automobile industry—the General Motors Technical Center.[3]

(373)

Previously the facilities for the General Motors technical staffs had been scattered all over the Detroit area, and it had been apparent for some time that they were inadequate. It was Alfred P. Sloan Jr., the president of the company, who launched the idea of combining all these facilities in one area. A site was acquired north of Detroit on Mound road in Warren Township, and upon the recommendation of Harley Earl, head of styling, the firm of Saarinen, Saarinen and Associates was chosen as architects.[4]

The award of such an important commission to the Saarinens was based upon the international reputation of Eliel Saarinen. Advanced years, however, were already creeping up on him. So far there was no indication that young Eero Saarinen was anything more than the son of a famous father. Intuitively, however, he sensed that it was the moment to assert himself, and he bent all his energies to the completion of the task. With the General Motors Technical Center he not only achieved a style that was distinctively his own, but also established himself as one of the top ranking architects in the nation.

From the beginning Saarinen was determined that the architecture of the center should be expressed in the technical terms of the product to which it was dedicated. Like the automobile, the twenty-five buildings of the complex were composed mainly of steel, aluminum, and glass. Standardized mass-produced units were the common denominator and permitted maximum flexibility. Since the research and engineering facilities of the client were at the disposal of the architects, the building techniques were well in advance of current architectural practice. The 'sandwich panels' of the wall construction were composed of enameled steel sides enclosing two inches of insulation, and neoprene gaskets instead of caulking were used to hold the windows and wall panels in place. Also, a light triangular steel truss with a span of fifty feet permitted flexible non-supporting partitions.

The construction of the center was begun in 1949 and completed in 1956. There are clusters of buildings for each of the five staff organizations: research, process development, engineering, styling, and service. The buildings are grouped in a landscaped setting around an artificial lake. Parking lots are hidden by shrubbery, and the entire complex is enclosed in a greenbelt of trees.

In this campus-like environment, so conducive to study and experimentation, Saarinen created a monument to the automotive age. He carried forward the tradition of industrial architecture established by Albert Kahn and gave it a new warmth and elegance. Here are the familiar long, low buildings with their interminable façades of glass, but to these were added end walls of vividly colored glazed bricks. The alternating glass and brick surfaces and the varying building heights have become the components of a massive orchestration. In contrast to these rectilinear forms, the oval mass of the stainless steel water tower hovers above the lake and complements the gleaming aluminum dome of the styling auditorium at the opposite end of the lake. *(376)*

Perfectionist that he was, Saarinen lavished the same care and attention to detail upon the interiors of the buildings as he did upon the exteriors. In each of the principal lobbies there is a spectacular staircase, each one distinctive in design, that provides a visual climax. *(375)*

Like his father, the younger Saarinen also believed in enriching architecture with sculpture. "A sculptor," he said, "brings to a building his special sensitivity."[5] In the central restaurant there is a magnificent gilded screen by Harry Bertoia, and in front of the Styling Administration Building stands the monumental Bird in Flight by Antoine Pevsner. As a finishing touch Alexander Calder created a water ballet with playing jets at the end of the lake. Small wonder that the center soon earned the sobriquet, the 'Industrial Versailles.' *(374)*

In such a setting 4,000 technicians, designers, engineers and executives of the General Motors Corporation are employed in planning the company's future products. "Functional requirements, however, were only part of the challenge," said Saarinen. "It meant also creating a beautiful and human environment in which men can give free rein to their intelligence and skills. It called for buildings that would symbolize industrial achievement and look as modern tomorrow as they do today."[6]

The accomplishment for General Motors brought Saarinen national recognition. Soon his talents were in demand for important commissions all over the country, and one brilliant triumph after another made architectural history. To mention only a few of his more important achievements, there are the U.S. Embassy (1960) in London, England, the Trans World Airlines Terminal (1962) in New York, the Dulles International Airport (1962) in Washington, the Columbia Broadcasting System Headquarters (1966) in New York, and the Jefferson National Expansion Memorial (1966) in St. Louis.

Shopping Centers

One of the inevitable results of the exodus to the suburbs of Detroit after World War II was the emergence of the shopping center. Their removal from arterial highways and their provision of adequate parking areas made these centers a distinct improvement over the earlier 'strip' shopping areas. The largest and best planned shopping centers in the metropolitan area are Northland, Eastland, and Westland Centers, which were developed by the J. L. Hudson Company, the largest department store in Detroit.

The choice of Victor Gruen of Los Angeles as architect for these vast projects was fortunate. Born and educated in Vienna, Austria, he came to the United States in 1938. Associating himself with a group of architects, planners, and engineers known as Victor Gruen Associates, he devoted himself not only to the design of individual buildings, but also to the solution of broader environmental and urban problems.

(372) Northland Center, which opened in 1954, was his first large shopping center and the first example in the country of the cluster type of planning.[7] Here pedestrians are completely separated from automobiles. One-story stores, shops, markets, and restaurants are grouped around garden courts and pedestrian malls surrounding a three-story Hudson department store. This cluster of buildings is ringed by parking areas accommodating 9,500 cars, and all trucking is done by means of underground tunnels. One of the most popular features at Northland is the fanciful outdoor sculpture which, combined with music and flowers, gives the courts and malls the air of a bazaar. Such radical innovations in merchandising at first met with resistance on the part of local merchants, but the understanding and support of enlightened clients, especially Oscar Webber, then president of the J. L. Hudson Company, helped to overcome the opposition, and the overwhelming response of the public dispelled any doubts.

(388)
(401) From the beginning Northland Center was envisioned as the nucleus of a larger commercial area which would be developed in a harmonious manner, and in recent years office buildings, apartment buildings, a hospital, and a hotel have been constructed on adjacent land.[8] These developments have been very successful commercially, but one could wish for a more coordinated plan and a higher general level of architecture.

(377) In 1957 Eastland Center was opened.[9] In many ways it is very similar to Northland. However, the clients had learned much from the experience at Northland. Consequently, more emphasis was placed on sculpture, one court was

enlarged for public gatherings, and a six-story medical building was designed by Gruen to be in harmony with the rest of the project.

In order to facilitate the construction of Northland and Eastland, Victor Gruen Associates established a branch office in Detroit. However, when West- *(378)* land Center was built, they worked jointly with the Detroit firm of Louis G. Redstone Architects. Opened in 1965, Westland Center differs radically from the two earlier projects by being contained under one roof. This permits pedestrian areas to be sheltered and air-conditioned. Fountains and sculpture add charm to large interior courts, and the controlled temperature encourages the growth of tropical vegetation.

The Civic Center

Ever since the founding of Detroit in 1701, the magnificent frontage on the Detroit River has been used mainly for commercial purposes. It was Mayor Hazen S. Pingree in 1890 who first suggested that a civic center be located at the foot of Woodward avenue. For many years the idea was bandied about, but little headway was made. Meanwhile the area under consideration continued to deteriorate. Finally, after World War I some progress was made. A plan was developed to build a river front civic center that would serve as a war memorial. Eliel Saarinen, who was then teaching at the University of Michigan, was commissioned by the American Institute of Architects to draw up a design in 1924.[10] *(381)* He envisioned a domical memorial hall with a long wing, which would serve as an exposition hall and a convention auditorium, in the foreground.[11] In the background rose a soaring tower which was reminiscent of the architect's earlier design for the *Chicago Tribune* tower. In 1925 the voters approved a public expenditure for the project, but no progress was made for lack of funds.[12]

At the end of World War II the idea of the civic center was revived. In 1947 Saarinen, Saarinen and Associates were engaged by the City Plan Commission to develop a new plan and act as consultants. Abandoning the old concepts of *(379)* monumentality and symmetry, the architects grouped public buildings around a landscaped plaza facing the river. Included in the scheme were a city-county building, a circular convention hall, an auditorium and music hall, and four government buildings for state, federal, and local functions.[13]

In 1950 the first unit of the Civic Center, the Veterans' Memorial Hall, was completed, fulfilling the dream for a war memorial. Begun before the Saarinens were called in as consultants, it was incorporated in their plan. Designed by Harley, Ellington and Day, it is a ten-story L-shaped building faced with white marble.

Following more or less the general outlines suggested in the Saarinen plan, the City-County Building was completed in 1955 on the northeast corner of *(382)* Woodward and Jefferson avenues. As a combined city hall and county building, the structure provides the office space, court rooms, and meeting rooms required by city and county government. Also designed by Harley, Ellington and Day, the building consists of two architectural masses. A clever use of black and white marble emphasized the verticality of the nineteen-story tower section, which stands out in marked contrast to the fourteen-story office section.

In their plans for the Civic Center, the Saarinens indicated a civic auditorium at the eastern end of the plaza. This became a reality in 1955 and is known as the *(384)* Henry and Edsel Ford Auditorium. Financing was provided by the city, the Ford family, and the dealers affiliated with the Ford Motor Company. Architects for the building were Crane, Kiehler and Kellogg, and O'Dell, Hewlett and Luckenbach. Members of the former firm had considerable experience in theater construction, having worked on many of Detroit's largest theaters, including the old Orchestra Hall.

Reflecting the latest trend in functional theater design, the Ford Auditorium is a large wedge-shaped mass projecting forward from the block of the stage and its loft. The curved front wall and the long walls of the stage enclosure are faced with mica-flecked blue granite which creates a shimmering effect at night. The side walls are of white marble. Severely plain on the interior, the auditorium has a seating capacity of 2,900.[14] It is now used principally for the performances of the Detroit Symphony Orchestra.

Perhaps even more than a new home for its symphony, Detroit needed new convention facilities. The Saarinens visualized a round convention hall at the western end of the Civic Center, but industrial leaders and automobile executives complained that there was no place to hold the National Automobile Show. They suggested that an exhibit hall be added to the convention hall and were willing to back their ideas with financial support. With city aid Mayor Albert E.

(383) Cobo enthusiastically helped them achieve their goal, and thus Cobo Hall was born. With the completion of the joint facilities of Cobo Hall and the Convention Arena in 1960, Detroit not only could hold its first National Automobile Show, but could also play the new role of being host to some of the larger national conventions.

In erecting a building for such convocations there is always the danger that it might turn out to look like an oversized barn. Architects Giffels and Rossetti avoided this pitfall by means of skillful design and interesting use of materials. The massive rectangular bulk of Cobo Hall defines the western extremity of the Civic Center, and its white marble façade provides a striking contrast to the dark green granite walls of the circular Convention Arena. An interesting aspect of the design of this complex is the way in which it was linked to the freeway system. The Lodge freeway dramatically plunges under Cobo Hall at the precise point where the glass-enclosed administrative offices are cantilevered out over the main entrance. At the rear of the building a graceful spiral ramp provides access from the freeway to a parking area on the roof. This area, combined with underground and surface space, can accommodate 3,430 cars.

On the interior of Cobo Hall there are 300,000 square feet of exhibition space and innumerable meeting rooms. A ballroom on the lower level and a large cafeteria above it take advantage of the site by providing a panoramic view of the Detroit River and Canada. With a maximum capacity of 12,000, the adjoining Convention Arena is used for meetings, large spectacles, and sports events.

The final unit of the Civic Center to be completed will be the Civic Center

(380) Plaza between the Veterans' Memorial Hall and the Ford Auditorium. Although the basic features of the original plan will be retained, changes will be made because of a decision to include an underground parking garage. When the plaza with its lagoon and landscaping is completed, Detroit will have a waterfront worthy of its magnificent site and its proud past.

Already the Civic Center has been adorned by an interesting piece of sculpture, The Spirit of Transportation, which the family of the late Alvan Macauley,

(313) president of the Packard Motor Car Company, commissioned in his memory. The work of Carl Milles, who was resident sculptor at the Cranbrook Academy of Art for many years, it is located in a small courtyard in front of Cobo Hall. This allegorical representation of an Indian carrying a canoe might seem incongruous in the "Motor City," but actually it is appropriate in that it harks back to

the earliest form of transportation used in the Great Lakes area, and leads one to ponder on the miraculous changes that have taken place in the years that separate the canoe from the automobile.

Commercial Buildings

For a city the size of Detroit, the downtown commercial area is surprisingly small. There is not the great concentration of activity to be found in New York or Chicago. Detroit is fundamentally an industrial center, and the automobile manufacturers do not require downtown office space. Long ago they discovered that it was to their advantage to locate their administrative offices away from the downtown congestion and preferably close to their factories. *(Frontispiece)*

As the Ford Motor Company expanded in the early part of the century, it pushed steadily out from the center of Detroit. When the main operations were moved from Highland Park to Dearborn, the administrative offices were likewise moved. To accommodate them, Albert Kahn built a large administration building adjacent to the burgeoning River Rouge plant in 1923. With the resurgence of the automobile industry after World War II, the Ford Motor Company built a Research and Engineering Center (1949–58) in Dearborn. Comparable to the General Motors Technical Center, it covers 750 acres and includes twenty major buildings and a test track. Architects for the complex were Voorhees, Walker, Foley and Smith of New York. Conservative in design, the buildings fit in well with their suburban surroundings. *(361)*

More interesting architecturally is the nearby Ford Administrative Center by the New York firm of Skidmore, Owings and Merrill. Replacing the earlier Administration Building in 1956, it consists of an eleven-story main building and the six-story Lincoln-Mercury Building, separated by the low slab of the parking garage. Looming above flat farmlands, these two towers draw 3,000 employees from the surrounding countryside. *(385)*

Architecturally the center exemplifies the most recent thinking in office building design and layout. In order to insure the flexibility of office partitions, it was necessary to clear the office space of all obstructions. Columns were placed outside the line of the curtain walls and inside the utility core. Since there was plenty of space, escalators were installed in order to relieve congestion in the elevators. The exterior wall panels were faced with white marble, and the columns were finished with stainless steel. Located at an important intersection, the Ford Administrative Center can be seen by thousands of motorists: a model of efficiency and a striking evidence of the post-war trend toward decentralization.[15]

It may be recalled that back in the twenties the General Motors Corporation erected a large office building in the New Center area of Detroit, and that at about the same time the Chrysler Corporation built general offices in Highland Park. The location of the administrative headquarters of Detroit's three major automobile companies in outlying areas may help to explain why there has never been a great demand for office space in the downtown district. The skyscrapers erected there during the twenties represent the characteristic overexpansion of the period, and for many years they were not completely filled. The long interval of economic depression and World War II brought about a stagnation of the building industry. It was not until after the war that an expanded economy led to a renewal of building activity. *(240)*

The first important structure erected downtown since the twenties was an eight-story annex to the Detroit branch of the Federal Reserve Bank of Chicago. *(386)*

The choice of Smith, Hinchman and Grylls as architects followed an established pattern, for they had been leaders in commercial practice in Detroit before the depression and, although the original partners were deceased, the firm continued to be one of the largest and most active in the city. Because of the large volume of construction in Detroit in normal times, this architectural firm was a magnet for design talent from other parts of the country. In 1945 Minoru Yamasaki was hired to be its chief designer. Born in Seattle, he had studied architecture at the University of Washington and had worked in New York in the offices of Shreve, Lamb and Harmon, and Harrison and Fouilhoux.[16] To many architects the prospect of building an addition to a twenty-three-year-old bank would have had a limited appeal, but to Yamasaki it offered interesting possibilities.

Located on the northeast corner of Fort and Shelby streets, the original building was erected in 1927 from plans by Graham, Anderson, Probst and White of Chicago. It was a compact mass of masonry-backed marble with a vertical emphasis. The new annex, completed in 1951, was set back thirty feet from the sidewalk, making room for attractive patches of greenery. In contrast to the older building, it was faced with a thin curtain wall of alternate bands of glass and marble veneer backed by only two inches of insulation. The lightness of the construction was emphasized by placing the columns three feet back from the wall. Although the design of the annex broke sharply with the mother building, unity was achieved by a continuity in the line of the spandrels and by the use of marble on both structures.[17] By introducing new concepts of design and construction and allowing space on the ground level for landscaping, Yamasaki ushered in a new era of commercial architecture in downtown Detroit.

It was a time for expansion. The main-office operations of the National Bank of Detroit were scattered in three buildings and were hampered by severe crowding. The late Albert Kahn had built the old main office building in the twenties. In order to improve efficiency and consolidate operations, a new build-ing was erected in 1959 across Woodward avenue from the old one. The archi-tects were Albert Kahn Associated Architects and Engineers, the firm once headed by Kahn.

(266)

(387)

The new bank building covers the entire block between Congress and Fort streets formerly occupied by a miscellaneous assortment of antiquated structures. Its handsome flank graces a three-block section of Woodward avenue, widened to create a dignified approach to the new Civic Center. The building was set back forty feet from the street to make way for an esplanade shaded by a double row of trees, behind which there is a covered arcade sheltering the vast glass wall of the two-story main banking room.

Above the arcade stretches the checkered pattern of the curtain wall which encloses twelve additional stories of office space. Marble was chosen as the mate-rial for the infill panels to harmonize with the nearby Civic Center. The span-drels were faced with gray porcelain enamel, and the framing members were made of aluminum. Since the building is air-conditioned and light controlled, the only function of the small windows is to meet the need of a view.[18]

The Federal Reserve Bank and the National Bank of Detroit illustrated ways of treating the curtain wall. Yamasaki was to return to this problem later, but in the meantime he was grappling with structural problems. In 1949 he and two of his colleagues from Smith, Hinchman and Grylls had formed a firm of their own, Leinweber, Yamasaki and Hellmuth. Their St. Louis Airport Terminal won the American Institute of Architects' first honor award in 1952. Consisting of three massive groined vaults, it gave a new dignity to the American airport building and served as a model for other architects.

Yamasaki's rise to fame was rapid, but the strain of the work took a toll on his health and he was forced to close his St. Louis branch office. Soon thereafter he established himself in suburban Birmingham, Michigan, with Joseph Leinweber, one of his former partners. In 1959 he designed the Reynolds Metals *(388)* Building in Southfield, across the Northwestern highway from Northland Center.[19] Serving as a sales office for the Reynolds Aluminum Company, this building provided an opportunity to demonstrate the architectural possibilities of aluminum. The richness of its façade and roof line was a protest against the flatness and monotony of the curtain wall. With characteristic thought and care, Yamasaki created a building that is as fresh and original in its concept as it is in its details.

The most striking feature is the gold-anodized aluminum screen wrapped around the two upper stories. This was made of sections of ordinary aluminum pipe and was intended to shield the broad expanse of windows from the sun. Columns supporting the building and the screen were clad with black anodized aluminum covers which contrast pleasingly with the gold screen. The building was set on a white terrazzo podium. From the glass enclosed lobby-display floor, one can look out over a surrounding reflecting pool, or upward at a skylighted well surrounded by balconies.[20]

There could be no more convincing evidence of Yamasaki's versatility than a comparison between his Reynolds Metals Building and his American Concrete *(389)* Institute (1958) completed a year earlier. To design two buildings simultaneously, each one demonstrating the imaginative use of a different product, is not an easy task; but to design them so that each one is unique, different, and hauntingly beautiful is ample evidence that Yamasaki is a man of no ordinary talent.

Located on West Seven Mile road, the American Concrete Institute headquarters is a small one-story building. In plan it consists of a simple rectangle with offices on either side of a central skylighted corridor. In keeping with the scale the architect wished to achieve lightness and delicacy with the material. A precast concrete folded plate roof was cantilevered out from the corridor walls and extended over the windows of the exterior walls. End walls were screens made up of concrete pipe sections, and the spandrel panels and pierced grilles for the basement windows were made of precast concrete. Privacy was maintained by a low surrounding wall made of faceted concrete blocks.[21]

The opportunity of a lifetime came to Yamasaki when he was commissioned to design a building for the Michigan Consolidated Gas Company.[22] The site was *(390)* a full block at the northwest corner of Woodward and Jefferson avenues overlooking the Civic Center. The architect and the client were in accord that the building should be a civic ornament. They could have erected a low, bulky structure occupying every available foot of the lot, but they chose to erect a lofty thirty-two story tower set back from Jefferson avenue behind reflecting pools bordered with planting.

Yamasaki wanted to create a distinctive building that people would enjoy. Completed in 1963, it rises from a marble platform like something out of *The Arabian Nights*. A thirty-foot high glass-enclosed lobby with marble columns is *(391)* reflected in the pools. At night sparkling blue lights suspended from the coffers of the lobby ceiling create a jewel-like effect, and on special occasions gas jets flicker over the pools, illuminating the bronze ballerina by Giacomo Manzù installed there.

Avoiding the monotony imposed by standardized products, Yamasaki gave an interesting form and texture to the exterior walls by the use of precast prestressed concrete panels. Two stories in height, the panels were joined at the center of the windows. These openings are extended hexagons, so designed to emphasize verticality and to eliminate the feeling of acrophobia when one is high in the building, even though the glass extends nearly to the floor. The shape of the windows was also intended to suppress the horizontal lines of the spandrels, but it does this effectively only at close range, since the cage-like character of the steel frame is clearly discernible at a distance.

The main mass of the building was terminated at the top by a lacy grille encompassing the twenty-seventh and twenty-eighth stories. Above this a four-story penthouse was built for air-conditioning and heating facilities. At night these areas are illuminated by colored lights that predict the weather and celebrate the season.[23] On the twenty-sixth story the Top of the Flame Restaurant permits the diner to gaze down upon the cities of Detroit and Windsor or to follow the slow progress of freighters along the river.

(392) In contrast to the fantasy of the Michigan Consolidated Gas Company building, the twenty-eight story Detroit Bank and Trust Company building strikes a note of restrained dignity befitting a bank. Erected in 1963 at the southeast intersection of Fort street and Washington boulevard, it adjoins the bank's (265) former main office which has been modernized. Architects Harley, Ellington, Cowin and Stirton do not seem to have been concerned with acrophobia. Dark-tinted floor-to-ceiling windows were set in precast concrete frames. Projecting from the glass, these frames combined to form a grid pattern which gives the building its essential character. An arcade at the ground level and a crowning colonnade completed the composition. Following the recent trend, the building was set back from the street to provide space for a landscaped plaza.[24]

Faced with dark granite, the First Federal Building by Smith, Hinchman and (393) Grylls went even further than the Detroit Bank and Trust Company in giving the impression of stability and permanency. After prolonged research the architects were able to make granite an economically feasible material by developing granite-veneered precast window units. The dark color lowered maintenance costs and provided a contrast to the other buildings in the downtown area. Completed in 1965, the building faces Kennedy Square, an open space in the heart of the city created by the demolition of the old City Hall. Early in the planning stage the officials of the First Federal Savings and Loan Bank had indicated that the size of their building would depend on the amount of available parking space. The decision of the City Council to build an underground parking garage under Kennedy Square paved the way for an ambitious undertaking.

The triangular lot, formed by the junction of Woodward and Michigan avenues, posed a problem to the architects. The lot had been the site of the (178) Majestic Building, one of Detroit's first skyscrapers. The architects wisely decided that the new structure should not follow the line of Michigan avenue, as its predecessor had done, but should stand at right angles to Woodward. Thus it could join with other buildings to form a unified rectilinear background on three sides of the new square.

The architects built an east tower on Woodward and a west tower on Michigan, linked by a utility core containing the elevator shafts. Rising above a landscaped plaza, the twenty-three story twin towers with their soaring vertical lines and dark granite surfaces make a strong architectural statement and add a new vitality to the core of the city.[25]

The consolidation of the city's air transportation facilities at the Detroit Metropolitan Airport necessitated an expansion program (1966–67). The original main terminal had been built by Giffels and Rossetti in 1958, but the architects placed in charge of the new construction were Smith, Hinchman and Grylls. Among other buildings they erected an impressive new terminal. According to the architects, this is the largest post-tensioned concrete structure in the world. Its bold functional forms capture some of the drama and excitement of the jet age. Horizontally curved beams on tapering cruciform columns support five huge concrete roof panels which were cantilevered out thirty-five feet to shelter the access driveway.[26] This building represents a new departure in reinforced concrete construction in Detroit. Although similar forms may not be found in the work of Kahn or Yamasaki, a study of the recent work of the brilliant Italian architect Pier Luigi Nervi will quickly reveal a precedent.[27] *(396)*

In the same year that Smith, Hinchman and Grylls were demonstrating the monumental potential of concrete in their airport terminal, Giffels and Rossetti were using this versatile material in quite a different way in their office complex for the Federal-Mogul Corporation in suburban Southfield. The staff building (1966) of this group is a two-story steel and glass cage surrounded by a delicately tapered grid of precast prestressed concrete. The upper portion of the building hovers above an all-glass lobby and is supported by cast-in-place columns which rest on a broad podium of textured concrete. Walls and columns in the lobby were faced with gray granite which contrasts pleasingly with a red carpet. The structure's lower level houses support facilities and was linked to the adjoining two-story divisional office unit.[28] *(394)*

The prosperity that followed World War II has left in its wake innumerable banks and branch banks in the Detroit area. One of the most glamorous of these is the Mount Clemens Federal Savings and Loan Association in Mount Clemens.[29] Built by Meathe, Kessler and Associates of Grosse Pointe in 1961, the main structure is a thin-shell concrete roof supported on four columns at the corners. Undulations in the roof give the building added strength, at the same time creating a dramatic effect. The space between the columns was filled with glass curtain walls, and the roof was pierced by a cluster of plastic skylights. A fountain in front adds a note of elegance, while at the rear a sunken garden provides a pleasing adjunct to the basement and serves as a buffer between the building and the parking lot. *(397)*

Hotels and Apartments

The Saarinens intended the Civic Center to be a nucleus for governmental buildings, but so far only the City-County Building has materialized as planned. Two important sites designated for governmental buildings were appropriated for commercial purposes. Certainly the Michigan Consolidated Gas Company building and the Hotel Pontchartrain add architectural luster to the Civic Center. The night life in these buildings also helps to enliven the area after dark.

In anticipation of the completion of Cobo Hall, a group of civic-minded businessmen purchased a block directly adjacent to it for the purpose of obtaining a new hotel for the city. Conrad Hilton intended to build one there in 1960, but he was unable to obtain the approval of his board of directors. Finally a group of local investors purchased the tract and proceeded with plans for the new hotel. The Detroit firm of King and Lewis was chosen as architects. The hotel, which drew its name from old *Fort Pontchartrain du Détroit*, was completed in 1965. Twenty-five stories high, it is the first major hotel built in Detroit in thirty-eight years. The main floor serves as a base for a glass-walled tower which contains 450 guest rooms. The glass walls are faceted so that each *(383)* *(398)* room has an angular bay commanding simultaneous views of the Detroit River and Canada to the south and the skyline of the city to the north. On the level above the main floor a terrace provides a swimming pool and sun-deck, while on the top floor there is a restaurant. The hotel was constructed entirely of reinforced concrete.

Along with new hotels and motels, new luxury apartments were changing the pattern of urban living in Detroit. Instead of the old rambling buildings with Gothic and Renaissance details, apartment dwellers were offered tall, clean slabs in park-like surroundings. Balconies and swimming pools were added attractions. *(399)* Overlooking the Detroit River on East Jefferson avenue, the thirty-story Jeffersonian Apartments were erected in 1965 by architects Giffels and Rossetti. Two *(401)* years later the twin nineteen-story North Park Towers were completed on the John Lodge freeway just north of Northland Center in Southfield. The architects were Levine-Alpern and Associates of Detroit, and Hirschfeld, Pawlan and Reinheimer of Chicago.

Public Housing

While the building of luxury apartments in a city follows the law of supply and demand, the provision of housing for the lowest income group falls into no such convenient economic pattern. On the contrary, studies have shown that this segment of the population is incapable of providing adequate housing for itself without some kind of government assistance. Public housing came into being during the administration of President Franklin D. Roosevelt. As a result of studies made by the City Plan Commission, federal funds were allocated to the city of Detroit in 1933 for slum clearance and the construction of low-rent housing. Immediately thereafter Mayor John W. Smith established the Detroit Housing Commission charged with the development and administration of federally-aided low-cost housing in the city.

In 1934 Mrs. Eleanor Roosevelt officiated at ceremonies which inaugurated the demolition of slum buildings on the near east side to make way for the Brewster Homes. By 1939 Brewster and Parkside Homes, Public Works Administration projects, were completed. Parkside was built on vacant land on the east side near Chandler Park. These two projects, consisting of two-story and three-story apartments arranged around open courts, were built by a group of architects supervised by George D. Mason.

The passage of the Wagner-Steagall Act of 1937 paved the way for housing on a permanent basis by the establishment of the National Housing Authority. In Detroit several projects were planned in outlying areas in the hope that these would provide a refuge for slum families before a frontal attack on the slums was made. The Parkside Homes addition was built in 1940 by the Parkside *(395)* Architectural Associates.[30] In the same year the Charles Terrace was done by the Michigan Housing Associates on the east side,[31] and in 1942 the Herman Gardens were completed by George D. Mason and Company on the far west side. These projects have gone a long way from the brickyard monotony of the earlier ones, and have taken on some of the design characteristics of northern European prototypes with their box-like masses and contrasting brick and stucco *(400)* surfaces. The John W. Smith Homes of 1942 on the far northwest side even suggest the Bauhaus in the crisp mechanical precision of their lines. Here architects Lyndon and Smith experimented with the use of plywood for exterior walls; unfortunately there were maintenance problems, and they were later covered with siding and asbestos shingles.

The principal objective of the Detroit Housing Commission in the years before World War II was to provide low-rent housing. Going beyond this immediate objective, however, it was able to introduce new standards of community planning. Schools, community centers, shopping facilities, and playgrounds were integrated with residential units in superblocks.

During the war the commission was preoccupied with temporary housing, being unable to secure material for permanent projects. The greatest need for housing was in the areas around the large defense plants which had sprung up outside the city limits. To accommodate the droves of workers from all over the country who were attracted by these plants, the Federal Public Housing Authority undertook a series of defense housing projects in outlying areas. Joining the ranks of prominent architects dedicating their talents to the war effort, Saarinen, Swanson and Saarinen designed the Kramer Homes (1942) in Center Line, Macomb County, to house the workers at the nearby war plants north of Detroit. Two-story row houses and one-story semi-detached houses surrounded a central playground. The houses were of wood construction and were sheathed with redwood stained different colors. A well-designed school and community house *(403)* was built at one end of the playground.[32]

In 1943 Norwayne was designed by Lyndon and Smith to the west of Detroit near Wayne. Two-story frame duplexes and one-story single dwellings surrounded cul-de-sacs. A shopping center and two schools were part of the de- *(404)* velopment. Simultaneously with Norwayne, two smaller projects were built for Negroes, the Carver Homes in Inkster and the Sojourner Truth Homes in Detroit.

Near the mammoth Willow Run bomber plant in the vicinity of Ypsilanti, an entire town with a population of 12,000 sprang up in 1942–43. Called Willow Run Village, it was designed by Saarinen, Swanson and Saarinen. Here temporary prefabricated houses were put up at the rate of twenty-five units a day. Three schools, a shopping center, and Willow Lodge, a complex of dormitories operated as a hotel for 3,000 single persons, were also built.[33]

After the war the Detroit Housing Commission resumed the task of building permanent housing with two projects on the sites of former slums: the Frederick Douglass Apartments, adjacent to the Brewster Homes, were built by Harley, Ellington and Day in 1951–55; and the Edward J. Jeffries Homes on the near west side were built by Smith, Hinchman and Grylls in 1952–55. High-rise apartments similar to those built in New York were introduced for the first time in Detroit public housing. However, the land values being lower than in the larger metropolis, it was possible to include two-story row houses in the projects, thus reducing the overall population density.

Residential Urban Redevelopment

Sporadic public housing in Detroit was only a prelude to a massive attack upon the slums. For many years the area directly east of the downtown district had been steadily declining. Its history began rather humbly back in the 1850s when a forest of small frame houses was thrown up to receive a wave of German immigrants. As these citizens dissolved into the larger community, the area was taken over by Negroes who came from the South to work in the factories.[34]

After World War II it became apparent that the only hope for the area was redevelopment. In 1946 plans were formulated for the clearance of 129 acres bounded by Gratiot, Dequindre, Hastings and Lafayette, and funds were appro-

priated by the city for land acquisition. The passage of the National Housing
Act of 1949 gave assurance of federal assistance. By the end of 1954 the land was
cleared. From the beginning the Housing Commission had intended the project
to be open to private developers, but it was no easy task to reverse the trend to
the suburbs, and at first the builders shied away from such an unconventional
venture.

Finally a group of citizens representing business, industry, and labor stepped
into the vacuum left by public apathy. Organized as the Citizens Redevelopment
Corporation, it attempted to promote the development of the Gratiot area. Con-
cluding that it was necessary to create a unique project in order to lure suburbanites back to the city, it proceeded to engage Oscar Stonorov, Victor Gruen
and Associates, and Leinweber, Yamasaki and Hellmuth to produce a plan. They
developed a scheme of high-rise apartments and low-rise housing with open
spaces intervening.[35]

In 1956 an offer to develop the area from two Chicago builders, Herbert
Greenwald and Samuel Katzin, radically changed the course of events. Having
engaged famed architect Ludwig Mies van der Rohe to build several apartments
for them in Chicago, they planned to continue with his services in Detroit and
called upon Ludwig Hilberseimer, his long-time companion and associate at the
Illinois Institute of Technology, to assist him in planning. The new team accepted the concept of mixed high- and low-rise housing. However, three superblocks were combined into one large superblock, and a central municipal park
(406) replaced an interior road. The twenty-two story Pavilion Apartments were completed in 1959, exemplifying the serene and classic discipline of Mies van der
Rohe.[36] Framed in concrete, they were faced with aluminum and gray glass.[37]
Around cul-de-sacs were grouped 186 low-rise apartments. These included two-
(405) story town houses and one-story court houses. Glass window walls and yellow
brick end walls were framed by the black outlines of exposed structural steel.
Brick-walled courts adjoining the one-story units provided private outdoor living
areas, and informal planting softened the architectural lines.

Mies van der Rohe's Lafayette Towers, completed in 1963, are similar in
design to the Pavilion Apartments with minor variations. They are twin twenty-
one story slabs separated by a low parking garage with a swimming pool on the
roof. Adjoining them is a shopping center designed by the local firm of King
and Lewis at the same time.

Originally the entire Gratiot project was to have been designed by Mies van
der Rohe, but the tragic death of Herbert Greenwald in a plane crash in New
York prevented the complete realization of his design. Only three of six apartment houses and half the town houses were built. The remainder of the project
was then developed piecemeal by other architects and builders. Although uniformity and in many cases quality were sacrificed, something was gained in
variety. On Antietam at the north end of the complex architect John Hans
Graham and Associates built the Four Freedoms House (1965), a twenty-one
story apartment building for the elderly sponsored by a group of labor unions.
Its brick walls and exposed concrete frame contrast pleasingly with the glass and
aluminum surfaces of the neighboring Miesian apartments.

Other developments took on the characteristics of elegant motels. Central
Park Plaza (1963) by Giffels and Rossetti consists of balconied walk-ups facing a
swimming pool in a landscaped court. A series of low peaked roofs create an
(402) undulating roof line. Regency Square (1966), a somewhat similar scheme by
Green and Savin, substitutes flat roofs for pitched ones, and offers the choice
between a walk-up or a six-story elevator apartment.[38]

If the Gratiot project had been allowed to remain an island of luxury in a sea of slums, its failure would have been assured. From the beginning, however, plans were made to acquire the adjoining areas for slum clearance so that eventually a vast model residential neighborhood could be created in the heart of the city. The Lafayette extension, an area between the Gratiot project and Jefferson avenue, was next to be redeveloped. Together the two projects came to be known as Lafayette Park.

The planning concepts already established were retained in the development of the Lafayette extension. Here architects Birkerts and Straub have planned an ambitious apartment project which, when completed, will include two high-rise apartments and seventy town houses. The first unit, a thirty-story apartment house known as 1300 Lafayette East, was built in 1964. Gunnar Birkerts, the *(407)* designing member of the firm, brought to his work a talent in keeping with the best traditions of Detroit architecture. Born in Riga, Latvia, he graduated from the *Technische Hochschule* in Stuttgart in 1949 and came to this country soon thereafter. He was among the gifted young architects who came to Detroit in the post-war period to benefit by the experience of working in the offices of Eero Saarinen or Minoru Yamasaki. He worked in both, becoming chief designer in the latter before founding his own firm with Straub in 1959.

"Concrete is not elegant in itself," Birkerts said, "but shape can give it elegance."[39] The elegance of 1300 Lafayette East lies in its tapering thinness. Wall surfaces were composed of precast window bays and tapering reinforced concrete columns spaced to correspond with differing room widths. The two halves of the building were offset, emphasizing even more the effect of thinness. Town houses in the development are the work of Hausner and Macsai of Chicago who have combined dark brown brick and wood siding in a handsome overall design.

By 1964, 126 acres immediately east of Lafayette Park were cleared and offered for sale. This prepared the way for the first stage of Elmwood Park, a 500-acre redevelopment project planned by Crane and Gorwic Associates. When *(409)* completed the project will accommodate 15,000 people. The success of the town houses in Lafayette Park led to the decision to build mainly low-rise units in the new project. However, three high-rise apartments will be located in a central twenty-two acre park, around which will be grouped several medium-rise apartments. Elmwood Park drive, a winding boulevard, will be the only through route in the project. Town houses will be reached by service drives at the rear, and landscaped walkways will lead from the fronts of the town houses toward the park.

Many builders submitted plans for developments in Elmwood Park No. 1, the area west of Chene street. Four of these were accepted by the Housing Commission because of excellence in design, and the first units of each development were opened in 1966. Each scheme consists of town houses clustered around service courts, and private walled gardens extend the living areas outdoors. Park North *(408)* by Eberle M. Smith Associates is particularly appealing because of the individualistic treatment of each unit, the varying roof levels, and the contrast of brick and redwood siding. Park West by Sanford Rossen and Park South by Green and Savin are well designed. However, Ronald E. Mayotte and Associates, the architects of Park East, succumbed to a suburban cliché in their use of steep mansard roofs.

The Medical Center

After World War II the area north of the downtown district in Detroit was a no man's land of dilapidated industrial, commercial, and residential buildings. In the midst of this milieu stood four of Detroit's most venerated medical institutions: Children's, Hutzel (formerly Woman's), Grace, and Harper Hospitals. Without some positive action, it was only a matter of time before these hospitals would be engulfed by the blight that surrounded them.

A promise of future growth came when the School of Medicine of Wayne State University expressed a desire to affiliate with these institutions in order to form a great center for medical education. In 1955 the Medical Center hospitals and the School of Medicine formed the Detroit Medical Center Citizens Committee. Its purpose was to create a great complex that would utilize the existing hospitals as a core around which to develop other facilities for medical care, teaching and research. This would involve problems of urban renewal, governmental financing, and the coordination of diverse institutions. But beyond this, imaginative planning was required to create a harmonious and efficient medical center that would meet the future needs of the community. To accomplish this herculean task, the committee engaged the services of Gerald Crane, architect and city planner.

English by birth, Crane studied architecture and city planning at the Southwest Essex School of Art and the University College in London. Completing his education with studies in regional planning at Cornell University in 1955, he was about to return to England when Charles Blessing, director of the Detroit City Plan Commission, convinced him that his destiny lay in Detroit. "Mr. Blessing's enthusiasm pulled me in," Crane explained later. "He has a remarkable view of Detroit's potential."[40]

The master plan of the new Medical Center was completed in 1956 and published in 1958. In 1961 Crane joined with Norbert Gorwic to form the firm of Crane and Gorwic Associates. A native of Poland, Gorwic studied architecture and city planning at the Warsaw Technical University and at Liverpool University in England, coming to Detroit in 1956. A revised master plan of the *(411)* Medical Center was published by Crane and Gorwic Associates in 1966.

(412) The plan embodies several basic objectives: blocks are assembled into superblocks for the best use of available land, vehicular and pedestrian traffic is separated, the street system is reorganized for greater efficiency, and provision is made for the expansion of the existing institutions. The center will be surrounded by four major traffic routes: the Walter P. Chrysler freeway, Woodward, Mack, and Warren. A medical core of 100 acres will be devoted entirely to medical care, teaching, and research. This will contain the existing hospitals and the Wayne State University School of Medicine. A landscaped walkway, extending the full length of the core, will replace Brush street. Vehicular access to the core will be accomplished by an internal ring road. Around the core will be a wide belt of land devoted entirely to residential, commercial, and related uses. Parking will be accommodated in above ground and underground structures and on surface lots.

Under the urban renewal program the federal government and the city share in the cost of making land available for redevelopment. The Medical Center project has been divided into four phases. Already the land in phases I and II has been cleared. The northwest corner of the center, to be developed in phase IV, does not qualify for federal assistance.[41]

Several new buildings have been completed on the cleared land. The most interesting architecturally are the Professional Office Tower and the Concourse Building by Crane and Gorwic, and the Wayne State University Medical Research Building by Smith, Hinchman and Grylls. The Professional Office Tower *(413)* is part of the proposed Professional Plaza. Completed in 1966, it is a square fifteen-story building. Elevators, stairwells, and washrooms were grouped at the center, thus eliminating long corridors and providing outside exposure for all offices. Floor space is clear of columns, which were placed inside the utility core or projected out from the tinted thermal glass of the curtain walls. Erected at the same time as the tower, the two-story Concourse Building, with its heavy concrete sunbreakers, provides an interesting contrast. Two more professional office towers and several more low-rise office and commercial buildings are planned for the Professional Plaza which will occupy fifteen acres on the southwest corner of the Medical Center.

The four-story Wayne State University Medical Research Building was completed in 1964. Research areas were grouped around a central longitudinal utility core which contains all the mechanical and electrical services. A grille of buff-colored precast concrete serves as a curtain wall and provides daylight for the peripheral corridors which give access to the laboratories. The building was cantilevered out over a fieldstone base which ties it to the site. *(414)*

The Wayne State University School of Medicine will occupy a prominent position in the medical core of the Medical Center. The first unit of this complex to be completed is the research building. Soon to be constructed, however, are the Shiffman Medical Library, the Basic Medical Science Building, and an outpatient clinic. The Webber Medical Center, which will be located between Harper and Grace Hospitals, is planned as a teaching hospital and will be closely associated with the School of Medicine.

In 1965 the Children's Hospital of Michigan acquired a site south of the School of Medicine, where it will erect the first entirely new hospital in the center. Designers of the building are Albert Kahn Associated Architects and Engineers. The Veterans Administration is currently engaged in a study to determine the feasibility of placing a new V.A. hospital in the medical core. Also under consideration is a new receiving hospital to be located on Woodward avenue north of Canfield.[41] *(410)*

The Cultural Center

The nucleus of a cultural center was established in Detroit early in the twentieth century. With considerable foresight, civic leaders purchased ideal sites for the future Detroit Public Library and Detroit Institute of Arts on opposite sides of Woodward avenue about two miles north of the downtown business district. Edward H. Bennett of Chicago and Frank Miles Day of Philadelphia were engaged by the City Plan and Improvement Commission to study the sites and prepare plans for developing them. These studies were published in 1913 in a brochure entitled *A Center of Arts and Letters*. It is interesting to note that even in these early plans there was an indication for related buildings to be clustered around the library and the art museum. Two of these were specifically referred to as a "school of design" and a "hall for music."

The completion of the Public Library (1921) and the Institute of Arts (1927) created for Detroit the distinguished so-called Art Center which satisfied the needs of the day. The idea of concentrating more buildings dedicated to the arts in the same area received a temporary setback, however, when the Orchestra Hall by C. Howard Crane was built further downtown on Woodward avenue in 1919. The Cultural Center area remained unchanged until 1941 when the Horace H. Rackham Educational Memorial by Harley, Ellington and Day was built on Farnsworth street directly south of the art institute. This monumental 'stripped classical' building houses the Engineering Society of Detroit and the Extension Division of the University of Michigan. *(247)* *(243)*

With the establishment of a master plan for Detroit in 1941, a new era in city planning was inaugurated. Studies were made of special areas with a view toward their future growth. In 1945 Professor Buford L. Pickens of Wayne University was engaged by the City Plan Commission to prepare plans for the future expansion of the Cultural Center. In the area east of the Institute of Arts he envisioned a museum of industry, a historical museum, a natural science museum, a social science museum, and a planetarium and astronomical institute. Included in the plan were suggestions for an adjoining medical science center to the east and an expanded Wayne University campus to the west.[42]

In 1948 the City Plan Commission published a brochure entitled *Cultural Center Plan.* In the meantime Buford L. Pickens had left town and the studies for the Cultural Center were continued by architect Suren Pilafian. In 1942 he had won the competition for the Wayne University campus plan. His designs for the campus were incorporated in the new brochure along with his version of the Cultural Center as a whole. Since the publication of this brochure many of the buildings or additions to buildings proposed on its pages have become a reality. In 1951 the Detroit Historical Museum by William E. Kapp was completed on the northwest corner of Woodward and Kirby, and in the same year the International Institute by O'Dell, Hewlett and Luckenbach opened its doors on the northwest corner of Kirby and John R. Although not included in the Cultural Center plan of 1948, the Society of Arts and Crafts located its Art School by Minoru Yamasaki on Kirby just east of John R. street in 1958.

(299)
(415)

The expansion of the collections and services of the Detroit Public Library necessitated the addition of two new wings (1963). Architects Francis J. Keally and Cass Gilbert Jr. of New York continued the lines of the old building in a simplified version of the original Italian Renaissance style. The same Vermont marble was used throughout with the addition of serpentine Italian marble trim.

In 1966 the new South Wing of the Detroit Institute of Arts was completed. Harley, Ellington, Cowin and Stirton were the architects, and Gunnar Birkerts was retained to work on the design. It would have been prohibitively costly to attempt to duplicate the white marble moldings and carvings of the old Italian Renaissance building, so the architects wisely decided to provide contrast by giving the new wing a decidedly contemporary treatment. The unbroken dark gray granite walls do not compete with the old building, but serve rather as a background to emphasize its fine details. With its lofty proportions, the wing continued the scale already established and at the same time provided an elegant contemporary setting for works of art. Nowhere is the contrast between old and new more dramatically emphasized than in the three-story Sculpture Court where jutting modern balconies provide a foil for the exquisitely detailed marble walls of the old building. While the South Wing is devoted largely to gallery space, the North Wing by the same architects (begun in 1966) will contain administrative offices, the art research library, a cafeteria, and other service facilities.

(416)

(417)

With additions to the Historical Museum, the Public Library, and the Institute of Arts completed or nearing completion, the City Plan Commission was faced with the problem of deciding what the next step should be in the development of the Cultural Center. The rapid growth of the Wayne State University campus to the west and the emergence of the Medical Center to the south emphasized the need for expanded cultural facilities. Looking forward to the day when the Cultural Center would serve as an inspiration to the entire metropolitan region, the City Plan Commission came forward in 1965 with a new plan for its development which is more comprehensive in scope than any previous plan.

(415)

In order to create an atmosphere of repose and to facilitate pedestrian circulation, the Cultural Center would be divided into three islands: Wayne State University, the Detroit Public Library, and the Cultural Center Park. Access to the islands would be provided from Woodward and Cass avenues and from a peripheral route consisting of Warren, Palmer, St. Antoine, and Third boulevards. In the landscaped setting of the Cultural Center Park, institutions devoted to the arts and sciences would be grouped around a reflecting pool, and would include a hall of man, a planetarium, a museum of science and technology, a center for the musical arts, a center for the theater arts, and the existing Institute of Arts.[43] In addition to providing Detroit with much-needed cultural institutions, the Cultural Center would then be an oasis of beauty in an area that has long been deficient in parks, and it would make the city a more desirable place in which to live.

Wayne State University

The meteoric rise of Wayne State University to its position as one of the largest universities in the country has been a truly miraculous phenomenon. No one could have prophesied that a small teacher-training class organized in 1881 would have developed into such a giant, but it was this class that later grew into the Detroit Teachers College, which was eventually to become the College of Education. It was not until 1933, however, that five scattered colleges—Education, Medicine, Law, Pharmacy, and Liberal Arts—were thrown together to form Wayne University. For many years the nascent university operated under the Detroit Board of Education, but in 1956 it came under state control and its name was lengthened to designate its new allegiance. The founding in 1868 of the medical school, the oldest of the colleges, is now accepted as the origin of the university.[43a]

The Liberal Arts College began as an outgrowth of the Detroit Junior College, an extension of Central High School. It was no happenstance, therefore, that the old high school on the southwest corner of Warren and Cass avenues became the first building on the Wayne campus, now known as Old Main. Designed by Malcomson and Higginbotham, the weathered yellow-brick building in the Romanesque Revival style was built in 1896. As the enrollment of the university increased, its plant expanded north along Cass avenue toward the Detroit Public Library.[44] Classes were held in old residences and garages. Recognizing this as a makeshift, the Board of Education held a competition for a campus plan in 1942.

There were forty-six entrants in the competition, but many had to withdraw because of the pressure of war work. Eleven completed plans were finally considered by a jury which included such notables as Joseph Hudnut, dean of the Harvard School of Design, and Walter R. MacCornack, dean of the School of Architecture at the Massachusetts Institute of Technology. Suren Pilafian, the winner, was a talented young architect of Armenian origin who had been educated at Pratt Institute, Columbia University, and New York University, and had been working as a designer in various architectural offices in New York.[45] The chief merit of his plan was the judicious arrangement of the buildings around open spaces. He revised the plan in 1948, enlarging the campus area from three blocks *(418)* or fifteen acres to eighty-five acres. Revisions were made again in 1950 and 1954 to bring the plan up to date.[46]

Fortunately there were no old college buildings of various periods inherited from the past, so an entire new campus could be built in the modern style. The first buildings, the work of Pilafian, established a precedent of good design early

377

in the program of campus development. The generous expanse of window areas and the uniform use of fawn-colored brick assured a certain stylistic consistency. The State Hall of 1948 was followed by the College of Engineering in 1952. Two of the most successful buildings by Pilafian are the General Library (1954)

(419) and the adjoining Kresge Science Library (1953) with sweeping horizontal lines and cantilevered upper stories. Pilafian was also the architect of an attractive group of buildings in the Community Arts Center, which included the Art and Music Buildings (1956), the Alumni House (1959) and the Auditorium (1959). The Science Hall of 1949, although designed by Ralph Calder, is similar in style to the buildings by Pilafian.

Planning at Wayne took a new turn in 1954 when Minoru Yamasaki completed a density study of the campus. The most radical innovation was the replacement of Second avenue by a pedestrian mall. Since the traditional rustic campus with sweeping lawns and stately oaks was out of the question, he planned instead a compact urban campus consisting of a series of courts linking low buildings no more than four stories in height. "In the superblock there will be no autos, no city traffic and confusion," said Yamasaki. "A walk from one building to another will be a series of delightful surprises. Each court will be different—one paved, one grassy; one with a fountain and statues, another with trees."[47]

Yamasaki's imaginative grasp of campus problems was soon to bear fruit. Plans were being formulated for a conference building to be erected as a gift of the McGregor Fund. It was to be more than simply a building for meetings and

(267) conferences: it was to be a memorial to Tracy W. and Katherine McGregor, the Detroit philanthropists who had established the fund in 1925. Yamasaki's buildings were already known for their poetic charm, and a happy meeting of liberal

(422) minds led to his selection as architect for the McGregor Memorial Conference Center. His American Concrete Institute headquarters had given him experience working with a precast concrete folded plate roof, and he saw in the McGregor Memorial an opportunity to carry his work to a logical conclusion by further exploiting the structural and aesthetic possibilities of this interesting form.

Completed in 1958, the McGregor Memorial is a two-story structure overlooking a sunken garden containing a reflecting pool.[48] End walls are of travertine marble. On the inside there are rows of conference rooms divided by a two-story lounge and reception area at the center. The triangular ends of the V-shaped ceiling beams are exposed inside and out, and form the basis of a decorative pattern that is repeated with variations throughout the building. At the top of the lounge is a skylight composed of glass pyramids, and at each end of the lounge is a glass cage penetrated by cast-aluminum doors. Everywhere the richness of the materials used is apparent—in the white marble columns and floors, in the teakwood doors, in the black leather Barcelona chairs, and in a turkey-red carpet.[49]

Although the McGregor Memorial is ostensibly modern in its impact, it owes much to the past. "Modern architects have been too self-conscious," observed Yamasaki. "We threw away everything of the past. Now we are reaching back and interpreting experience gained from old buildings in our own terms, solving the needs of our own generation."[50] Clearly much of the inspiration for the McGregor Memorial came from the impressions absorbed by Yamasaki on his world travels: the use of a consistent decorative theme harks back to the Gothic cathedral; the monumental proportions and exquisite detail recall the Taj Mahal; and the pool, with its islands of chipped marble and its sculpturesque rocks, brings to mind the serene enclosure of a Japanese temple courtyard.

After the splendor of the McGregor Memorial, Yamasaki's College of Educa- *(420)*
tion (1960) comes as somewhat of an anticlimax. They share frontages on the
sunken garden of the Community Arts Center and provide an interesting study
in contrasts. The concept of the College of Education derived from the period
when Yamasaki was working on the density study of the campus. He believed
that square structures with major rooms on the interior met the requirements of
the high density of building necessary to accommodate the rapid growth of the
university. Windowless interior classrooms could be air-conditioned, were especially suitable for audio-visual methods of instruction, and the distractions of
windows facing restricted exterior areas thronged with students would be
avoided.

Besides affording Yamasaki an opportunity to demonstrate his ideas in class-
room planning, the College of Education also provided another occasion to experiment in the use of precast concrete, which he regarded as a means of achieving
an economical and expressive method of construction. Beams, columns, and exterior walls were composed of this material. Taking advantage of modern technology, he was able to have huge (40 x 5 feet) wall units cast, combining columns
and spandrels in one piece. Three stories in height, these 'trees' were hoisted in
place by giant cranes. The plasticity of the material gave the architect a certain
freedom in design and permitted a richness of surface that was integral rather
than applied.[51]

It would, perhaps, be expecting too much of any architect to assume that all
his efforts could meet with equal success. In comparison to the McGregor
Memorial, the College of Education seems fussy and amorphous, and its repetitious
pointed arches remind one too readily of the 'Steamboat Gothic' of another era.
The ideas that went into the concept of this building still seem tentative. Time
was needed to mould them into a cohesive and effective statement, and this is
precisely what happened when Yamasaki did his Michigan Consolidated Gas *(390)*
Company building in 1963.

Returning to the Wayne campus the same year, Yamasaki again tried his
hand at academic architecture, this time with the Meyer and Anna Prentis Building which houses the School of Business Administration (1964). Here precast *(421)*
concrete wall panels were used, but in contrast to the College of Education,
however, there was a clear differentiation between the ground floor arcade and
the upper stories, the fenestration was arranged in neat horizontal tiers, and a
certain elegance of proportion was enhanced by the delicately tapering columns.
An archway on the ground level leads one through the Prentis Building to a
courtyard where the Helen L. DeRoy Auditorium (1964) seems to be moored in
the middle of a lagoon. Here Yamasaki tried to conceal an uninteresting building
by means of applied ornament.

In spite of their discrepancies, however, the buildings by Yamasaki as a whole
add considerable character and beauty to the campus. Nevertheless, it was not
his intention to design the entire campus, as he felt that other minds and other
talents would add richness and variety. University officials, recognizing the
wealth of architectural talent in the area, called upon leading architects to design
various buildings.

Albert Kahn Associated Architects and Engineers were responsible for the
handsome Life Sciences Research Center of .1960. Here tall narrow windows *(425)*
were divided by projecting columns of poured concrete which double as sun
baffles; wall panels of quartz aggregate provide textural richness; a recessed
arcade on the ground level enhances the visual appeal; and a graceful crown of
precast concrete, concealing mechanical equipment, adds interest to the silhou-

ette. The interplay of flat and projecting surfaces and the contrasts of light and shadow create a pleasing overall effect.[52]

In general the recent buildings at Wayne State are slab-like in structure, but variety is achieved by the individual design approaches of the different architects. The Richard Cohn Memorial Building (1959) by Harley, Ellington and Day favors thin curtain walls with strip windows; the façade of the Law School Building (1966) by O'Dell, Hewlett and Luckenbach is characterized by concrete window panels with projecting brick piers; and the Physics Research Building (1965) by Smith, Hinchman and Grylls achieves a pleasing effect by resorting to heavy brick walls and an interesting treatment of window openings.

(424)   By far the most unusual building yet to grace the Wayne campus is the Shapero Hall of Pharmacy (1965) by Paulsen, Gardner and Associates. Looking like a fortress with firing slits, this inverted stepped-pyramid of concrete seems to defy the laws of gravity. Yet once one has become reconciled to its seeming irrationality, positive attributes become more apparent. Certainly it offers a refreshing change of pace from its ground-hugging neighbors and deserves salvos for its sheer audacity. More important, it is completely functional. The laboratories, which need the most space and the most isolation, have been placed in the two upper stories, while the activities that involve the most traffic are centered in the two-story base, which includes a lobby and a 160-seat lecture hall. To those who are disturbed by the proportions of the design, consolation will come with the knowledge that in a second phase of construction a low building will encircle the main building, partially shielding its narrow base.

(423)   It is true that classrooms are the most essential requisite of a university campus, but attractive dining facilities help to create a pleasant atmosphere as a background for student life. The completion of the University Center Building in 1968 marked a new era in the development of the Wayne campus. The choice of Alden B. Dow of Midland, Michigan, as architect was fortunate; for, having studied under Frank Lloyd Wright after receiving a degree at Columbia University, he was an experienced hand at creating sprawling buildings with low horizontal lines and warm, inviting interiors. A student cafeteria and a snack bar are readily accessible on the lower floors behind a long arcade, and on the third floor a more formal dining room for students and faculty opens on an outdoor terrace. The building also houses student activities and the Charles Grosberg Religious Center.

Recently completed on the new athletic field is the Matthaei Physical Education Building (1967), also by Alden B. Dow Associates. Other buildings under construction or soon to be constructed are for biology (by Glen Paulsen and Associates), foreign languages and speech classrooms, and general lectures (both by Jickling and Lyman), and a natural sciences complex (Ralph Calder and Associates). The latter will include a chemistry building and a seven-story science library.

The rapid increase of building projects in the sixties grew out of a new concept of the university as a whole. While three separate campus plans were made in the forties and fifties, this planning was done in the framework of a commuter college as opposed to an urban university. It was necessary to consider growth potential and to plan in terms of land requirements and building needs. Additional facilities must be built for research, and provision must be made for housing, physical education, and parking. In recognition of the expansion problems of the urban university, the Federal Housing Act of 1959 broadened its urban renewal section (Sect. 112) to encourage municipalities to assist institutions of higher learning located within their boundaries. With this encouragement, the Detroit Housing and City Plan Commissions drew up the "University City General Neighborhood Renewal Plan." The total project will take in 304 acres bounded by the Ford and Lodge freeways, and Canfield, Twelfth, and Fourteenth. To be developed in five phases, this area will be devoted to physical education, student housing, private housing, commercial development, and schools. Not only will the project meet the campus expansion needs of Wayne State University, but it will also improve the quality of the surrounding environment and encourage private development.[53]

In order to work out the details of campus planning, in 1965 Wayne State University engaged Sasaki, Dawson, DeMay Associates, landscape architects of Watertown, Massachusetts, as planning consultants. Their master plan of the university includes a land use plan and a site plan. The many fine plans for the future growth of Wayne State envision the day when it will be a great urban university in the total sense of the phrase.

Other Universities and Colleges

The University of Detroit shares the distinction with Wayne State University of being one of the older established institutions of higher learning in Detroit. Founded in 1877, it is a Roman Catholic institution conducted by the Jesuit order. The main campus was located downtown on East Jefferson avenue until *(168)* 1927 when six buildings were completed on a new campus at the intersection of McNichols road and Livernois avenue. Designed by Malcomson and Higginbotham, the new structures, following the eclectic tendencies of the day, were styled in an adaptation of the Spanish Renaissance.[54]

Very little growth was discernible at the university for several decades. In the fifties, however, the increasing population and expanding economy precipitated an extensive building program. With the advent of the sixties, some very distinguished buildings began to appear on the campus. Noteworthy is the Fisher Administrative Center (1966) designed by Gunnar Birkerts and Associates. This *(427)* building, which is of concrete construction, was divided into three elements: the ground floor, which serves as a podium; four office floors; and the fifth floor penthouse, which contains executive offices and conference rooms. Projecting columns in gray slate, blending with the dark tinted glass of the window areas, support the floors. The roof was suspended from the center core by concrete encased cables.[55]

Entirely different in concept but equally distinguished is the Ford Life Sciences Building (1967) by Glen Paulsen and Associates, who created a monumen- *(426)* tal effect with plain brick walls and projecting stair towers. Since the building contains interior classrooms reached by peripheral corridors, only minimal window area was required.

While Wayne State University and the University of Detroit felt the influence of the expanding population, it was actually in the Oakland–Macomb county area north of Detroit that the greatest growth was taking place. Cut off from expansion south and east because of the Detroit River and Lake St. Clair, industry had surged north after World War II, and in its wake entire communities sprang up and became part of metropolitan Detroit. The need for a university in the region was apparent for a number of years. No one was more aware of this than Matilda Dodge Wilson, widow of the automotive pioneer John F. Dodge. In 1957 she and her husband Alfred G. Wilson offered their estate near Rochester as a campus for Michigan State University–Oakland. The gift in-

(307)   cluded their manorial Tudor mansion Meadow Brook Hall and funds for the first two new buildings of the university. In the decade that has elapsed since then, an entire new campus has materialized. While the buildings are generally unremarkable in themselves, they are well laid out on the gently rolling terrain and create a harmonious ensemble.

In the meantime, the University of Michigan at Ann Arbor was answering the need for higher education in the Detroit area. A shortage of college-trained manpower to direct and service expanding industry had become a matter of national concern. The university had already initiated the idea of extending its facilities to local communities, and then it turned to the problem of combining this approach with a program in which local industry would cooperate in the training of students. A stretch of grassy farmland on the Ford Fair Lane estate offered by the Ford Motor Company made an ideal site for such an experiment. By 1960 the Dearborn Center of the University of Michigan had become a reality, and a cluster of low buildings by Giffels and Rossetti were ready to receive their first students.

(430)   While the Dearborn Center accommodates only juniors and seniors, the adjoining Henry Ford Community College, opened about the same time, is a junior college. Operated by the Board of Education of Dearborn, it also occupies a site given by the Ford Motor Company. Buildings designed by Eberle M. Smith Associates have been grouped around a plaza; the largest one, containing classrooms and a library, was constructed of concrete and was faced with precast concrete panels.

(433)   Schoolcraft College in Livonia joined the ranks of community colleges in the Detroit area in 1965. Smaller and more informal than the Henry Ford Community College, it was also designed by Eberle M. Smith Associates. Low brick buildings surround a quadrangle. Metal roofs with flaring eaves supported on laminated wood beams give character to the ensemble, and fieldstone retaining walls between the grade levels add a note of rusticity.[56]

(429)   More formal in its architectural treatment, Macomb County Community College (1965) was completed in the same year in Warren. Rows of similar buildings were joined by an arcade of shallow precast concrete arches around a quadrangle. The walls of the buildings themselves were composed of similar but taller arches, each of which was filled with textured cinder-block panels surrounded by narrow window areas. The architects for the college were Harley, Ellington, Cowin and Stirton.

Schools and Libraries

The deterioration of the central core of Detroit after World War II created acute educational problems. The exodus to the suburbs had lowered tax revenues, and the increasing services to the underprivileged were a severe strain on the school system. In 1956 Dr. Samuel M. Brownell, superintendent of the Detroit Public Schools, asked George Romney, then head of American Motors Corporation, to form a citizens advisory committee to study the needs of the system. Following the recommendations of the committee, Brownell spearheaded a building program that produced fifty-three schools during the ten years of his administration.[57] For the first time in its history the Board of Education relinquished control of school architecture and talented architects were given a free hand in school design. The most pressing need was for elementary schools. Various architects found different solutions to the problem of placing buildings on small lots in congested areas.

Linn Smith Associates kept their Tendler Elementary School (1961) as far from congested East Vernor highway as possible, turned blank brick walls toward the thoroughfare, and faced window areas toward the side streets. Louis G. Redstone Architects put small interior courts in their Glazer Elementary School *(431)* (1966) on Ford street between Twelfth and Fourteenth. An attractive feature is a glazed brick mural by Narenda Patel in one of the courts.

In 1961 Meathe, Kessler and Associates built the Fleming Elementary School *(428)* on Waltham street in the Gratiot-Seven Mile road area. With more land than usual at their disposal, they grouped hexagonal classrooms around a hexagonal court. This imaginative scheme minimized noise and congestion.[58] On the other hand, economy of plan and materials was a primary consideration in the construction of the Woodward Elementary School (1963) on Wreford street near *(432)* Northwestern High School. Also designed by Meathe, Kessler and Associates, it is a square box with the gymnasium and auditorium located in the center. A recessed first floor helped to avoid a boxy look, the precast concrete panels of the second floor contrast with the dark brick of the first floor, and concrete 'eyebrows' and T-shaped columns add interest.[59]

One of the most unusual schools in the Detroit area is the fortress-like Amelia Earhart Junior High School on West Lafayette avenue near Clark Park *(434)* designed by Meathe, Kessler and Associates (1963). It consists of a central core building for major functions and two separate identical houses for classrooms and laboratories. The massive poured concrete walls of the former, eventually to be covered with ivy, provide an interesting contrast to the precast concrete panels of the latter, and the buildings are connected by glass-enclosed passages.[60]

Different in concept is the Knudsen Junior High School (1962) located on Leland street between Chene and Grandy. Of concrete construction, it was faced with precast concrete panels surfaced with dark pebbles. An attractive formica mural by Edith Pirtle faces the main entrance, and the library overlooks an interior court. Eberle M. Smith Associates were the architects. The Philip Murray Senior High School by the same architects is somewhat similar but on a *(436)* larger scale. Completed in 1965, it is on Warren avenue between Twelfth and Fourteenth streets, on the western edge of the future University City. Dark brown bricks alternate with precast concrete panels on the exterior wall surfaces. In the two-story academic section on Warren the academic houses were grouped around the library and the lecture forum facility. At the rear is a one-story laboratory and manipulative skills section which also contains the dining room and gymnasium. The appearance of heavy massiveness was avoided and congestion reduced through the use of open courts and the appropriate location of special use areas.[61]

Although similar in construction to the Murray High School, the Eastern Senior High School (1966) by Linn Smith Associates is more monumental in *(437)* appearance because of the extensive use of dark brown brick wall surfaces and round brick arches. Contrast was provided by the exposed concrete fascia and spandrels. Laboratory and manipulative facilities were grouped around an audio-visual lecture hall on the first floor, while academic classrooms were grouped in houses around an instructional materials center and an audio-visual lecture hall on the second floor. Each house was articulated as a separate building and contains its own dining hall.[62] Eastern Senior High School is on East Lafayette avenue and is part of the Elmwood No. 2 urban renewal project.

Without the limitations of space found in the city, suburban high schools tend to be campus-like in character. The East Hills Junior High School (1962) *(438)* in Bloomfield Hills is a case in point. Here architects Tarapata-MacMahon Associates loosely grouped four main elements around a landscaped court with connecting enclosed passageways. The gymnasium and the cafetorium were located near the parking area for public access, and the academic wing and the arts unit, requiring more quiet, were situated in the rear. All the buildings are well adapted to the rolling terrain.[58]

(435) Requiring less space than high schools, suburban elementary schools are often ingeniously planned. The Meadowlake Elementary School (1963) in Bloomfield Township by Linn Smith Associates is simple in plan but appealing because of the visual awareness of the interlocking character of all its components. A continuous loop corridor was built around a central block containing the library, music rooms, kitchen and multi-purpose space, and the classrooms were placed outside the loop. Small interior courts and generous window areas in the corridors create an airy, sunny effect.[63] The Westchester Elementary School (1962) (443) in Birmingham is notable for its crisp clear-cut design and commendable grouping of classrooms around open courts. The architects were Eberle M. Smith Associates.[58]

Many branch public libraries were built in Detroit after World War II, but limitations of space and funds precluded much architectural experimentation. To find interesting library buildings, one must turn to the suburbs. Grosse Pointe can claim the distinction of persuading Marcel Breuer, an architect of international reputation, to build the Grosse Pointe Public Library in 1953.[64] A preliminary survey had recommended that it be placed in the shopping district for accessibility. Breuer carried this idea further by making an inviting reading room visible to the passerby through a large glass area. It was his conviction that art should be combined with architecture: he put a Mobile by Alexander Calder at one end of the two-story reading room, and at the other end he placed a colorful tapestry designed by Wassily Kandinsky against teakwood paneling.[65] Herbert Matter was commissioned to create a photomural of the history of printing for the adult reading room.

(439) With their Carl Sandburg Branch Library (1964) in Livonia, Tarapata-MacMahon Associates demonstrated the advantages of clerestory lighting. The side walls were glazed, but the front and rear walls were penetrated only by narrow openings between the book bays. In this way readers are spared the distractions of the street and the parking lot. An interesting feature of the design is the roof of inverted pyramids in the central section.[66]

(440) The West Bloomfield Township Library (1963) by Stickel, Jaroszewicz and Moody is a charming solution of the problem of a small library in a rural setting. The library facility is a flat roofed area with solid walls, while the room for civic and social gatherings was roofed with a triple barrel vault and faced with a glazed wall overlooking the surrounding meadows. Wood beams and steel columns were left exposed.[67]

Churches

There was both an economic and an aesthetic basis for the widespread acceptance of modern religious architecture in Detroit after World War II. The traditional styles, if they were to be at all convincing, were financially burdensome, and the point had been reached when the public began to tire of the repetitious and the imitative. No one could deny that modern architecture was capable of generating the desired spiritual atmosphere, and few denominations were willing to deny themselves the aesthetic satisfactions that come from the exciting forms and lighting effects of modern religious architecture. Pioneer architects in Europe and America had already pointed the way: using new engineering techniques, they had created a wealth of monuments from which to draw inspiration.

It is perhaps no accident that one of the more technically advanced churches *(441)* in the Detroit area is in Center Line near the General Motors Technical Center. The structure of St. Clement's Church (1961) by Diehl and Diehl consists of two thin intersecting parabolic shells of concrete rising directly from the ground. Parabolic vaults of poured concrete had been used in churches as early as the twenties in Europe, and later in Latin America. What makes St. Clement's unique is the method of construction: the concrete was pumped in place with a hose onto a form made of wood ribs covered with acoustical cement and wood fiber decking. When the concrete dried the form was left in place, and green sheet-aluminum roofing was applied on the exterior. The ends of the shells were then filled in with precast concrete window panels glazed with stained glass. These were undulated for acoustical reasons. Near the entrance to the church is a slender campanile of poured concrete.[68] The structure of the church is eminently practical. The unobstructed vaults are sixty-five feet high with a span of eighty feet, and the cruciform plan seats 1,600 people. However, the aesthetic potentiality of the parabola has not been fully realized, and the interior of the church, although light and airy, is somewhat amorphous.

Our Shepherd Lutheran Church (1966) in Birmingham, by Glen Paulsen and *(445)* Associates, is more traditional in feeling without specifically resorting to traditional forms. Eliel Saarinen had introduced modern Scandinavian religious architecture to America with his Tabernacle Church of Christ (1942) in Columbus, Indiana, and his son Eero continued the tradition with his chapel for Concordia Lutheran Senior College (1958) in Fort Wayne, Indiana. Paulsen had worked in the office of the younger Saarinen and the influence is clearly visible. As in the earlier Saarinen churches, Paulsen's work emphasized unadorned interior wall surfaces and hidden light sources to epitomize spiritual values. The shed roof and the rugged brick and wood textures help to create an atmosphere of austere Nordic grandeur.

We have seen in the work of Diehl and Diehl and of Glen Paulsen an emphasis upon roof construction. With the abandonment of the traditional belfry, it is the roof which has given the modern church its distinguishing characteristic. Two well-known American architects opened up new possibilities in the treatment of the gabled roof in church construction. When he built the First Unitarian Meeting House (1951) in Madison, Wisconsin, Frank Lloyd Wright pitched the ridge of the roof upward to a peak at one end; then he filled in the gable behind the pulpit with glass. In Sarasota, Florida, Victor Lundy swept the roof of his St. Paul's Lutheran Church (1960) up to a sharp peak supported on arches of laminated wood.

The influence of Wright is evident in the design of the Christus Victor *(446)* Lutheran Church (1964) in Dearborn Heights. Here architects Merritt, Cole and McCallum placed a stained glass window behind the altar at the end of the church and covered the roof with copper. A variation of this form may be found in the design by Swanson Associates of the St. John Fisher Chapel (1966) *(444)* near Rochester, Michigan.[69]

The Wrightian formula has found monumental expression in the Congregation Shaarey Zedek synagogue in Southfield (1962) by Albert Kahn Associated *(450)* Architects and Engineers, and Percival Goodman, associate architect. The sanctuary juts out like a giant Hebrew tabernacle or tent on a bluff overlooking Northwestern highway. Stained glass windows symbolizing the burning bush follow the slope of the roof. On the interior of the sanctuary is a forty-foot marble ark of the scrolls.

Alden B. Dow, a disciple of Frank Lloyd Wright, has developed many of Wright's concepts of religious architecture into a personal expression of his own. After building several churches in Midland, Michigan, he was commissioned to *(448)* design the First Presbyterian Church of Dearborn (1965). The church is hexagonal in plan and is traversed by a narrow copper-covered clerestory, supported on concrete columns, which terminates in a tall window behind the altar.

The Chapel of Our Lady of Orchard Lake (1963) by Walter J. Rozycki *(447)* follows the prototype established by Victor Lundy. The roof arches of laminated wood were designed as quadrant segments of a circle placed back-to-back in order to create pleasing upward curved lines, and the copper roof projecting forward serves as both an entrance porch and a canopy for an enormous copper statue of Our Lady of Orchard Lake by Clarence Van Duzer.[70] The walls of the chapel were made of fieldstone.

A Novitiate Chapel is part of the Detroit Province Sisters of Mercy complex *(451)* located on a 150-acre tract near Farmington. Completed in 1966, the complex was designed by Giffels and Rossetti. Somewhat similar to the Chapel of Our Lady of Orchard Lake, the Novitiate Chapel and the adjoining Novitiate are dramatically located on a bluff overlooking a small lake. A narrow stained glass window behind the altar rises to the soaring peak of the gable, dividing a rugged wall of fieldstone at the center.

The most recent religious edifice to have been built in the Detroit area is also *(449)* the most radical departure from familiar models. The Congregation B'Nai David synagogue (1966) in Southfield is a square building, on each side of which is a sweeping segmental arch springing from the corners. The roof line is made up of similar arches reversed. Seen through the lower arches is the cylindrical sanctuary whose walls are a continuous stained glass window ranging in color from cool greens and blues to warm yellows and oranges. The architect was Sidney Eisenshtat of Beverly Hills, California.

Residences

In many parts of the country the last stronghold of resistance to contemporary architecture is the private residence. It is difficult to know where to place the blame; whether the public has been victimized by the realtors or vice versa. In any case, when confronted with the problem of choosing his own personal surroundings, the average citizen almost invariably turns to the comfortable security of the past. In fact, even the thought of introducing the modern world into the living room, far from arousing the pleasure of anticipation, seems to bring grave doubts and fears.

No one in the Detroit area thought of hiring a good modern architect to design a house until the thirties. By then architect Alden B. Dow of Midland had gained such prestige that a few bold spirits were willing to take the plunge. His *(454)* Gordon Saunders house (1937) in Bloomfield Hills carried on the tradition of organic planning which Dow had inherited from Frank Lloyd Wright. The plunging roofs and varying floor levels, conforming to the irregular topography, seem to express the prodigality of nature. A special feature is a pond at the level of the window sills which transmits its quivering reflections into the interior of *(458)* the house. The next year Dow built a house for Millard Pryor in Grosse Pointe (1938). This cinder-block structure is unusual for Dow in that it leans toward the so-called 'International Style' in its box-like quality and uncompromisingly white exterior. A Wrightian flavor persists in the two-story living room where space extends upward to the balcony and outward into the one-story dining area. A wall of glass blocks admits light to the living room and at the same time assures privacy. A small corner window, however, affords a glimpse of the walled terrace and the long horizontal pergola that ties the house to the site.

By the forties Detroit was ready for the great master Frank Lloyd Wright himself. In 1942 Gregor Affleck commissioned him to design a house in Bloom- *(453)* field Hills. Noting Wright's proclivity for building some of his most interesting houses on property that nobody else wanted, Affleck chose a wooded lot traversed by a gully. The house that soon took form juts out boldly from the hillside and seems to hover as if suspended in the dense woodland. Patches of summer sunshine filtering through the foliage make patterns on the tawny cypress and pinkish brick walls.

Simultaneously with the Affleck house, Wright's Carl Wall house material- *(452)* ized on a hillside near Plymouth (1942). Looking like the bridge of a ship, the glass-enclosed hexagonal living room with its deep overhangs snuggles on top of a prow-like brick rampart overlooking the rolling countryside. Demonstrating that he was capable of designing a modest residence of simple construction, Wright completed the Melvyn Maxwell Smith house in Bloomfield Hills in *(455)* 1951.[71] Here he reverted to his L-shaped Usonian type of house. Resting on a concrete slab, it is of wood construction with a brick utility core.

Minoru Yamasaki's feeling for natural materials and for the interpenetration of space is in the tradition of Frank Lloyd Wright, but his delicacy of articulation in domestic work and his control of environment are closer to the Japanese ideal. In 1950 he built a house in Grosse Pointe for Daniel W. Goodenough in *(456)* collaboration with Alexander Girard. Located in a pine grove, it is T-shaped in plan and is on three levels. A small interior court opens up the center of the house, and the glass walls of the living-dining area command a splendid view of towering pines.

The residence that Yamasaki built for S. Brooks Barron (1955) in the Palmer *(457)* Woods area of Detroit is also T-shaped in plan. Part of the charm of the house stems from the intimate relation between the interior and a series of outdoor areas: on the east is the entrance court with its limpid pond filled with water plants, on the west is a Japanese rock garden, and to the north sweeps an expanse of lawn studded with shade trees. A generous skylight brings light into the center of the house. The entrance hall and dining area, both with travertine floors, open into the living area where a sunken carpeted section in front of the fireplace helps to create an atmosphere of elegance and charm.

The buildings of famed architect Edward Durrell Stone of New York have charmed many people. Detroiter Carney D. Matheson was so taken by his work that he asked Stone to design his house on a small lake in Bloomfield Hills *(460)* (1953). From the road the house appears unpretentious—long and low—decorated only by the brick grillework that is Stone's trademark. Since the house is on a hillside, the entrance is on the second floor, from which an open staircase descends into a two-story living room with a two-story glass wall overlooking the lake. Shoji screens conceal the bedrooms which open off the balcony. Adding to the exotic flavor is a fountain in a pool surrounded by luxuriant tropical vegetation.

The house that architect Glen Paulsen built for himself in Bloomfield Hills *(459)* (1954) is a demonstration that handsome modern architecture can be within the reach of the home-owner operating on a limited budget. The house is rectangular in plan and of wood construction. Its nine by eight foot module conformed to milled lumber lengths, and all columns were left exposed. Sliding glass doors and windows were standard.

(463) The Alan Schwartz summer residence (1961) follows the "much with little" philosophy of Mies van der Rohe. Designed by Birkerts and Straub, it is a square glass box set in the midst of an apple orchard near Plymouth. A raised deck surrounds the house and is accessible through sliding glass doors from most rooms. Broad overhangs with deep fascias shade the interior and the decks. At the center of the house is the utility core lighted by clerestory windows. A special decorative feature is the sunken pit fireplace above which a cylindrical flue is suspended.

Philip J. Meathe and William H. Kessler, who had both worked in the office of Minoru Yamasaki, organized the firm of Meathe, Kessler and Associates in 1955. The private house became one of their specialties. During the fifties and sixties they designed a series of residences that are notable for the ingeniousness of their construction and design.

(461) Their Arthur Beckwith house (1960) was built in a wooded area near Farmington. The interesting saw-tooth pattern of the roof was derived from the practical wooden A-frame truss construction, and the plan was based on a series (462) of fifteen-foot bays with exterior walls mainly of glass. The interior was carefully zoned and provides an interesting sequence of spaces. For the Dr. Hilbert (464) DeLawter house in Bloomfield Hills (1962), Meathe-Kessler concentrated the living area in a glazed central section flanked by wings with walls of plywood. The jagged pattern of the roof was framed by the outlines of the wood braces that hold the roof trusses in place. A sculpturesque fireplace and the circular walls of the room add further interest to the living area. The house and terrace command a splendid view of a dense woodland.

(465) Meathe, Kessler and Associates completed a house for W. Hawkins Ferry in Grosse Pointe on Lake St. Clair in 1964.[72] In order to take the maximum advantage of the view a two-story house was desirable. This required a more rigid framing system than the architects had found necessary for one-story residential work. A modular system of precast concrete columns 15½ feet on center was used. All columns were exposed on both the exterior and the interior, and concrete floors were supported on steel beams. On the east side glass walls face a series of terraces descending to the lake. The other three sides of the house were sheathed with cyprus wood and, except for two large glass areas, were broken only by narrow window openings. A seven-foot overhang shields the house from the sun. On the interior the living room and the library, both two stories high, create an effect of spaciousness; and a balcony, reached by a handsome spiral staircase, adds to the number of vantage points from which dramatic views may be enjoyed. The house affords an ideal setting for the owner's collection of contemporary art.[65]

(466) In 1959 William H. Kessler, the designing member of the firm, built a small residence for himself on a narrow lot in Grosse Pointe. Here the same careful detailing and interesting spatial relationships are to be found as in his larger houses. The division of the structure into bays, each with its own gable, was a variation of the scheme followed in the construction of the Beckwith house. In this case, however, there are no trusses, and solid cedarwood decking rests directly on the metal frames of the window walls. There is a delightful relationship between the interior of the house and the outdoor areas. The living room opens upon an inviting patio that is screened from the street by a textured brick

wall, and the dining room and the family room face a lawn surrounded by shrubbery at the rear of the house.

The private residence may be the last stronghold of resistance against modern architecture, but it is in this field that some of the most interesting experimentation is taking place—experimentation that is pointing the way to a pleasanter environment for the individual. When this last stronghold of resistance is overcome, the cycle will be complete: man will have accepted in its totality the image of the modern metropolis that is the hope of the future.

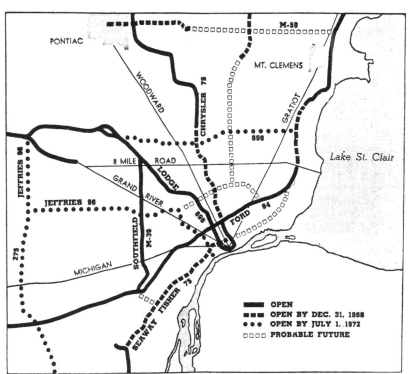

(371) Metropolitan Detroit Freeway System (DFP)

(372) Northland Center, *V. Gruen Assoc.*, 1954 (JLH)

(373-376) General Motors Technical Center, *Eero Saarinen et al.*, 1956 (GMC)(WA)

(377) Eastland Center,
V. Gruen Assoc., 1957 (JLH)

(378) Westland Center,
V. Gruen et al., 1965 (BK)

(379) Civic Center project, *Saarinen, Saarinen & Assoc.*, 1947 (CPC)

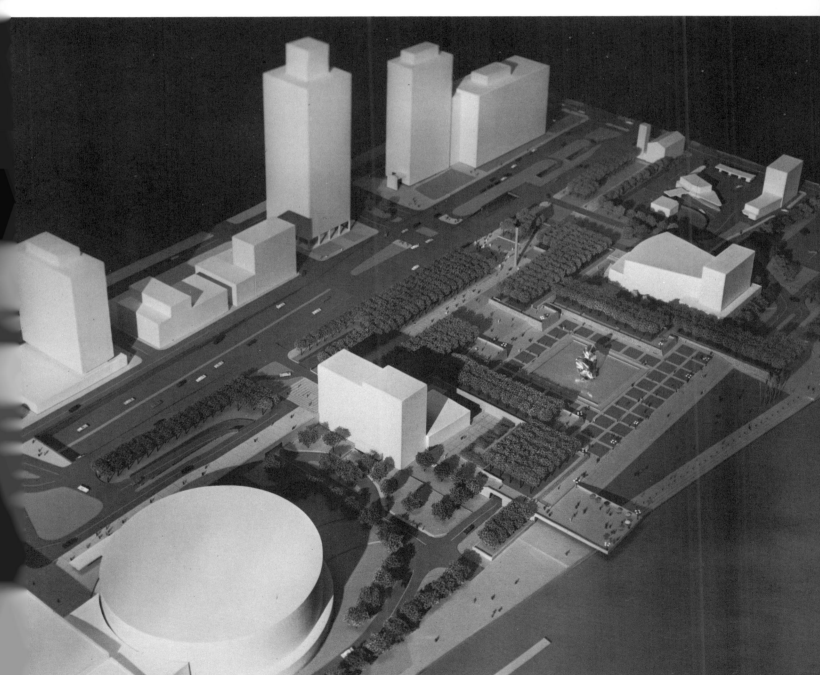

(380) Civic Center Plaza project, *Smith, Hinchman & Grylls*, 1967 (SHG)

(381) Civic Center project,
Eliel Saarinen, 1924 (SC)

(382) City-County Building,
Harley, Ellington & Day, 1955 (OP)

(383) Cobo Hall, *Giffels & Rossetti*, 1960 (DRI)
(384) Ford Auditorium, *O'Dell, Hewlett & Luckenbach et al.*, 1955 (BK)

(385) Ford Administrative Center,
Skidmore, Owings & Merrill, 1956 (FMC)

(386) Federal Reserve Bank Annex,
Smith, Hinchman & Grylls, 1951 (L-A)

(387) National Bank of Detroit, *A. Kahn Assoc.*, 1959 (BK)

(388) Reynolds Metals Building, *M. Yamasaki & Assoc.*, 1959 (BK)

(389) American Concrete Institute, *Yamasaki, Leinweber & Assoc.*, 1958 (BK)

(390) Michigan Consolidated Gas Co., *M. Yamasaki et al.*, 1963 (BK)

(391) Michigan Consolidated Gas Co., lobby (BK)

(392) Detroit Bank & Trust Co., *Harley, Ellington, Cowin & Stirton,*
1963 (C-C)

(393) First Federal Building,
Smith, Hinchman & Grylls, 1965 (BK)

(394) Federal-Mogul Staff Offices, *Giffels & Rossetti*, 1966 (GR)

(395) Charles Terrace, *O'Dell, Hewlett & Luckenbach*, 1940 (FPH)

(396) Metropolitan Airport Terminal, *Smith, Hinchman & Grylls*, 1966 (SHG)

(397) Mount Clemens Federal Savings Building, *Meathe, Kessler & Assoc.*, 1961 (BK)

8) Pontchartrain Hotel,
g & Lewis, 1965 (BK)

(399) Jeffersonian Apartments,
Giffels & Rossetti, 1965 (L-A)

(400) John W. Smith Homes,
Lyndon & Smith, 1942 (MB)

(401) North Park Towers, *Levine-Alpern et al.*, 1967 (LA/B-K)

(402) Lafayette Park Regency Square, *Green & Savin*, 1966 (B-K)

(403) Kramer Homes School, *Saarinen, Swanson & Saarinen*, 1942 (WHF)

(404) Norwayne Homes School, *Lyndon & Smith*, 1943 (ELA)

(405) Lafayette Park Court Houses, *L. Mies van der Rohe*, 1959 (WA)

(406) Lafayette Park Pavilion Apartments, *L. Mies van der Rohe*, 1959 (WA)

(407) 1300 Lafayette East, *Birkerts & Straub*, 1964 (BK)

(408) Elmwood Park North, *E. M. Smith Assoc.*, 1966 (BK)

(409) Elmwood Park project, *Crane & Gorwic*, 1964 (DB)

(410) Children's Hospital, *A. Kahn Assoc.*, c. 1970 (AKA)

(411) Medical Center project, *Crane & Gorwic*, 1966 (CG)

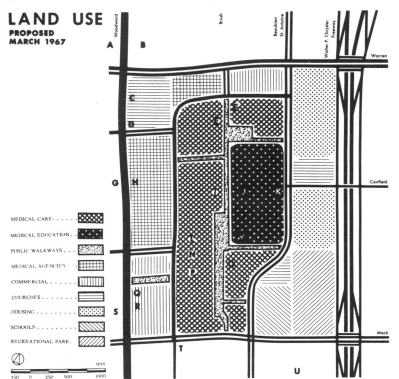

LAND USE
PROPOSED
MARCH 1967

MEDICAL CARE . . . . .
MEDICAL EDUCATION . . .
PUBLIC WALKWAYS . . .
MEDICAL AGENCIES . . .
COMMERCIAL . . . . . .
CHURCHES . . . .
HOUSING . . . .
SCHOOLS . . . .
RECREATIONAL PARK .

250   0   250   500   1000   feet

(412) Medical Center plan, *Crane & Gorwic*, 1967 (CG)

(413) Medical Center Professional Plaza, *Crane & Gorwic*, 1966 (C-C/CG)

(414) W.S.U. Medical Research Building, *Smith, Hinchman & Grylls*, 1964 (SHG)

(415) Cultural Center Park project, 1965 (CPC)

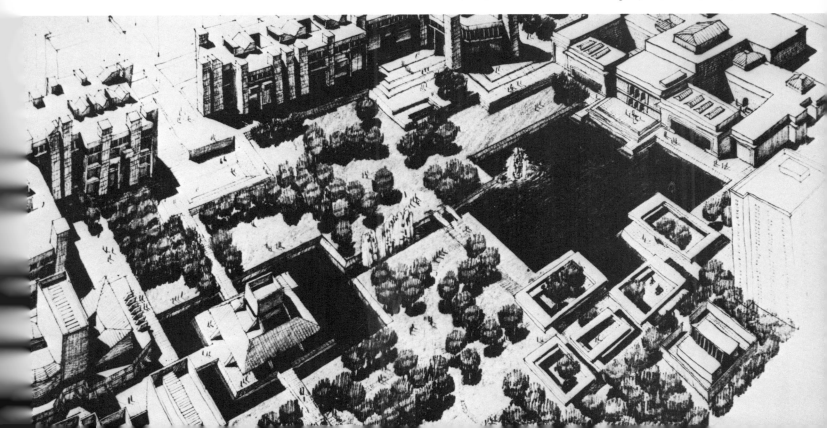

(416-417) Detroit Institute of Arts South Wing, *Harley, Ellington, Cowin & Stirton et al.*, 1966 (C-C)

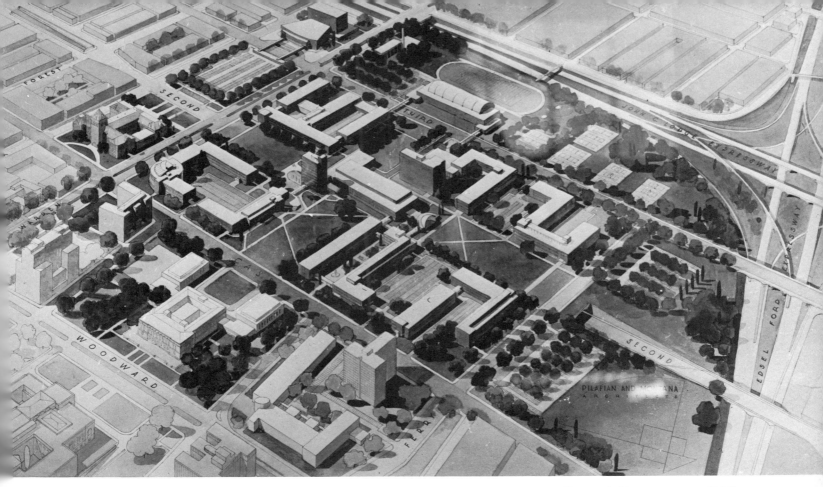

(418) Wayne University Campus project, *Pilafian & Montana*, 1948 (PM)

(419) Kresge Science Library, *Pilafian & Montana*, 1953 (H-B)

(420) W.S.U. College of Education, *Yamasaki, Leinweber & Assoc.*, 1960 (BK)

(421) Prentis Building, *M. Yamasaki & Assoc.*, 1964 (WSU)

(422) McGregor Memorial Conference Center, *M. Yamasaki & Assoc.*, 1958 (CHE/JKJ)

(423) W.S.U. University Center, *A. B. Dow Assoc.*, 1968 (ABD)

(424) Shapero Hall of Pharmacy, *Paulsen & Gardner*, 1965 (BK)
(425) W.S.U. Life Sciences Research Center, *A. Kahn Assoc.*, 1960 (BK)

(426) Ford Life Sciences Building, *G. Paulsen & Assoc.*, 1967 (L-A)
(427) Fisher Administrative Center, *G. Birkerts & Assoc.*, 1966 (BK)

(428) Fleming Elementary School, *Meathe, Kessler & Assoc.*, 1961 (BK)

(429) Macomb County Community College, *Harley, Ellington, Cowin & Stirton*, 1965 (C-C)

(430) Henry Ford Community College, *E. M. Smith Assoc.*, 1960 (L-A)

(431) Glazer Elementary School,
L. G. Redstone Assoc., 1966 (DB)

(432) Woodward Elementary School,
Meathe, Kessler & Assoc., 1963 (BK)

(433) Schoolcraft College, *E. M. Smith Assoc.*, 1965 (L-A)

(434) Earhart Junior High School, *Meathe, Kessler & Assoc.*, 1963 (BK)

(435) Meadowlake Elementary School, *L. Smith Assoc.*, 1963 (L-A)

(436) Murray Senior High School,
E. M. Smith Assoc., 1965 (BK)

(437) Eastern Senior High School,
L. Smith Assoc., 1966 (L-A)

(438) East Hills Junior High School,
Tarapata-MacMahon Assoc., 1962 (BK)

(439) Carl Sandburg Library,
Tarapata-MacMahon Assoc., 1964 (BK)

(440) West Bloomfield Library, *Stickel, Jaroszewicz & Moody*, 1963 (L-A)

(441) St. Clement's R.C. Church, *Diehl & Diehl*, 1961 (BK)

(442) Grosse Pointe Public Library, *M. Breuer*, 1953 (SP)

(443) Westchester Elementary School, *E. M. Smith Assoc.*, 1962 (L-A)

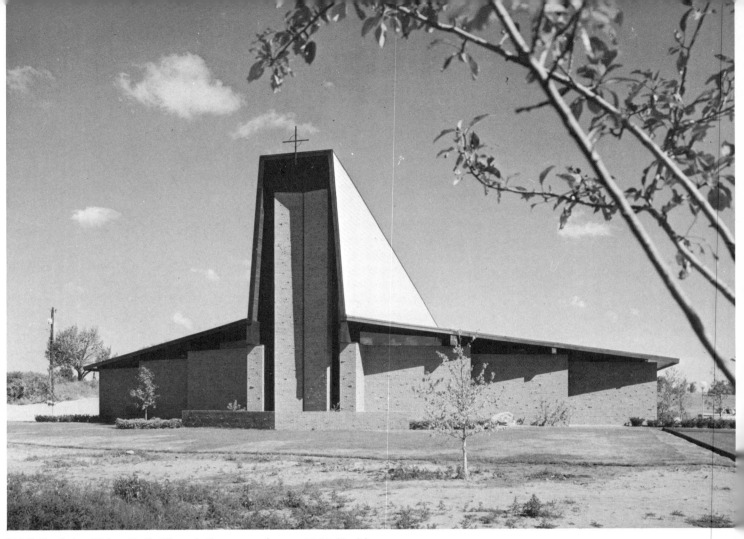

(444) St. John Fisher R.C. Chapel, *Swanson Assoc.*, 1966 (L-A)

(445) Our Shepherd Lutheran Church, *G. Paulsen & Assoc.*, 1966 (BK)

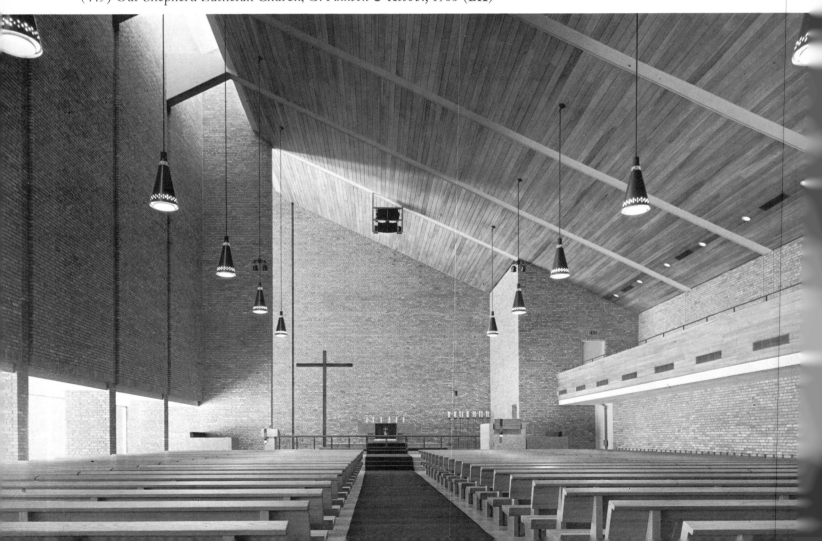

(446) Christus Victor Lutheran Church,
Merritt, Cole & McCallum, 1964 (JPM)

(447) Our Lady of Orchard Lake
R.C. Chapel, *W. J. Rozycki,* 1963 (JPM)

(448) First Presbyterian Church of Dearborn
A. B. Dow Assoc., 1965 (JPM)

(449) Congregation B'Nai David, *S. Eisenshtat & Assoc.*, 1966 (JPM)

(450) Congregation Shaarey Zedek, *A. Kahn Assoc. et al.,* 1962 (JPM)

(451) Sisters of Mercy R.C. Novitiate Chapel, *Giffels & Rossetti*, 1966 (JPM)

(452) Carl Wall House, *F. L. Wright*, 1942 (WHF)

(453) Gregor Affleck House, *F. L. Wright*, 1942 (WHF)
(454) S. Gordon Saunders House, *A. B. Dow*, 1937 (ABD/JKJ)

(455) Melvyn M. Smith House, *F. L. Wright*, 1951 (WA)

(456) Daniel W. Goodenough House, *Yamasaki & Girard*, 1950 (MB)

(457) S. Brooks Barron House, *Yamasaki, Leinweber & Assoc.*, 1955 (H-B)

(458) Millard Pryor House, *A. B. Dow,* 1938 (WHF)

(459) Glen Paulsen House, *G. Paulsen & Assoc.*, 1954 (GP)

(460) Carney D. Matheson House, *E. D. Stone*, 1953 (CDM)

(461-462) Arthur Beckwith House, *Meathe, Kessler & Assoc.*, 1960 (BK) (DFP)

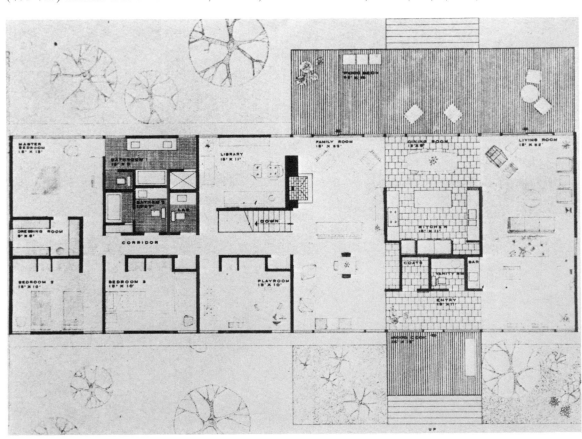

(463) Alan E. Schwartz House, *Birkerts & Straub*, 1961 (BK)

(464) Hilbert DeLawter House, *Meathe, Kessler & Assoc.*, 1962 (BK)

(465) W. Hawkins Ferry House, *Meathe, Kessler & Assoc.*, 1964 (BK)

(466) William H. Kessler House, *Meathe, Kessler & Assoc.*, 1959 (BK)

Selected Chronology

With Map References

Symbols

†	Destroyed
*	Altered
‡	Relocated
§	Not built
■	Building (or block)
®	Church (or religious building)
●	House (residence)
★	Plant (factory)

Some works are placed under their approximate dates: refer to index or illustrations (numbers in parentheses). Estimated dates of completion follow 1968.

1701   *A. Cadillac*   Fort Pontchartrain (2)† Cf. [2C] map 1
      Ste. Anne's R.C. ® (2A)†
1703   Ste. Anne's R.C. ®†
1709   Ste. Anne's R.C. ®†
1723   Ste. Anne's R.C. ®†
1728   Huron Mission House (3)†
1730   Hurron Mission ® (4)† Map 3
1740   Old Moran ● (11)†
1745   Baudry-Cass ● (7)† Map 1
1747   Old Lafferty ●†
1755   Ste. Anne's R.C. ® (9)† Map 1
1757   Old Campau ● (8)†
1764   Citadel (14)† Map 1
1778   Campau (®) (8)†
1779   Fort Lernoult (Ft. Shelby) (13)† Map 1
1780   Old Labadie ● (12)†
1790   Knaggs-Hubbard ● (15)†
1800   E. Brush ●†
      A. Grant ●†
1802   J. F. Hamtramck ● (18)†
1805   J. May ●†
1807   Council House (19)† Map 1
      W. Hull ● (20)† Map 1
      Stockade†
      Woodward Plan (16)§ (17)
1813   J. Campau ● (21)† Map 1
1815   Knaggs Windmill (10)†
1818   Catholepistemiad ■ (25)† Map 1
1826   C. C. Trowbridge ● (37)* Map 2
1827   *Letourno & Wait*   Indian Agency ● *

1828   Ste. Anne's R.C. ® (27)† Map 1
      A. Merrill   St. Paul's P.E. ®† (see 1836)
      O. Wait   Court House & Capitol (35)† Map 1
1829   *F. Letourno?*   J. Palmer ● (26)† Map 1
1830   *F. Letourno*   T. Palmer ●†
1835   J. Abbott ● (44)† Map 1
      American (Wales') Hotel (22)† Map 1
      First Brick Bap. ® (28)† Map 1
      F. Letourno   Mich. Exchange Hotel†
      A. Merrill   First Presb. ® (32)† Map 1
      A. White   City Hall (33)† Map 1
1836   *C. Lum*   Bank of Mich. ■ (34)† Map 1
      Merrill & Elliott   St. Paul's P.E. ® (53)† Map 1
1840   *R. T. Elliott*   J. A. Welles ●†
1845   *R. T. Elliott*   St. Mary's R.C. ®† Site (116) map 1
      C. Stewart   Stewart-Newland ● (64)† Map 1
1848   T. H. Hinchman ●†
      Mich. Central R.R. Depot (49)† Map 1
      Mrs. S. Sibley ● (38) Map 2
      H. Leroy   F. Palms ● (43)† Map 1
      F. Letourno   SS. Peter & Paul's R.C. ® (31) Maps 1–2
      M. C. Meigs   Fort Wayne Barracks (29) Map 3 (30)
1849   Biddle House (47)† Map 1
      C. N. Otis   Mariners' P.E. ® (54)‡ Maps 1–2
1850   A. Chene ● (39)* Map 2
      G. V. N. Lothrop ● (Summerside)†
      Mich. Central R.R. Roundhouse (50)†
      Newberry-Walker ● (48)† Map 1
      A. Merrill   First M.E. ® (36)† Map 1
1851   Firemen's Hall (83)† Map 1
1852   *C. N. Otis*   St. Paul's P.E. ® (51)‡ Maps 1–3
1853   Congregational-Unitarian ® (45)† Map 1
1854   Newberry Warehouse (41)† Map 1
      A. H. Jordan   First Cong. ® (80)† Map 1
1855   *A. H. Jordan*   First Presb. ® (81)† Map 1
      A. H. Jordan   Jefferson Ave. Presb. ® (60)†
      O. & A. Jordan   Fort Street Presb. ® (52) Maps 1–2
1856   E. Brush ● (The Pines)†
      A. J. Davis   Baughman-Scotten ● (66)†
      A. J. Davis   B. Hubbard ● (Vinewood) (73)†
      A. J. Davis   C. Reeve ●†
      A. H. Jordan   Chapel in Elmwood Cem. (®)
1857   *Jordan-Anderson-?Young*   Marine Hosp.†
      Jordan & Anderson   Russell House (33)† Map 1

1858 *Jordan & Anderson* Z. Chandler ● (76)† Map 1
1859 Merrill ■ (82)† Map 1
1860 D. Preston ● (40)†
G. B. Russel ● (42)†
E. B. Ward ● (77)†
Jordan-Anderson-Young Custom House (79)† Map 1
1861 *Jordan & Anderson* St. John's P.E. ® (56)‡ Maps 1–2
1862 J. F. Joy ● (46)† Map 1
G. W. Lloyd A. H. Dey ● (68)† Site nr. (70) map 2
1863 *G. W. Lloyd* Christ P.E. ® (57) Map 2
G. W. Lloyd S. T. Douglass ® (Little Cote) (69)*
Map 3
1864 F. Buhl ● (75)†
G. W. Lloyd S. D. Miller ● (63)†
1867 *G. W. Lloyd* Central M.E. ® (61)* Maps 1–2
G. W. Lloyd St. Andrew's P.E. ®
G. W. Lloyd St. James's P.E. ®
1868 *G. W. Lloyd* T. A. Parker ● (70) Map 2
1869 J. J. Bagley ● (71)† Map 1
E. W. Smith C. Du Charme ● (96)†
S. & M. L. Smith Det. Opera House (86)† Map 1
1870 *G. W. Lloyd?* S. D. Elwood ● (67)†
G. W. Lloyd? F. Moore ● (65)†
M. L. Smith? D. Whitney ● (91)†
1871 *J. Anderson* City Hall (85)† Map 1
M. L. Smith Godfrey ■†
1872 *G. W. Lloyd* Congregational ®
G. W. Lloyd G. W. Lloyd ● (140) Map 3
R. Rogers Soldiers' & Sailors' Mon. (85) Maps 1–3
1873 *F. G. Himpler* St. Joseph's R.C. ® (62) Map 2
1874 T. W. Palmer ● (72)† Site nr. (247) map 2
J: P. Phillips ● (94)†
G. W. Lloyd C. J. Whitney & Co. ■ (124)† Map 1
1875 W. Boeing ● (93)†
Store ■ (137)† Map 1
Brush & Smith Hillsdale College
G. W. Lloyd J. McMillan ● (Lake Terrace)†
G. W. Lloyd J. S. Newberry ● (101)†
G. W. Lloyd J. S. Newberry ● (Lake Terrace)
(142)†
G. W. Lloyd A. Shelden ● (114)†
G. W. Lloyd Whitney Opera House† Site (169)
map 1
1876 *H. T. Brush* C. Lafferty ● (95)†
Brush & Mason R. Gillis ● (111)* Map 2
Brush & Smith G. O. Robinson ● (112)†
J. Hess Mich. ■ (143)†
E. E. Myers P. Parsons ● (100)†
J. Hess St. Mary's R.C. Parsonage (107) Map 2
W. Scott Wayne County Savings Bank (88)† Map 1
M. L. Smith R. H. Fyfe ● (145)†
1877 *Brush & Smith* Det. Pub. Lib. (132)† Map 1
Hess & Mendelssohn Schloss Bros. ■ (109)† Map 1
G. W. Lloyd H. P. Baldwin ● (97)† Map 1
J. E. Sparks Waterworks (104)†
J. A. M. Whistler Peacock Room (191)‡ Site (193)
map 2
1878 *E. E. Myers* Mich. State Capitol (90)
M. L. Smith J. Black ● (118)†
1879 *G. W. Lloyd* Board of Trade ■†
G. W. Lloyd Burnham, Stoepel & Co. ■ (108)†
Map 1
G. W. Lloyd Newberry & McMillan ■ (87)† Map 1
G. W. Lloyd A. Shelden & Co. ■†
M. L. Smith Ferry ■ (128)† Map 1
1880 *G. W. Lloyd* J. B. Dyar ●†
G. W. Lloyd Heavenrich Bros. ■†
G. W. Lloyd J. McMillan ● (113)†

G. W. Lloyd T. Schmidt ●†
Mason & Rice Central Market ■ (106)† Map 1
M. L. Smith T. P. Hall ● (Tonnancour) (144)†
1881 *A. Chapoton* Russell House (106)† Map 1
G. W. Lloyd Edson, Moore & Co. ■ (125)† Map 1
G. W. Lloyd Moore-Ferry ● (139)† Site nr. (247)
map 2
G. W. Lloyd Palms ■ (126)† Map 1
Lloyd & Pearce Westminster Presb. ® (117)† Site
(412S)
Mason & Rice D. M. Ferry & Co. ■ (110)† Map 1
1882 *G. W. Lloyd* H. B. Ledyard ● (Cloverleigh) (141)†
G. W. Lloyd H. McMillan ● (Cloverleigh) †
Mason & Rice J. H. Berry ● (Edgemere) (147)†
1883 Art Loan Exhibition ■ (120)† Map 1
H. S. Pingree ● (92)† Site (412B)
C. L. W. Eidlitz Mich. Central R.R. Sta. (123)†
Map 1
G. W. Lloyd Parker (B. Siegel Co.) ■ (127) Map 1
Mason & Rice Store & Residence ■ (157)†
Mason & Rice Y.M.C.A. ■†
Smith & Brown Campau ■ (105)† Map 1
1884 *Donaldson & Meier* Belle Isle Casino (177)†
G. W. Lloyd Police H.Q. ■†
E. E. Myers Harper Hosp. (115) Map 2
1885 L. S. Moore ● (119) Map 2
P. Dederichs St. Mary's R.C. ® (116) Maps 1–2
G. W. Lloyd R. A. Alger ● (130)† Map 1
G. W. Lloyd Grand Circus ■ (129)† Map 1
1886 Lake St. Clair (Old) Club (183)† Map 3
W. E. Brown Grosse Pointe Club (185)†
H. H. Richardson Bagley Mem. Armory (173)†
Map 1
Spier & Rohns Ann Arbor R.R. Sta.
1887 *L. Coquard* Ste. Anne's R.C. ® (122) Map 2
J. V. Gearing Det. Athl. Club (162)†
G. W. Lloyd D. M. Ferry & Co. ■ (170) Map 1
G. W. Lloyd H. B. Ledyard ●†
Mason & Rice Mackinac Island Grand Hotel (199)
H. H. Richardson Bagley Mem. Fountain (154)‡
Maps 1–2
W. & J. Scott S. J. Murphy ● (131)† Site nr. (243)
map 2
M. L. Smith Woodward Ave. Bap. ® (136)*
Maps 1–2
1888 *J. Balfour* Det. Museum of Art (171)†
B. L. Gilbert Newberry Mem. Chapel (®) (152)†
Mason & Rice C. A. Du Charme ● (158)†
Mason & Rice G. W. Lee ● (159)†
Mason & Rice W. C. McMillan ● (The Cottage)
(189)†
Mason & Rice Kingsville R.R. Sta. (166)
Mason & Rice Walkerville R.R. Sta. (167)†
Rogers & MacFarlane Banner Cigar ★†
1889 J. N. Bagley ● (155) Map 2
L. Kamper Exposition Pavilion (187)†
Mason & Rice G. G. Booth ● (249)†
Mason & Rice Det. Business Univ. ■†
Mason & Rice First Presb. ® (149)* Map 2
Mason & Rice Mettawas Hotel & Casino (190)†
1890 *Donaldson & Meier* First Unit. ® (146)* Map 2
H. W. J. Edbrooke Hammond ■ (176)† Map 1
W. Eyre+ C. L. Freer ● (193) Map 2
Mason & Rice A. L. Stephens ● (164)†
Scott-Kamper-Scott F. J. Hecker ● (272) Map 2
1891 *W. Eyre* Det. Club (163) Map 1
J. L. Faxon First Congregational ® (148) Map 2
B. L. Gilbert Jefferson Ave. Presb. ® (153)†

G. W. Lloyd   Det. College (U.D.) (168) Maps 1–2
Malcomson & Higginbotham   Cass Ave. M.E. ®
(150) Map 2
Malcomson & Higginbotham   Central Christian ®
(151)†
Mason & Rice   J. E. Scripps ● (282) Map 2
M. L. Smith   J. L. Hudson Co. ■ (175)† Map 1
1892   *Mason & Rice*   Trinity P.E. ® (314) Map 2
Mason & Rice   H. Walker & Sons Off. ■ (225) Map 3
1893   *J. V. Moran* ● (Maplehurst) (184)†
Mason & Rice   Belle Isle Police Sta. (182) Map 3
Mason & Rice   W. Livingstone ● (269) Map 2
Spier & Rohns   Sweetest Heart R.C. ® (121) Map 2
J. Stewart+   Union R.R. Sta. (165) Map 2
1894   *Brede & Mueller*   Hurlbut Mem. Gate (242) Map 2
Donaldson & Meier   Det. Boat Club (181)†
G. W. Lloyd   D. Whitney ● (161) Map 2
Mason & Rice   Masonic Temple†
Mason & Rice   T. W. Palmer ■ (174) Map 1
J. H. Windrim   Federal ■ (169)† Map 1
1895   *J. H. Walker* ● (251)†
Donaldson & Meier   Union Trust ■ (180)† Map 1
Mason & Rice   W. M. Freer ● (250)†
Spier & Rohns   Chamber of Commerce ■ (179) Map 1
Stratton & Baldwin   W. B. Stratton ● (290)†
1896   *E. H. Parker* ● (195)†
D. H. Burnham   Majestic ■ (178)† Map 1
Malcomson & Higginbotham   W.S.U. Old Main ■
(418) Map 2
Malcomson & Higginbotham   Holy Rosary R.C. ®
1897   Det. Cornice & Slate Co. ■ (135) Maps 1–2
Donaldson & Meier   J. T. Melchers ● (198) Map 2
J. & A. Scott   Wayne County Jail (230)† Map 1
1898   *Kahn & Nettleton*   J. E. Scripps Lib. (284)†
L. Kamper   H. Scherer ● (196)
G. D. Mason   Det. Opera House (226)† Map 1
1899   *Spier & Rohns*   St. Thomas's R.C. ®
1900   *A. Kahn*   Boyer Machine Co. ★†
McKim-Mead-White   Peoples State Bank ■ (229)
Map 1
S. White   Bicentennial Mem. (245)§
1901   *Carrère & Hastings*   Merrill Fountain (244)‡
Maps 1, 3
1902   *A. W. Chittenden*   Det. Boat Club
C. A. Platt   Yondotega Fountain (256)‡ Maps 1–2
Rogers & MacFarlane   D. C. Whitney ● (Ridgemont)
(197)†
J. & A. Scott   Wayne County ■ (227) Map 1
Stratton & Baldwin   J. Hamilton ● (287) Map 2
1903   *Mason & Kahn*   Palms Apts.
Mason & Kahn   U.M. Engr. ■
1904   *Chittenden & Kotting*   J. B. Ford ●‡
Field-Hinchman-Smith   Ford M.C. ★ (201) Map 2
A. Kahn   Burroughs Adding Machine Co. ★
1905   *Donaldson & Meier*   Penobscot ■I Cf. (354) map 1
A. Kahn   Packard M.C. ★ (Ten) (203)* Map 2
A. Kahn   C. M. Swift ● (286)
G. D. Mason   Cadillac M.C. ★
1906   *Chittenden & Kotting*   W. T. Barbour ● (Briarbank)
A. Kahn   A. Kahn ● (295) Map 2
A. Kahn   E. C. Walker ● (Willistead) (288) Map 3
Stratton & Baldwin   J. Sparling & Co. ■ (206)† Map 1
1907   *A. Kahn*   Chalmers M.C. ★
A. Kahn   Country Club of Det. (214)†
A. Kahn   Trussed Concrete ■†
G. D. Mason   Pontchartrain Hotel (232)† Map 1
Stratton & Baldwin   Pewabic Pottery Co. ■ (297)
Map 2

1908   *A. Kahn*   Grinnell ■
Stratton & Baldwin   F. M. Alger ● (By Way) (293)†
Stratton & Baldwin   Baldwin-Murphy ● (The
Hedges) (289)†
1909   *D. H. Burnham*   Ford ■ (213) Map 1
R. Carey   J. M. Dwyer ● (Lakewood Court) (335)‡
M. Grabowsky   Maxwell M.C. ★ (365) Map 3
A. Kahn   G. G. Booth ● (Cranbrook House) (296)
Map 3
A. Kahn   Ford M.C. Off. ■ (207)†
Trowbridge & Ackerman   L. S. Trowbridge ●
(Elmsleigh) (294)†
1910   *D. H. Burnham*   Dime ■ (212) Map 1
A. Kahn   C. G. Edgar ● (261)
A. Kahn   Hudson M.C. Off. ■†
A. Kahn   H. B. Joy ● (Fair Acres) (224)†
L. Kamper   L. Kamper ● (255) Map 2
C. A. Platt   R. A. Alger ● (The Moorings) (259)
Map 3
Postle & Mahler   D. J. Healy Co. ■ (208)* Map 1
1911   *Cram-Goodhue-Ferguson*   St. Paul's P.E. Cath. ®
(316) Map 2
A. Heun   H. D. Shelden ● (Deeplands) (263)†
A. Kahn   J. S. Newberry ● (Lake Terrace) (333)†
L. Kamper   J. B. Book ● (253) Map 2
1912   *A. Kahn*   H. E. Dodge ● (Rose Terrace) (323)†
A. Kahn   P. H. McMillan ● (Elsinore) (223)
G. D. Mason   L. W. Bowen ● (324) Map 2
1913   *Chittenden & Kotting*   F. W. Hubbard ● (Shadow
Lawn) (334)
Donaldson & Meier   Cass Theater
A. Kahn   Boulevard ■ (211)* Map 2
A. Kahn   Old Free Press ■
A. Kahn   U.M. Hill Auditorium (218) Map 3
C. A. Platt   Mrs. H. Stephens ● (275)
J. & A. Scott   H. N. Torrey ● (Clairview) (254)†
Warren & Wetmore+   Mich. Central R.R. Sta. (264)
Map 2
1914   *Chittenden & Kotting*   J. B. Nichols ●†
A. Kahn   Dodge Bros. Corp. ★
A. Kahn   Ford M.C. ★ (205)* Map 3
A. Kahn   Kales (Kresge) ■
G. D. Mason   A. L. Stephens ● (252)†
G. B. Post   Statler-Hilton Hotel (231) Map 1
Smith-Hinchman-Grylls   Shubert (Orpheum)
Theater†
A. H. Spahr   E. D. Speck ● (Fairholme) (325)†
Trowbridge & Ackerman   T. H. Newberry ● (Dry
Brook) (331)†
1915   *Baxter-O'Dell-Halpin*   T. B. Rayl Co. ■ (210)* Map 1
D. H. Burnham   David Whitney ■ (215) Map 1
A. Kahn   Det. Athl. Club (237) Map 1
A. Kahn   Det. Trust Co. ■ (265) Map 1
A. Kahn   Woodward ■ (216) Map 1
A. H. Spahr   J. B. Schlotman ● (Stonehurst) (326)
Trowbridge & Ackerman   D. M. Ferry ● (329)†
W. H. Van Tine   H. Ford ● (Fair Lane) (332) Map 3
H. A. Walsh   R.C. Cath. ® (318) Map 3
1916   *C. H. Crane*   Madison Theater
Donaldson & Meier   Penobscot ■II Cf. (354) map 1
A. Kahn   Det. News ■ (358)   Map 1
A. Kahn   U.M. Nat. Sci. ■ (221) Map 3
G. D. Mason   Pontchartrain Hotel (add.) (232)†
Smith-Hinchman-Grylls   Woman's Exchange ■ (291)
Map 1
A. H. Spahr   E. L. Ford ● (327)†
Stratton & Grylls   Soc. of Arts & Crafts ■ (299) Map 2

1917   *A. Kahn*   Det. Golf Club (302) Map 3
     A. Kahn   Ford M.C. Riv. Rouge ★ (362) Map 3 (361)
     A. Kahn   A. Kahn ● (Walnut Lake) (222) Map 3
     L. Kamper   Book ■ (236) Map 1
     L. Kamper   M. W. Sales ● (Edgeroad) (248)
     G. D. Mason   Lincoln M.C. ★
     G. D. Mason   F. Woodruff ● (217)

1918   *G. G. Booth*   Cranbrook Meeting House (®) (301)*
      Nr. (296) map 3
     L. Kamper   Cadillac Sq. ■

1919   *C. H. Crane*   Orchestra Hall Cf. (412S)
     A. Kahn   Finsterwald ■ (209)* Map 1
     A. Kahn   U.M. Gen. Lib. (220) Map 3
     Smith-Hinchman-Grylls   Fyfe's Shoe Store ■ (321)
      Map 1

1920   *Smith-Hinchman-Grylls*   J. F. Dodge ● (306)†

1921   *C. Gilbert*   Det. Pub. Lib. (243) Map 2
     A. Kahn   Cadillac M.C. ★

1922   *C. H. Crane*   Capitol Theater
     A. Kahn   Gen. Motors ■ (240) Maps 2–3
     A. Kahn   Nat. Bank ■ (266) Map 1
     E. Saarinen   Chicago Tribune project (349)§

1923   *A. Kahn*   Clements Lib. (U.M.) (239) Map 3
     A. Kahn   Country Club of Det.† Site (303) map 3
     A. Kahn   Det. Free Press ■ (356) Map 1
     A. Kahn   Ford M.C. Admin. ■ (361) Map 3
     A. Kahn   Police H.Q. ■ (238) Map 1
     L. Kamper   Washington Blvd. ■
     G. D. Mason   E. S. George ● (Cedarholm) (300) Map 3

1924   *M. R. Burrowes*   R. H. Booth ● (330)
     B. Fleming   W. Seyburn ● (277)
     L. Kamper   Book-Cadillac Hotel (233) Map 1
     H. T. Keyes   C. A. Dean ● (Ridgeland) (260)
     E. Saarinen   Civic Center project (381)§

1925   *C. H. Crane*   State Theater
     R. O. Derrick   S. T. Miller ● (340)
     R. O. Derrick   R. H. Webber ●
     C. Gilbert   J. Scott Fountain (246) Map 3
     A. Kahn   U.M. Angell Hall (268) Map 3
     H. T. Keyes   W. P. Harris ●
     Rapp Bros.   Mich. Theater
     Smith-Hinchman-Grylls   Bankers Trust Co. ■ (353)
      Map 1
     Smith-Hinchman-Grylls   Buhl ■ (351) Map 1
     Smith-Hinchman-Grylls   Jefferson Ave. Presb. ®
      (319) Map 2
     W. B. Stratton   J. H. Harris ● (315)

1926   *R. O. Derrick*   E. H. Brown ● (281)
     R. O. Derrick   W. L. Mitchell ● (337)
     L. Kamper   Book Tower ■ (234) Map 1
     G. D. Mason   H. G. Higbie ● (270)
     Smith-Hinchman-Grylls   Country Club of Det. (303)
      Map 3
     Tilton & Githens+   McGregor Pub. Lib. (267) Map 3

1927   *Bonnah & Chaffee*   Cadillac (Barlum) Tower ■
     P. P. Cret+   Det. Inst. of Arts (247) Map 2
     R. O. Derrick   Grosse Pointe Club
     R. O. Derrick   Hannan Mem. Y.M.C.A. (338) Map 2
     W. Frost   J. P. Bowen ● (280)
     Graham-Anderson-Probst+   Fed. Res. Bank ■ (386)*
      Map 1
     A. Kahn   E. B. Ford ● (312)
     A. Kahn   Kresge Admin. ■ (360) Map 2
     A. Kahn   Maccabees ■ (355) Map 2
     G. Lowell   Grosse Pointe Yacht Club (262) Map 3
     Malcomson & Higginbotham   Univ. of Det. Nr.
      (427) map 3
     J. R. Pope   R. D. Chapin ● (336)

     Rapp Bros.   Det. Leland Hotel
     E. Saarinen   Cranbrook School (370) Map 3
     W. B. Stratton   W. B. Stratton ● (305)

1928   *R. Carey*   H. F. Smith ●
     C. H. Crane   Fox Theater (350) Map 1
     C. H. Crane   United Artists Theater
     B. G. Goodhue+   Christ P.E. ® Cranbrook (317)
      Map 3
     Graven & Mayger   Fisher Theater (348)* Map 2
      (359)
     A. Kahn   Chrysler Corp. Engr. ■ Nr. (365) map 3
     A. Kahn   Fisher ■ (359) Map 2
     A. Kahn   Harper Hosp. add. (410) Nr. (115) map 2
     A. Kahn   Plymouth M.C. ★
     G. D. Mason+   Masonic Temple (322) Map 2
     Smith-Hinchman-Grylls   Penobscot ■III (354) Map 1

1929   *Booth-Burrowes-Booth*   Brookside School (301) Nr.
      (296) map 3
     R. O. Derrick   Henry Ford Museum (346) [310]
      Map 3
     R. O. Derrick   J. B. Moran ●
     Donaldson & Meier   David Stott ■ (352) Map 1
     A. Kahn   Det. Times ■
     A. Kahn   A. Macauley ● (313)
     L. Kamper   Industrial Bank ■
     E. Saarinen   E. Saarinen ●
     Smith-Hinchman-Grylls   Guradian ■ (357) Map 1
     Smith-Hinchman-Grylls   J. L. Hudson Co. ■ Sites
      (81) (128) map 1
     Smith-Hinchman-Grylls   A. G. Wilson ● (Meadow
      Brook) (307) Map 3

1930   *R. O. Derrick*   Jennings Mem. Hosp.
     R. O. Derrick   Punch & Judy Theater

1931   *R. Carey*   G. B. Pingree ● (343)
     R. O. Derrick   F. C. Walker ● (341)
     A. Kahn   New Center ■
     E. Saarinen   Kingswood School (368) Nr. (296)
      map 3
     Smith-Hinchman-Grylls   Univ. Club (311) Map 2

1932   *W. B. Stratton*   E. S. Bennett ● (339)

1933   *E. Saarinen*   Cranbrook Inst. of Sci. Nr. (296) map 3

1934   *R. Carey*   G. M. Holley ● (342)
     R. O. Derrick   S. Backus ● (309)†
     H. T. Keyes   E. W. Clark ● (344)
     C. A. Platt   Mrs. R. A. Alger ● (345)†
     H. Trumbauer   Mrs. H. E. Dodge ● (Rose Terrace)
      (279)
     Wetmore & Derrick   Federal ■ Site (169) map 1

1935   *A. Kahn*   Ford M.C. Rotunda (361)† Map 3

1936   *A. Kahn*   Chrysler-De Soto Press Shop (★) (363)
      Map 3

1937   *A. B. Dow*   S. G. Saunders ● (454)
     A. Kahn   Chrysler-Dodge Truck ★ (364)* Map 3

1938   *A. B. Dow*   M. Pryor ● (458)

1939   *G. D. Mason+*   Brewster Homes Cf. (412U)
     G. D. Mason+   Parkside Homes

1940   *A. Kahn*   Chrysler Tank Arsenal (★) (367) Map 3
     O'Dell-Hewlett-Luckenbach   Charles Terrace (395)
      Map 3
     Palmer-Schilling-Ditchy+   Parkside Homes add.

1941   *Harley-Ellington-Day*   Rackham Mem. ■ Cf. (412B)
      (415)
     F. Miles   J. L. Booth ● (347)

1942   *Lyndon & Smith*   John W. Smith Homes (400)*
      Map 3
     G. D. Mason+   Herman Gardens
     S. Pilafian   W.(S.)U. Campus plan Cf. (418)§
     Saarinen-Swanson+   Kramer Homes (403) Map 3

F. L. Wright   G. Affleck ●(453)

F. L. Wright   C. Wall ● (452)

1943   *A. Kahn*   Ford M.C. Willow Run Bomber ★ (366)*
Map 3

Lyndon & Smith   Norwayne Homes (404)* Map 3

E. Saarinen   Cranbrook Acad. of Art (369) Nr. (370)
map 3

Saarinen-Swanson+   Willow Run Village

1947   *Saarinen-Saarinen*+   Civic Center project (379)§

1948   *S. Pilafian*   W.S.U. State Hall

1949   *R. Calder*   W.S.U. Sci. Hall

J. L. Pottle   J. L. Booth ● (Lakecrest)

1950   *Harley-Ellington-Day*   Veterans' Mem. Hall (380)
Maps 1–2

Yamasaki & Girard   D. W. Goodenough ● (456)

1951   *W. E. Kapp*   Det. Hist. Museum Cf. (418)

O'Dell-Hewlett-Luckenbach   International Inst.

Smith-Hinchman-Grylls   Fed. Res. Bank annex (386)
Maps 1–2

F. L. Wright   M. M. Smith ● (455)

1952   *Pilafian & Montana*   W.S.U. College of Engr. ■

1953   *M. Breuer*   Grosse Pointe Pub. Lib. (442) Map 3

Pilafian & Montana   W.S.U. Kresge Sci. Lib. (419)
Map 2

E. D. Stone   C. D. Matheson ● (460)

1954   *V. Gruen*+   Northland Center (372) Map 3

G. Paulsen+   G. Paulsen ● (459)

Pilafian & Montana   W.S.U. Gen. Lib.

1955   *Harley-Ellington-Day*   City-County ■ (382) Maps 1–2

Harley-Ellington-Day   Frederick Douglass Apts.
Cf. (412U)

O'Dell-Hewlett-Luckenbach+   Ford Auditorium
(384) Maps 1–2

Smith-Hinchman-Grylls   Edward J. Jeffries Homes

Yamasaki-Leinweber   S. B. Barron ● (457) Map 3

1956   *Saarinen-Saarinen*+   Gen. Motors Tech. Center (373)
Map 3

Skidmore-Owings-Merrill   Ford M.C. Admin. Center
(385) Map 3

1957   *V. Gruen*+   Eastland Center (377) Map 3

1958   *Giffels & Rossetti*   Met. Airport Terminal Nr. (396)
map 3

Rowland & Mason+   Kirk-in-the-Hills (®) (320)
Map 3

Voorhees-Walker-Foley+   Ford M.C. Res. & Engr.
Center

Yamasaki-Leinweber   American Concrete Inst. (389)
Map 3

M. Yamasaki+   McGregor Mem. Conf. Center (422)
Maps 2–3

M. Yamasaki+   Soc. of Arts & Crafts Art School
(415) Map 2

1959   *A. Kahn*+   Nat. Bank of Det. ■ (387) Maps 1–2

Meathe-Kessler   W. H. Kessler ● (466)

Harley-Ellington-Day   W.S.U. Cohn Mem. ■

L. Mies van der Rohe   Lafayette Park Pavilion
(Apts.) (406) Map 2

S. Pilafian   W.S.U. Community Arts Center

M. Yamasaki+   Reynolds Metals ■ (388) Map 3

1960   *Giffels & Rossetti*   Cobo Hall & Arena (383) Maps 1–2

Giffels & Rossetti   U.M. Dearborn Center Nr. (430)
map 3

A. Kahn+   W.S.U. Life Sci. Res. Center (425) Map 2

Meathe-Kessler   A. Beckwith ● (461)

E. M. Smith+   Henry Ford Community College
(430) Map 3

Yamasaki-Leinweber   W.S.U. College of Educ. ■
(420) Map 2

1961   *Birkerts & Straub*   A. E. Schwartz ● (463)

Diehl & Diehl   St. Clement's R.C. ® (441) Map 3

Meathe-Kessler   Fleming Elem. School (428) Map 3

Meathe-Kessler   Mount Clemens Fed. Savings ■
(397) Map 3

L. Smith+   Tendler Elem. School

1962   *A. Kahn*+   Congregation Shaarey Zedek (®) (450)
Map 3

Meathe-Kessler   H. DeLawter ● (464)

E. M. Smith+   Knudsen Jr. High School

E. M. Smith+   Westchester Elem. School (443)
Map 3

Tarapata-MacMahon   East Hills Jr. High School
(438) Map 3

1963   *Giffels & Rossetti*   Lafayette Park Plaza

Harley-Ellington-Cowin+   Det. Bank & Trust Co.
■ (392) Maps 1–2

Keally & Gilbert   Det. Pub. Lib. Cass Ave. add.
Cf. (243) map 2

King & Lewis   Lafayette Park Shopping Center

Meathe-Kessler   Earhart Jr. High School (434)
Maps 2–3

Meathe-Kessler   Woodward Elem. School (432)
Map 2

L. Mies van der Rohe   Lafayette Towers (Apts.)

W. J. Rozycki   Our Lady of Orchard Lake R.C.
Chapel (®) (447) Map 3

L. Smith+   Meadowlake Elem. School (435) Map 3

Stickel-Jaroszewicz-Moody   W. Bloomfield Township
Lib. (440) Map 3

M. Yamasaki+   Mich. Cons. Gas. Co. ■ (390)
Maps 1–2

1964   *Birkerts & Straub*   1300 Lafayette E. (Apts.) (407)
Map 2

Meathe-Kessler   W. H. Ferry ● (465)

Merritt-Cole-McCallum   Christus Victor Luth. ®
(446) Map 3

Smith-Hinchman-Grylls   W.S.U. Med. Res. ■ (414)
Map 2

Tarapata-MacMahon   Carl Sandburg Lib. (439)
Map 3

M. Yamasaki+   W.S.U. DeRoy Auditorium

M. Yamasaki+   W.S.U. Prentis ■ (421) Map 2

1965   *A. B. Dow*+   First Presb. ® of Dearborn (448)
Map 3

Giffels & Rossetti   Jeffersonian Apts. (399) Map 2

J. H. Graham+   Four Freedoms (Apt.) House

Gruen & Redstone   Westland Center (378) Map 3

Harley-Ellington-Cowin+   Macomb County
Community College (429) Map 3

King & Lewis   Pontchartrain Hotel (398) Maps 1–2

Paulsen-Gardner   W.S.U. Shapero Hall (424) Map 2

E. M. Smith+   Murray Sr. High School (436) Map 2

E. M. Smith+   Schoolcraft College (433) Map 3

Smith-Hinchman-Grylls   First Fed. ■ (393) Maps 1–2

Smith-Hinchman-Grylls   W.S.U. Physics Res. ■

1966   *G. Birkerts*+   U.D. Fisher Administration Center
(427) Map 3

Crane & Gorwic   Med. Center Professional Plaza
(413) Map 2

S. Eisenshtat+   Congregation B'Nai David (®)
(449) Map 3

Giffels & Rossetti   Federal-Mogul Staff ■ (394) Map 3

Giffels & Rossetti   Sisters of Mercy Chapel (®)
(451) Map 3

Green & Savin   Elmwood Park S. S. of (408) map 2

Green & Savin   Lafayette Park Regency Sq. (402)
Map 2

Harley-Ellington-Cowin+   Det. Inst. of Arts S. Wing (416) Cf. (247) map 2
Hausner & Macsai   Lafayette Park E.
R. E. Mayotte+   Elmwood Park E.
O'Dell-Hewlett-Luckenbach   W.S.U. Law School ■
G. Paulsen+   Our Shepherd Luth. ® (445) Map 3
L. G. Redstone+   Glazer Elem. School (431) Map 3
S. Rossen   Elmwood Park W.
E. M. Smith+   Elmwood Park N. (408) Map 2
Smith-Hinchman-Grylls   Met. Airport Terminal (396) Map 3
L. Smith+   Eastern Sr. High School (437) Map 2
Swanson+   St. John Fisher R.C. Chapel (®) (444) Map 3

1967   *A. B. Dow*+   W.S.U. Matthaei Physical Educ. ■
Levine-Alpern+   North Park (Apt.) Towers (401) Map 3

G. Paulsen+   U.D. Ford Life Sci. ■ (426) Nr. (427) map 3

1968   *A. B. Dow*+   W.S.U. Univ. Center ■ (423) Map 2

1969   *R. Calder*+   W.S.U. Nat. Sci. Complex
Jickling & Lyman   W.S.U. Language Classrooms ■

1970   *Giffels & Rossetti*   W.S.U. Basic Med. Sci. ■ Cf. (412J)
Jickling & Lyman   W.S.U. Gen. Lectures ■
A. Kahn+   Children's Hosp. (410) Map 2
O'Dell-Hewlett-Luckenbach   W.S.U. Shiffman Med. Lib. Cf. (412I)

1972   *Smith-Hinchman-Grylls*   W.S.U. Med. Clinics ■ Cf. (412M)
Smith-Hinchman-Grylls   Webber Med. Center. Cf. (412N)

1975   *Smith-Hinchman-Grylls*   Grace Hosp. Cf. (412L)

Maps

The numbers on the maps are those of the illustrations. In general only works illustrated, and except for the historical map of downtown Detroit (Map 1) still standing, are located on the maps. On all three maps locations are approximate. Those of most houses still used as residences outside the city limits of Detroit are not given.

Base Map 1 is used by courtesy of the Automobile Club of Michigan; base Maps 2 (including inset) and 3 were kindly furnished by the Detroit City Plan Commission. For other maps, see illustrations (2) (5) (9) (13) (16) (17) (371) (412).

Map 1. Historical Map of Downtown Detroit

All numbers refer to illustrations. Numbers in parentheses are on the map; those in brackets do not locate the building on the map. Base map of about 1930, courtesy of the Automobile Club of Michigan.

(A) [85] Soldiers & Sailors Mon. 1872

[2C] [5A] Cadillac's ho. 1701, traditional site (21)

(7) Baudry-Cass ho. c. 1745 (moved to site 1836)

(9) [5C] Ste. Anne's R.C. Chu. 1755

(13) Fort Shelby 1779, + sites (48) (169) (229) (265)

(14) Citadel 1764

(19) Council House c. 1807, site of [83] (54)

(20) Gov. Hull's ho. 1807, site of [22] [47]

(21) Jos. Campau ho. 1813, site of ? [5A]

[22] Wales' Hotel 1835, site (20)

(25) Catholepistemiad 1818

(26) J. Palmer ho. 1829, site of [354]

(27) Ste. Anne's R.C. Chu. 1828

(28) First Baptist Chu. 1835, site of [212]

(31) SS. Peter & Paul's R.C. Chu. 1848

(32) First Presbyterian Chu. 1835

(33) City Hall 1835, site of [106]

[33] Russell House 1857, site (232)

(34) Bank of Michigan 1836

(35) Court House & Capitol 1828

(36) First Methodist Chu. 1850, site of [127]

(41) Newberry Whse. 1854, site of [383]

(43) F. Palms ho. 1848, site of [168]

(44) J. Abbott ho. 1835, site of [176] [387]

(45) Congregational Unitarian Chu. 1853

(46) J. F. Joy Ho. 1862

[47] Biddle House 1849, site (20)

(48) Newberry-Walker ho. c. 1850, site of (13) [386]

(49) Mich. Central R.R. Depot 1848, site of [123]

(51) St. Paul's P.E. Chu. 1852, moved (see map 2)

(52) Fort st. Presbyterian Chu. 1855

(53) St. Paul's P.E. Chu. 1828

(54) Mariners' P.E. Chu. 1849, moved to site (19)

(56) St. John's P.E. Chu. 1861

(61) Central Methodist Chu. 1867

(64) Stewart-Newland ho. 1845

(71) J. J. Bagley ho. 1869, site of [231]

(76) Z. Chandler ho. 1858, site of (358)

(79) Federal Bldg. 1860

(80) First Congregational Chu. 1854

(81) First Presbyterian Chu. 1855, site of [175]

(82) Merrill Block 1859, site of [382]

[83] Firemen's Hall 1851, site (19)

(85) City Hall 1871, site of Kennedy Sq.

(86) Det. Opera House 1869, site of [226]

(87) Newberry & McMillan Bldg. 1879, site of [390]

(88) Wayne County Savings Bank 1876

(97) H. P. Baldwin ho. 1877

(105) Campau Block 1883

[106] Central Market Bldg. 1880, site (33)

[106] Russell House 1881, site (232)

(108) Burnham, Stoepel & Co. 1879

(109) Schloss Bros. Block 1877

(110) D. M. Ferry & Co. 1881, site of [170]

(116) St. Mary's R.C. Chu. 1885

(120) Art Loan Exhibition Bldg. 1883, site of [382]

[123] Mich. Central R.R. Sta. 1883, site (49)

(124) C.J.Whitney & Co. 1874, site of [212]

(125) Edson, Moore & Co. 1881

(126) Palms Block c. 1881, site of [398]

(127) Parker Block 1883, site (36)

(128) Ferry Bldg. 1879

(129) Grand Circus Bldg. 1885, site of [215]

(130) R. A. Alger ho. 1885

(132) Det. Public Library 1877

(135) Det. Cornice & Slate Co. 1897

(136) Woodward ave. Baptist Chu. 1887

(137) Store Bldg. c. 1875

(154) Bagley Mem. Fountain 1887, moved to site (244)

(163) Det. Club 1891

[168] Det. College 1891, site (43)

(169) Federal Bldg. 1894, site of (13)

[170] D. M. Ferry & Co. 1887, site (110)

(173) Bagley Mem. Armory 1886

(174) T. W. Palmer Block 1894

[175] J. L. Hudson Co. 1891, site (81)

[176] Hammond Bldg. 1890, site (44)

(178) Majestic Bldg. 1896, site of [393]

(179) Chamber of Commerce Bldg. 1895

(180) Union Trust Bldg. 1895, site of [387]

(206) J. Sparling & Co. 1906

(208) D. J. Healy Co. 1910

(209) Finsterwald Bldg. 1919

(210) T. B. Rayl Co. 1915

[212] Dime Bldg. 1910, sites (28) (124)

(213) Ford Bldg. 1909

[215] David Whitney Bldg. 1915, site (129)

(216) Woodward Bldg. 1915

(226) Det. Opera House 1898, site (86)

(227) Wayne County Bldg. 1902

(229) Peoples State Bank 1900, site of (13)

(230) Wayne County Jail 1897, site of [238]

[231] Statler Hotel 1914, site (71)

(232) Pontchartrain Hotel 1907, site of [33] [106] [266]

(233) Book-Cadillac Hotel 1924

(234) Book Tower 1926

(236) Book Bldg. 1917

(237) Det. Athletic Club 1915

[238] Police Hq. 1923, site (230)

(244) Merrill Fountain 1901, moved (see map 3), site of (154)

(256) Yondotega Club Fountain 1902, moved (see map 2)

(265) Det. Trust Co. 1915, site of (13)

[266] National Bank Bldg. 1922, site (232)

(291) Woman's Exchange 1916

(321) Fyfe's Shoe Store 1919

(350) Fox Theater 1928

(351) Buhl Bldg. 1925

(352) David Stott Bldg. 1929

(353) Bankers Trust Co. 1925

[354] Penobscot Bldg. 1928, site (26) +

(356) Det. Free Press 1923

(357) Guardian Bldg. 1929

(358) Det. News 1916 + site (76)

(380) Veterans Mem. Hall 1950

[382] City-County Bldg. 1955, sites (82) (120) +

[383] Convention Arena 1960, site (41)

(384) Ford Auditorium 1955

[386] Federal Reserve Bank 1927, site (48)

[387] National Bank of Det. 1959, sites (44) (180) +

[390] Mich. Cons. Gas Co. 1963, site (87) +

(392) Det. Bank & Trust Co. 1963

[393] First Federal Bldg. 1965, site (178)

[398] Pontchartrain Hotel 1965, site (126) +

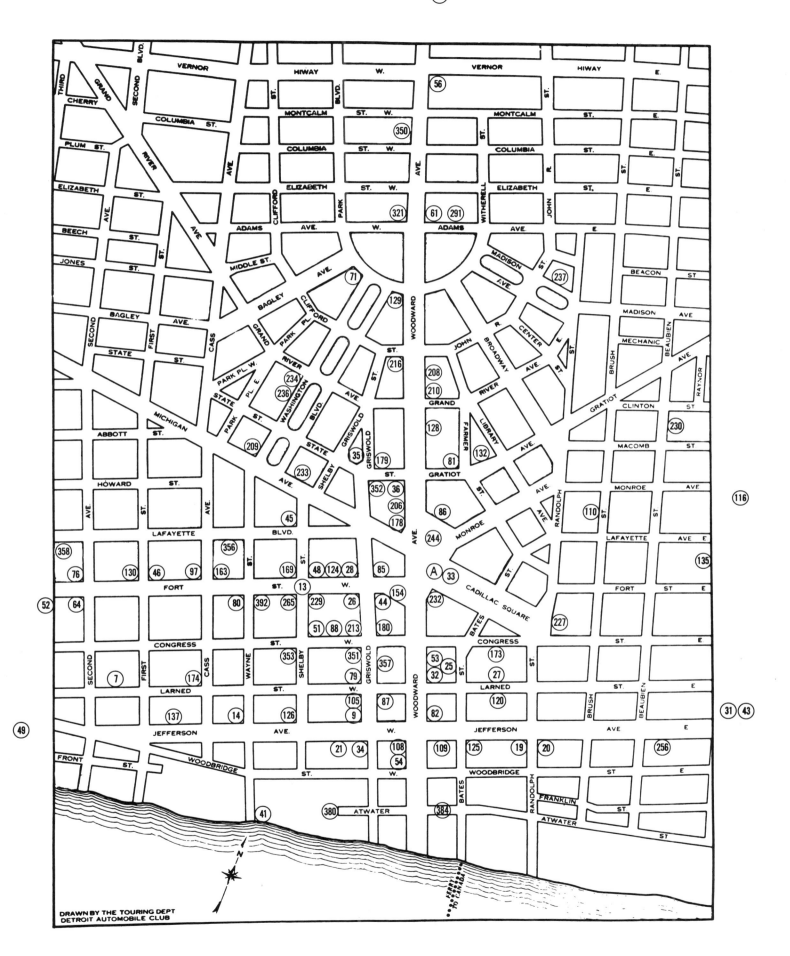

DRAWN BY THE TOURING DEPT
DETROIT AUTOMOBILE CLUB

Map 2. Detroit Inner City

Map 2 is of the so-called inner city, the area bounded by Grand boulevard. The numbers of four group illustrations are used to locate specifically: (85) Soldiers and Sailors Monument, (380) Veterans Memorial Hall, (415) Art School, and (418) W.S.U. Old Main. The inset on Map 2 includes the Indian Village area around Jefferson avenue east of Grand boulevard and north of Belle Isle.

References

Special Abbreviations

AIA—American Institute of Architects
arch., archit., archt.—architectural, architecture, architect
BHC—Burton Historical Collection, Detroit Public Library
Det.—Detroit
DHM—Detroit Historical Museum
DHS(B)—Detroit Historical Society *(Bulletin)*
DIA(B)—Detroit Institute of Arts *(Bulletin)*
DPL(AF)—Detroit Public Library *(Among Friends)*
HSM—Historical Society of Michigan, Lansing
MHC *(Mich. Hist.)*—Michigan Historical Commission *(Michigan History)*
MSA(B)—Michigan Society of Architects *(Weekly* or *Monthly Bulletin)*
MS(U)(P)—Michigan State (Univ.)(Press), East Lansing
UD(P)—University of Detroit (Press)
UM(P)—University of Michigan (Press), Ann Arbor
v.a.—verbal attribution
v.i.—verbal information
W(S)U(P)—Wayne (State) Univ. (Press), Detroit

Short Names and Titles

This is virtually a selected bibliography. In the notes, generally in the case of multi-volume works, volume number is not given for first one or continuous pagination (e.g., Farmer); most citations of Andrews, Hanawalt, McKee *(HABSM)*, Robinson, and Woolfenden are editorial cross-references rather than sources; and references are not exhaustive, particularly to Farmer.

Advertiser (Adv.), Free Press, Journal (Jour.), News, Post, Times, Tribune (Trib.), etc., are Detroit newspapers
Andrews AIM—Wayne Andrews, *Architecture in Michigan*, Det., WSUP, 1967
Bald, Det.—F. Clever Bald, *Detroit's First American Decade*, Ann Arbor, UMP, 1948
Bald, Mich.—F. C. Bald, *Michigan in Four Centuries*, N.Y., Harper, 1954
Barcus, Det.—Frank Barcus, *All Around Detroit*, Det., Barcus, 1939
Beasley, Det.—Norman Beasley and George W. Stark, *Made in Detroit*, N.Y., Putnam, 1957
Bingay, Det.—Malcolm W. Bingay, *Detroit is my own Home Town*, Indianapolis, Bobbs, 1946
Burton, City—Clarence M. Burton, *The City of Detroit, Michigan*, Det., Clarke, 1922, 5 v.
Burton, Det.—C. M. Burton, *When Detroit was Young*, Det., Burton, 1951
Carlisle, Chron.—Frederick Carlisle, *Wayne County . . . Chronography*, Det., Gulley, 1890
Catlin, Det.—George B. Catlin, *The Story of Detroit*, Det., News, 1923
Christ-Janer, Saarinen—Albert Christ-Janer, *Eliel Saarinen*, Chicago, Univ., 1948
Colby, Art—Joy H. Colby, *Art and a City, a History of the Detroit Society of Arts and Crafts*, Det., WSUP, 1956
Condit, Rise—Carl W. Condit, *The Rise of the Skyscraper*, Chicago, Univ., 1952
DAB—*Dictionary of American Biography*, N.Y., Scribner, 1928-58
Det. Dir.—Detroit city directories pub. under various titles by MacCabe, 1837; Wellings, 1845–46; Advertiser, 1850; Shove, 1853; Johnston, 1854–61; Clark, 1863–72; Hubbell, 1873; Weeks, 1874–85; Polk, 1886–

Det. Illus.—Detroit-Illustrated, Det., Hook, 1891

Det. in Hist.—James J. Mitchell, *Detroit in History and Commerce*, Det., Rogers, 1891

DIWS—Rae E. Rips, *Det. in its World Setting*, Det., DPL, 1953

Downing, Newport—Antoinette F. Downing and Vincent J. Scully Jr., *The Architectural Heritage of Newport, Rhode Island*, Cambridge, Harvard, 1952

Farmer, Hist.—Silas Farmer, *History of Detroit and Wayne County and Early Michigan*, Det., Farmer, 1890, 2 v. (other ed.)

Ferry AQ—W. Hawkins Ferry, "The Gothic and Tuscan Revivals in Detroit, 1828–75," *Art Quarterly*, Summer 1946, pp. 234–56

Ferry DIAB—W. H. Ferry, "Representative Detroit Buildings," *DIAB*, Mar. 1943, pp. 45–64

Ferry MSAB—W. H. Ferry, "The Mansions of Grosse Pointe," *MSAB*, Mar. 1956, pp. 5–23

Goodrich, Front.—Calvin Goodrich, *The First Michigan Frontier*, Ann Arbor, UM, 1940

HABSM—Harley J. McKee, *Historic American Buildings Survey: Michigan*, Lansing, HSM, 1967 (repr. fr. *Mich. Hist.*, Mar. 1966, pp. 1–49)

Hall GP—Theodore P. Hall, *Grosse Pointe on Lake Sainte Claire*, Det., Farmer, 1886

Hamlin, Arch.—Talbot F. Hamlin, *Architecture Through the Ages*, N.Y., Putnam, 1940

Hamlin, Gk. Rev.—T. F. Hamlin, *Greek Revival Architecture in America*, N.Y., Oxford, 1944

Hanawalt POL—Leslie L. Hanawalt, *A Place of Light: The History of Wayne State University*, Det., WSUP, 1968

Hitchcock, Rich.—Henry-Russell Hitchcock Jr., *The Architecture of H. H. Richardson and his Times*, N.Y., Little, 1936

Hubbard, Mem.—Bela Hubbard, *Memorials of a Half-Century*, N.Y., Putnam, 1888

Koyl AAD—George S. Koyl, *American Architects Directory*, N.Y., Bowker, 1955

Larkin, Art—Oliver W. Larkin, *Art and Life in America*, N.Y., Rinehart, 1949

Lloyd—Ernest F. Lloyd, son of Gordon W. Lloyd

Malbin, Mrs.—Mrs. Lydia Winston Malbin, daughter of Albert Kahn

Marquis BOD—Albert N. Marquis, *The Book of Detroiters*, Chicago, Marquis, 1908

Mich. Guide—Harold Titus, *Michigan: A Guide to the Wolverine State*, N.Y., Oxford, 1941

Moore GP—Kenneth L. Moore, MS. "History of Grosse Pointe," 1950 (Grosse Pointe Pub. Lib.)

Nelson, Kahn—George Nelson, *Industrial Architecture of Albert Kahn*, N.Y., Arch., 1939

Nevins, Ford—Allan Nevins, *Ford; the Times, the Man, the Company*, N.Y., Scribner, 1954

Nevins, Ford, 2—A. Nevins and Frank E. Hill, *Ford . . . 1915–33*, N.Y., Scribner, 1957

Nevins, Ford, 3—A. Nevins and F. E. Hill, *Ford . . . 1933–62*, N.Y., Scribner, 1962

Newcomb, Arch.—Rexford Newcomb, *Architecture of the Old Northwest Territory*, Chicago, Univ., 1950

Palmer, Det.—Friend Palmer, *Early Days in Detroit*, Det., Hunt, 1906

Pevsner, Pion.—Nikolaus Pevsner, *Pioneers of Modern Design*, N.Y., Simon, 1949

Pickens AQ—Buford L. Pickens, "Early City Plans for Detroit," *Art Qu.*, Winter 1943, pp. 35–50

Pickens AR—B. L. Pickens, "Treasure Hunting at Detroit," *Architectural Review* (Lon.), Dec. 1944, pp. 169–76

Pound, Det.—Arthur Pound, *Detroit, Dynamic City*, N.Y., Appleton, 1940

Quaife, Det.—Milo M. Quaife, *This is Detroit*, Det., WUP, 1951

Quaife, Mich.—M. M. Quaife and Sidney Glazer, *Michigan*, N.Y., Prentice, 1948

Robinson FIA—Francis W. Robinson, "Detroit, 1701–1840," *The French in America*, Det., DIA, 1951, pp. 185–202

Ross, Det.—Robert B. Ross and George B. Catlin, *Landmarks of Detroit*, Det., News, 1898

Shaw, Call—Virginia W. V. Shaw, *O, Call Back Yesterday*, Det., Herold, 1936–37, 2 v.

Simonds, Ford—William A. Simonds, *Henry Ford; his Life, his Work, his Genius*, Indianapolis, Bobbs, 1943

Tallmadge, Arch.—Thomas E. Tallmadge, *The Story of Architecture in America*, N.Y., Norton, 1936

Tallmadge, Chi.—T. E. Tallmadge, *Architecture in Old Chicago*, Chicago, Univ., 1941

Warner, Det.—Charles F. Warner, *Picturesque Detroit and Environs*, Northampton, Picturesque, 1893

Westcott, Cent.—Thompson Westcott, *Centennial Portfolio*, Philadelphia, Hunter, 1876

Withey, Dict.—Henry F. and Elsie R. Withey, *Biographical Dictionary of American Architects*, Los Angeles, New Age, 1956

Woodford, Cass—Frank B. Woodford, *Lewis Cass*, New Brunswick, Rutgers, 1950

Woolfenden CAID—William E. Woolfenden, MS. "A Study of Nineteenth Century Church Architecture in Detroit, Michigan," Det. 1941 (WSU Lib.)

Notes

Chapter 1

1 I have relied for historical background mainly on *Bald, Mich.,* & *Quaife, Mich.*
2 *Mich. Guide,* pp. 25–26.
3 Quoted, Wilbert B. Hinsdale, *Primitive Man in Mich.,* UMP, 1925, p. 19.
4 *Hubbard, Mem.,* p. 228.
5 *A New Discovery of a Vast Country in America,* London, 1699, p. 61.
6 *The Western Country in the 17th Cent.,* Chicago, 1947, pp. 8–10.
7 *Catlin, Det.,* pp. 5–6.
8 Glenn G. Stille, "The Indians of Cadillac's Det.," *DHSB,* Nov. 1955, pp. 4–8.
9 Jacques C. Sabrevois de Bleury, "Memoir on the Savages of Canada as Far as the Mississippi River," *Wisc. Hist. Coll.,* v. 16, 1902, pp. 363–76.
10 Reuben G. Thwaites, *The Jesuit Relations,* Cleveland, v. 69, 1900, p. 305.
11 *Robinson FIA,* p. 192, no. 522.
12 *Goodrich, Front.,* p. 58.
13 *Farmer, Hist.,* pp. 367, 529–30.
14 *Robinson FIA,* p. 190, no. 514 (cf. 512).
15 See *Burton, Det.,* pp. 22–23.
16 *Catlin, Det.,* p. 10.
17 *Farmer, Hist.,* p. 374.
18 *Goodrich, Front.,* p. 78.
19 Cadillac, *Western Country,* pp. 10–11 n.
20 John Drury, *Midwest Heritage,* N.Y., 1948, p. 64.
21 *Hubbard, Mem.,* p. 131.
22 *Farmer, Hist.,* pp. 368–69.
23 *Quaife, Det.,* p. 15.
24 *Trib.,* 2 Oct. 1886.
25 *Farmer, Hist.,* p. 372.
26 *Jour.,* 1 Feb. 1890.
27 *Bald, Det.,* p. 18.
28 *Palmer, Det.,* p. 24.
29 *Goodrich, Front.,* p. 105 n.
30 *Burton, Det.,* pp. 24–25.
31 *Robinson FIA,* p. 192, no. 521.
32 *Bald, Mich.,* p. 81.
33 *Robinson FIA,* p. 191, no. 520.

34 *Pickens AQ,* p. 38.
35 *Bald, Det.,* pp. 31, 41, 92.
36 Milo M. Quaife, *The John Askin Papers,* DPL, 1928, pp. 7–15.
37 *Hall GP,* p. 77.
38 *Ross, Det.,* pp. 255–56.
39 *News Trib.,* 22 May 1898.
40 *Bald, Det.,* p. 39.
41 *Robinson FIA,* p. 192, no. 523.
42 *Pickens AQ,* pp. 39–45.
43 *Farmer, Hist.,* pp. 472–73.
44 *Burton, Det.,* p. 96.
45 Quaife, *Askin Papers,* p. 15.
46 *Free Press,* 19 Feb. 1876.
47 *Pittsburg Commonwealth,* 12 Aug. 1807.
48 *Newcomb, Arch.,* p. 114.
49 See legend on Hurd-Martin's bird's-eye news of Det. in 1818, Det., 1906.
50 *Woodford, Cass,* p. 115.
51 *Sketches of a Tour to the Lakes,* Baltimore, 1827, pp. 113–14.
52 *Carlisle, Chron.,* pp. 48–50.
53 *Sun. News,* 29 Mar. 1891.
54 *Hubbard, Mem.,* pp. 132–33.
55 *Robinson FIA,* p. 196, no. 526.
56 See Palmer scrapbook 19: 67 (BHC)
57 *Det. Sat. Night,* 28 May 1923.
58 *Masonic World,* Apr. 1947, p. 9.
59 M. M. Quaife in *DAB,* v. 3, p. 446.
60 *Woodford, Cass,* pp. 122–39.
61 Henry R. Schoolcraft, *Jour. of Travels,* Albany, 1821, p. 383.
62 *Woodford, Cass,* p. 128.
63 *Woodford, Cass,* pp. 146–47.
64 Thomas L. McKenney & James Hall, *The Indian Tribes of North America,* Edinburgh, 1933, p. 98.
65 Edsel K. Rintala, *Douglass Houghton,* WUP, 1954, pp. 10–68.
66 *Hubbard, Mem.,* pp. 21, 66.
67 *Hubbard, Mem.,* p. 132.
68 *Hubbard, Mem.,* p. 225.
69 *Catlin, Det.,* pp. 266–68.

70 Robert F. Bauman, "Kansas, Canada or Starvation," *Mich. Hist.*, Sept. 1952, pp. 293, 297.
71 *Farmer, Hist.*, p. 225.

Chapter 2

1 *Bald, Mich.*, pp. 145–46.
2 *Bald, Mich.*, pp. 152–53.
3 *Palmer, Det.*, p. 232.
4 *Catlin, Det.*, p. 259.
5 *Bald, Mich.*, pp. 151–56.
6 *Burton, Det.*, p. 51.
7 *Bald, Mich.*, pp. 175–82.
8 Wilfred B. Shaw, *A Short Hist. of the Univ. of Mich.*, Ann Arbor, 1934, p. 24.
9 *Farmer, Hist.*, pp. 728–32.
10 *Robinson FIA*, p. 197, no. 527.
11 See *Quaife, Det.*, p. 168.
12 See A. Hyatt Verrill, *Along New England Shores*, N.Y., 1936, pp. 36, 149, 184.
13 *Hamlin, Arch.*, pp. 563–64.
14 *Free Press*, 28 Aug. 1860; for hotel, see *Quaife, Det.*, p. 67.
15 *Palmer, Det.*, p. 782.
16 *Farmer, Hist.*, p. 376.
17 See John Drury, *Midwest Heritage*, N.Y., 1948, p. 144.
18 Emil Lorch, "The Archit. of the Indian Agency House," *Mich. Hist.*, Mar. 1956, pp. 56–59.
19 Mentor L. Williams, "They Wrote Home About It," UM Alumni Assoc. *Qu. Rev.*, Summer 1945, pp. 337–38.
20 George W. Pierson, *Tocqueville & Beaumont in America*, N.Y., 1938, p. 230.
21 *Society in America*, London, 1837, p. 313.
22 *Farmer, Hist.*, pp. 480–85.
23 *Woolfenden CAID*, p. 6.
24 *Farmer, Hist.*, p. 606.
25 *Woolfenden CAID*, p. 4.
26 *Farmer, Hist.*, p. 533.
27 *Robinson FIA*, p. 197, no. 528.
28 *Newcomb, Arch.*, p. 121.
29 *Farmer, Hist.*, p. 539.
30 *HABSM*, p. 48.
31 *Woolfenden CAID*, p. 11.
32 Charles A. Place, *Charles Bulfinch*, Boston, 1925, pp. 127–31.
33 At UD. See George S. May, *Pictorial Hist. of Mich.*, Grand Rapids, 1967, p. 219.
34 *HABSM*, p. 47; *Mich. Guide*, p. 271.
35 *DHSB*, July 1956, pp. 4–7.
36 *Hamlin, Arch.*, pp. 562–76.
37 William W. Bishop, "Judge Woodward and the Catholepistemiad," UM Alumni Assoc. *Qu. Rev.*, Summer 1945, pp. 323–36.
38 *Farmer, Hist.*, pp. 473–75.
39 *Hamlin, Gk. Rev.*, p. 291.
40 *Bald, Mich.*, p. 253.
41 *Quaife, Det.*, p. 138.
42 Richard R. Elliott, "Capt. Alpheus White of Det. During the Thirties," *Mich. Pion. & Hist. Coll.*, v. 26, 1894, pp. 267–72.
43 *Woolfenden CAID*, p. 8.
44 *Farmer, Hist.*, p. 595.
45 *Det. Dir.*, 1850, p. 45.

46 *Woolfenden CAID*, p. 13.
47 *Farmer, Hist.*, p. 566.
48 *Farmer, Hist.*, p. 626.
49 *Woolfenden CAID*, p. 14.
50 *Quaife, Det.*, p. 130.
51 *Farmer, Hist.*, pp. 859, 867.
52 *Farmer, Hist.*, v. 2, p. 1034.
53 M. Woolsey Campau, "The Trowbridge House," *DHSB*, May 1948, pp. 5–7.
54 M. M. Quaife, "The Abbotts of Det.," *DHSB*, Feb. 1945, p. 12.
55 *Palmer, Det.*, p. 737.
56 Palmer scrapbook 3: 85 (BHC).
57 *Hamlin, Gk. Rev.*, p. 292.
58 *Burton, City*, v. 3, pp. 24–30.
59 *Sun. Trib.*, 25 Jan. 1914.
60 *Palmer, Det.*, p. 752.
61 *HABSM*, p. 49.
62 *Free Press*, 18 Aug. 1946.
63 M. Woolsey Campau, "The Sibley House," *DHSB*, May 1948, pp. 8-9.
64 *HABSM*, p. 49.
65 *Farmer, Hist.*, p. 415.
66 *News*, 29 Aug. 1926; *Trib.*, 19 Aug. 1906.
67 Henry D. Brown, "The Biddle House," DHS ser. of hist. repro.
68 *Catlin, Det.*, p. 370.
69 *Farmer, Hist.*, pp. 898–900.
70 *Quaife, Mich.*, pp. 239–41.
71 *Hamlin, Gk. Rev.*, p. 290.

Chapter 3

1 D. D. Runes & H. G. Schrickel, *Ency. of the Arts*, N.Y., 1946, p. 865.
2 *Hamlin, Arch.*, pp. 577–82.
3 *Palmer, Det.*, pp. 987–91.
4 *Farmer, Hist.*, p. 581; *Woolfenden CAID*, p. 19.
5 Letter, 12 July 1827, N. Moon to James Abbott (St. Paul's P.E. Church MSS., BHC).
6 Richard R. Elliott, "Judge Robert T. Elliott," *Mich. Pion. & Hist. Coll.*, v. 26, 1896, pp. 553–68.
7 *Daily Adv.*, 22 Dec. 1849; both *HABSM*, pp. 16, 48, & *Woolfenden CAID*, p. 23, apparently on inconclusive evidence, give it to Albert Jordan.
8 George H. Stowits, *Hist. of the 100th Regt. of N.Y. State Volunteers*, Buffalo, 1870, p. 386.
9 John T. Frederick, *Illinois Guide*, Chicago, 1939, p. 339.
10 *Farmer, Hist.*, p. 584.
11 *Daily Adv.*, 8 Oct. 1855; given to O. & A. Jordan by both *Ferry AQ*, p. 238, & *Woolfenden CAID*, p. 24.
12 Everard M. Upjohn, *Richard Upjohn*, N.Y., 1939, fig. 54.
13 See photo of interior (BHC).
14 *Free Press*, 2 Aug. 1901.
15 See Johnston's *Det. Dirs.* & Geer's *Hartford Dirs.*
16 *Free Press*, 17 Nov. 1855; *HABSM*, pp. 46–47; drawings at DIA bear name of firm.
17 See A. H. Gardner, *Outline of English Archit.*, London, 1947, no. 41B.

18 *Woolfenden CAID*, p. 25, cites it as "the finest example of Gothic Revival in Det."

19 Drawing of interior bears names O. & A. Jordan; see also *Det. Dir.* 1855–56, p. 39; *Woolfenden CAID*, p. 27.

20 *News*, 2 Oct. 1903; see also *Det. Dir.*, 1856–57.

21 *Trib.*, 27 Apr. 1860; *Andrews AIM*, no. 23; *HABSM*, p. 48; *Woolfenden CAID*, p. 27.

22 *Farmer, Hist.*, pp. 585–86.

23 *News*, 15 June 1937.

24 *Free Press*, 25 Dec. 1904.

25 Basil F. S. Clarke, *Church Builders of the 19th Cent.*, London, 1938, pp. 158–59.

26 Lloyd, v.i.

27 Given to DIA by E. F. Lloyd; cf. Augustus Pugin, *Gothic Ornaments*, London, 1844.

28 Clarke, *Builders*, pp. 128–30; George G. Scott, *Personal & Prof. Recollections*, London, 1879, p. 175.

29 *Andrews AIM*, no. 24; *HABSM*, p. 46; *Woolfenden CAID*, p. 28 (also cites church of 1845 by Joseph Busby, p. 21).

30 *Free Press*, 9 Apr. 1863.

31 *Adv. & Trib.*, 16 Nov. 1867; *Woolfenden CAID*, p. 29.

32 *Free Press*, 9 May 1936; *News*, 7 June 1936.

33 Upjohn, *Upjohn*, pp. 178–80.

34 Designation of Lloyd's churches outside Det. was given by E. F. Lloyd, v.i.

35 *Ferry AQ*, fig. 9.

36 *Ferry AQ*, fig. 11.

37 *Ferry AQ*, fig. 10.

38 *Andrews AIM*, no. 13.

39 *Nat. Cyc. of Amer. Biog.*, v. 18, N.Y., 1922, p. 43; *Woolfenden CAID*, p. 32, gives F. X. Himpler as archt. (cites *Post & Trib.*, 9 Nov. 1882), as does *Hist. & Dict. of Churches in U.S.*, Det., 1877, p. 76; *News*, 13 Oct. 1889, gives James Himpler; *Ferry AQ*, fig. 8, & John A. Russell, *The Germanic Influence in the Making of Mich.*, UD, 1927, p. 287, give William Himpel; church's *100 Years of Service 1856–1956*, n.p., says J. X. Himpler; Francis G. Himpler is sole Himpler (there is no Himpel) in *Withey, Dict.*, p. 288.

40 *Larkin, Art*, pp. 172–74.

41 *The Archit. of Country Houses*, N.Y., 1851, pp. 26–27.

42 Carl Carmer, *The Hudson*, N.Y., 1939, pp. 234–35.

43 *Country Houses*, p. 101.

44 *Free Press*, 22 Oct. 1905.

45 *Farmer, Hist.*, pp. 374, 395.

46 *Farmer, Hist.*, p. 382.

47 *Andrews AIM*, no. 12.

48 Mrs. Louis P. Hall, his daughter, v.i.

49 *Country Houses*, p. 29.

50 *Det. Dir.*, 1850, p. 53.

51 *Daily Adv.*, 21 July 1851.

52 *Farmer, Hist.*, pp. 520–23.

53 *Palmer, Det.*, p. 985.

54 *Farmer, Hist.*, p. 359.

55 Roger H. Newton, *Town & Davis, Archts.*, N.Y., 1942, pp. 244–45.

56 Henry-R. Hitchcock Jr., *Rhode Island Archit.*, Providence, 1939, p. 48.

57 *Country Houses*, pp. 285–86.

58 Newton, *Town & Davis*, pp. 268–69.

59 Mrs. Alanson Brooks, his daughter, v.i.

60 *Free Press*, 14 June 1896.

61 MS. letter, 30 Aug. 1853, Bela Hubbard to A. J. Davis (Metropolitan Museum of Art).

62 *Andrews AIM*, illus. C (drawing of 1854).

63 See *Det. Art Loan Catalog*, Det., 1883.

64 See MS. account book of A. J. Davis, p. 150 (Met. Mus.); cf. *Andrews AIM*, illus. B (drawing of 1853).

65 See Newton, *Town & Davis*, p. 24.

66 *News Trib.*, 28 June 1896.

67 See MS. account book, p. 135; cf. *Andrews AIM*, illus. A (drawing of 1852).

68 *Shaw, Call*, pp. 88–89.

69 *Shaw, Call*, pp. 90–91.

70 *Shaw, Call*, pp. 100–01.

71 Hitchcock, *R. I. Archit.*, p. 49.

72 Newton, *Town & Davis*, p. 247.

73 *Trib.*, 21 Dec. 1913.

74 *Daily Adv.*, 29 Mar. 1858.

75 *Catlin, Det.*, pp. 498–99.

76 *Det. Dir.*, 1859, pp. 25–26; *Free Press*, 11 Oct. 1857; *Daily Adv.*, 18 May 1858; *Ferry AQ*, fig. 17; *HABSM*, p. 46.

77 *Hamlin, Gk. Rev.*, pp. 106–08.

78 *Det. Dir.*, 1857–58, p. 98.

79 *Free Press*, 14 Aug. 1857.

80 *Daily Adv.*, 28 Mar. 1853; *Woolfenden CAID*, p. 14.

81 *A Half-Cent. Hist. of the Farmington Ave. Congregational Church . . . in Hartford, Conn.*, n.d., pp. 19–24.

82 See *Connecticut* (Amer. Guide Ser.), Boston, 1938, illus. bet. pp. 150–51.

83 *Daily Adv.*, 8 Oct. 1855.

84 *Daily Democrat & Inquirer*, 8 Sept. 1855; *Woolfenden CAID*, p. 16.

85 *Free Press*, 11 Nov. 1860.

Chapter 4

1 *Bald, Mich.*, pp. 226–28.

2 *Quaife, Mich.*, pp. 218–19.

3 *Quaife, Mich.*, pp. 228–32.

4 *Farmer, Hist.*, p. 802.

5 *Catlin, Det.*, pp. 650–51.

6 *Catlin, Det.*, pp. 651–53.

7 *Burton, City*, pp. 545–49.

8 *Catlin, Det.*, pp. 545, 650.

9 *Farmer, Hist.*, pp. 773–79.

10 *Catlin, Det.*, p. 593.

11 *Pound, Det.*, pp. 225–57.

12 MS. (Harvard Univ. Lib.).

13 *Free Press*, 18 Aug. 1882.

14 *Free Press*, 10 Jan. 1869.

15 MS. diary of Edith Ferry, daughter of D. M. Ferry.

16 *Arch. Details*, N.Y., 1873.

17 *Homes of America*, N.Y., 1879, p. 148.

18 *Free Press*, 29 Aug. 1880.

19 H.-R. Hitchcock, *Early Victorian Archit. in Britain*, New Haven, 1954, p. 202.

20 *HABSM*, p. 46.

21 *Post*, 4 July 1871.

22 *Adv. & Trib.*, 9 June 1869.

23 *Free Press*, 15 Jan. 1908; *Scribner's*, Oct. 1928, p. 396.

24 MS. letter, 7 Nov. 1929, John M. Donaldson to C. M. Burton (BHC).

25 *Farmer, Hist.*, p. 312.

26 Charles R. Tuttle, *Gen. Hist. of the State of Mich.*, Det., 1873, pp. 540–42.

27 Ihna T. Frary, *They Built the Capitol*, Richmond, 1940, pp. 226–27.

28 Albert T. E. Gardner, *Yankee Stonecutters*, N.Y., 1945, p. 71; e.g., Bela Hubbard's Ruth Gleaning, T. W. Palmer's Nydia, & H. S. Pingree's Lost Pleiad, all now at DIA.

29 *Free Press*, 30 Mar. 1869.

30 *Adv.*, 4 May 1868.

31 *Adv.*, 13 Mar. 1869.

32 *Det. in Hist.*, pp. 114–15.

33 *Det. Illus.*, p. 170.

34 *Free Press*, 14–15 Feb. 1871.

35 *Trib.*, 11 Sept. 1875.

36 *Free Press*, 17 Dec. 1876.

37 Emil Lorch, v.i.

38 *Farmer, Hist.*, p. 483; *Quaife, Det.*, p. 70.

39 *Det. Illus.*, p. 149.

40 *Hist. of Hillsdale County, Mich.*, Philadelphia, 1879, pp. 90–93.

41 *HABSM*, pp. 55–56.

42 *Cyc. of Mich.*, N.Y., 1900, pp. 314–15; George D. Mason, v.i.

43 *Free Press*, 31 July 1898.

44 *Farmer, Hist.*, p. 425.

45 Clarence B. Smith, his son, v.a.

46 *Free Press*, 15 Dec. 1876.

47 *Farmer, Hist.*, p. 439.

48 *Farmer, Hist.*, p. 402.

49 *Woodford, Cass*, pp. 218–219.

50 Lloyd, v.i.

51 *Post*, 27 May 1869.

52 Hugh Morrison, *Louis Sullivan*, N.Y., 1935, p. 284.

53 *Free Press*, 17 Oct. 1875.

54 *Free Press*, 15 Sept. 1876.

55 *Carlisle, Chron.*, p. 297.

56 Cf. *Hints*, Boston, 1872, pl. 26.

57 George D. Mason, v.i.

58 *Hamlin, Arch.*, pp. 586–87.

59 Hitchcock, "Victorian Monuments of Commerce," *Arch. Rev.* (Lon.), Feb. 1949, pp. 61–74.

60 *Stones of Venice*, Boston, n.d., p. 291.

61 *Stones of Venice*, pp. 68–72.

62 *Larkin, Art*, p. 244.

63 *Tallmadge, Arch.*, pp. 150–51.

64 *Free Press*, 20 July 1899, 15 Dec. 1876.

65 *Free Press*, 19 Dec. 1876.

66 *Free Press*, 18 Aug. 1882.

67 *Eve. News*, 6 June 1882.

68 Lloyd, v.a.

69 *Free Press*, 22 Apr. 1879.

70 *Free Press*, 2 Jan. 1886.

71 *News*, 7 Mar. 1937.

72 Frank B. Woodford & Philip P. Mason, *Harper of Det.*, WSUP, 1964, p. 164.

73 *Carlisle, Chron.*, pp. 443–44.

74 *Free Press*, 23 Jan. 1887.

75 *Post & Trib.*, 19 May 1878.

76 Clarence B. Smith, v.i.

77 *Woolfenden CAID*, p. 37 (also cites 1845 church by Robert T. Elliott, p. 9).

78 John A. Russell, *The Germanic Influence in the Making of Mich.*, UD, 1927, p. 287.

79 Lloyd (v.a.) was of the opinion that it must have been designed by John Pearce, an Englishman who was G. W. Lloyd's partner at the time, since it was so unlike any of his other work; cf. *Woolfenden CAID*, p. 35.

80 Walter H. Kilham, *Boston after Bulfinch*, Cambridge, Mass., 1946, p. 77; pl. 29.

81 *News*, 8 Dec. 1891; *Quaife, Det.*, p. 128; *Woolfenden CAID*, p. 31.

82 Emil Lorch, "William C. Rohns," *MSAB*, 2 Apr. 1946, pp. 1–3.

83 *Mich. Guide*, pp. 271–72.

84 Carroll L. V. Meeks, *The Railroad Station*, New Haven, 1956, pp. 21–24; figs. 92, 109, 133.

85 *Hamlin, Arch.*, p. 588.

86 *Illus. of Iron Archit. Made by the Arch. Iron Works of the City of New York*, N.Y., 1865.

87 *Cast Iron Buildings, their Construction & Advantages*, N.Y., 1856, pp. 4, 9.

88 *Free Press*, 6 Mar. 1874.

89 *Free Press*, 4 Dec. 1898.

90 "Sugaring off the Palms Millions," *Mich. Mfr. & Fin. Rec.*, 10 Nov. 1923.

91 *News Trib.*, 14 July 1895.

92 *Det. in Hist.*, pp. 65–66.

93 *Free Press*, 24 Nov. 1893.

94 *Free Press*, 17 Mar. 1883.

95 *Free Press*, 28 Apr. 1894.

96 *Eve. News*, 5 May 1892.

97 Det. Cornice & Slate Co., v.i.

98 *Farmer, Hist.*, p. 760.

99 Richard H. Howland & Eleanor P. Spencer, *The Archit. of Baltimore*, Baltimore, 1953, p. 139.

100 *Free Press*, 20 Jan. 1887; cf. *Woolfenden CAID*, p. 32.

101 *Pevsner, Pion.*, pp. 77–78.

102 *News*, 9 Feb. 1935.

103 *Pevsner, Pion.*, pp. 32–35.

104 *Free Press*, 2 Sept. 1882; *Quaife, Det.*, p. 150.

105 *News*, 26 May 1889.

106 *Carlisle, Chron.*, pp. 440–41.

107 *Burton, City*, v. 3, pp. 274–77.

108 *Inland Archt.*, Nov. 1887.

109 *Farmer, Hist.*, pp. 360–61.

110 *Free Press*, 1 Sept. 1883.

111 *Det. Art Loan Catalog*, Det., Eby, 1883.

112 *Free Press*, 29 Dec. 1869.

113 Hitchcock, *Victorian Archit.*, p. 31.

114 *Archit. of Country Houses*, N.Y., 1856, pp. 123–25.

115 *Downing, Newport*, pp. 127, 133–35.

116 *Shaw, Call,* pp. 28–33.
117 *Hall GP,* p. 38.
118 Emil Lorch, v.a.
119 *Hall GP,* p. 39.
120 Lamb, *Homes,* pp. 205–06.
121 *Farmer, Hist.,* pp. 453, 1151–53.
122 *Hall GP,* p. 94.
123 Gustavus Arnold, "The Remodeling of Chateau de Tonnancour," *MSAB,* June 1956, p. 41.
124 Marie C. W. Hamlin, *Legends of Le Détroit,* Det., 1884, pp. 17–21.
125 Lloyd, qualified v.a.
126 John Maass, *The Gingerbread Age,* N.Y., 1957, p. 167.
127 César Daly, *L'Archit privée au XIXme siècle,* Paris, 1868–72, v. 2, sec. 1, pl. 10.
128 *Westcott, Cent.,* p. 40.

Chapter 5
1 *Westcott, Cent.,* p. 17.
2 *A.A.&.B.N.,* 28 Apr. 1877.
3 *Eve. Jour.,* 18 Dec. 1886.
4 George D. Mason, v.i.
5 *Burton, City,* v. 3, p. 696.
6 *Eve. Jour.,* 9 Sept. 1885.
7 *Shaw, Call,* v. 2, pp. 38–40.
8 *Tallmadge, Arch.,* pp. 168–72.
9 *Tallmadge, Arch.,* pp. 173–75.
10 *Woolfenden CAID,* p. 41.
11 *Woolfenden CAID,* p. 42.
12 *Hitchcock, Rich.,* pp. 262–63.
13 *Woolfenden CAID,* p. 45.
14 *News,* 30 Nov. 1890.
15 Now at DIA.
16 *Burton, City,* v. 3, p. 644.
17 *Free Press,* 30 Jan. 1891; *Woolfenden CAID,* p. 44.
18 *Trib.,* 18 Oct. 1891; *Woolfenden,* p. 44.
19 *Eve. News,* 10 Feb. 1896.
20 *News,* 12 Oct. 1931; *Free Press,* 10 Apr. 1923.
21 *Quaife, Det.,* p. 139.
22 *Trib.,* 18 Oct. 1891; *Woolfenden CAID,* p. 46.
23 *News,* 14 Apr. 1889.
24 *Barcus, Det.,* p. 25.
25 *Free Press,* 5 May 1887.
26 *Eve. Jour.,* 27 Feb. 1886; *Andrews AIM,* no. 27.
27 Mrs. Frances Bagley Wallace, v.i.
28 Charles E. Jenkins, "Mason & Rice," *Arch. Reviewer,* 30 Sept. 1897, pp. 48–79.
29 *Free Press,* 19 Apr. 1891.
30 Albert Kahn, v.i.
31 Donald M. Davies, "Million Dollar Office Boy," *This Week,* 5 May 1940, p. 6.
32 *Beasley, Det.,* pp. 74–78.
33 *Free Press,* 4 Feb. 1894.
34 *News,* 30 Oct. 1887.
35 *Quaife, Det.,* p. 194.
36 *Free Press,* 19 July 1891; *Andrews AIM,* no. 29.
37 Vincent J. Scully, Jr., *The Shingle Style,* New Haven, 1955, pp. 36, 121.
38 *Eve. Jour.,* 25 Feb. 1885.
39 DHS, v.i.
40 *Free Press,* 22 Jan. 1893.
41 *Free Press,* 18 Apr. 1890.
42 Carroll L. V. Meeks, *The Railroad Station,* New Haven, 1956, p. 146.
43 *Free Press,* 12 Aug. 1894, 18 June 1890.
44 *Burton, City,* pp. 851–52.
45 *Free Press,* 22 Aug. 1888.
46 *Catlin, Det.,* p. 564.
47 *Det. Sat. Night,* 2 Aug. 1913.
48 *Times,* 27 May 1885? (cf. Det. Mus. of Art, *Cat. of the Scripps Coll.,* Det., 1889, p. iii).
49 "The 100th Anniv. of James Edmund Scripps," *DIAB,* Mar. 1935, pp. 73–75.
50 *Free Press,* 13 Nov. 1891, 26 Nov. 1939.
51 *Hitchcock, Rich.,* p. 78.
52 *Trib.,* 4 Aug. 1888.
53 *Hitchcock, Rich.,* pp. 282–83.
54 Emil Lorch, v.a.; *Det. in Hist.,* p. 50.
55 *Free Press,* 7 Oct. 1887.
56 Lloyd, v.i.
57 *Eve. News,* 16 Sept. 1891.
58 *Free Press,* 10 Dec. 1942.
59 *Free Press,* 3 Nov. 1889.
60 *Quaife, Det.,* p. 90.
61 See construction drawings at DIA.
62 *Pickens AR,* p. 176.
63 *Tallmadge, Chi.,* pp. 193–97.
64 *Condit, Rise,* p. 140.
65 *Eve. News,* 1 May 1895.
66 *News Trib.,* 12 Aug. 1894.
67 Emil Lorch, "William C. Rohns," *MSAB,* 2 Apr. 1946, pp. 1–3.
68 *News Trib.,* 4 Oct. 1896.
69 *News Trib.,* 2 June 1895.
70 *Tallmadge, Chi.,* pp. 203–05.
71 *Condit, Rise,* p. 147.
72 *Tallmadge, Arch.,* p. 181.
73 *Jour.,* 20 Jan. 1915.
74 Christopher Tunnard & Henry H. Reed, *American Skyline,* N.Y., 1956, pp. 108–11.
75 *Burton, City,* pp. 454–57, 430–34.
76 Burton scrapbook, v. 2, p. 40 (BHC).
77 *Burton, City,* p. 461.
78 *Jour.,* 17 Feb. 1887.
79 *News,* 25 June 1954; Det. Com. of Parks & Boulevards, *Annual Rep.,* 1895–96, p. 8.
80 *Peculiarities of American Cities,* Philadelphia, 1883, p. 184.
81 *Burton, City,* pp. 437–38.
82 *Tallmadge, Arch.,* pp. 187–88.
83 Scully, *Shingle Style,* pp. 71, 88.
84 Office of Donaldson & Meier, v.i.
85 *Free Press,* 3 Mar. 1908.
86 Boat Club *News,* Dec. 1952, pp. 3–4.
87 Jenkins, "Donaldson & Meier," *Arch. Reviewer,* 30 Sept. 1897, pp. 116–37.
88 Dexter M. Ferry Jr., v.i.
89 *Hall GP,* p. 26.
90 *Moore GP,* pp. 10–11.
91 *Free Press,* 13 Nov. 1887.
92 *Sun. News Trib.,* 6 June 1897.
93 Louis Kamper, v.i.
94 *Ross, Det.,* pp. 628–29.
95 *Free Press,* 26 Sept. 1919.
96 *Free Press,* 13 Sept. 1921.
97 *Andrews AIM,* no. 28.

98 *News*, 26 Feb. 1956.
99 *News*, 26 Nov. 1943.
100 Scully, *Shingle Style*, pp. 22–37.
101 Lawrence G. White, *Sketches & Designs by Stanford White*, N.Y., 1920, pp. 6–22.
102 *Free Press*, 12 June 1898.
103 Kenneth L. Moore, v.i.
104 *Eve. Jour.*, 9 Sept. 1885.
105 Mrs. Margaret Longyear Palmer, v.i.
106 Mrs. Frances Bagley Wallace, v.i.
107 Biog. file (BHC).
108 *Marquis BOD*, p. 260.
109 Mrs. Harley G. Higbie, v.i.
110 Whitney Estate, v.i.
111 *Warner, Det.*, p. 107.
112 *MSAB*, Aug. 1955, p. 21.
113 *Andrews AIM*, no. 25.
114 *Hamlin, Gk. Rev.*, pp. 260–62.

Chapter 6

1 *News*, 5 Feb. 1915.
2 *Nevins, Ford*, pp. 154–57.
3 *Pound, Det.*, pp. 267–75.
4 *Burton, City*, pp. 566–69.
5 *Pound, Det.*, pp. 276–81.
6 *Burton, City*, pp. 1504–08.
7 Albert Kahn, "Industrial Archit.," *MSAB*, 27 Dec. 1939, pp. 5–7.
8 *Nevins, Ford*, pp. 265–66.
9 Unidentified clipping (DPL).
10 MS. "Saga of Packard, 1899–1949," p. 16 (Automotive Hist. Coll., DPL).
11 *Times*, 12 Nov. 1922.
12 *Burton, City*, pp. 557–62.
13 *News Trib.*, 5 May 1912.
14 *Burton, City*, pp. 581–82.
15 Saga of Packard, pp. 12–16.
16 *Motor Age*, 14 Apr. 1904.
17 Sigfried Giedion, *Space, Time & Archit.*, Cambridge, Mass., 1943, pp. 247, 250.
18 Ada L. Huxtable, "The Packard Plant," *Progressive Archit.*, Oct. 1957.
19 *Nelson, Kahn*, p. 17.
20 *News Trib.*, 20 Sept. 1908.
21 *Marquis BOD*, p. 259.
22 *News*, 5 Nov. 1942.
23 *Engineering Record*, 17 Nov. 1906.
24 *Burton, City*, pp. 572–73.
25 *Trib.*, 23 Nov. 1903.
26 *Trib.*, July/Aug. 1904? (clipping, DPL).
27 *Free Press*, 28 June 1914.
28 *Nevins, Ford*, p. 340.
29 *Bingay, Det.*, p. 307.
30 *Nevins, Ford*, pp. 451–52.
31 *Nevins, Ford*, pp. 453–76, 587.
32 Hugh Morrison, *Louis Sullivan*, N.Y., 1935, pp. 142–47, 172–74, 194–96.
33 Emil Lorch, "Frank Conger Baldwin," *MSAB*, 15 Jan. 1946, p. 4.
34 *Withey, Dict.*, pp. 33, 578.
35 *Free Press*, 9 Jan. 1910.
36 *Free Press*, 2 May 1915.
37 Leonard K. Eaton, "The Louis Sullivan Spirit in Michigan," *Mich. Alumnus*, 24 May 1958.
38 *Det. Sat. Night*, 14 Aug. 1909.

39 *Free Press*, 10 Mar. 1957.
41 *Western Archt.*, Oct. 1916.
42 *Detroiter*, Jan. 1914; *Andrews AIM*, no. 49.
43 *Free Press*, 3 Sept. 1911.
44 *Tallmadge, Arch.*, pp. 198–99.
45 *Withey, Dict.*, p. 99.
46 Mrs. Lydia Winston Malbin, daughter of Albert Kahn, kindly allowed me to examine his sketchbooks in her possession.
47 *Andrews AIM*, no. 52.
48 *Andrews AIM*, no. 51.
49 Mrs. Malbin, v.i.
50 *Moore GP*, pp. 14–15.
51 *Times*, 3 Dec. 1922.
52 *Free Press*, 30 July 1933.
53 *Free Press*, 9 Apr. 1935.
54 *Det. Sat. Night*, 10 Mar. 1928.
55 *Free Press*, 2 Oct. 1955.
56 *Marquis BOD*, p. 309.
57 Henry E. Candler, sometime owner of the house, kindly allowed me to examine the blueprints.

Chapter 7

1 *Tallmadge, Arch.*, p. 196.
2 Russell Lynes, *The Tastemakers*, N.Y., 1954, p. 140.
3 *The Decoration of Houses*, N.Y., 1919, pp. 197–98.
4 Lawrence G. White, *Sketches & Designs by Stanford White*, N.Y., 1920, pp. 24–26.
5 Wharton, *Decoration*, p. xxii.
6 *The Autobiography of an Idea*, N.Y., 1949, pp. 324–25.
7 *The Life & Times of Charles Follen McKim*, Boston, 1929, pp. 308–09.
8 Vincent J. Scully, *The Shingle Style*, New Haven, 1955, p. 149.
9 Wayne Andrews, *Archit., Ambition & Americans*, N.Y., 1955, p. 186.
10 Albert C. McDonald of George D. Mason & Co., v.i.
11 *Trib.*, 25 Jan. 1914; *Free Press*, 6 Oct. 1957.
12 Charles E. Jenkins, "Mason & Rice," *Arch. Reviewer*, 30 Sept. 1897, pp. 48–79.
13 *Withey, Dict.*, p. 544.
14 Emil Lorch, v.i.
15 *Mich. Guide*, p. 243.
16 *Free Press*, 20 Oct. 1901.
17 *News*, 1 Jan. 1897.
18 White, *White*, p. 19.
19 *Free Press*, 3 July 1898.
20 *Quaife, Det.*, p. 80.
21 *Free Press*, 27 Oct. 1907.
22 *Free Press*, 13 Mar. 1920.
23 *Beasley, Det.*, pp. 13–14.
24 *Trib.*, 26 Oct. 1913.
25 *Det. Sat. Night*, 24 Apr. 1926.
26 *Detroiter*, 2 July 1917.
27 *Hotel Bull.* (Chicago), Jan. 1925.
28 In the possession of Mrs. Malbin.
29 *Bingay, Det.*, p. 23.
30 *Det. Sat. Night*, 3 Feb. 1923.
31 *Mich. Alumnus*, 17 Apr. 1943, p. 339; *Andrews AIM*, no. 53.
32 *Andrews AIM*, no. 48.

33 *Det. Sat. Night,* 14 Oct. 1922.
34 Halsey C. Ives, *The Dream City,* St. Louis, 1893.
35 Charles Moore, *Daniel H. Burnham,* Boston, 1921, pp. 86–87.
36 Moore, *Burnham,* pp. 97, 101–02, 113.
37 Charles Moore, *The Promise of American Archit.,* Washington, 1905, p. 5.
38 *Washington Star,* 12 Jan. 1936.
39 *Free Press,* 11 Nov. 1941.
40 *New York Times,* 3 Mar. 1924.
41 *Amer. Hist. Rev.,* Jan. 1943, pp. 454–55.
42 *News Trib.,* 15 Oct. 1911.
43 Frank B. Woodford, *A Life of Justice Woodward,* E. Lansing, 1953, p. 40.
44 *Preliminary Plan of Det.,* Det. City Plan & Improvement Com., 1915.
45 *Modern Civic Art,* N.Y., 1903, p. 167.
46 Other sculptors: Adolph A. Weinman (Macomb), Henry M. Shrady (Williams), Albert Weinert (Mason).
47 *Free Press,* 17 July 1901.
48 *Free Press,* 24 Aug. 1893.
49 Biog. file (BHC); *MSAB,* 24 Aug. 1937.
50 *Mon. . . . to Commemorate the 200th Anniv. of . . . Det.,* Det., 1900.
51 *Bingay, Det.,* pp. 280–83.
52 *News,* 10 July 1914.
53 *Withey, Dict.,* pp. 233–34.
54 *Art & Archaeology,* Mar. 1924, p. 87.
55 *Andrews AIM,* no. 32.
56 *Mich. Guide,* pp. 256–58.
57 *Andrews AIM,* no. 33.
58 *News,* 27 Apr. 1930.
59 *Burton, City,* p. 853.
60 *Withey, Dict.,* p. 149.
61 *Westcott, Cent.,* p. 1.
62 *Art & Archaeol.,* Mar. 1924, p. 99.
63 E. P. Richardson, "Foreword," *Treasures from the DIA,* Det., 1966, p. 7.
64 *Det. Sat. Night,* 20 Mar. 1926.
65 *DIAB,* Oct. 1919, p. 6.
66 *Marquis BOD,* p. 260.
67 See *The Work of McKim, Mead & White,* N.Y., 1914–17, v. 3, pls. 285, 290.
68 *Downing, Newport,* p. 160; pl. 218.
69 Charles Moore in *DAB,* v. 15, pp. 1–2.
70 Fiske Kimball, *Amer. Archit.,* Indianapolis, 1928, pp. 171–87.
71 *Andrews AIM,* no. 62.
72 *The Place of Art in Civilization,* Washington, 1905, pp. 21–23.
73 Carroll L. V. Meeks, *The Railroad Station,* New Haven, 1956, p. 131.
74 George H. Edgell, *The Amer. Archit. of Today,* N.Y., 1928, p. 345.
75 *Free Press,* 12 Mar. 1922.
76 Prof. Ralph Hammet of UM, v.i.
77 *Mich. Guide,* p. 293.
78 *Free Press,* 2 Mar. 1924.
79 Alan Burnham, "The N.Y. Archit. of Richard M. Hunt," Soc. of Arch. Hist. *Jour.,* May 1952, pp. 11–14.
80 John Drury, *Old Chicago Houses,* Chicago, 1941, pp. 50, 68, 134, 291.
81 *Free Press,* 2 Aug. 1953.
82 *Free Press,* 25 May 1890.

83 *Free Press,* 23 Dec. 1898.
84 *News,* 23 Dec. 1898.
85 *Free Press,* 27 June 1927.
86 George D. Mason, v.i.; cf. Kahn sketchbooks owned by Mrs. Malbin.
87 *Hitchcock, Rich.,* fig. 82.
88 *Andrews AIM,* no. 61.
89 *Free Press,* 13 Apr. 1910.
90 *Landscape Archt.,* Jan. 1947.
91 *Downing, Newport,* p. 162; pl. 228.
92 Edgell, *Amer. Archit.,* pp. 130–31.
93 *Free Press,* 16 Aug. 1959.
94 *MSAB,* Aug. 1956, p. 24.
95 *Ladies' Home Jour.,* Sept. 1957, pp. 60, 176.
96 Det. Athl. Club *News,* Dec. 1935.
97 Garden Club of Amer., *37th Annual Meeting,* Det., 1950, p. 23.

Chapter 8
1 *Pevsner, Pion.,* p. 20.
2 Walter C. Behrendt, *Modern Building,* N.Y., 1937, pp. 51, 55.
3 Paul Bloomfield, *William Morris,* London, 1934, pp. 104–06, 185–86, 242–44.
4 *Colby, Art,* pp. 4–8.
5 Cranbrook Alumni *News,* Apr. 1958.
6 *News,* 11 Apr. 1949.
7 Leonard Bahr, "Printed by Hand," *DPLAF,* Spring 1960, pp. 4–8.
8 *Colby, Art,* p. 13.
9 *Free Press,* 12 Jan. 1941; *News,* 22 Sept. 1957.
10 *Burton, City,* v. 5, p. 576.
11 *Colby, Art,* pp. 11, 15–18, 23–33, 50–51, 57, 67.
12 Behrendt, *Building,* pp. 63–64.
13 *Downing, Newport,* pp. 142–46.
14 *News,* 29 May 1906, 21 Nov. 1926, 24 July 1927, 1 Dec. 1938.
15 *News Trib.,* 13 Sept. 1896; *Jour.,* 11 Mar. 1915.
16 *Jour.,* 27 Jan. 1916; *Burton, City,* v.5, p. 576.
17 Behrendt, *Building,* pp. 65–66.
18 Emil Lorch, "Frank C. Baldwin," *MSAB,* 15 Jan. 1946.
19 *Free Press,* 14 Sept. 1960.
20 *Western Archt.,* Oct. 1916.
21 *New York Times,* 28 Sept. 1950.
22 *Colby, Art,* pp. 17–18.
23 Quoted, ibid. pp. 18–20 (June 1917).
24 *Andrews AIM,* no. 47.
25 *News,* 11 Apr. 1949.
26 Henry S. Booth, v.i.
27 *Colby, Art,* p. 53.
29 *Free Press,* 1 July 1923.
30 *Free Press,* 19 Oct. 1925.
31 *Andrews AIM,* no. 60.
32 *Free Press,* 22 Oct. 1933.
33 *News,* 22 May 1927, 5 Sept. 1941.
34 *Withey, Dict.,* pp. 559–60.
35 William E. Kapp, v.i.
36 *Andrews AIM,* nos. 63–64.
37 *News,* 3 Jan. 1957.
38 *Free Press,* 6 Mar. 1961.
39 Univ. Club *Bull.,* May 1961.
40 Robert O. Derrick, v.i.
41 *Strange Commissions for Henry Ford,* York (Eng.), 1934, p. 21.

42 *Nevins, Ford,* 2, p. 501.
43 William A. Simonds, *Henry Ford & Greenfield Village,* N.Y., 1938, pp. 208–09.
44 Morton, *Strange Com.,* pp. 21–23.
45 *Countryman* (Oxfordshire), Apr. 1931.
46 MS. "Interview with E. J. Cutler," 23 June 1955 (Henry Ford Mus.).
47 *Andrews AIM,* nos. 54–57.
48 *The Edsel B. Ford Lake Shore Estate at Grosse Pointe Shores, Mich.,* Det. (n.d.).
49 *Andrews AIM,* no. 58.
50 Mrs. Alvan Macauley, v.i.
51 *Town & Country,* 1 May 1933; now owned by Alfred R. Glancy Jr.
52 *Trinity Church Det.,* Det. (n.d.), p. 7.
53 *Woolfenden CAID,* p. 30.
54 Ralph A. Cram, *My Life in Archit.,* Boston, 1936, p. 72.
55 *Tallmadge, Arch.,* pp. 257–61.
56 *Andrews AIM,* no. 30.
57 *Free Press,* 16 Apr. 1911.
58 Cram, *Life,* pp. 78–80.
59 *Andrews AIM,* no. 31.
60 *Pathfinding in Cultural & Creative Educ.,* Cranbrook Foundation (n.d.), pp. 41–43.
61 *Afterglow,* Nov. 1927; *Amer. Mag. of Art,* June 1929.
62 *Mich. Catholic,* 3 Mar. 1938; the towers were completed in 1951 by Diehl & Diehl *(MSAB,* Oct. 1957, p. 35).
63 *News,* 2 Dec. 1946.
64 Wirt C. Rowland, MS. "A Letter on Gothic Archit.," pp. 5a–6a, 1–2 (owned by Miss Florence Davies).
65 Miss Florence Davies, v.i.
66 *Free Press,* 22 Nov. 1958.
67 Rowland letter, pp. 7–31.
68 *News,* 30 Nov. 1958.
69 *Ency. Brit.,* 11th ed., 1911, v. 18, p. 100.
70 *Burton, City,* v. 3, p. 15; v. 5, p. 576.
71 *Masonic News,* Nov. 1926; cf. *DIWS,* pp. 248–49.

Chapter 9

1 Banister Fletcher, *A Hist. of Archit.,* London, 1931, pp. 777–78.
2 Albert C. McDonald of George D. Mason & Co., who prepared drawings for both the Bowen & Albert Stephens houses, v.i.
3 *Burton, City,* v. 4, p. 312.
4 *Ladies' Home Jour.,* Sept. 1957, pp. 61, 176–78.
5 Arthur Pound, *Salt of the Earth, Story of Capt. J. B. Ford & Mich. Alkali Co.,* Boston, 1940, pp. 33, 58, 61.
6 Dexter M. Ferry Jr., my father, v.i.
7 *Arch. Review,* Apr. 1919, pp. 89–92.
8 *Times,* 19 July 1931.
9 *Free Press,* 21 June 1931.
10 *News,* 21 June 1931.
11 Paul L. Grigaut & Ernst Scheyer, v.i.
12 *Nevins, Ford,* pp. 583–85.
13 Finis Farr, *Frank Lloyd Wright,* N.Y., 1961, p. 116.
14 MS. letter, E. G. Liebold to Henry Ford, 3 Mar. 1914 (Ford Archives).

15 *Nevins, Ford,* p. 585.
16 MS. letter, M. L. Benedum to Ford, 22 Jan. 1914 (Ford Archives).
17 MS. letter, Fred S. Sly to William Lucking, 9 Mar. 1914 (Ford Archives).
18 MS. letter, Liebold to Ford, 7 Mar. 1914 (Ford Archives).
19 R. Ruddell, MS. "Guide to Fair Lane Papers," 16 Apr. 1952 (Ford Archives).
20 Fletcher, *Archit.,* pp. 773, 778–85.
21 *Pevsner, Pion.,* p. 35.
22 *Town & Country,* 7 Dec. 1912, pp. 43–44.
23 *Bald, Mich.,* pp. 342, 346.
24 *Archit.,* Oct. 1913, pp. 243–45, 254–56; pl. 113–26.
25 Virginia W. B. Shaw, *Memories of Harriet Barnes Newberry,* Chicago, 1944, pp. 62–64.
26 *News,* 8 Oct. 1950.
27 *The Work of Charles A. Platt,* N.Y., 1913, pp. 120–28.
28 Ernest Wilby, v.i.
29 *Nat. Archt.,* Aug. 1946, p. 5.
30 John S. Newberry Jr., v.i.
31 *News,* 26 Sept. 1956.
32 Gustavus Arnold on Chittenden in *MSAB,* Jan. 1957, pp. 44–47.
33 Talmage C. Hughes and Gilbert B. Pingree, v.i.
34 Mrs. B. E. Hutchinson, wife of a later owner, v.i.
35 "Our Domestic Archit.," *Town & Country,* Dec. 1946, p. 110.
36 *Who's Who in Amer.,* 1930–31.
37 *New York Times,* 7 Oct. 1925.
38 *Time,* 6 Sept. 1937.
39 *Free Press,* 3 May 1959.
40 *Free Press,* 4 June 1961.
41 *Mich. Mfr. & Fin. Rec.,* 30 Aug. 1930.
42 Now owned by Walter B. Ford.
43 *Ferry MSAB,* no. 33.
44 Now owned by Roy D. Chapin Jr.
45 Now owned by Mrs. Wendell Anderson.
46 *Ferry MSAB,* no. 43, builder identified.
47 Platt also designed the Allen F. Edwards & Mrs. Arthur McGraw houses.
48 *Det. Sat. Night,* 18 Sept. 1937; Keyes also designed the Dr. J. Stewart Hudson, Mrs. Gilbert Lee, & Robert H. Tannahill houses.
49 Now owned by Allan Shelden III.
50 William C. Richards, *The Last Billionaire, Henry Ford,* N.Y., 1948, pp. 179–84.
51 Kenneth N. Metcalf, librarian, Henry Ford Mus., v.i.
52 William A. Simonds, *Henry Ford & Greenfield Village,* N.Y., 1938, pp. 154–55.
53 *Mich. Guide,* p. 226.

Chapter 10

1 *Catlin, Det.,* pp. 445–46.
2 *Quaife, Det.,* p. 130.
3 *Jour.,* 9 May 1914.
4 *Detroiter,* 14 Sept. 1925.
5 *Detroiter,* 20 Sept. 1926.
6 *Catlin, Det.,* p. 702.
7 *Free Press* and *News,* 15 Aug. 1958.

8 Ben M. Hall, *The Best Remaining Seats,* N.Y., 1961, pp. 136, 141.
9 *Free Press,* 22 Aug. 1926.
10 Hall, *Seats,* p. 142.
11 *Free Press,* 20 Mar. 1927.
12 *Free Press,* 29 Jan. 1928.
13 *Free Press,* 3 Sept. 1928.
14 *Fox News,* Mar. 1928.
15 Hall, *Seats,* p. 110.
16 *Mich. Mfr. & Fin. Rec.,* 27 Oct. 1928. See *American Archt.,* 20 Feb. 1929.
17 *New York Times,* 17 Jan. 1931.
18 *Tallmadge, Arch.,* p. 289.
19 *Tallmadge, Arch.,* p. 292.
20 Sheldon Cheney, *New World Archit.,* N.Y., 1930, p. 144.
21 *The Metropolis of Tomorrow,* N.Y., 1929, p. 78.
22 *Ralph Walker, Archt.,* N.Y., 1957, p. 15.
23 *Koyl AAD,* p. 583.
24 *Arch. Record,* July 1929.
25 *Walker,* p. 21.
26 *Detroiter,* 7 Feb. 1927.
27 William E. Kapp, v.i.
28 *MSAB,* 10 Sept. 1946.
29 MS. "A Letter on Gothic Archit.," (n.d.) p. 26 (coll. Miss Florence Davies).
30 *Det. Sat. Night,* 2 May 1925.
31 *Farmer, Hist.,* p. 463.
32 *Carlisle, Chron.,* pp. 262–63.
33 *Burton, City,* v. 3, pp. 274–75.
34 *Mich. Mfr. & Fin. Rec.,* 15 May 1929.
35 *Free Press,* 20 Dec. 1932.
36 *News,* 31 Mar. 1929.
37 *Mich. Mfr. & Fin. Rec.,* 15 May 1929; *News,* 31 Mar. 1929.
38 J. L. Hudson Co., *For a Greater Det.,* Det., 1927, p. 22.
39 *Free Press,* 4 Mar. 1928.
40 *Metropolis,* p. 46.
41 "Arch. Trend," Md. Acad. of Sci. *Jour.,* Apr. 1931, p. 120.
42 Lee White, *The Det. News, 1873–1917,* Det., 1918, p. 26.
43 Md. Acad. *Jour.,* p. 108.
44 *Nat. Archt.,* Aug. 1946.
45 Ernest Wilby, v.i.
46 Md. Acad. *Jour.,* p. 131.
47 *Andrews AIM,* no. 50.
48 Alfred J., Charles T., Edward F., Frederick J., Howard A., Lawrence P., & William A. Fisher.
49 *News,* 24 Aug. 1927.
50 Md. Acad. *Jour.,* p. 122.
51 Alfred C. Bossom, *Building to the Skies,* N.Y., 1934, p. 62.
52 Cheney, *New World,* p. 154.
53 *News,* 21 June 1950.
54 "Dual-Purpose Plants," *Arch. Forum,* Feb. 1952.
55 *Nevins, Ford,* p. 453.
56 Ada L. Huxtable, "River Rouge Plant," *Progressive Archit.,* Dec. 1958, p. 120.
57 *Nevins, Ford,* pp. 200–09.
58 *Mich. Guide,* p. 275.
59 *Pound, Det.,* p. 293.
60 *Bald, Mich.,* p. 364.

61 *Cadillac Clearing House,* 1 Jan. 1920.
62 Joseph N. French of Albert Kahn Assoc., v.i.
63 *Maxwell Motor Cars* brochure, c. 1914 (DPL).
64 Designated on drawing at Chrysler Corp.
65 John Holmes, MS. "Hist. of Maxwell Orgn." (DPL).
66 MS. "Some Facts About Chrysler Corp." (DPL).
67 *N.Y. Geneal. & Biog. Rec.,* v. 72, 1941, pp. 91–93.
68 MS. "Notes Gathered from Conversation with C. W. Fisher, Charles Walker, etc." (DPL).
69 *Automotive Topics,* 6 Mar. 1926.
70 Plymouth plant, v.i.
71 *Saxon Days* brochure, 1916 (DPL).
72 *Nelson, Kahn,* pp. 48–49.
73 *Nelson, Kahn,* pp. 82–83; *Andrews AIM,* no. 59.
74 *Nevins, Ford,* 2, p. 289.
75 *Nelson, Kahn,* pp. 80–81.
76 *MSAB,* 30 Mar. 1943, p. 31.
77 *Simonds, Ford,* pp. 330–32.
78 *Nevins, Ford,* 3, p. 211.
79 *Christ-Janer, Saarinen,* pp. 4–6.
80 *Christ-Janer, Saarinen,* pp. 7–12.
81 *Christ-Janer, Saarinen,* pp. 13–19.
82 *Christ-Janer, Saarinen,* pp. 32–54, 133.
83 *Christ-Janer, Saarinen,* pp. 54–58.
84 *Christ-Janer, Saarinen,* pp. 59–65.
85 *Crane,* 11 Apr. 1947.
86 *Andrews AIM,* no. 67.
87 *Colby, Art,* p. 17.
88 Cranbrook *Bull.,* Winter 1944–45.
89 *Cranbrook School in Bloomfield Hills* brochure (n.d.).
90 *Andrews AIM,* no. 66.
91 *Christ-Janer, Saarinen,* pp. 70–78.
92 *Andrews AIM,* nos. 69–73.
93 *Christ-Janer, Saarinen,* pp. 71–73.
94 *Andrews AIM,* no. 74.
95 Cranbrook Acad. of Art *Acad. News,* May 1939.
96 *Andrews AIM,* no. 65.
97 *Christ-Janer, Saarinen,* pp. 80–81.

Chapter 11

1 *De America,* Milan, 1954, p. 193 (my tr.).
2 *Arch. Forum,* June 1965.
3 *Andrews AIM,* nos. 76–85.
4 Alfred P. Sloan Jr., *My Years with Gen. Motors,* N.Y., 1964, pp. 259–63.
5 *Look,* 30 Sept. 1958, p. 67.
6 *Free Press,* 13 May 1956.
7 *Andrews AIM,* no. 97.
8 Victor Gruen, *The Heart of Our Cities,* N.Y., 1964, pp. 194, 200–03.
9 *Andrews AIM,* no. 96.
10 *Detroiter,* 30 June 1924.
11 *Christ-Janer, Saarinen,* pp. 59, 62.
12 *Free Press,* 20 May 1944.
13 *Arch. Forum,* Apr. 1949.
14 *Arch. Record,* Nov. 1951.
15 *Arch. Forum,* Dec. 1950.
16 *Time,* 18 Jan. 1963.

17 *Arch. Forum*, Mar. 1950.

18 *Arch. Forum*, Feb. 1957.

19 *Andrews AIM*, no. 91.

20 *Arch. Forum*, May 1957; *Arch. Rec.*, Nov. 1959.

21 *Arch. Rec.*, Aug. 1956; *Progressive Archit.*, Oct. 1958.

22 *Andrews AIM*, nos. 94–95.

23 *Arch. Forum*, May 1963.

24 *Free Press*, 3 Feb. 1965.

25 *Arch. Rec.*, Apr. 1963.

26 *Arch. Forum*, Aug. 1966.

27 See *Arch. Forum*, May 1960.

28 Giffels & Rossetti's *Projects & Activities*, Oct. 1966.

29 *Andrews AIM*, no. 101.

30 C. William Palmer, Edward A. Schilling, Clair W. Ditchy, & Nelson B. Hubbard *(Ferry DIAB*, p. 59).

31 Augustus O'Dell, Thomas H. Hewlett, & Owen A. Luckenbach *(Ferry DIAB*, p.60).

32 *Christ-Janer, Saarinen*, p. 139.

33 *News*, 30 Aug. 1943.

34 *Arch. Forum*, Mar. 1955.

35 *Arch. Forum*, Jan. 1955.

36 *Andrews AIM*, nos. 88–89.

37 *Arch. Forum*, Apr. 1956.

38 *Arch. Forum*, Jan.–Feb. 1967.

39 *Free Press*, 4 Feb. 1965.

40 *Free Press*, 27 Jan. 1963.

41 Crane & Gorwic, *Med. Cen. Progress Rep.*, Det., 1966; cf. *Hanawalt POL*, pp. 339–43, 423.

42 *Free Press*, 4 Feb. 1945.

43 City Plan Com., *Det. Cultural Cen.*, Det., 1965.

43a *Hanawalt POL*, pp. 43, 107, *passim*.

44 *Mich. Guide*, pp. 260–61; cf. *Hanawalt POL*, p. 229.

45 *Pencil Points*, Sept. 1942; cf. *Hanawalt POL*, pp. 234–37.

46 "Suren Pilafian, Archt.," *MSAB*, Feb. 1955, pp. 41–56; cf. *Hanawalt POL*, pp. 263–64.

47 *Free Press*, 11 May 1958.

48 *Andrews AIM*, nos. 92–93; *Hanawalt POL*, pp. 258, 419–21.

49 *Arch. Forum*, Dec. 1957.

50 *Free Press*, 28 Sept. 1958.

51 Minoru Yamasaki, "The College of Educ. Bldg.," WSU *Graduate Comment*, Apr. 1961.

52 *Arch. Forum*, Sept. 1961.

53 Douglas R. Sherman, MS. "WSU Campus Development & Urban Renewal," Jan. 1965 (WSU Lib.).

54 *Mich. Guide*, pp. 280–81.

55 *MSAB*, Apr. 1967.

56 *MSAB*, July 1965.

57 *Newsweek*, 5 Sept. 1966.

58 *MSAB*, Oct. 1962.

59 *Arch. Forum*, Nov. 1963.

60 *Free Press*, 15 Jan. 1966.

61 Eberle M. Smith Assoc.'s *Philip Murray Sr. H.S. Design Manual*.

62 Linn Smith Assoc.'s *Eastern Sr. H.S. Des. Man.*

63 *Arch. Forum*, Aug. 1963.

64 *Andrews AIM*, no. 90.

65 *The W. Hawkins Ferry Coll.*, Det., DIA, 1966, nos. 46–47.

66 *Arch. Forum*, May 1964.

67 *Arch. Rec.*, Apr. 1963.

68 Gerald G. Diehl, v.i.

69 *Andrews AIM*, nos. 98–99.

70 *Impresario* (Det.), May–June 1965.

71 *Andrews AIM*, no. 36.

72 *Andrews AIM*, nos. 102–04.

Index
of Persons, Places and Buildings

Arabic numbers not in parentheses or brackets are page numbers; arabic numbers of three digits or less in parentheses refer to the illustrations; dates in parentheses refer to the Selected Chronology. In the index the colon (:) always means see or see also. It does not mean an entry architect, for example, was the sole author or even an author at all of the cited work(s); the text must be consulted. To facilitate quick identification of types of buildings, four symbols are used: ▪ Building or Block (name); ® Church, Chapel, or Religious edifice; ● House (residence); and ★ Plant (factory).

For architectural styles and types of buildings, use list of Contents—as a rule such terms are not indexed. In general the individual names of architects and builders, rather than those of their firms, which are given in the text, are indexed, and are in *italics* when Detroit area buildings are involved. Places on Map 3 with indexed works are listed under Suburbs. In addition, a classified breakdown is given under City of buildings which are or were within the present city limits of Detroit. (Current usage as opposed to original purpose is sometimes reflected in this list.)

W. Hawkins Ferry was educated at the Grosse Pointe University School, at Cranbrook, and at Harvard University (B.A. 1939). He pursued graduate studies at the Harvard School of Design, worked as an architectural designer, and has served as an instructor in art and architectural history at Wayne State University.

Mr. Ferry is an honorary curator of architecture, chairman of the Friends of Modern Art, and a trustee of the Founders Society at the Detroit Institute of Arts, and an honorary member of the Michigan Society of Architects.

The manuscript was edited by Charles H. Elam.

The list of illustrations, selected chronology, and index were compiled, the maps were prepared, and the notes were augmented by the editor.

The book was designed by Richard Kinney and Donald Ross. The text typeface is Linotype Janson cut by Nicholas Kis about 1690. The display face is Bookman originally cut for Linotype about 1936.

The regular edition of the book is printed on Mohawk's Patrician paper and bound in Columbia Mills Riverside Chambray cloth. The limited edition of 200 copies is bound in genuine blue Morocco leather.